Techniques and Tools for the Design and Implementation of Enterprise Information Systems

Angappa Gunasekaran
University of Massachusetts-Dartmouth, USA

IGI PUBLISHING
Hershey • New York

Acquisition Editor: Kristin Klinger
Development Editor: Kristin Roth
Senior Managing Editor: Jennifer Neidig
Managing Editor: Jamie Snavely
Assistant Managing Editor: Carole Coulson
Copy Editor: Alana Bubnis
Typesetter: Michael Brehm
Cover Design: Lisa Tosheff
Printed at: Yurchak Printing Inc.

Published in the United States of America by
        IGI Publishing (an imprint of IGI Global)
        701 E. Chocolate Avenue
        Hershey PA 17033
        Tel: 717-533-8845
        Fax: 717-533-8661
        E-mail: cust@igi-global.com
        Web site: http://www.igi-global.com

and in the United Kingdom by
        IGI Publishing (an imprint of IGI Global)
        3 Henrietta Street
        Covent Garden
        London WC2E 8LU
        Tel: 44 20 7240 0856
        Fax: 44 20 7379 0609
        Web site: http://www.eurospanbookstore.com

Library of Congress Cataloging-in-Publication Data

Techniques and tools for the design and implementation of Enterprise Information Systems / Angappa Gunasekaran, editor.
    p. cm.
  Summary: "This book enables libraries to provide an invaluable resource to academicians and practitioners in fields such as operations management, Web engineering, information technology, and management information systems, providing insight into the effective design and implementation of enterprise information systems to improve communication and integration between partnering firms to achieve an integrated global supply chain"--Provided by publisher.
  ISBN 978-1-59904-826-0 (hardcover) -- ISBN 978-1-59904-829-1 (e-book)
  1. Management information systems. I. Gunasekaran, Angappa.
  T58.6.T435 2008
  658.4'038--dc22
                            2007040903

British Cataloguing in Publication Data
A Cataloguing in Publication record for this book is available from the British Library.

All work contributed to this book is originial material. The views expressed in this book are those of the authors, but not necessarily of the publisher.

Advances in Enterprise Information Systems (AEIS) Series

ISBN: 1935-3111

Editor-in-Chief: Angappa Gunasekaran, University of Massachusetts – Dartmouth, USA

Modelling and Analysis of Enterprise Information Systems Vol. I

Angappa Gunasekaran, University of Massachusetts - Dartmouth, USA

IGI Publishing * copyright 2007 * 392pp * H/C (ISBN: 978-1-59904-477-4) * US $89.96 (our price)

Insight into issues, challenges, and solutions related to the successful applications and management aspects of enterprise information systems may provide to be a hardship to researchers and practitioners. Modelling Analysis of Enterprise Information Systems presents comprehensive coverage and understanding of the organizational and technological issues of enterprise information systems.

Modelling Analysis of Enterprise Information Systems covers current trends and issues in various enterprise information systems such as enterprise resource planning, electronic commerce, and their implications on supply chain management and organizational competitiveness.

Techniques and Tools for the Design and Implementation of Enterprise Information Systems Vol. II

Angappa Gunasekaran, University of Massachusetts-Dartmouth, USA

IGI Publishing * copyright 2008 * 303pp * H/C (ISBN: 978-1-59904-826-0) * US $89.96 (our price)

Inter-organizational information systems play a major role in improving communication and integration between partnering firms to achieve an integrated global supply chain. Current research in enterprise resource planning and electronic commerce is crucial to maintaining efficient supply chain management and organizational competitiveness.

Techniques and Tools for the Design & Implementation of Enterprise Information Systems enables libraries to provide an invaluable resource to academicians and practitioners in fields such as operations management, Web engineering, information technology, and management information systems, providing insight into the effective design and implementation of enterprise information systems to improve communication and integration between partnering firms to achieve an integrated global supply chain.

The Advances in Enterprise Information Systems (AEIS) Book Series aims to expand available literature in support of global markets and the globalized economy surrounding Enterprise Information Systems. The Series provides comprehensive coverage and understanding of the organizational, people and technological issues of EIS. Design, development, justification and implementation of EIS including ERP and EC will be discussed. Global markets and competition have forced companies to operate in a physically distributed environment to take the advantage of benefits of strategic alliances between partnering firms. Earlier, information systems such as Material Requirements Planning (MRP), Computer-Aided Design (CAD) and Computer-Aided Manufacturing (CAM) have widely been used for functional integration within an organization. With global operations in place, there is a need for suitable Enterprise Information Systems (EIS) such as Enterprise Resource Planning (ERP) and E-Commerce (EC) for the integration of extended enterprises along the supply chain with the objective of achieving flexibility and responsiveness. Companies all over the world spend billions of dollars in the design and implementation of EIS in particular ERP systems such as Oracle, Peoplesoft, SAP, JD Edwards and BAAN with the objective of achieving an integrated global supply chain. Inter-organizational information systems play a major role in improving communication and integration between partnering firms to achieve an integrated global supply chain. The Advances in Enterprise Information Systems (AEIS) Book Series endeavors to further this field and address the growing demand for research and applications that will provide insights into issues, challenges, and solutions related to the successful applications and management aspects of EIS.

Hershey · New York
Order online at www.igi-global.com or call 717-533-8845 x 10 –
Mon-Fri 8:30 am - 5:00 pm (est) or fax 24 hours a day 717-533-8661

Techniques and Tools for the Design and Implementation of Enterprise Information Systems

Table of Contents

Preface

Enterprise resource planning (ERP) system is an enterprise-wide information system. ERP systems automate business processes and provide access to data from global operations. These systems have been used to integrate business processes along the supply chain. It is hard to imagine a well-integrated supply chain without the application of ERP. Techniques and tools play a major role in the design, development and implementation of enterprise information systems (EIS). In the past, many companies have reported failures with reference to the implementation of ERP systems. Most companies had problems with the design and implementation of ERP due to lack of adequate techniques and tools to design and implement the EIS. Considering the importance of ERP in global enterprise environments, and the competitiveness of companies in global markets, this edited book focuses on the techniques and tools for the design, development and implementation of EIS.

Effective communication along the supply chain is essential to provide high-level customer service by delivering the right products, at the right time and in the right quantity and price. In order to avoid any quality and delivery problems of materials, a real-time and shared information system such as ERP is important. The objective of EIS is to facilitate a smooth flow of information along the supply chain. Many companies have failed in their attempt to successfully implement ERP due to lack of proper planning and having the right techniques and tools for the design and implementation of EIS. Implementation of ERP starts with whether a company needs such a system and then selecting the right system considering the nature of its business and the overall scope of the market. Hence, there is a need to carefully align the business model with information model or system. For this, companies need suitable techniques and tools for the development and implementation of ERP systems. This edited book presents some useful strategies, techniques and tools for the design, development and implementation of EIS. It is our hope that both academic researchers and practitioners will benefit from the strategies, techniques and tools presented for the design and implementation of EIS. An overview of the chapters is presented hereunder.

Chapter I, *Applying Collaboration Theory for Improving ERP System-User Interaction*, by Lucas, Babaian, and Topi argues that ERP systems remain difficult to learn and use, however, despite the vast resources devoted to employee training and the reams of documentation provided by their manufacturers. To enhance the usability, and thereby increase the usefulness of ERP systems in organizations, it proposes the application of collaboration theory to ERP system design. Conceptualizing the relationship between the user and the system as one in which the system works in partnership with the user provides a development framework targeted at helping users achieve their system-related goals.

Chapter II, *A Component-Based Tool Architecture for Performance Modelling and Optimization*, by Syrjakow, Syrjakow, and Szczerbicka elaborates on the design of a powerful optimization component and its integration into existing modelling and simulation tools. For that purpose, it proposes a hybrid integration approach, being a combination of loose document-based and tight invocation-based integration concepts. Beside the integration concept for the optimization component, it also gives a detailed insight into the applied optimization strategies.

Chapter III, *The Critical Success Factors Across ERP Implementation Processes*, by Lai reports a study that consists of two phases: (i) a questionnaire survey among experienced ERP consultants in order to identify the key successful factors of each step within ERP implementation models and (ii) experienced ERP consultants are interviewed to examine why these factors are important at each of the implementation steps and what are the difficulties of using Western ERP implementation models in China. This study provides guidance to ERP consultants on how to utilize their limited resources by considering these factors at each step within the ERP implementation models.

Chapter IV, *Integrated Design System: An Information Processing Approach for Knowledge-Based Product Development,* by Yang and Reidsema discusses the structure and development of a design information system that can convert descriptive information into forms that are suitable for embedding within decision-making algorithms. Information in such a system is sorted in terms of its nature into three groups: input data information, constraint information and objective information, all having different representations. Information is also mapped to the relevant design objectives and ranked in importance to facilitate the trade-off analysis after a series of processing activities.

Chapter V, *Behavioral Aspects in Strategic Transformation of Organizations,* by Mandal stresses on behavioral issues, particularly how human behavior impacts on transforming organizations through implementing large IT systems such as ERP systems. The current business environment is forcing IT managers to use more and more "collective thinking power," generated by team activities, to make strategic decisions, or even to run day–to-day operations. Here, the chapter focuses on broader issues managed through people's cooperation and efforts.

Chapter VI, *Decisional DNA and the Smart Knowledge Management System: A Process of Transforming Information into Knowledge,* by Sanin and Szczerbicki shows how Decisional DNA is constructed through the implementation of the Smart Knowledge Management System (SKMS). SKMS is a hybrid knowledge-based decision support system that takes information and sends it through four macro-processes: diagnosis, prognosis, solution, and knowledge, in order to build the Decisional DNA of an organization. The SKMS implements a model for transforming information into knowledge by using *Sets of Experience Knowledge Structure.* Fully developed, the SKMS will improve the quality of decision-making, and could advance the notion of administering knowledge in the current decision-making environment.

Chapter VII, *Organizational Readiness to Adopt ERP: An Evaluation Model for Manufacturing SMEs,* by Raymond, Rivard, and Jutras presents the results of a study that proposes and validates a framework for evaluating the level of readiness for ERP adoption in manufacturing SMEs. The framework conceptualizes readiness to adopt an ERP as including four dimensions:

the organizational context, external forces, perception of ERP, and business processes. A field study of eleven manufacturing SMEs was conducted. The framework led to the classification of these firms in three clusters: "committed adopters," "uncommitted adopters," and "late adopters."

Chapter VIII, *Design and Development of ISO 9001:2000-Based Quality Management Information System,* by Sakthivel, Devadasan, Vinodh, Raghu Raman, and Sriram reports on a quality management information system (QMIS) that has been designed by referring to clause 4 of ISO 9001:2000. After designing this QMIS, its development in real-time environment was examined by conducting a study at an ISO 9001:2000 certified high technology oriented company. Also, a validation study was conducted by gathering the opinions and assessment of the managing partner of the company on QMIS. These studies revealed the feasibility and possibility of implementing QMIS in ISO 9001:2000 certified companies.

Chapter IX, *Motivational Aspects of Legitimate Internet File Sharing and Piracy,* by Smith examines potential and active customers' intrinsic and extrinsic values associated with selected legal, ethical, and economic impacts of file sharing, especially in relationship to potential impacts on customer relationship management (CRM). The pros and cons of file sharing are highlighted in a conceptual model and empirically tested through graphical and statistical analysis through hypothesis testing, via factor analysis and principal component analysis (PCA) techniques. Recommendations on the potential growth of file sharing industry, through the lens of price, competition, increased selection, and regulation, are included.

Chapter X, *The Next Generation of Customer Relationship Management (CRM) Metrics,* by Shea, Brown, White, Curran, and Griffin contends that the limitations of mostly internally-focused, marketing-based, efficiency-oriented CRM metrics has hindered both the understanding of why CRM systems often fail as well as led to the perception of failed CRM implementations. Only through the development, application and use of CRM metrics can organizations hope to better understand CRM implementations or achieve their CRM goals. To make matters more difficult, the growing capabilities of CRM applications over the past few years has been raising the expectations and sophistication of customers. A new generation of CRM metrics is needed—a generation of relevant, enterprise-wide, and customer-centric metrics.

Chapter XI, *Development of Intelligent Diagnosis and Maintenance System using JESS: Java Expert System Shell Technology,* by Yao, Lin, and Trappey describes the development of a rule-based intelligent equipment troubleshooting and maintenance system using JAVA Expert System Shell (JESS) technology. The main modules of the system include diagnosis knowledge management, project or case management and system administration. Further, a Thin-Film Transistor Liquid-Crystal Display (TFT-LCD) production equipment diagnosis and maintenance system is designed and implemented to demonstrate the intelligent maintenance capability.

Chapter XII, *Measuring of Web Performance as Perceived by End-Users,* by Borzemski presents a Wing free service that has been developed for the purpose of Web transaction visualization. Its Web client that probes a target Web site is a real Web browser (MS IE), so the user can observe how a particular browser uses the network. Wing can be a good analysis tool for Web page and network application developers. It also introduces the MWING system, which is based on their experiences from Wing project. MWING is a generic automated distributed multiagent-based measurement framework for running different measurement, testing and diagnosing tasks related to the Internet; for example, in Internet topology discovering, Web benchmarking, or grid services performance studies. One of possible agents can be Wing-like agents downloading different Web pages in periodic experiments from many agent locations.

Chapter XIII, *Information System Development: Using Business Process Simulation as a Requirements Engineering Tool,* by Elliman, Hatzakis, and Serrano discusses the idea that even though information systems development (ISD) approaches have long advocated the use of integrated organisational views, the modelling techniques used have not been adapted accordingly and remain focused on the automated information system (IS) solution. This chapter uses the findings from three different case studies to illustrate the ways BPS has been used at different points in the ISD process, especially in the area of requirements engineering. It compares the results against IS modelling techniques, highlighting the advantages and disadvantages that BPS has over the latter. The research necessary to develop appropriate BPS tools and give guidance on their use in the ISD process is also discussed.

Chapter XIV, *Selfish Users and Distributed MAC Protocols in Wireless Local Area Networks,* by Guha and Rakshit considers the effect of "selfishness" on distributed MAC protocols in wireless local area network (WLAN). The inherently contention-based medium access in distributed systems is modelled as a non-cooperative game: "access game." Both quality of service (QoS) and battery power (BP) are incorporated in modelling the game. It is shown that the Nash equilibrium (NE) for incomplete information games is usually inefficient compared to the NE of complete information games. It investigates whether fairness can be achieved by selfish users. Then it computes the constrained NE (CNE) for the access game.

Enterprise information systems have become an essential part of the global supply chain. Effective design, development and implementation of ERP will make a great difference in organizational performance and competitiveness. Nevertheless, suitable techniques and tools are critical for the successful development and implementation of ERP in real-life enterprises. An outstanding collection of the latest research associated with the effective techniques and tools for the development and implementation of ERP systems, *"Advances in Enterprise Information Systems,"* provides insight and assistance in learning how to design and develop enterprise information systems with suitable techniques and tools.

My sincere thanks go to all the authors of this edited book whose timely submissions and revisions of chapters have made this book possible. I am thankful to Dr. Medhi Khosrow-Pour, executive editor of IGI Global, Ms. Kristin Roth (managing editor) and Ms. Deborah Yahnke (assistant development editorial), for their constant support throughout editing the book.

I am grateful to my wife, Latha Parameswari and son, Rangarajan for their support and understanding during this book project.

Angappa Gunasekaran, PhD

Editor

Angappa Gunasekaran is a professor of operations management and the chairperson of the Department of Decision and Information Sciences in the Charlton College of Business at the University of Massachusetts (North Dartmouth, USA). Previously, he has held academic positions in Canada, India, Finland, Australia and Great Britain. He has BE and ME from the University of Madras and a PhD from the Indian Institute of Technology. He teaches and conducts research in operations management and information systems. He serves on the editorial board of 20 journals and edits a journal. He has published about 200 articles in journals, 60 articles in conference proceedings and 3 edited books. In addition, he has organized several conferences in the emerging areas of operations management and information systems. He has extensive editorial experience that includes the guest editor and editor of many journals. He has received outstanding paper and excellence in teaching awards. His current areas of research include supply chain management, enterprise resource planning, e-commerce, and benchmarking. He is also the director of the Business Innovation Research Center (BIRC) at the University of Massachusetts - Dartmouth.

Chapter I

Applying Collaboration Theory for Improving ERP System-User Interaction

Wendy Lucas, Bentley College, USA

Tamara Babaian, Bentley College, USA

Heikki Topi, Bentley College, USA

Abstract

Enterprise resource planning (ERP) systems automate business processes and provide access to data from worldwide operations. These systems remain difficult to learn and use, however, despite the vast resources devoted to employee training and the reams of documentation provided by their manufactures. Oftentimes, even well trained employees will appeal to more knowledgeable users for help or will augment their system use with other software, such as spreadsheet or database applications. The need for such practices has a negative impact on employee performance and the ability of companies to reap the full benefits afforded by ERP systems. To enhance their usability, and thereby increase their usefulness to organizations, we propose the application of collaboration theory to ERP system design. Conceptual-

izing the relationship between the user and the system as one in which the system works in partnership with the user provides a development framework targeted at helping users achieve their system-related goals.

Introduction

Anecdotal evidence of the problems encountered by users interacting with enterprise resource planning (ERP) systems abounds, and recent studies confirm the poor usability characteristics of these systems. A study of ERP users in one division of a Fortune 500 company identified the following six categories of usability problems: difficulty in identifying and accessing the correct functionality, lack of transaction execution support, system output limitations, inadequate support in error situations, incompatibility between the users' and the system's terminology, and usage-related problems arising from the overall complexity of the system (Topi, Babaian, & Lucas, 2005). Although these users had undergone training on the use of the system and had access to manufacturer-supplied documentation, they relied heavily on extensive sets of informal notes on system usage prepared by fellow employees (Topi, Lucas, & Babaian, 2006), sought out "power users" from within the organization for answers to their questions, and sometimes turned to outside applications, such as Microsoft Excel®, for meeting unfulfilled reporting needs (Topi et al., 2005).

Usability issues can have a detrimental effect on business performance and, in particular, on end-user productivity (Iansiti, 2007). Recent studies from Forrester Research on enterprise usability (Ragsdale, 2004) and business application usability (Herbert, 2006) also note the negative effect of poorly designed user interfaces on the bottom line, with costs arising from increases in new user training time, decreases in productivity, and poor user adoption rates. Hamerman (2007) notes that usability is not a strong suit of ERP applications, with newer versions of the leading packages showing only minor usability improvements over their predecessors, and includes lack of usability as one of five major challenges facing ERP customers. It appears that little progress has been made since an earlier Forrester Research evaluation of eleven ERP products (Chew, Orlov, & Herbert, 2003), which found that poor usability characteristics and the unintuitive user interfaces of these systems contribute to decreased productivity and increased costs for businesses using them. The overall conclusion was that "users should demand better usability," which, according to Hamerman (2007), is what they are now doing.

The lack of attention paid to addressing the significant usability shortcomings of ERP systems by both manufacturers and the usability community motivates the research initiative described here. Given the time, effort, and money expended on implementation and training, it is surprising that so little attention has been focused on understanding the ways in which users interact with ERP software and the degree to which the interaction model supports the tasks being performed. In this chapter, we suggest that applying the principles of collaboration (Bratman, 1992) to systems development provides a means for addressing the gap between the capabilities of the ERP system and harnessing those capabilities to meet each user's individual objectives. By "collaboration," we refer to the collaboration between the user and the system, as opposed to collaboration between people that is supported by computing technology, which is commonly referred to as computer-supported cooperative work (CSCW). The novelty of our research lies in its emphasis on the relationship between collaborative support, task performance, and satisfaction. We believe that the more aligned the technology is with the users' goals, the better able it will be to respond in a collaborative manner to the users' needs, enhancing both user performance and satisfaction with the system.

Our long-term research goal is to improve the usability of enterprise systems by increasing the collaborative capabilities of their interfaces. This research currently includes the following components:

- Field studies focusing on the nature of the users' everyday needs and interactions with these systems
- Development of enterprise system design guidelines based on collaboration theory
- Development of interface evaluation techniques based on collaboration theory
- Implementation of prototype ERP interfaces for validating the design and evaluation methodologies we are developing

In this chapter, we elucidate the role of collaboration theory in our research and illustrate the benefits gained by applying it to ERP design and evaluation. In the next section, we discuss the most important approaches that have been followed to date for usability design and evaluation in the fields of human-computer interaction and enterprise systems and position the collaborative view in the context of these approaches. We then describe the principles of collaboration theory and illustrate how they can be used for establishing guidelines for usability design and evaluation. This is followed by an example scenario of a user performing a typical ERP task and a discussion of how the interface could be improved by taking a collaboration-based approach to its design. A prototype implementation that embodies this approach is then presented. This chapter concludes with directions for future work.

Related Research

Few studies focus on interface design and usability in the context of enterprise systems. Bishu et al. (1999), however, raise some of the human factors issues associated with ERP systems, including the lack of attention paid to training and the maze of screens one has to navigate. Building on the rich research tradition associated with the technology acceptance model (TAM) and its successors for predicting and explaining user acceptance of information technologies (Venkatesh et al., 2003), Calisir and Calisir (2004) examine the effects of interface usability characteristics, perceived usefulness, and perceived ease of use on end-user satisfaction with ERP systems in a study with 51 users in 24 companies. The usability characteristics under investigation are system capability, compatibility, flexibility, user guidance, learnability, and minimal memory load. The authors find that perceived usefulness has the strongest impact on end-user satisfaction, while learnability has a relatively smaller but still significant effect. Perceived ease of use exerts an indirect effect on satisfaction via perceived usefulness, indicating that users rate ERP systems as less useful if they find them difficult to use. System capability also has a strong impact on perceived usefulness, and the authors recommend that ERP system designers should pay more attention to user requirements analysis in order to incorporate relevant materials and functions into their systems. The study also finds that a good user guidance scheme improves the learnability of the system and reduces the mental workload, suggesting that easy-to-understand error messages, the possibility of making use of the system without having to learn all of it, the availability of undo and reverse control actions, and the presence of confirming questions before the execution of risky commands may increase both perceived usefulness and learnability.

While there is little research from the usability community that directly addresses ERP system design, research on human-computer interaction in general has made considerable advances, as evidenced by comprehensive collections of state-of-the-art articles on usability, such as one by Jacko and Sears (2003), and by the large number of innovative interface types. Although many experimental interfaces have found their way into practice, to the best of our knowledge they have not yet been used in the context of ERP systems. Applying the scientific and technological advancements that have been made in user interface research to these systems holds great promise for improving their usability.

It is virtually impossible to create a highly usable system without addressing usability issues from the start: that is, at the requirements analysis and design stages (Maguire, 2001). This approach is known as user-centered design. Although methods employed for this type of design differ significantly in their underlying theories, the key component of all modern usability design and evaluation techniques is a clear understanding of the users' goals and tasks. These goals and their associated tasks can be of different granularities, ranging from broadly defined ones like "retrieve, relate, and report financial, production, and personnel data in order to persuade [a] manager to allocate effort and resources differently" (Mirel, 1996, p. 16), to very specific ones involving a few clearly articulated changes to an existing document.

The broad scope of ERP and other enterprise-wide systems creates its own special requirements for usability analysis. Rather than evaluating usability one function at a time, it is necessary to analyze the integrated use of the multiple system features required for achieving a comprehensive goal. Few existing usability methodologies are appropriate for this type of analysis. Model-based approaches such as GOMS (Card et al., 1983), for example, cannot be applied due to the obvious difficulty of specifying complex tasks and respective user behaviors at a detailed level. While task analysis (Redish & Wixon, 2003) can be used to model a hierarchy of goals and tasks at a high level, it does not address the interactions between the system and its users. Therefore, task analysis cannot be effectively used in the design of user interfaces.

Although it is theoretically possible to evaluate the interactions involved in performing a comprehensive task using inspection methods (e.g., Nielsen, 1993; Wharton et al., 1994), Cockton et al. (2003, p. 1121) report that this type of verification is overwhelmingly left out of usability evaluations. This can be attributed to the fact that the guidelines on which the methods are based do not address the dynamics of the interaction between the system and its users, but rather focus on the more static aspects of the system. User-based methods (Dumas, 2003) work well for uncovering usability problems but typically focus on specific features of the existing implementation. Therefore, they tend to elicit information that is boxed within the framework of the specific tool being evaluated, leading to localized fixes rather than system-wide alterations of the design.

Constantine (2006a) argues for a newer approach referred to as activity modeling for representing the users, their system-related roles, and the system itself. This approach builds upon activity theory and usage-centered design (Constantine, 2006b). The former provides a conceptual framework for human activity, while the latter focuses on user performance and the creation of tools that enhance the efficiency and dependability of that performance. Activity modeling is, therefore, more concerned with the activities in which users are engaged and the tasks they want to perform within those activities, rather than on the users themselves, who are the focus of user-centered design.

Of the above approaches, activity modeling is the one that is most closely aligned with collaboration theory because it focuses on user interactions with the system and the activities in which the user and the system are involved. The collaborative view of a system-user interaction also explicitly includes the user and the system in the single model of interactions involved in completing a task. However, the system's role is expanded in that it must act as a partner to help the user achieve his or her system-related goals. This changes the dynamic from the user being the only one with responsibilities and knowledge about the process to one that incorporates the system as a partner in completing that process. This naturally leads to specific requirements regarding the knowledge and behavior of the system, as described next.

Collaboration Theory for Interface Design and Evaluation

The core thesis of this chapter is that collaboration theory can be applied as a set of guiding principles to the design and evaluation of ERP systems. In this section, we discuss the overall characteristics of this theory and illustrate how taking a collaborative view of user-system interactions influences the design and evaluation processes and leads to enhanced system usability.

Terveen (1995) defines collaboration as the process of two or more agents working together to achieve shared goals, and human-computer collaboration as collaboration involving at least one human and one computational agent. Grosz (1996) and Shieber (1996) build on Terveen's framework, suggesting that human-computer interaction should move from a master-slave model, in which the human user issues commands to the system, to a model based on collaboration between the system and the user in order to provide an adequate level of support to users in the increasingly complex environments of modern applications. In other words, the computer system should be designed to act as the user's partner in the process of goal achievement. This view of a system-collaborator, supported by a philosophical account of cooperative activity (Bratman, 1992) and by more formal mathematical frameworks for collaboration (Grosz & Kraus, 1996), has already been used in the design and implementation of several prototype interfaces in the intelligent agents community (e.g., Babaian, Grosz, & Shieber, 2002; Rich, Sidner, & Lesh, 2001). None of these, however, have been interfaces to enterprise-wide administrative systems.

It should be noted that the phrase "system-partner" is not to be taken literally here. Computing technology does not yet have the capability to implement a collaborative partner with human-like abilities. Rather, moving towards more collaborative behavior on the part of the system can be accomplished by a careful design based on the principles of collaboration. As defined by Bratman (1992) and further elaborated for computational use by Grosz and Kraus (1996), these principles are:

- **Commitment to the joint activity:** Each party recognizes the joint activity and is committed to it. As part of this commitment, the parties need to be aware of the context surrounding their collaboration because it may be important in determining the finer details of that activity.
- **Mutual responsiveness:** Each participant seeks to adjust his behavior based on the behavior of the other and guided by his commitment to the joint activity. Mutual responsiveness, in conjunction with this commitment, means that the parties may have to adapt their actions for the benefit of the more optimal joint outcome.
- **Commitment to mutual support:** Each party is committed to supporting the efforts of the other. When an agent knows the other party may need help in performing a subtask related to their shared activity and is able to provide such help, the agent is ready to assist and the other party

recognizes and supports such assistance. Commitment to mutual support also implies communication with the purpose of sharing information that is essential for the completion of the joint activity.

- **Meshing subplans:** The parties should seek to decompose the task into mutually meshing, although independent, subplans. The parties must thus engage in communication to coordinate their independent subplans at certain times, as the need arises.

To illustrate how these principles can change the approach taken to the design and evaluation of systems, we first describe a well-known usability evaluation method called the cognitive walkthrough (Wharton et al., 1994), and then show how taking a collaborative view of user-system interaction would affect it. The basis for the cognitive walkthrough method is a theory of exploratory learning called CE+ (Polson & Lewis, 1990), which was developed to guide the design of interfaces that are easily learnable. This work, therefore, bears similarity to our proposed usage of collaboration theory as a set of guiding design and evaluation principles.

A cognitive walkthrough involves an analyst evaluating an interface by creating a scenario of its usage for a particular task. During the walkthrough, the following questions, taken directly from Wharton et al. (1994), must be answered in order to assess an untrained user's success in invoking the appropriate system action at each step of the way:

Will the users try to achieve the right effect?

Will the user notice that the correct action is available?

Will the user associate the correct action with the effect trying to be achieved?

If the correct action is performed, will the user see that progress is being made toward solution of the task?

(Wharton et al., 1994, p. 112)

The answers to these questions then form the basis for predicting a user's success in either properly completing the task or failing to do so.

Taking a collaborative view of user-system interactions would affect the formulation of each of these questions. Keeping in mind that this view requires us to think of the system as an equal partner in the process, let us consider the first question ("Will the users try to achieve the right effect?"). It is designed to capture the users' ability to recognize the relationship between the structure of the task and the system's known functions. The example Wharton et al. (1994) use to illustrate this question is a user whose task is to print a document, but he cannot achieve this goal without first selecting a printer. The question therefore becomes: Will the user know that his next immediate step should be to select the printer?

Evaluating this situation from the collaboration perspective brings us to a different conclusion regarding the relevant question to ask. It is not whether or not the user knows to select the printer. Rather, it is whether or not the system has been designed in such a way that it knows the next step in the printing process is the selection of a printer and will act in accordance with this knowledge. The system must therefore be aware of the overall "recipe" for printing, which connects the two actions of selecting the printer and sending the document to it. Once the user has identified the goal of printing a document, the system should proceed with an action that enables the user to select a printer, either by choosing one from a system-generated list or by specifying a new one. It is the commitment to mutual support that causes the system to aid the user with the printer selection process. It would not be collaborative for the system to send the document to any printer without first consulting with the user for a number of reasons, including the fact that the user must know where to pick up the printed document and that the default option may not be the best choice in this particular instance.

Thus, the first question can be modified according to the principles of collaboration to read as follows:

Based on the user's overall goal, will the system recognize the next step in the process and either act to perform that step or, if the user's input is necessary, present a set of alternative actions from which the user may make a selection?

A similar viewing of the three remaining questions in light of collaboration theory leads us to the following possible versions of questions two through four:

Does the system help the user identify the next action and present it in a highly visible manner?

Does the system present a meaningful set of alternative actions based on the user's overall goal?

Will the system keep the user informed about the consequences of actions taken by either the user or the system, as they relate to progress made toward the achievement of the task?

In transforming the walkthrough questions to reflect the collaborative view of system-user interaction, we have shifted the focus from the actions, knowledge, and capabilities of the user alone to include the system as an equal partner in the process. If a system is designed with this view in mind and evaluated using questions based on the principles of collaboration, the nature of the relationship between the user and the system will change. We believe that the collaborative view of the user-system relationship will result in interactions that allow users to achieve their goals with less effort and frustration and with more accuracy, due to the additional support provided by the system.

While the example we have used in this evaluation (namely, selecting a printer prior to printing) is a very narrow task compared to many of those that are encountered in the enterprise system environment, it makes the point that even the simplest of tasks can benefit from the application of the principles of collaboration. The benefits of user-system collaboration would be significantly greater with more complex organizational tasks, as the system could provide knowledge and assistance for those cases where the correct sequence of events is not readily discernable by even the most educated of users. Given the lack of transparency in performing enterprise system transactions, an approach that sheds light on the recipes for successful task completion holds great promise for improving user productivity through enhanced system usability.

Transaction Task Example

To illustrate the use of collaboration principles in the context of an ERP system, we apply these principles to a common ERP transaction task. In this walkthrough scenario, we point out how a fictitious materials management system that closely resembles a well-known and widely used ERP system fails to support the user in achieving her goal. In the subsequent discussion, we suggest how that system could be modified to be a better collaborator. This is followed by a snapshot of our prototype implementation and a description of how collaboration theory has been used to influence its design.

Scenario

Pat is an engineer and a relatively new user of a large enterprise system. As part of her engineering assignment, Pat needs to order a certain hardware component. She tries to create a purchase requisition, but is stymied when she can't specify the item to be ordered because it is not listed in the Material Master.

The option of adding a new material to the Material Master is not available in the purchase requisition interface, although its implementation exists and is available elsewhere in the system. Interface design based on collaboration should recognize the broader context in which the task of creating a purchase requisition may occur. Based on the mutual support principle, the system should provide easy access to related or prerequisite tasks, such as adding a new item in the context of creating a purchase requisition:

Pat has to scrap the unfinished purchase requisition, enter the item into the Material Master, and then proceed to create the purchase requisition again. To create a new purchase requisition, Pat follows this menu path: Logistics—Material Master—Purchasing—Purchase Requisition—Create. She enters information regarding the delivery date, the plant to which this material must be delivered, the storage location, and the purchasing group.

When Pat presses Ok to move to the next screen, the system complains: "Date period D is not valid." Pat goes back to the date field and tries to modify the date specification. Reading the system-provided help files on various formats fails to explain how the D, T, W, or M options affect the format of the date to be entered (particularly since Pat does not recognize that the use of the letter 'T' for 'Date' is not based on the English language). She remains puzzled for a while until she stumbles upon the Possible Entries option that is available for the date field. Selecting this option results in the system displaying a calendar from which Pat selects a date, which is then correctly entered for her by the system into the date field.

The interface includes the very useful option of selecting the date from a calendar, but this option is not offered and remains obscured even though the system has detected and reported the user's error. Commitment to mutual support and mutual responsiveness would require a system-collaborator that has the ability to offer such help when it can provide it, instead of merely informing the user about a failure:

A colleague then suggests that Pat select the Model service specifications option, which displays the actual names of all items listed in the form in addition to their numeric identifier. Pat finds this option to be very helpful, for both clarity and verification purposes, and opts to use it.

Commitment to mutual support requires that the collaborating parties share the knowledge that is relevant to the success of the joint activity. In the previous example, even though displaying the item names in addition to the identifiers would be more informative from the perspective of a human user and is very easy for the system to do, the interface does not provide this information without a specific request. Typically, new users are not aware of all of the available options, and thus fail to take advantage of these types of capabilities:

Pat verifies that the information she has entered, including the destination plant for the material, is correct, confirms this to the system, and is taken to the next screen, where she is asked to list the items to be ordered. Unfortunately, Pat has forgotten the exact ID number of the material she just entered into the Material Master.

If the system kept track of the steps Pat had previously taken, it could use this information to examine the context of the current interaction. It would then be able to recognize that, having just entered a new material; Pat is likely to need to refer to this item's information when she follows up with the purchase requisition:

Pat tries to find the ID number by reviewing the item descriptions using the Possible Values option for the item field. At some point during this review process, the information on the screen changes completely. Pat is unsure what she has done to cause this change and wonders whether or not the information on the purchase requisition is still available.

The rapid and drastic change to the screen's contents creates an impression that the purchase requisition task has been abandoned. Pat is now unsure of whether the system is still committed to the joint activity of creating a purchase requisition. This situation demonstrates the need for the system to convey the future steps (i.e., the plan) for performing the task as well as the history of the steps performed and the context of the most current interaction. Collaborators need to communicate in order to make sure their mutual plans for achieving the shared goal are coordinated:

After an initial moment of panic, Pat discovers that she can still get to the list of items in the purchase requisition by using the Go Back button and heaves a sigh of relief.

There would be no need to panic if Pat knew exactly where she was in the process. She should be kept aware of the plan by the system-collaborator and be able to get back to the previous steps:

There are more than 12 available options for displaying the material lists—too many for Pat to make use of them all.

Pat has just provided the system with information regarding the plant for which the material is being ordered. The system should be able to infer that the list of parts for this plant should be most useful for the search and perhaps rate that option higher than other searches for parts:

Feeling overwhelmed by choices, Pat finally notices an option for displaying materials by plant and, in reviewing the material list for the destination plant, locates the description of the item. Upon specifying the quantity, Pat has finished creating this document. She feels unsure, however, if the information she has entered is complete because there is no confirmation that she has in fact completed the process. After consulting the help desk, Pat concludes that the purchase requisition is complete and saves it.

The system knows when a process has been completed and should clearly communicate this knowledge to the user.

Discussion

As is evident from the above scenario, the numerous data and process dependencies built into an ERP system are largely hidden from the user. Coupled with the vastness of these systems, it is virtually impossible for any user to know about all, or even most, of these dependencies. Yet, users are often required to be familiar with at least some of these dependencies in order to fully understand the ramifications of their actions, determine what the next step should be in order to carry out a business process, or diagnose and fix an error. The mutual responsiveness principle of collaboration requires that the system share with its users any information that is necessary for the achievement of their goals in a clear and effective manner. The system is better equipped than a human user for "remembering" such a large and complex set of relationships spanning multiple domains. Thus, the system that is committed to supporting its users should assume responsibility for guiding them through the interrelated processes and helping them find the relevant data. One way to achieve this is by having the system make the recipes for complex business tasks available to its users. Moreover, the system must be designed to be aware of the broader business context of each user-computer interaction in order to recognize (figuratively speaking) the high-level goal that the user is trying to achieve and guide her through a multiple-step business process.

In the case of human errors and uncertainty over how to proceed (such as Pat's confusion about how to correctly enter the date), it is critical that an ERP system clearly communicates possible causes and/or alternative courses of action instead of simply reporting that an error has occurred. Effective communication is a hallmark of successful collaboration, and mechanisms must be built in for enabling clear communication from the system to the user. To be truly effective, this communication should be based on the business vocabulary employed by the organization.

The scenario also shows that the principles of collaboration influence the design of both the static components of the interface and the dynamic elements resulting from the human-computer interaction. Including an "*Add new material*" option in the purchase requisition interface and displaying information about which fields are required are examples of modifications to the static components of the interface. Recognizing that the number for a newly added item may be used in the purchase requisition that follows is an example of keeping track of a dynamic element and considering the broader context for each simple interaction. Collaboration principles should be used to guide system behavior in both static and dynamic contexts.

Illustrative Prototype

We are currently working on the design and implementation of a prototype involving several categories of ERP tasks for demonstrating how collaboration principles can be used to create efficient and usable interfaces to enterprise tasks. The snapshot shown in Figure 1 illustrates some of the important features of that interface.

This figure captures a moment in the process of the user creating a purchase requisition. The main screen on the right is where the user enters the data required for the current step in the process. In this case, default values that were specified by the user in the previous step for fields such as *Material Group* and *Plant* have been automatically entered by the system but can be overridden. The *Lookup* buttons provide access to listings of available data

Figure 1. Prototype implementation

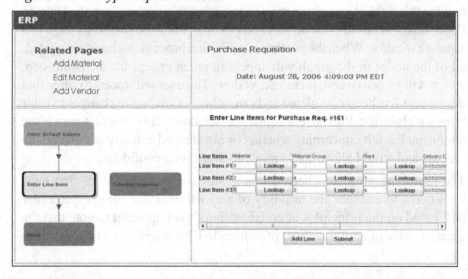

items for each required field. If the user specifies an invalid date, such as in the *Delivery Date* field, a pop-up calendar will automatically appear, from which the user can then select a valid entry.

The left-hand portion of the screen is composed of two sections: related pages and a process graph. The related pages portion contains links to tasks that are most closely related to the current activity and may be required for its successful completion. In the transaction task example from the prior section, Pat could have selected the *Add Material* link, which would have opened the New Materials page in a separate window from the Purchase Requisition. This allows for quick navigation to related tasks without the user losing context for the current activity.

The process graph depicts the steps required for completing part of a business process using the system; in this case, it shows the tasks required for creating a purchase requisition. The status of each task is depicted by a color scale, with green indicating *completed*, yellow indicating *in progress*, and red indicating *not yet started*. Here, the user has already entered default values and is in the process of entering line items. The black border around the *Enter Line Item* node shows that this is the currently active step. The user may return to a prior step to review or make changes and can look ahead to view future steps (but cannot enter any data until all preceding steps have been completed).

Other tasks may appear in the process graph as needed. For example, because the cursor is currently in the *Material* field, an *Edit/Add Material* node has appeared in the process graph and will disappear once a value has been specified for this field. As an alternative to selecting this option from the Related Pages link, Pat could click on this node to open the New Materials page in a separate window. When the purchase requisition process has been completed, all of the nodes in the graph will appear in green except for the *Done* step, which will be active and, therefore, yellow. The user will receive notice that the process has been completed and can either review/make changes to prior steps or close the Purchase Requisition window. This would remove the confusion Pat felt concerning whether or not she had actually completed the process and would allow her to move forward with confidence

The prototype presented here demonstrates some simple steps that have been taken to enhance the usability of an ERP interface for one particular task based on the principles of collaboration. It is important to note that the greatest value of applying these principles to ERP interfaces will come from the system's ability to support users in performing a broad range of tasks spanning multiple business processes.

Conclusion and Future Work

Improving the usability of ERP systems provides benefits that extend well beyond meeting the needs of individual users. It benefits the organization as a whole by reducing the length of the training time, improving employee satisfaction, and providing valuable information on overall system usage. This chapter has argued that collaboration theory is a highly relevant conceptual framework that can be used effectively to guide the design and evaluation of user-system interaction in the context of large-scale enterprise systems. While the examples we have shown here for improving user interaction do not necessarily extend beyond those that may already exist in individual implementations, it is the application of the principles of collaboration for methodically addressing system usability as a whole that is the unique contribution of this work.

It has been argued by usability researchers as well as by those in the collaborative interfaces community that design for usability cannot be achieved by a local change in the interface. Collaboration cannot be "patched on" and must be designed in from the start. The influence on the design is not limited to the system's front-end: to implement the collaborative nature of the interaction generally requires appropriate support in the data model and the algorithmic modules of a system.

Investigating the design principles and the resulting representational and algorithmic needs stemming from the user-system collaboration model of the interface is especially interesting and important in the context of enterprise-wide systems, and not only because of the obvious shortcomings of ERP interfaces. These systems span an enormously broad domain of organizational tasks, with most tasks involving multiple logical and physical system modules. In addition, there are multiple users with varying demands and levels of expertise. All of these factors increase the challenge of enhancing system usability.

We believe that collaboration theory is an excellent foundation for usability design and evaluation because:

- It directly addresses the process of collaborative problem solving in a systematic way by suggesting a set of requirements and procedures that must be in place to achieve successful collaboration.

- It provides a framework for analyzing many existing user interface practices and developments that improve system usability and helps in explaining their benefits.

- In addition to its role as an evaluation framework, it can simultaneously be used to guide design choices [identified as one of the challenges of usability research by John (1996)].

One of the core ideas of this chapter is that large-scale enterprise systems are a particularly useful domain for applying the principles of collaboration to user-system interactions. To explore the validity of this claim, it is important to conduct systematic field studies that focus on the users' perceptions regarding the usability of enterprise systems. In-depth case studies based on interviews and observations as well as surveys should be used to improve our understanding of the factors that affect usability perceptions. Field-based research, together with laboratory studies, will allow a comprehensive evaluation of the opportunities that collaboration theory offers for improving the usability of these systems.

To date, we have applied the principles of collaboration to the design and evaluation of enterprise systems through the use of scenarios, case examples, and the aforementioned ERP field study of ERP users (Topi et al., 2005). Work on our prototype is on-going; when completed, this prototype will be tested in user studies aimed at evaluating the effects of the process graph components and other interface enhancements on usability. We have also augmented the design of the prototype to support the automatic logging of all user inputs (Babaian, Lucas, & Topi, 2007). This will enable us to study the actual workflow process (Aalst, Weijter, & Maruster, 2004) and determine the areas that could benefit the most from additional user support.

Future research on ERP and enterprise system usability should address both the technical issues related to user interface design as well as the overall impact of ERP interfaces on organizational decision-making.

Acknowledgment

This work was funded by a grant from Bentley College. We gratefully acknowledge this support. An earlier version of this paper appears in the *International Journal of Enterprise Information Systems,* 2(3) (July-September 2006).

References

Aalst, W.M.P.v.d., Weijter, A.J.M.M., & Maruster, L. (2004). Workflow mining: Discovering process models from event logs. *IEEE Transactions on Knowledge and Data Engineering, 16*(9), 1128-1142.

Babaian, T., Grosz, B.J., & Shieber, S.M. (2002). A writer's collaborative assistant. In *Proceedings of the 2002 International Conference on Intelligent User Interfaces (IUI-02),* New York, NY (pp. 7-14).

Babaian, T., Lucas, W., & Topi, H. (2007). A data-driven design for deriving usability metrics. In *Proceedings of the 2nd International Conference on Software Data Technologies*. Barcelona, Spain.

Bishu, R.R., Kleiner, B.M., & Drury, C.M. (2000). Ergonomic concerns in enterprise resource planning (ERP) systems and its implementations. In *Proceedings of the Fourth International Conference on the Design of Information Infrastructure Systems for Manufacturing (DIISM 2000),* Melbourne, Victoria, Australia (pp. 146-155). Kluwer.

Bratman, M.E. (1992). Shared cooperative activity. *The Philosophical Review, 101*(2), 327-341.

Calisir, F., & Calisir, F. (2004). The relation of interface usability characteristics, perceived usefulness, and perceived ease of use to end user satisfaction with enterprise resource planning (ERP) systems. *Computers in Human Behavior, 20*(4), 505-515.

Card, S.K., Moran, T.P., & Newell, A. (1983). *The psychology of human-computer interaction*. Hillsdale: Lawrence Erlbaum.

Chew, J., Orlow, L., & Herbert, L. (2003). *App user interfaces still need work: A technology brief by Forrester Research*. Retrieved July 2, 2007, from http://www.forrester.com/Research/PDF/0,,16184,00.pdf.

Cockton, G., Lavery, D., & Woolrych, A. (2003). Inspection-based evaluations. In J. A. Jacko & A. Sears (Eds.). *The human-computer interaction handbook: Fundamentals, evolving technologies, and emerging applications* (pp. 1118-1138). Mahwah, NJ: Lawrence Erlbaum.

Constantine, L. (2006a). Activity modeling: Toward a pragmatic Integration of activity theory with usage-centered design, *Keynote Presentation at the 2ⁿᵈ National Conference in Interacção Person-Machine*, Braga, Portugal.

Constantine, L. (2006b). Users, roles, and personas. In Pruitt & Aldin (Ed.), *The persona lifecycle*. San Francisco, CA: Morgan-Kaufmann.

Dumas, J.S. (2003). User-based evaluation. In J.A. Jacko & A. Sears (Eds.). *The human-computer interaction handbook: Fundamentals, evolving technologies, and emerging applications* (pp. 1093-1117). Mahwah, NJ: Lawrence Erlbaum.

Grosz, B.J. (1996). Collaborative systems. *AI Magazine, 17*(2), 67-85.

Grosz, B.J., & Kraus, S. (1996). Collaborative plans for complex group action. *Artificial Intelligence, 86*(2), 269-357.

Hamerman, P. (2007). *ERP applications 2007: Innovation rekindles*. Forrester Research. Retrieved June 28, 2007, from http://www.forrester.com/Research/Document/0,7211,41883,00.html.

Herbert, L. (2006). *Put business applications to the usability test*. Forrester Research. Retrieved June 28, 2007, from http://www.forrester.com/Research/PDF/0,,39636,00.pdf.

Iansiti, M. (2007). *ERP end-user business productivity: A field study of SAP & Microsoft*. Keystone Strategy. Retrieved June 28, 2007, from http://download.microsoft.com/download/4/2/7/427edce8-351e-4e60-83d6-28bbf2f80d0b/KeystoneERPAssessmentWhitepaper.pdf.

Jacko, J.A., & Sears, A. (Eds.). (2003). *The human-computer interaction handbook: Fundamentals, evolving technologies, and emerging applications*. Mahwah, NJ: Lawrence Erlbaum.

John, B.E. (1996). Evaluating usability evaluation techniques. *ACM Computing Surveys, 28*(4), 139-139.

Maguire, M. (2001). Methods to support human-centred design. *International Journal of Human-Computer Studies, 55*(4), 587-634.

Mirel, B. (1996). Contextual inquiry and the representation of tasks. *The Journal of Computer Documentation, 10*(1), 14-21.

Nielsen, J. (1993). *Usability engineering*. San Diego, CA: Academic Press.

Polson, P., & Lewis, C. (1990). Theory-based design for easily learned interfaces. *Human-Computer Interaction, 5*, 1-48.

Ragsdale, J. (2004). *Put enterprise applications to the usability test*. Forrester Research.

Redish, J., & Wixon, D. (2003). Task analysis. In J.A. Jacko & A. Sears (Eds.), *The human-computer interaction handbook: Fundamentals, evolving technologies, and emerging applications* (pp. 922-940). Mahwah, NJ: Lawrence Erlbaum.

Rich, C., Sidner, C., & Lesh, N. (2001). COLLAGEN: Applying collaborative discourse to human-computer interaction. *AI Magazine, 22*(4), 15-26.

Shieber, S.M. (1996). A call for collaborative interfaces. *ACM Computing Surveys, 28*(4), 143-143.

Terveen, L.G. (1995). An overview of human-computer collaboration. *Knowledge-Based Systems Journal, Special Issue on Human-Computer Collaboration, 8*(2-3), 67-81.

Topi, H., Babaian, T., & Lucas, W. (2005). Identifying usability issues with an ERP implementation. In *Proceedings of the Seventh International Conference on Enterprise Information Systems*, Miami, FL.

Topi, H., Lucas, W., & Babaian, T. (2006). Using informal notes for sharing corporate technology know-how. *European Journal of Information Systems, 15*(5), 486-499.

Venkatesh, V., Morris, M.G., Davis, G.B., & Davis, F.D. (2003). User acceptance of information technology: Toward a unified view. *Management Information Systems Quarterly, 27*(3), 425-478.

Wharton, C., Rieman, J., Lewis, C., & Polson, P. (1994). The cognitive walkthrough method: A practitioner's guide. In J. Nielsen & R.L. Mack (Eds.), *Usability inspection methods* (pp. 105-141). New York, NY: John Wiley & Sons.

Chapter II

A Component-Based Tool Architecture for Performance Modeling and Optimization

Michael Syrjakow, Brandenburg University of Applied Sciences, Germany

Elisabeth Syrjakow, SWR Baden-Baden, Germany

Helena Szczerbicka, University of Hanover, Germany

Abstract

Most of the available modeling and simulation tools for performance analysis do not support model optimization sufficiently. One reason for this unsatisfactory situation is the lack of universally applicable and adaptive optimization strategies. Another reason is that modeling and simulation tools usually have a monolithic software design, which is difficult to extend with experimentation functionality. Such functionality has gained in importance in recent years due to the capability of an automatic extraction of valuable information and knowledge out of complex models. One of the most important experimentation goals is to find model parameter settings, which produce optimal model behaviour. In this chapter we elaborate on the design of a powerful optimization component and its integration into existing modeling and simulation tools. For that purpose we propose a hybrid integration approach being a combination of loose document-based and tight invocation-based integration concepts. Beside the integration concept for the optimization component we also give a detailed insight into the applied optimization strategies.

Introduction

Complexity of computer software is constantly growing, both in the size of developed systems and in the intricacy of its operations. This general observation particularly applies to modeling and simulation tools, which have grown enormously over the past decades. Today the most prominent approaches to master the complexities of large-scale software development are object-orientation and component technology. Component approaches being usually built up on object-orientation concentrate design efforts on defining interfaces to pieces of a system and describing an application as the collaborations that occur among those interfaces. Implementers of a component can design and build the component in any appropriate technology as long as it supports the operations of the interface and is compatible with the component execution environment. For that reason the interface is focal point for all analysis and design activities of component-based software development (Szyperski, 1999; Brown, 2000). Component technology has also deeply influenced the area of computer simulation. Here we can distinguish two main fields of activity: component-oriented development of simulation models and component-oriented development of modeling and simulation (M&S) tools.

For a component-oriented development of distributed simulation models, the U.S. Department of Defense (DoD) Modeling and Simulation Office (DMSO) has adopted a global standard called high level architecture (Kuhl et al., 2000). Contrary to the area of component-oriented development of simulation models, where a standard is available today and where a variety of research activities can be observed, the field of component-oriented development of M&S tools yet remains rather untouched. This is a very unsatisfactory situation because many M&S tools still have a monolithical software design, which is difficult to maintain and to extend and which doesn't correspond any more to the modern distributed Web-centered technologies of today. In order to illustrate this unsatisfactory situation in more detail, we take a look at some existing and widely used M&S tools. We focus on Petri Net tools because they are a quite suitable example to explain the disadvantages of a monolithical software design. It should be mentioned for fairness that these observations also apply to other prominent classes of M&S tools, for example Queuing Network tools.

Having surveyed the software architecture of existing Petri Net tools in the second section, a hybrid integration approach for legacy M&S tools based on a component architecture is presented in the third section. The fourth section focuses on the architecture and implementation of a universally applicable optimization component. Finally, in the fifth section we summarize and draw some conclusions.

Disadvantages of Current Architectures of Petri Net Based Performance Modeling Tools

More than 100 different Petri Net tools are available today. A comprehensive database can be found at http://www.informatik.uni-hamburg.de/TGI/PetriNets/. Altogether these tools offer about 75 different graphical Petri Net editors, about 50 different token game animations, about 50 different implementations for structural analysis, and about 40 different implementations for performance analysis. This variety in fact is not bad because it opens many possibilities to deal with Petri Nets. The monolithical software design however makes it almost impossible to combine, for example, an outstanding Petri Net evaluation module from one tool with a nice graphical Petri Net editor from another tool. Beyond that, all these tools are difficult to maintain and to extend. Another significant disadvantage is the lack of interoperability. A user who has edited a Petri Net with one tool usually cannot analyse this Petri Net with another tool. The reasons for that incompatibility are the following: every Petri Net tool uses its own proprietary file format and often supports only a specific type of Petri Nets. To overcome this unsatisfactory situation, international standards are going to be established regarding:

- A mathematical semantic model, an abstract mathematical syntax, and a graphical notation for High-Level Petri Nets. The standards group of the International Organization for Standardization (ISO) relevant for the Petri Nets standardization effort is called ISO/IEC JTC1/SC7/WG11. An overview of the current activities of that group is available at http://www.informatik.uni-hamburg.de/TGI/PetriNets/standardisation/.

- A general Petri Net interchange format that supports all features of existing and forthcoming Petri Net tools. An overview of the ongoing standardization efforts of an XML-based Petri Net interchange format is given in the third section.

- A component architecture for M&S tools. In addition to the two standards mentioned above, appropriate component architecture for M&S tools is of great importance.

One main focus of this chapter is a component architecture for performance M&S tools, which will be described in detail in the following section.

Towards a Component-Oriented Design of Performance Modeling Tools

Contrary to the HLA, which provides with the RTI a very demanding infrastructure for a tight coupling of highly interdependent simulation components, component architecture for M&S tools should support a much looser component coupling. This is justified because M&S tools usually consist of a very limited number of quite self-sufficient and coarse-grained components. From the user's point of view, usually the following software parts can be identified within an M&S tool:

- **Model editor:** A model editor allows the modeller to edit new and to modify existing models. We can distinguish textual and graphical editors. Modern Web-based modeling tools may allow collaborative online editing of models. A model editor basically can be realized as an independent stand-alone component. Its output is a model description in a specific description format, which is characterized by the supported modeling technique.

- **Model analysis/evaluation modules:** These modules are used to analyse/evaluate models generated by the model editor. In case of High-Level Petri Nets (Jensen, 1991), we can distinguish between a mathematical analysis of structural properties (place-invariants, transition-invariants, boundedness, etc.) and performance evaluations (stationary or transient analyses). Performance evaluation can be computed either analytically or by (discrete-event) simulation. An evaluation module may also provide some animation features, for example, a token game animation in case of Petri Nets.

- **Experimentation modules:** These modules are optional. They allow goal-driven experimentation with a model, for example to find optimal parameter settings, to determine sensitive model parameters, to perform a model validation, and so forth. To fulfil all these tasks usually a lot of model evaluations (experiments) are required.

Figure 1. M&S tool components and their interdependencies

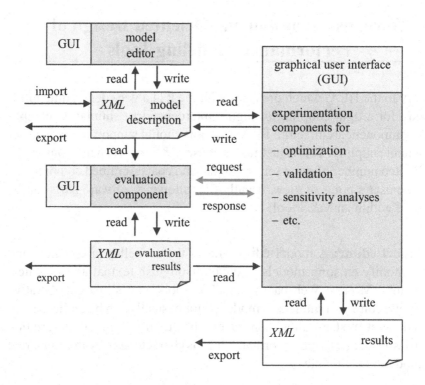

Figure 1 shows the different M&S tool components and their interdependencies. As we have described, the collaboration of these components is based on two kinds of interactions: exchange of documents and invocation of model evaluation functionality. For that reason an obvious and pragmatic integration approach for M&S tool components is a hybrid one being a combination of loose document-based and tight invocation-based integration techniques. For remote invocations, universal component "wiring" standards like CORBA (Common Object Request Broker Architecture), RMI (Remote Method Invocation) or DCOM (Distributed Component Object Model) can be used. A specialized standard like the HLA, which focuses on the specific requirements of tightly coupled simulation models (federation management, time management, etc.), is not needed in this case. For document-based integration standardized document interchange formats are required. Today, the most promising ones are XML-based approaches.

Advantages of the hybrid integration approach described above are manifold:

1. It enables a flexible distribution of the involved components within a computer network.

2. It allows user access by traditional application clients or by Java-based Web clients.

3. It enables an easy integration of existing monolithical tools as a whole by transformation of the proprietary model description format into a standardized XML-based format or partially by appropriate component wrappers.

4. It considerably simplifies tool modifications and extensions (for example to achieve HLA compliance).

5. It represents a good basis for agent-based approaches.

6. Beside all these technical advantages, component-orientation opens several economic and organizational advantages (software reuse, clear separation of concerns, etc.).

Figure 2 shows an example realization of a component-oriented M&S tool based on a modern distributed 4-tier architecture. The first tier contains client components, which allow access (Web- or application-based) to server components residing on the other tiers behind. The application server contains

Figure 2. Example realization of a component-oriented M&S tool based on a distributed 4-tier architecture

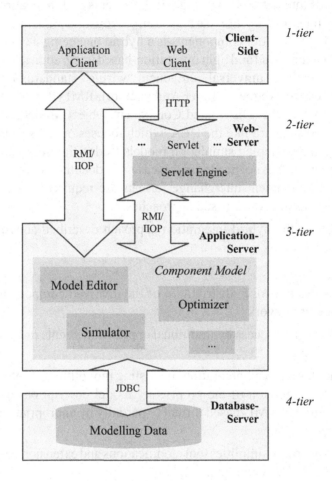

the M&S tool components shown in Figure 1. For their component-oriented realization several component models can be applied, for example J2EE/EJB, CCM (CORBA Component Model) or (D)COM/COM+ ((Distributed) Component Object Model). Persistent modeling data are saved on a database-server representing the fourth tier of the distributed architecture.

In the following two sections we will explain in more detail two important sub areas of our approach: 1) an XML-based interchange format for models of a specific modeling technique (in our case High-Level Petri Nets), and 2) experimentation components allowing the modeller to automatically extract information about the behaviour of complex simulation models. The presented methods and concepts have been already successfully used for the prototypical realization of a component-oriented Stochastic Petri Net M&S tool (Syrjakow et al., 2002; Syrjakow, 2003). A detailed description of Stochastic Petri Nets (SPN), being a particular type of High-Level Petri Nets, can be found in Lindemann (1998).

An XML-Based Model Interchange Format for High-Level Petri Nets

The idea of a standardized interchange format for Petri Nets is not new. However, the attempts to define such a standard file format were not very successful in the past. The main reasons for that are the following:

1. Each Petri Net tool usually supports a particular version of Petri Nets.
2. As a consequence, each Petri Net tool provides a specific file format, which solely satisfies the needs of the supported Petri Net type.
3. The lack of appropriate description techniques being flexible enough to cover both the common essence of all existing Petri Net types and beyond that, the specific features of any particular Petri Net extension.

Recently however, the idea of a standardized Petri Net interchange format got a new boost due to the availability of the Extended Markup Language (XML). Today XML seems to have the power to become a major means for a homogeneous and standardized exchange of information. XML allows the specification of specialized markup languages for the convenient exchange of information in specific areas of research or business. Examples of recent markup languages based on XML are the Chemical Markup Language (CML), the Mathematical Markup Language (MathML) or the Astronomical Instrument Markup Language (AIML).

In the area of Petri Nets several research groups are currently working on an XML-based model interchange format, which of course should be based on the ISO/IEC Petri Net standard. Beyond that, this format should be generic and extensible to be able to cover all existing and forthcoming Petri Net classes. A preliminary proposal for such an interchange format can be found in Jüngel et al. (2000). The proposed format consists of two parts:

1. A general part called Petri Net Markup Language (PNML), which captures the common features of all existing Petri Net versions.

2. A specific part called Petri Net Type Definition (PNTD), which allows specifying additional features. This part is of great importance because it provides openness for future Petri Net extensions.

We have proposed a PNTD for Stochastic Petri Nets in Syrjakow and Syrjakow (2003). An overview of the ongoing standardization efforts of an XML-based Petri Net interchange format can be found at http://xml.coverpages.org/xmlAndPetriNets.html.

As shown in Figure 1, XML-based description formats for models and modeling results are an integral part of our proposed M&S tool architecture. They allow a simple document based integration of tool components, which is usually much easier to realize than invocation-based approaches. Beyond that, existing monolithically designed M&S tools can be easily integrated into our architecture without any expensive software modifications. For that purpose only appropriate file converters (C) have to be realized being able to convert the proprietary file formats of the legacy tools into the XML-based model interchange format (see Figure 3). This has been proven to be a very simple and efficient way to achieve compatibility between several legacy M&S tools allowing the mutual use of parts (editors, evaluation components, etc.) of them.

Figure 3. Necessary format conversions with an XML-based model interchange format

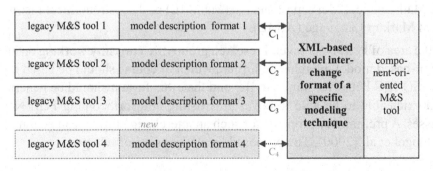

Figure 4. Necessary format conversions without an XML-based model interchange format

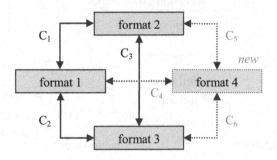

As shown in Figure 3 for the integration of a new legacy tool the realization of only one additional file converter is required. Without such a standardized interchange format the number of required file converters would not increase linearly but quadratically. As indicated in Figure 4 for n different file formats, $(n^2-n)/2$ file converters would be required to achieve compatibility between the n corresponding M&S tools.

Experimentation Components

M&S tool developers often neglected or in the worst case just ignored experimentation components in the past. This was mainly caused by the monolithical software design of the existing M&S tools, which made a later integration of additional experimentation functionality rather intricate and expensive. With the enormous increase of model complexity however these components have gained great importance because experimentation goals like finding optimal or sensitive model parameters cannot be reached by hand any more. Following our hybrid integration approach it is very easy to provide an existing M&S tool with additional functionality for experimentation, which can be used to automatically extract valuable information and knowledge out of complex models. In the following, we take a detailed look at a parameter optimization component, which provides efficient and universally applicable methods to optimize the behaviour of complex simulation models.

Figure 5. Parameter optimization of a simulation-based goal function

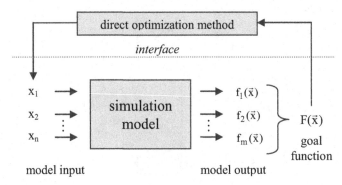

Tool Support for Model Optimization

Introduction to Model Optimization

This section gives a brief introduction to the fascinating field of model optimization. In the following, the instance of an optimization problem is formalized as a pair (S,F). The solution space S denotes the set of all possible problem solutions. The goal function F, which has to be optimized, is a mapping defined as $F : S \to R$. In this paper we focus on parameter optimization problems where the search space is a subset of R^n ($S \subset R^n$) and the goal function is defined through a performance model, which is analysed by discrete event simulation. Such a goal function is called simulation-based goal function in the following.

As shown in Figure 5, a performance model maps a vector $\vec{x} = (x_1, x_2, ..., x_n), x_i \in R$, $i \in \{1,..., n\}$ of model input parameters onto several model outputs $f_j(\vec{x})$, $j \in \{1,...,m\}$. Often the relation between input and output of a performance model is so complex that it cannot be described by mathematical expressions any more. In this case the performance model represents a so-called "black-box" system.

A function $f : S \subset Rn \to Rm$ that is defined through a model is referred to as model function. In case of a performance model the model inputs can be roughly classified into system and workload parameters. The model outputs describe the system behaviour (performance, reliability, consumption of resources, etc.). As indicated in Figure 5, the goal function F may be either one or a composition of several model outputs. The formulation of F usually is rather difficult, especially if contradictory goals are involved. Very frequently F is defined as a weighted sum of model outputs

$$F(\vec{x}) = \sum_{k=1}^{m} \omega_k \cdot f_k(\vec{x}), \; \omega_k \in R$$

$$(1)$$

The overall goal of optimizing a simulation-based goal function is to find a parameter vector $\vec{x}^* \in S$ which satisfies:

$$\forall \vec{x} \in S : F(\vec{x}) \circ F(\vec{x}^*) = F^*, \text{ with } \circ \in \{\leq, \geq\}$$

$$(2)$$

A solution $\vec{x}^*$ is called global optimum point. The goal function value $F(\vec{x}^*) = F^*$ is referred to as global optimum of F. Beside global optimum points there may exist local optimum points $\vec{x}^\wedge$, having the property that all neighbouring solutions have the equal or a worse goal function value. A local optimum $F^\wedge = F(\vec{x}^\wedge)$ is defined as follows:

$$\exists \varepsilon > 0, \forall \vec{x} \in S : \left\| \vec{x} - \vec{x}^\wedge \right\| < \varepsilon \Rightarrow F(\vec{x}) \circ F(\vec{x}^\wedge) = F^\wedge, \text{ with } \circ \in \{\leq, \geq\}.$$

$$(3)$$

Goal functions with several global and/or local optimum points are called multimodal functions. An optimization problem is either a minimization ($\circ = \geq$) or a maximization ($\circ = \leq$) problem. Minimization problems can be easily transformed into maximization problems and vice versa, because $\min\{F(\vec{x})\} = -\max\{-F(\vec{x})\}$.

Optimization of a simulation-based goal function has been proven to be a demanding task. The main challenges are the following:

- **Black-box situation:** Usually the relation between input and output of performance models being analysed by discrete event simulation cannot be described mathematically. For that reason classical mathematical optimization methods, which require analytical information like gradients or other problem specific knowledge, are not applicable any more.

- **Expensive model evaluation process:** Evaluation of a simulation model usually requires a lot of computation time, which in practice may last from several minutes until many hours or even days. For that reason the optimization process should only require a very limited number of simulation runs (goal function evaluations) to reach the optimization goal.

- **Inaccurate simulation results:** The model outputs of probabilistic performance models being evaluated by discrete event simulation may be considerably distorted by stochastic inaccuracies. For that reason the applied optimization methods should be robust against inaccurately evaluated goal function values.

- High dimensional search space with complex parameter restrictions.

- Multimodal goal function with many local and/or global optimum points.

Summing up, for optimization of simulation models methods are required, which first of all are able to deal with the black-box situation. For that reason only optimization methods are applicable which solely use goal function values to guide the optimization process (blind search). Methods with this property are called direct optimization methods. As shown in Figure 5, direct optimization methods work iteratively. A parameter vector $\bar{x}$ generated by the direct optimization process is passed on to the simulation process, where a simulation tool evaluates the optimized simulation model. Afterwards, the calculated goal function value $F(\bar{x})$ is sent back to the optimization process. Outgoing from $F(\bar{x})$, a new parameter vector is generated, which is in turn transferred to the simulation process. This way, the goal function is improved step by step until a termination condition is fulfilled. Because the evaluation of a simulation-based goal function usually requires considerable computational resources the optimization goal should be reached with a minimum number of iteration steps.

Genetic algorithms (Goldberg, 1989; Michalewicz, 1992), evolution strategies (Schwefel, 1981), and simulated annealing (Aarts & Korst, 1989) are the most common and powerful direct methods for global optimization today. All these methods apply probabilistic search operators that imitate principles of nature. Although these operators have been proven to be well suited for global search, the required computational effort (number of goal function evaluations) and the quality of the generated optimization results still remain a big problem. In the following, an approach for further improvement of direct optimization methods is presented. Our considerations are restricted to global optimization of continuous parameter optimization problems. In order to make direct optimization more efficient and to achieve high quality solutions, we propose a combination of existing global and local optimization methods. The structure of the resulting combined 2-phase optimization strategy is described in the next section. The excellent heuristic properties of this hybrid method allow using it as the basic component of a multiple-stage optimization strategy, which is presented next. Then, several methods to reduce goal function evaluations are presented. Following that, a section describes an approach to deal with misleading problems. The next segment is about the realization of our developed optimization algorithms. Finally, some optimization results achieved with our optimization strategies are presented.

Combined 2-Phase Optimization

To be able to cope with the non-trivial task of model optimization described above, we have developed a new kind of direct optimization algorithm called combined 2-phase optimization strategy. The basic idea of this hybrid method is to split the optimization process into two phases: pre-optimization with a probabilistic global optimization method and fine-optimization performed by a deterministic local Hill-Climber. The task of pre-optimization is to explore

Figure 6. Basic structure of a combined 2-phase optimization strategy

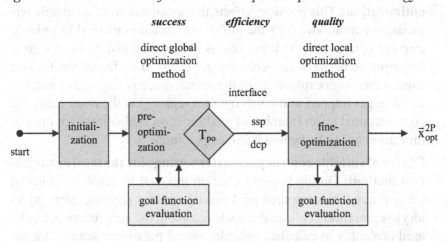

the search space in order to get into the direct neighbourhood (catchment area) of a global optimum point. The catchment area of an extreme point represents all the search points in its neighbourhood from which the extreme point can be localized by a local optimization method. Outgoing from the best solution found by pre-optimization (pre-optimization result) the task of fine-optimization is to efficiently localize the neighbouring extreme point with a user-defined accuracy. Thus, pre-optimization is predominantly responsible for optimization success, whereas fine-optimization has to ensure the quality of the optimization result.

Figure 6 shows the basic structure of a combined 2-phase optimization strategy, which is referred to as os_{2P} in the following. For pre-optimization os_{2P} uses a direct global optimization method. For fine-optimization a direct local optimization method is applied. The two strategies are coupled by an interface, comprising a method to select starting points (SSP) as well as a method to derive control parameter values from optimization trajectories (dcp). The result of a combined 2-phase optimization strategy as well as the required computational effort mainly depend on the specific capabilities of the employed global and local optimization method but also on the:

- **Choice of suitable control parameter settings for the global optimization method:** For pre-optimization control parameter settings have to be used rather forcing exploration of the search space than convergence towards a search space region. This can be achieved by emphasizing the probabilistic search operators of the global optimization method.

- **Choice of an advantageous switch-over point from pre- to fine-optimization:** This problem affects the specification of a suitable termination condition T_{po} for the global optimization method in order to stop pre-optimization in time. This is not a trivial task because a good compromise between two contrary goals has to be found. On the one hand, a thorough exploration of the search space is required in order to avoid to get trapped into a sub-optimal region. On the other hand, the computational effort (number of goal function evaluations) for pre-optimization has to be kept as small as possible.

- **Choice of suitable control parameter settings for the local optimization method:** During pre-optimization the goal function is evaluated many times. The computed goal function values (optimization trajectory), representing collected knowledge about the goal function, can be used profitably to calculate suitable control parameter settings for the local optimization method. For this purpose a method to derive control parameter settings from optimization trajectories (dcp) was developed. It is based on analysing the optimization trajectory of the global optimization method by application of cluster analysis methods. From the size and form of the found clusters appropriate step sizes for the local optimization method can be derived. Well-suited initial step sizes are very important to keep the required number of goal function evaluations for local search small.

- **Selection of a favourable starting point** $\vec{x}_{start}$ **for the local optimization method (SSP):** The simplest way to solve this problem is to choose the best solution found during pre-optimization as the starting point $\vec{x}_{start}$ for fine-optimization. A more complex approach is described in detail later in the chapter.

As already mentioned, the specification of an appropriate termination condition T_{po} is decisive for the efficiency of a combined 2-phase strategy. On principal T_{po} may be based on the following criteria:

- **The number of generated search points:** This criterion allows specifying the maximum number of goal function evaluations that should be spent for pre-optimization.

- **Search point constellations:** Specific search point constellations (regional accumulations of search points in the search space) indicate convergence of the global optimization method towards a search space region. Applying standard cluster analysis methods, this property can be exploited profitably to compute switch-over points of good quality.

- **The improvement of the goal function:** This criterion has been proven to be the most powerful one. Pre-optimization is stopped if the goal function could not be improved p%, $p \in R^+$ over a specified number of iteration steps.

Table 1. Powerful direct optimization methods for global and local search

	global	local
direct optimization methods	genetic algorithm (GA) simulated annealing (SA)	pattern search (PS) of Hooke and Jeeves (1961)

- **A priori knowledge about the goal function:** A priori knowledge about the goal function usually provides advantageous hints to improve efficiency. Hence, if available, it should be exploited in any case.

Of course, it is also possible to specify termination conditions that combine several of the criteria listed above.

Table 1 shows some powerful direct optimization methods for global and local search that are well suited for realization of a combined 2-phase optimization strategy. Outgoing from the optimization methods presented in Table 1 there exist the following realization possibilities:

- genetic algorithm + pattern search (GA+PS)
- simulated annealing + pattern search (SA+PS)

Both realization alternatives have been already implemented and thoroughly examined (Syrjakow, 1997; Syrjakow & Szczerbicka, 1997, 1999). Some quantitative optimization results achieved with GA+PS are presented later in the chapter.

Multiple-Stage Optimization

All optimization strategies considered so far localize only one optimum point when executed. Outgoing from these so-called single-stage optimiza-

Figure 7. Basic structure of a multiple-stage optimization strategy

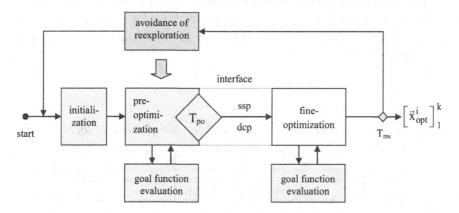

tion strategies, we want to present an optimization algorithm that is able to detect several optimum points of a given (multimodal) optimization problem. The basic structure of such a multiple-stage optimization algorithm, which is referred to as osms in the following, is shown in Figure 7.

The main component of a multiple-stage optimization strategy is a combined 2-phase strategy os_{2p}. os_{2p} is embedded in an exterior iteration process, which generates step-by-step a sequence of optimum points $\vec{x}_{opt}^1, \vec{x}_{opt}^2, ..., \vec{x}_{opt}^k, k \in N$. An iteration step of a multiple-stage optimization strategy is called optimization stage. os_{ms} stops if the termination condition T_{ms} is fulfilled. A good termination criterion has been proven to be: stop, if a new optimum point could not be located over a specified number of optimization stages. If T_{ms} is not fulfilled, a method called avoidance of reexploration (AR) is applied. The task of AR is to avoid that previously found optimum points are located again in subsequent optimization stages. This is done by making already explored regions of the search space unattractive for the global optimization method used for pre-optimization. For that purpose attractiveness values are introduced and related to each search point of the search space. Attractiveness values are computed by means of an attractiveness function

$$av(\bar{x}) = \prod_{i=1}^{k} \left[1 - (1 + \alpha \cdot d_i)^{-\beta} \right] \tag{4}$$

with $d_i = \sqrt{(\bar{x} - \bar{x}_{opt}^i)^2}$; α, β: scaling factors; k: number of already found optimum points.

Multiple-stage optimization can be viewed as a substantial improvement compared to conventional optimization methods because not only one optimal solution is localized but a sequence of the most prominent extreme points of the given optimization problem. This enables the modeller to get a comprehensive overview of the behaviour of the optimized system. For a further description of multiple-stage optimization we refer to Syrjakow and Szczerbicka (1994) and Syrjakow (1997).

Methods for Reduction of Goal Function Evaluations

As already mentioned, simulation-based goal functions may require a lot of time for evaluation. Thus, for direct optimization of these functions additional methods to reduce goal function evaluations are of great importance. A very simple and obvious way to save goal function evaluations is to avoid reevaluations of search points, which are generated several times during the optimization process. This can be done very easily by search of the optimization trajectory, which comprises all generated search points together with their corresponding goal function values.

Within a combined 2-phase strategy the pre-optimization phase offers an additional possibility to save goal function evaluations. This is due to the primary goal of pre-optimization, which is not to exactly localize a globally optimal solution but only to get into its catchment area. This property as well as the robustness of probabilistic global optimization strategies against inaccurately evaluated goal function values makes it possible to also use goal function approximations. The goal function value of a search point can be approximated if there are several search points in its direct neighbourhood, which have been already evaluated. Through goal function approximation a lot of possibly very expensive goal function evaluations can be saved without a substantial loss of optimization success. Especially multiple-stage optimization makes the application of a goal function approximator very advantageous. In this case with each optimization stage some more information about the goal function

Figure 8. Acceleration of pre-optimization through goal function approximation

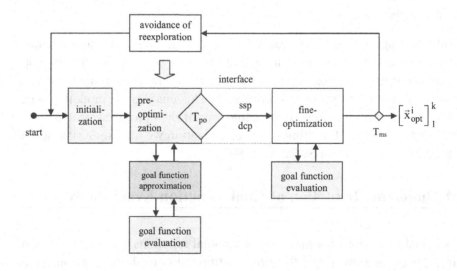

Figure 9. Repeated start of fine-optimization

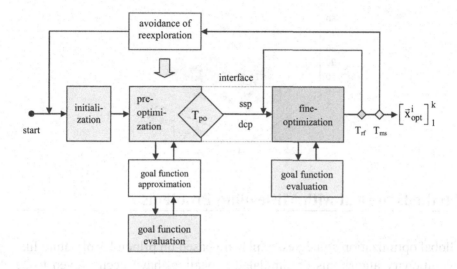

is gathered, which in turn can be exploited in subsequent optimization stages for approximation. Figure 8 shows the multiple-stage optimization strategy of Figure 7 extended by a goal function approximator, which is embedded between the pre-optimization process and the process of goal function evaluation. For approximation we use a simple grid-based technique as well as a special kind of neural networks called rectangular basis function networks (Berthold & Huber, 1995). A more detailed description of our approach to accelerate pre-optimization by goal function approximation can be found in Syrjakow et al. (1996).

Another possibility to save goal function evaluations is to start fine-optimization not only once after a pre-optimization run but several times. This repeated start of fine-optimization, which is shown in Figure 9, has been proven to be very successful, especially in case of multimodal goal functions with many global and/or local extreme points. Then, the probability is rather high that during pre-optimization several similar good solutions are found being located in the catchment areas of different extreme points. These extreme points can be obtained with only one pre-optimization run through the repeated start of fine-optimization.

Figure 10. Misleading problem for evolutionary algorithms

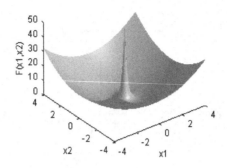

Methods to Deal with Misleading Problems

Global optimization strategies, which are based on principles of nature like evolutionary algorithms or simulated annealing, have been proven to be very suitable for pre-optimization in many cases. However, there also exist problems that are very difficult to solve with these strategies. "Very difficult" for a particular optimization strategy means that pure Monte Carlo search works better on average. Problems with this property are called misleading for the considered optimization strategy in the following. An example of a misleading problem for evolutionary algorithms is presented in Figure 10.

This problem is difficult to solve because the catchment area of the global optimum point, which is located exactly in the middle of the search space is much smaller than the catchment areas of the surrounding four local optimum points. To solve this problem with an evolutionary algorithm the catchment area of the globally optimal solution has to be found very early in the optimization process. Otherwise the evolutionary algorithm converges quickly towards one of the four locally optimal solutions at the edge of the search space. The more the evolutionary algorithm converges towards one of the locally optimal solutions, the less the probability will be to get back to the catchment area of the globally optimal solution. This is not the case when pure Monte Carlo search is applied because here the generated search points are equally distributed all over the search space.

An obvious possibility to improve the optimization success of a multiple-stage optimization strategy in case of misleading problems is to cyclically apply several pre-optimization methods. This possibility is depicted in *Figure 11* where a genetic algorithm (GA), simulated annealing (SA), evolution strate-

Figure 11. Application of different pre-optimization strategies in cyclical change

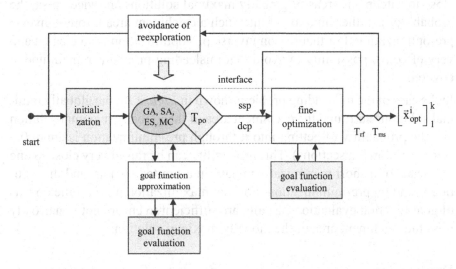

gies (ES) and pure Monte Carlo (MC) search are applied cyclically one after the other. This collection of pre-optimization strategies has been proven to be very suitable because several different search principles are applied. That way the overall performance of multiple-stage optimization might slightly decrease in case of good-natured problems. However, the risk is considerably lowered to work on a particular problem with a completely unsuited optimization strategy.

As already mentioned the misleading problem presented in *Figure 10* can be solved on average more successfully with pure Monte Carlo search than with evolutionary algorithms. However, pure Monte Carlo search certainly is also not a very good choice because the observable performance difference is far away from being substantial and more and more shrinking with increasing problem dimension (see the following sections). A much more promising approach has been proven to be a slight modification of the multiple-stage strategy presented in *Figure 11*. The modification is that the search objective (minimization or maximization) of pre-optimization remains not always the same but changes from time to time. Pre-optimization with the inverse search objective is called inverse pre-optimization in the following. When maximizing the goal function depicted in *Figure 10*, inverse pre-optimization means that the applied pre-optimization algorithm is not looking for the global maximum but for the global minimum. Because misleading problems usually have a function surface where globally minimal solutions are located close to catchment areas of globally maximal solutions and vice versa, the probability is rather high to get into such a catchment area through inverse pre-optimization. For that reason inverse pre-optimization is an elegant and very effective possibility to avoid that misleading problems remain undiscovered.

In the case of the misleading problem shown in *Figure 10*, the globally minimal solutions surround the catchment area of the globally maximal solution and the probability of getting into it through pre-minimization is about 0.5 (see the following sections). This probability can be raised very close to one by means of a short maximization phase in a limited area around the solution found by pre-minimization. For that maximization phase some dozens of goal function evaluations usually are sufficient to ensure not to narrowly miss the catchment area of the globally maximal solution.

Realization

All the optimization strategies described above have been already implemented and integrated into the parameter optimization component shown in Figure 12. Such a parameter optimization component can be viewed as a special kind of experimentation component. As already depicted in Figure 1, the extension of an M&S tool by an experimentation component requires—in addition to the exchange of standardized documents—also a more tight invocation-based integration concept. This is unavoidable because the two alternating processes of experimentation (generation of model input parameters) and model evaluation have to be coupled with each other allowing data exchange as well as process synchronisation.

Figure 12 shows the interactions of a direct parameter optimization component with a model evaluation component. For specification of the optimization problem the optimization component has access to two files: the model description and the evaluation results. The model description comprises all existing model parameters allowing the user to select the parameters that have to be optimized. To define the goal function the user has to select one or to combine several model outputs, which can be found in the evaluation results file. In each iteration step of the optimization process the direct search strategy generates a vector of parameter values that are entered into

Figure 12. Interactions between the components for model evaluation and optimization

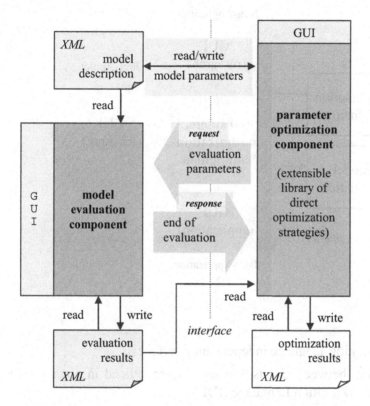

the model description. Subsequently, the optimization component sends a request to the evaluation component containing several evaluation parameters. In case of a discrete-event simulation component, for example, the simulation run length, kind of confidence interval method and so forth has to be defined. After model evaluation the evaluation component sends a response message to the optimization component to indicate that the required model outputs have been calculated and are now available in the evaluation results file. Outgoing from these outputs the optimization strategy generates a new parameter vector. This alternating process continues until a termination criterion is fulfilled.

For realization of the required invocations of the model evaluation component, universal middleware standards like CORBA, RMI or DCOM can be used. In our case we have used CORBA because it provides the following main advantages:

Figure 13. Graphical user interface (GUI) of the optimization component

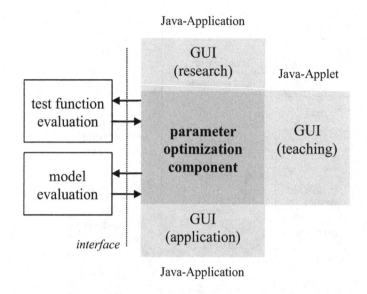

- Programming-language independent interface
- Interfaces between clients and servers are defined in a standardized Interface Definition Language (IDL)
- Using IDL, programmers can encapsulate existing applications in wrappers and use them as objects on the ORB (Object Request Broker)
- Rich set of distributed object services and facilities

To allow a flexible and platform independent usage the parameter optimization component was implemented in Java. Beside the optimization algorithms our optimization component offers a powerful graphical user interface (GUI). As depicted in Figure 13 the GUI is divided into three parts. Each part is designed for a particular kind of user group to ensure a comfortable dealing with the implemented optimization algorithms.

Altogether the following kinds of use are supported:

- **Getting advanced knowledge about complexity, behaviour, and performance of the implemented optimization strategies:** For that purpose a lot of mathematical test functions are offered. Compared to simulation-based goal functions mathematical test functions have the great advantage that they can be evaluated very quickly. This property allows making a large number of optimization experiments in a short time, which is a basic prerequisite for statistically sound performance analyses of probabilistic optimization strategies.

- **Getting familiar with the implemented optimization strategies:** For that purpose the complex search processes of several direct optimization methods are visualized. To ease the access to this version we have implemented it as a Java-Applet. It is available on the Web at http://ces. univ-karlsruhe.de/goethe/syrjakow/anim_env3/start_environ-ment. html.

- **Application of the implemented optimization algorithms to optimization problems from practice:** For this purpose the GUI allows the specification of model optimization problems. Afterwards a personal assistant (wizard) supports the user to choose an appropriate optimization strategy. Finally, the user has the possibility to observe the ongoing optimization process and to look at the computed optimization results.

Evaluation

Some very important theoretical results regarding direct optimization strategies are summarized in the so-called "No Free Lunch" theorems for optimization (Wolpert & Macready, 1997), which can be viewed as a framework to explain the connection between effective direct optimization algorithms and the problems they solve. These theorems, loosely speaking, say that all algorithms that search for an extremum of a goal function perform exactly the same, when averaged over all possible goal functions. In other words no direct optimization algorithm, when averaged across all possible goal functions, is able to outperform pure Monte Carlo search. This in turn means that without any structural assumptions on an optimization problem it doesn't make any difference what kind of direct optimization algorithm is chosen.

At first sight this looks unpleasant because pure Monte Carlo search gets the same rating as much more sophisticated nature-analogous optimization methods like genetic algorithms or simulated annealing, which don't use chance completely arbitrarily but in a goal-driven way. Fortunately however, many simulation-based goal functions from practice are structured that way that nature-analogous optimization methods perform better than Monte Carlo search (Droste et al., 1999). Such good-natured optimization problems can be characterized as follows:

1.   The search space comprises only a limited number of extreme points.
2.   Each extreme point has an extensive catchment area.
3.   The goal function surface above the catchment area of an extreme point is not a thin peak.

The properties listed above usually are fulfilled if the system that has to be optimized is a technical system. This is not surprising because in this case a well-defined (non-chaotic) system behaviour can be assumed.

As already mentioned our proposed optimization methods usually perform well on good-natured problems. However, there also exist some exceptions. In the following, we consider a mathematical test problem, which in the 2- and 3-dimensional case fulfils the simplifying assumptions above. Even so, it isn't easy to optimize. This problem, which was already investigated in a previous section, is specified in Table 2. The problem specification comprises the definition of the solution space S and the goal function F. Beyond that, the function surface for the 2-dimensional case (S2, F2) is presented. For all problem dimensions $n \in N$ test problem (Sn, Fn) has exactly one globally maximal solution at $\vec{x}^* = (0, 0, ..., 0)$, which is surrounded by four locally maxi-

Table 2. Test problem (S^n, F^n)

Specification of test problem (S^n, F^n)	Function surface of (S^2, F^2)
Solution space: $$S^n = \left\{ \vec{x} \in R^n \mid -a_i \leq x_i \leq a_i; i \in \{1,...,n\} \right\}$$ Goal function: $$F^n(\vec{x}) = \sum_{i=1}^{n} x_i^2 + \frac{1}{0.02 + \sum_{i=1}^{n} x_i^2}$$	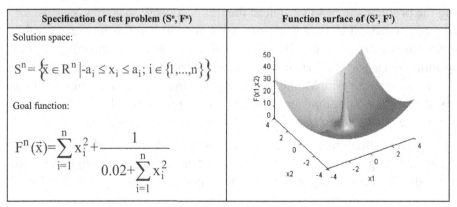

Table 3. Constants ai, i∈{1,...,n} of test problem (Sn, Fn), n∈{2,3,4}

problem dimension n	2	3	4
constants a_i	4	2.5	2

mal solutions. Although the function surface fairly well fulfils the simplifying assumptions it can be shown that evolutionary algorithms solve this problem less successfully than pure Monte Carlo search.

In the following, this is shown empirically by means of a comprehensive optimization experiment where we study not only the 2-dimensional but also the 3- and 4-dimensional case. The values of the constants ai, $i\in\{1,...,n\}$, which restrict the search space and determine the goal function values of the four locally maximal solutions of (Sn, Fn), $n\in\{2,3,4\}$, are presented in Table 3.

To solve the test problem specified in Table 2 a multiple-stage optimization strategy osms was applied. Within the multiple-stage strategy a combined 2-phase optimization algorithm os2P was used consisting of a genetic algorithm (being a special kind of evolutionary algorithm) for pre-maximization and pattern search for fine-maximization. The demanded accuracy of the pattern search algorithm was set to 0.01 for each coordinate. In order to get a representative overview of the performance behaviour of osms 200 independent optimization runs were carried out for each considered problem dimension $n\in\{2,3,4\}$. In each of these 200 multiple-stage runs a sequence of 20 maximum points was generated with osms.

Diagram 1 summarizes the results of this experiment, which is referred to as E1 in the following. The x-axis of Diagram 1 shows the problem dimension $n\in\{2,3,4\}$. The bars represent the average number of goal function evaluations required in one optimization stage (optimization effort oe). The white bars show the optimization effort of the GA, the grey ones represent the optimization effort of PS. The lines show the optimization success os(s) achieved after $s\in\{1,2,...,5\}$ optimization stages, which is defined as follows:

$$os(s)=\sum_{i=1}^{s}p_{\bar{x}^i,\varepsilon}^i \qquad (5)$$

Diagram 1. Results of optimization experiment E_1

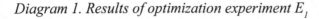

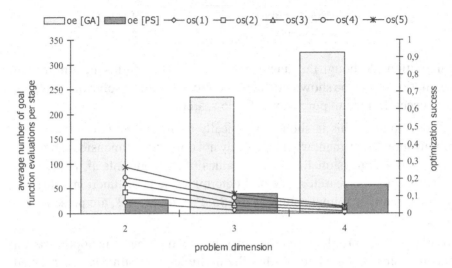

problem dimension

In the expression above s denotes the optimization stage and $p^i_{\bar{x}^*,\varepsilon}$ is the empirical probability of finding the global maximum point $\bar{x}^*$ for the first time in optimization stage i with accuracy ε:

$$p^i_{\bar{x}^*,\varepsilon} = \frac{\text{number of first } (\bar{x}^*,\varepsilon)\text{-hits in stage i}}{\text{total number of stage i optimization runs}} \qquad (6)$$

The results presented in Diagram 1 impressively show that it is very difficult for the genetic algorithm to get into the catchment area of the globally maximal solution. Already for the 2-dimensional problem (S^2, F^2) the optimization success after the first optimization stage is very low and cannot be increased considerably with additional optimization stages. With increasing problem dimension the success curves os(s), $s \in \{1,2,...,5\}$ quickly drop towards zero.

To get more evidence that (Sn, Fn) is really a misleading problem for genetic algorithms another comprehensive optimization experiment was made. In this experiment, which is referred to as E2 in the following, the same multiple-stage optimization strategy as in E1 was used except that for pre-optimization the genetic algorithm was replaced with pure Monte Carlo search. The results of E2 are summarized in Diagram 2. They confirm that (Sn, Fn) actually is

Diagram 2. Results of optimization experiment E_2

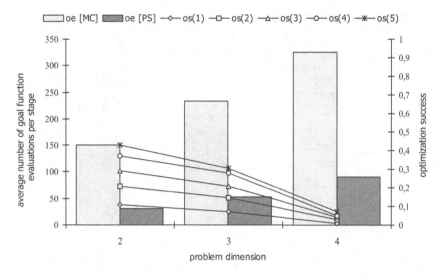

a misleading problem for genetic algorithms because, with exactly the same pre-optimization effort, pure Monte Carlo search works better on average than genetic algorithms. However, the difference between the success curves shown in Diagram 1 and 2 is rather small and drops with increasing problem dimension. For that reason pure Monte Carlo search cannot be considered as a really good substitute for genetic algorithms.

The results of the next optimization experiment E3 show that it is quite possible to solve test problem (Sn, Fn) both successfully and efficiently. The optimization strategy used in E3 is the same as in E1 apart from the fact that for pre-optimization the genetic algorithm is used inversely, that is, the genetic algorithm is used for minimization instead of maximization. The results of E3 are summarized in Diagram 3. With exactly the same control parameter settings as in E1 the genetic algorithm gets into the catchment area of the globally maximal solution in the first optimization stage with a probability of almost 0.5 independently of the problem dimension. The success curves os(i), $i \in \{2,3,...,5\}$ show that with each additional optimization stage the optimization success can be increased considerably. After five optimization stages the optimization success has almost reached the maximal value of 1 for all considered problem dimensions. The success curve os(1) presented in Diagram 3 can be further improved if after pre-minimization a short maximization phase is carried out in a limited area around the solution

Diagram 3. Results of optimization experiment E3

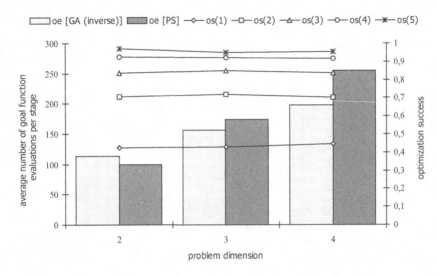

problem dimension

found by pre-minimization. That way it is possible to raise os(1) almost to 1 by spending only some dozens of goal function evaluations.

Finally, it should be mentioned that the optimization results presented in this section could be further improved through application of the methods to reduce goal function evaluations described in the previous sections. In the experiments described above only the very simple method to avoid reevaluations of previously evaluated search points was applied in order to save goal function evaluations. Through application of goal function approximation and repeated fine-optimization it is possible to further reduce the optimization effort of os_{ms} considerably. Quantitative results regarding this can be found in Syrjakow et al. (1996) and Syrjakow (1997).

Conclusion

In this chapter we presented a hybrid integration approach for M&S tool components being a combination of loose document-based and tight invocation-based integration concepts. The core of our approach is an XML-based model interchange format, which allows a homogeneous and standardized information exchange between tool components. For the tight coupling of tool components universal component "wiring" standards are used. Our integration concept has been proven to be very flexible and applicable to all kinds of M&S tools. For its validation we have applied it to realize a component-oriented SPN-based M&S tool. A great advantage of M&S tools with a component-oriented software design is their openness for all kinds of extensions. As a result tool developers can fully concentrate on the development of such extensions and are not any longer needlessly stressed with their integration.

Today, especially experimentation components are of great importance because they allow to automatically extract valuable information and knowledge about the behaviour of complex simulation models, which isn't possible by hand any more. In this chapter an experimentation component was presented in detail, which provides efficient and universally applicable methods to optimize the behaviour of complex simulation models. Beside common direct strategies for global and local search our optimization component offers combined 2-phase and multiple-stage optimization being a substantial improvement compared to existing nature-analogous optimization methods like genetic algorithms, simulated annealing, and hill-climbing. Combined 2-phase strategies are combinations of global and local search methods trying to exploit their advantages. The excellent heuristic properties of combined 2-phase optimization are an important prerequisite for multiple-stage optimization allowing to efficiently localize not only one but a sequence of prominent extreme points of a given goal function. Altogether our optimization component offers a powerful modular assembly system of direct optimization strategies, which can be flexibly adapted to a broad range of optimization problems. The achieved optimization results show that our developed optimization methods work very well on a variety of good-natured problems. Even misleading problems can be solved efficiently through inverse pre-optimization. In our future work we intend to further improve our optimization algorithms. At the moment we are looking for local fine-optimization strategies that could replace the deterministic pattern search algorithm. A promising candidate seems to be the probabilistic SPSA (simultaneous perturbation stochastic approximation) method (Spall, 1998). Beyond that, we will develop other kinds of experimentation components, for example, for sensitivity analysis or model validation. And finally, we will further apply our hybrid integration concept to build powerful and innovative M&S tools.

Acknowledgment

We want to thank Professor D. Schmid for his encouragement and support of our work. We also thank our students, especially S. Schillinger, F. Schmidt, H. Renfranz, T. Sommer, D. Haag, C. Bentz, J. Gramlich, and A. Kehl for their engagement and contributions.

References

Aarts, E., & Korst, J. (1989). *Simulated annealing and Boltzmann machines*. New York: John Wiley & Sons.

Berthold, M.R., & Huber, K.-P. (1995). Extraction of soft rules from RecBF networks. *Advances in Intelligent Data Analysis, 1*, 11-15.

Brown, A.W. (2000). *Large-scale, component-based development*. Prentice Hall.

Droste, S., Jansen, T., & Wegener, I. (1999). Perhaps not a free lunch but at least a free appetizer. In *Proceedings of the Genetic and Evolutionary Computation Conference*, Orlando, Florida, USA (pp. 833-839).

Goldberg, D.E. (1989). *Genetic algorithms in search, optimization and machine learning*. Addison-Wesley.

Goldberg, D.E., & Sastry, K. (2007). *Genetic algorithms: The design of innovation*. Berlin: Springer.

Heineman, G.T., & Council, W.T. (2001). *Component-based software engineering - putting the pieces together*. Addison-Wesley.

Hooke, R.A., & Jeeves, T.A. (1961). Direct search solution for numerical and statistical problems. *Journal of the ACM, 8*, pp. 212-221.

Jensen, K. (1991). *High-Level Petri Nets: Theory and application*. Springer.

Jüngel, M., Kindler, E., & Weber, M. (2000). The Petri Net Markup Language. In *Proceedings of the AWPN-Workshop*. Koblenz, Germany.

Kuhl, F., Weatherly, R., & Dahmann, J. (2000). *Creating computer simulation systems - an introduction to the high level architecture*. Prentice Hall.

Lindemann, C. (1998). *Performance modelling with deterministic and stochastic Petri Nets*. New York: John Wiley & Sons.

Michalewicz, Z. (1992). *Genetic algorithms + data structures = evolution programs*. Springer-Verlag.

Price, K.V., Storn, R., & Lampinen, J. (2005). *Differential evolution - a practical approach to global optimization*. Berlin: Springer.

Schwefel, H.-P. (1981). *Numerical optimization of computer models*. New York: John Wiley & Sons.

Spall, J.C. (1998). An overview of the simultaneous perturbation method for efficient optimization. *Johns Hopkins APL Technical Digest, 19*, 482–492.

Syrjakow, M., & Szczerbicka, H. (1994). Optimization of simulation models with REMO. In *Proceedings of the European Simulation Multiconference*, Barcelona, Spain (pp. 274-281).

Syrjakow, M., Szczerbicka, H., Berthold, M.R., & Huber, K.-P. (1996). Acceleration of Direct Model Optimization Methods by Function Approximation. In *Proceedings of the 8th European Simulation Symposium*, Genoa, Italy (Vol. II, pp. 181-186).

Syrjakow, M. (1997). *Verfahren zur effizienten Parameteroptimierung von Simulationsmodellen*. Dissertation at the Institute for Computer Design and Fault Tolerance at the University of Karlsruhe. Shaker-Verlag, Aachen.

Syrjakow, M., & Szczerbicka, H. (1997). Efficient methods for parameter optimization of simulation models. In *Proceedings of the 1st World Congress on Systems Simulation*, Singapore, Republic of Singapore (pp. 54-59).

Syrjakow, M., & Szczerbicka, H. (1999). Efficient parameter optimization based on combination of direct global and local search methods. In L. D. Davis, K. De Jong, M. D. Vose, & L. D. Whitley (Eds.), *Evolutionary Algorithms*. Ima Volumes in Mathematics and Its Applications (Vol. 111, pp. 227-249). New York: Springer Verlag.

Syrjakow, M., Syrjakow, E., & Szczerbicka, H. (2002). Towards a component-oriented design of modeling and simulation tools. In *Proceedings of the International Conference on AI, Simulation and Planning in High Autonomy Systems*, Lisbon, Portugal.

Syrjakow, M. (2003). *Web- und Komponenten-Technologien in der Modellierung und Simulation*. Habilitation at the Faculty of Informatics at the University of Karlsruhe.

Syrjakow, E., & Syrjakow, M. (2003). XML for data representation in modeling and simulation environments. In *Proceedings of the IASTED International Conference on Modelling, Simulation, and Optimization*, Banff, Alberta, Canada (pp. 100-107).

Szyperski, C. (1999). *Component software - beyond object-oriented programming*. Addison-Wesley.

Wolpert, D.H., & Macready, W.G. (1997, April). No free lunch theorems for optimization. *IEEE Transactions on Evolutionary Computation, 1*(1), 67-82.

Zomaya, A.Y. (2006). *Handbook of nature-inspired and innovative computing - integrating classical models with emerging technologies*. Springer.

Chapter III

The Critical Success Factors Across ERP Implementation Processes

Ivan K.W. Lai, Macau University of Science and Technology, China

Abstract

It is very important to identify what are the key factors across different steps within enterprise resource planning (ERP) implementation models. This study consists of two phases. The first phase involves a questionnaire survey among experienced ERP consultants in order to identify the key successful factors of each step within ERP implementation models. In the second phase, experienced ERP consultants are interviewed to examine why these factors are important at each of the implementation steps and what are the difficulties of using Western ERP implementation models in China. The results suggest that ERP implementation is likely to be more successful if ERP implementation models address implementation challenges and leverages. This study provides guidance to ERP consultants on how to utilize their limited resources by considering these factors at each step within the ERP implementation models.

Introduction

An ERP implementation is usually a large and complex project involving large groups of people and other resources working together under considerable time pressure and facing many unforeseeable developments (Davenport, 1998). Over the past few years, critical success factors (CSFs) of ERP implementation have been well studied (Esteves & Pastor, 2001), but very little attention has been paid to ERP implementation models. On the other hand, the compound annual growth rate of the China ERP market was estimated to be triple the worldwide growth rate, and the China ERP market was forecasted to reach a half billion U.S. dollars in 2008 (IDC, 2004b). However, previous studies on ERP implementation were focused mainly on large companies in Europe and the U.S.; very few have been focused on enterprises in China (He, 2004). Therefore, there is a gap in the study of CSFs across ERP implementation models for ERP implementation in China.

ERP implementations are particularly worth continuing to research because the software and technology bases themselves are changing quickly with time, presenting new risks and issues (Plant & Willcocks, 2007). The purpose of this chapter is to investigate what and why CSFs are relatively important in each step within selected ERP implementation models. Results of this study also help understand the cultural issues of using Western ERP implementation models for ERP implementation in China and, consequently, help to improve ERP implementation success in China.

This chapter commences by summarizing previous research findings relating to the CSFs of ERP implementation. The second part examines different types of ERP implementation models found in the existing literature. A research framework then is developed. Empirical ERP implementation models are selected in order to help to assess major ERP challenges. Finally, the vendor ERP implementation models then are embedded with data from a question-naire survey and personal interviews in order to illustrate contributions of CSFs across ERP implementation models and the cultural issues of using Western ERP implementation models in China.

Background Literature

Enterprise resource planning (ERP) systems are configurable information systems packages that integrate information and information-based processes within and across functional areas in an organization (Kumar & van Hillegersberg, 2000). ERP systems have become popular in a rapidly changing business environment since the 1990s (Chung & Snyder, 2000). ERP systems provide a new class of comprehensive packaged application software designed to integrate the core corporate activities of the organization (Tsamatanis & Kogetsidis, 2006). Generic ERP software packages are already increasingly tailored to specific market segments (e.g., refinery, hospital, automotive assembly, law office, etc.) (Jacobs & Weston, 2007). With ERP systems, firms are able to manage their resources (i.e., physical or intangible assets, finances, human resources, production, etc.) more effectively (Nah & Delgado, 2006).

Many of the most experienced IT organizations have failed in their ERP implementations. Implementation failures may include cancellation before completion or never successfully integrating them into the business on implementation (Standish, 1999). Approximately 20% of systems are terminated before implementation (Computerworld, 2001). Even the project can be started, delayed and negative results are a possibility (Ferratt, Ahire, & De, 2006). More than 50 European companies revealed that an overwhelming 92% were dissatisfied with the results achieved from their ERP implementations (PA, 2000). More than 70% of ERP implementations failed to meet stated objectives such as staying within budget, finishing on schedule, and system performing well (Buckhout, Frey, & Nemec, 1999).

The reasons for these failures are that the implemented ERP systems suffer from system integration problems; the lack of alignment between people, processes, and the new technology; and precluding organizations from realizing anticipated benefits or even to recover the cost of the implementation effort (Davenport, 1998). ERP implementation problems were influenced by a clash between the customer's culture (defined by the stakeholder's norms), values, and beliefs, and the changes in culture that arise from the imposition of the ERP package (Krumbholz & Maiden, 2001).

However, many organizations still are planning to invest heavily in ERP systems. Companies have expressed multiple reasons to implement ERP (Nadkarni & Nah, 2003). ITtoolbox (2004) conducted an online survey from ITtoolbox network in March 2004 in order to gain insight into current ERP implementation trends among companies worldwide. The survey results demonstrated that many companies are looking to improve functionality in 2004 by adding new ERP packages. IDC (2004a) reported that the ERP market rose 5% in 2003 to reach nearly US$25 billion and was estimated to hit US$36 billion by 2008.

There are many motivations for investing in an ERP system. A successful ERP system makes it possible to develop and implement a variety of flexible supply chain options that can create significant cost and value advantages (Hayes, Hunton, & Reck, 2001). ERP system helps to provide better service to customers as well as strengthen supplier partnerships (Willis, Willis-Brown, & McMillan, 2001). Also, it standardizes a firm's data (Mabert, Soni, & Venkataramanan, 2000) and provides decision rules for both management and operations (Davenport, 2000). It provides a way to increase management control (Beeson & Rowe, 2001) and to increase IT infrastructure capacity and business flexibility and to reduce IT costs (Shang & Seddon, 2002).

Given the high unsuccessful rate, it calls for a better understanding of its CSFs (Somers, Nelson, & Ragowsky, 2000). Much research (ITtoolbox, 2004; Nah, Lau, & Kuang, 2001; Somers & Nelson, 2001; Zhang, Lee, Zhang, & Banerjee, 2003) has been conducted on the CSFs for successful ERP implementation since the early 1990s.

Critical Success Factors for ERP Implementation

CSFs initially were devised as a tool for identifying what organizations must do well in order to succeed, and to determine the information needs of top executives (Rockart, 1979).

Somers and Nelson (2001) conducted a meta-study of more than 110 ERP implementation cases and provided a well-grounded ranked list of 22 CFSs for ERP implementation (as shown in Table 3). The top five CFSs are top management support, project team competence, interdepartmental co-operation, clear goals and objectives, and project management.

Nah, Lau, and Kuang (2001) identified 11 CSFs for ERP implementation success. They are appropriate business and IT legacy systems; business plan and vision; business process re-engineering (BPR); change management program and culture; communication; ERP teamwork and composition; monitoring and evaluation of performance; project champion; project management; software development, testing, and troubleshooting; and top management support. Nah, Zuckweiler, and Lau (2003) conducted a questionnaire survey on those CSFs. The results indicate that the top five CSFs for ERP implementation are top management support, project champion, ERP teamwork and composition, project management, and change management program and culture.

Zhang, Lee, Zhang, and Banerjee (2003) classified 10 CSFs into five categories: organizational environments; people characteristics; technical problems; vendor commitment; and cultural impact. They conducted a hypothesized research and concluded that the top five CSFs for ERP implementation are top management support, business process reengineering, effective project management, education and training, and suitability of software and hardware.

ITtoolbox (2004) has conducted an online survey from ITtoolbox network and identified the top five challenges to successful ERP implementation as inadequate definition of requirements, resistance to change/lack of buy-in, inadequate resources, inadequate training and education, and lack of top management support.

These studies on the CFSs of ERP implementation provide possible influences on success. CSFs exist within a complex social organization with interactions among various stakeholders, and are naturally subjective (Parr, Shanks, & Darke, 1999; Williams & Ramaprasad, 1996). There is, however, no general consensus as to which set of factors is the key to success in ERP implementation. The priority of these CSFs may change over the course of ERP implementation because of the dynamics of project life cycle and, consequently, they may not be winning tools at any time (Deloitte Consulting, 1999). ERP systems are enterprise-wide in scope, have a high level of complexity, and require a different implementation methodology. While most studies have concentrated on the CSFs for ERP implementation, limited study has been conducted in the ERP implementation models.

ERP Implementation Models

Managing an ERP project is not the same as implementing a small scale IT system (Ghosh, 2002). A special implementation model is required in the areas of scope, change, budgeting, planning and staffing (Rose & Kræmmergaard, 2006). Most ERP vendors and consultants (e.g., SAP and Ernst & Young) have embedded implementation models that represent their capabilities and best solutions (Bruges, 2002). The model embedded in an ERP system may serve as a basis for matching the system with the requirements (Soffer, Golany, & Dori, 2003). Different ERP systems, in order to maximize their capabilities, will have different implementation models.

For the manufacturing industry, Symix has created four FOCUS models designed to properly structure and manage its ERP implementation. These models are Business Objective, Rapid, Supported, and Self-Directed (as shown in Figure 1). FOCUS models consist of five phases and seven steps. Figure 2 shows these steps and their sequence in the implementation process.

Table 1. FOCUS implementation models

Models	Design to
Business Objective	Support the achievement of client's stated business objectives, such as enhanced information system capabilities and business process improvement.
Rapid	Support a quick implementation that is driven by speed more than business process changes.
Supported	Facilitate implementations and establish responsibilities of the project and how best to support all project activities.
Self-Directed	Meet the needs of the self-sufficient customer.

Figure 1. FOCUS implementation models

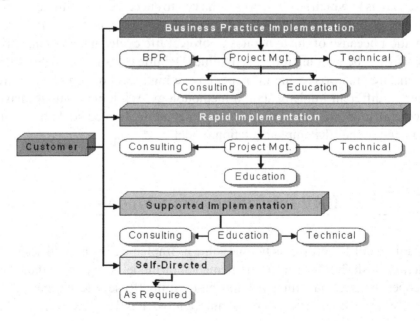

Figure 2. FOCUS implementation steps

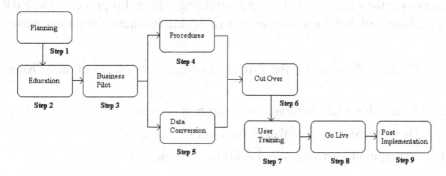

Phase 1: Project and Education Planning

Step 1: Implementation Planning

The implementation planning is a crucial step in setting mutual expectations and in establishing a successful working relationship with the customer. It is crucial that the consultant shows confidence and a methodical control of the FOCUS methodology process.

Step 2: Education Planning

Education is a key component in FOCUS methodology. It is a step to train the implementation team. The team members, as students, must have a clear understanding of the purpose and expectations of the education. After the training, the team members will have a solid foundation to understand the ERP system and to make meaningful and constructive contributions throughout the project.

Phase 2: Business Pilot and Procedures

Step 3: Business Pilot (Conference Room Pilot and Business Simulations)

The team members now are beginning to formulate how the business will be run using an ERP system in their organization. There is a great deal of emotion associated with this process, because, as in buying a new car, this will be the first real drive of the ERP system. There is also a great deal of fear by the users over their possible failure in performing within this process. The ERP consultant will direct and oversee the following business simulation steps:

1. Planning Session for the Process (structure, dates, times, data, roles, etc.)
2. Simulation Planning (data elements and outputs)
3. Business System Simulation Activities
4. Managing Open Issues and Additional Topics

Step 4: Developing and Writing Operating Procedures

Procedures represent an overview of the business flow and provide structure and control over individual and departmental processes. Procedures often are developed in accordance with or from workflow charts. The first process step in writing procedures should be to outline the lines of integrations between and within departments. This is done through workflow mapping. The procedure-building process usually takes place as business processes are finalized during the business pilot. It is one of the most time-consuming tasks of the implementation project.

Phase 3: Cutover and Training

Step 5: Data Conversion

Data conversion includes data mapping and actual conversion programming in order to convert existing data to the new system in preparation for the final cutover. Specifications for data conversion programs are developed in order to protect and reuse existing data and to minimize entry and validation efforts.

Step 6: Cutover Planning

Cutover planning ensures that the completed system is fully functional and satisfies the customer's data requirements. Cutover planning entails the sequenced detail steps, responsibilities, and estimated duration. The necessary steps are accomplished through a consulting session with the implementation team in order to outline the possible steps and their inherent advantages and drawbacks. Cutover planning also acts as a checklist for the project in order to determine the company's readiness to go live.

Step 7: End-User Training Process

User training and cutover mark the final preparation steps prior to *going live*. End-users must be trained and a conversion plan is created in order to determine the necessary cutover steps. These two activities will allow a smooth transition from the pilot phase to the cutover phase. Both steps require an equal amount of effort in order to prevent a false start or a dangerous cutover with untrained personnel. Each component of the phases requires unique processes and planning efforts. Companies that are cross training will be striving for efficiency from all members of the team or group in all tasks.

Phase 4: Go Live

Step 8: Go Live Assistance

It is important to have technical representation during the final cutover. The goal of this step is less structured but not less important than the others. It is used to ensure that any issue that arises during the final cutover can be addressed quickly and decisively.

Phase 5: Post Implementation

Step 9: Post-Implementation Review

The post-implementation review provides a formal review of the customer's system implementation. It provides a method in which to review and bring closure to all functions of the implementation (i.e., training, functionality, business practices, and month-end closing procedures). It performs 30 to 60 days after going live.

MAPICS consultants have been using FOCUS implementation models for successful implementations of their ERP systems more than 20 years. The same as most vendor ERP implementation models, FOCUS implementation models are very useful, because MAPICS has gained from experience to improve these implementation models.

CSFS Across the ERP Implementation Model

Somers and Nelson (2004) integrated the CSFs approach with the six-stage IT implementation stage model that was developed by Rajagopal (2002). The six-stage model of IT implementation consists of initiation, adoption, adaptation, acceptance, routinization, and infusion. CSFs, of course, can be temporal (i.e., their relative importance changes with the stage of the project life cycle) (Rockart, 1979).

Somers and Nelson (2004) conducted a mail survey and reported by a cross-section of 116 organizations that completed an ERP implementation experience. They found that the temporal nature of CSFs is being less understood than their overall importance. They summarized that the results for the latter stages of implementation are in consonance with the literature, even though such behavior is not fully understood, because most IT implementation research has focused on the adoption and acceptance of IT in an organization (Bacon, 2002). The level of ERP implementation in different industry sectors may have some variability; for instance, different conditions and situations and different requirements among industry sectors (Wu & Wang, 2002).

ERP has been popular since the 1990s. Then, many researchers conducted their studies on the CSFs for successful ERP implementation in Europe and the U.S. They provided different sets of CSFs in different implementation environments. Somers and Nelson (2001) provided a well-grounded ranked list of 22 CFSs for ERP implementation. Later, Somers and Nelson (2004) integrated these 22 CSFs with the six-stage IT implementation stage model and identified the importance of CSFs across six-stage IT implementation stage model. However, the six-stage IT implementation stage model is a genetic model that is not designed for ERP implementation. In China, Western ERP packages took up a large market share. The organizational cultures between China and Western countries are very different. Therefore, a qualitative study on the CSFs across vendor ERP implementation models for ERP implementation in China is considered to be important.

Research Approach

The primary objective of this study is to identify the CSFs of each step within ERP implementation models. The secondary objective of this study is to examine why these CSFs are important on each step within ERP implementation models. The third objective is to understand the difficulties of using Western ERP implementation models in China. The research questions are as follows:

1. What are the critical successful factors of each step within ERP implementation models?
2. Why are these CFSs important on each step within ERP implementation models?
3. What are the difficulties of using Western ERP implementation models in China?

An empirical study was undertaken in order to view the indubitable experience on the external world; data are collected systematically and collated as the route to knowledge (Ackroyd & Hughes, 1992). This research is based heavily on the experience from ERP consultants. It is important to choose a group of ERP consultants with experience in their implementation models. For convenience reason, MAPICS consultants were selected to participate in this research. Based on an extensive review of existing literature on CSFs for successful ERP implementation, a set of 26 CSFs was identified and integrated with FOCUS implementation models in order to complete a comprehensive research model suggested by Somers and Nelson (2004) (as shown in Figure 3).

A survey questionnaire that contains these 26 CSFs was performed in order to measure the relative importance of these CSFs with each step within FOCUS implementation models. After analyzing the data collected from the questionnaire survey, semi-structured interviews were conducted to ask why these CSFs are relatively important to each step within FOCUS implementa-

Figure 3. The integration of CSFs with ERP implementation models

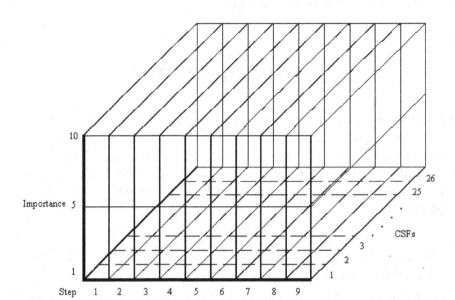

tion models and what the difficulties are in using FOCUS implementation models in China.

Data Collection and Findings

Twelve questionnaires were distributed and collected among MAPICS project management and implementation consultants in Hong Kong and China from September 1 to October 10, 2004. Their experiences on ERP projects are summarized in Table 2. The results of data analysis from the survey questionnaire are summarized in Table 3.

Personal interviews were conducted with six MAPICS project management and implementation consultants in Hong Kong and China from November 1 to November 16, 2004. A table of top five CSFs with an average higher than seven for each step with ERP implementation models was used in order to provide a uniform base for all interviews (as shown in Table 4). Interview questions focused on why these factors are critical for each implementation step. The results of personal interviews were analyzed by content analysis techniques.

This study is regarded as a qualitative research. The results derived from the data analysis were discussed, accompanied by literature to describe the phenomenon about the CSFs for ERP implementation.

CSFS of Each Step within ERP Implementation Models

Management of expectations is highly important at earlier steps (step 1, 2, 3, 4) within ERP implementation models. Before implementing an ERP system, management and users of client organization do not have much knowledge about their ERP system. In general, they have overestimated the benefits of their ERP system or have underestimated the efforts needed to implement their ERP system. ERP consultants should encourage them to provide positive contributions in the earlier steps in order to meet their expectations. After completing the developing and writing operating procedures (step 4), the whole picture of their ERP system appeared. In this case, it is easy to understand why management of expectations becomes less important in the remaining steps within ERP implementation models.

Many previous studies considered *top management support* as the most relevant factor for ERP implementation (Brown & Vessey, 1999; ITtoolbox, 2004; Nah, Lau, & Kuang, 2001; Somers & Nelson, 2001; Zhang, Lee, Zhang, & Banerjee, 2003). This study, however, discovered that top management support appears to be important in steps 1, 6, 7, and 8. During the early part of the ERP project, top management provides direction to the implementation teams (Bingi, Sharman, & Godla, 1999) and allocates valuable resources to the implementation project (Hong & Kim, 2002; Shanks, Parr, Hu, Corbitt, Thanasankit, & Seddon, 2000; Somers & Nelson, 2001). Top management also provides commitments to the board of director. After finishing the data analysis and conversion step, the ERP system is going to go live. Managers and users of different departments will generate more resistances in order to protect their existing benefits against each other in the final steps. Top management must resolve conflicts among departments and monitor the progress of the ERP project.

Table 2. Experiences on ERP projects

	Lowest	Highest	Average
No. of years experience on ERP implementation	1	20	9
No. of years experience on FOCUS implementation models	1	18	6
No. of ERP projects participated	1	60	15

Table 3. CSFs across FOCUS implementation models

Critical successful factor	Step								
	1	2	3	4	5	6	7	8	9
(1) Top management support	8.58	7.75	5.83	5.58	3.83	8.25	1.58	8.25	7.58
(2) Project team competence	3.33	8.25	6.75	7.58	5.5	5.58	6.67	7.33	4.42
(3) Interdepartmental co-operation	6.67	6.42	7.58	7.67	4.17	7.5	3.67	7.25	5.75
(4) Clear goals and objectives	7.58	5.5	7.83	6.25	1.75	4.42	3.58	5.75	2.5
(5) Project management	7.33	6.67	6.75	4.08	7.25	6.25	4.58	6.58	4.83
(6) Interdepartmental communication	6.67	5.58	7.67	6.67	4.17	8.33	3.33	7.5	5.33
(7) Management of expectations	9.75	8.58	9.58	7.58	2.83	5.83	3.75	7.42	1.25
(8) Project champion	5.67	8.33	7.5	7.17	6.58	7.25	5.25	7.67	7.83
(9) Vendor support	5.42	7.75	7.5	3.83	1.67	7.75	3.92	5.33	2.75
(10) Careful package selection	0	0	0	0	0	0	0	0	0
(11) Data analysis and conversion	2.83	1.83	6.75	5.33	8.33	5.33	1.58	1.58	1.75
(12) Dedicated resources	5.67	6.67	3.67	7.33	5.25	8.25	5.5	9.58	2.42
(13) Steering committee	8.25	7.58	5.67	3.83	3.67	7.67	3.75	7.5	7.25
(14) User training	1.83	5.5	1.75	1.67	2.75	5	8.42	3.25	1.67
(15) Education on new business processes	7.42	8.42	7.67	6.25	1.58	7.67	5.25	4.67	3.67
(16) BPR	6.5	7.33	7.58	7.17	2.58	6.58	2.83	6.83	4.58
(17) Minimal customization	4.58	7.25	7.67	4.58	1.5	4.83	1.67	7.75	1.75
(18) Architecture choices	6.75	5.83	6.75	0	0	1.58	0	1.58	0
(19) Change management	7.67	8.75	6.42	7.42	1.58	7.75	5.75	7.83	7.42
(20) Vendor partnership	6.67	5.58	5.5	4	1.5	5.67	4.5	5.75	4.67
(21) Vendor's tools	2.83	7.75	5.58	5.58	4.58	5.83	4.42	4.42	3.42
(22) Use of consultants	8.5	9.67	8.83	5.17	3.42	7.58	2.83	8.25	8.67
(23) Company-wide support	7.58	7.83	5	7.08	5.25	7.25	4.58	6.83	7.25
(24) User involvement	7.25	7.67	4.83	7.42	1.67	7.67	9.67	7.83	7.75
(25) Organizational culture	6.58	7.5	6.08	4.83	3.42	7.67	5.83	8.5	7.67
(26) Monitoring and evaluation of performance	6.5	6.92	4	6.17	6.25	7.75	5.67	7.5	7.42

Table 4. Top 5 important factors for each step within ERP implementation models

Rate	Step 1	Step 2	Step 3	Step 4	Step 5	Step 6	Step 7	Step 8	Step 9
1	Management of expectations	Use of consultants	Management of expectations	Interdepartmental co-operation	Data analysis and conversion	Interdepartmental communication	User involvement	Dedicated resources	Use of consultants
2	Top management support	Change management	Use of consultants	Project team competence Management of expectations	Project management	Top management support Dedicated resources	User training	Organizational culture	Project champion
3	Use of consultants	Management of expectations	Clear goals and objectives			Vendor support		Top management support Use of consultants	User involvement
4	Steering committee	Education on new business processes	Interdepartmental communication Education on new business processes	Change management User involvement		Monitoring and evaluation of performances Change management		Organizational culture	
5	Clear goal and objectives Change management	Project champion	Minimal customization					User involvement Change management	Top management support

Use of Consultants spans the first three steps and final two steps. IT staff of client organizations is not system implementer. Third-party ERP consultants are often used to help on ERP project (Brown & Vessey, 1999). ERP consultants can either be a knowledge provider or a facilitator during the implementation (Wang, Lin, Jiang, & Klein, 2007). ERP consultants have good experience and knowledge in clients' business environment, their ERP system, and ERP project management. They easily can manage and control each step in the ERP project. At the implementation planning step (step 1), ERP consultants provide expertise in the ERP system and produce project schedule. They develop and ensure education strategies at the education planning step (step 2). They also ensure smooth running of pilot strategies and direct simulation activities at the business pilot and procedures step (step 3). ERP consultants provide continued problem solving in the go-live assistance (step 8) and post-implementation step (step 9).

The *steering committee* usually is formed prior to the initial step with a combination of senior management and end-users from different departments. It is important in the first step to ensure appropriate involvement of all departments at the beginning of the ERP project. It provides guidance and facilitates the implementation effort. Somers and Nelson (2004) agreed that it is very important in the initiation phase. But they added that it is also important in the adoption and acceptance phases. This is not observed in this study. Some interviewees shared that the impact of the steering committee is weaker in the event that everybody is willing to contribute their best in the rest of the implementation steps. Other interviewees did not agree; they believed that the members of the steering committee do not contribute well and were absent most steering committee meetings in the rest of the implementation steps. So a steering committee does not exercise well as proposed.

Clear goals and objectives appear to be important in steps 1 and 3. They provide management, end-users, and ERP consultants with the purpose of their ERP project in the early steps. Effective ERP implementation requires a well-known business vision that establishes the goals and the business model behind the implementation project (Holland & Light, 1999). After completion of the business pilot (step 3), everybody begins to work on a clear business vision and commits to use the system for achieving business aims.

ERP systems introduce large-scale change that can cause resistance, confusion, redundancies, and errors if not management effectively (Somers & Nelson, 2004). In order to stay competitive, recognizing the need for change is very important (Falkowski, Pedigo, Smith, & Swanson, 1998). *Change management* appears to be important in steps 1, 2, 4, 6 and 8. Potential changes happen in the most steps within the ERP implementation models. ERP consultants should communicate effectively and regularly with the super users to smooth the way of ERP implementation.

Education on new business processes appears to be important in steps 2 and 3. There is a need for business process change during the implementation of an ERP system (Motwani, Mirchandani, Madan, & Gunasekaran, 2002; Al-Mashari & Zairi, 2000). Education on new business processes is essential for managers (Mahapatra & Lai, 1998). It should be considered a priority form the beginning of the project (Roberts & Barrar, 1992). One reason to employ an ERP system is that it can support new business processes. ERP consultants introduce new business processes and educate managers on how to use their system in order to perform new business processes in the education planning and business pilot steps.

Project champion appears to be important in steps 2 and 9. The project champion should be an advocate for the project (Robey, Ross, & Boudreau, 2002). The role of project champion is to provide strategic input for the project team and to market the benefits of project back to business (Parr, Shanks, & Darke, 1999). It plays a critical role in acceptance of the technology (Somers & Nelson, 2004). It is important in the education planning step (step 2). The success of project champion can facilitate the post-implementation (step 9) process and produces good view to the business.

Interdepartmental communication is critical during steps 3 and 6. In the business pilot step (step 3), departments work together to simulate their operations in the ERP system. In the cutover planning step (step 6), departments collaborate to ensure the smooth running of the ERP system.

Successful ERP implementations are often the result of *minimal customization* (Somers & Nelson, 2004; Yakovlev & Anderson, 2001). The decision of customization occurs within the business pilot step (step 3) when management or end-users reject the business processes that are built into the ERP system. Customization not only increases the cost of ERP implementation but also increases the risk in ERP project. It also causes longer implementation time and reduces the benefit from the vendor's software maintenance and upgrades (Nah & Delgado, 2006).

Interdepartmental cooperation appears to be important in the developing and writing operating procedures step (step 4). The development of operating procedures is a cross-functional activity that involves all departments in order to outline their business processes. It helps to establish a successful working relationship with each department.

Project team competence appears to be important in the developing and writing operating procedures step (step 4). The project team provides expertise in areas of business and technological competence (Mendel, 1999).

User involvement refers to participation in the implementation processes. It is important in the developing and writing operating procedures (step 4), end-user training process (step 7), and go-live assistance (step 8). Users should be involved in procedure writing. It helps users to understand the new business processes and the capabilities of the ERP system. Users also can help to identify and resolve potential issues in early stages, thereby improving implementation quality (Brown, 2001). User involvement also helps to reduce user resistances, raise user responsibilities, and improve user satisfaction when a system goes live.

Data conversion (step 5) is one of the most complex and risky activities within the ERP implementation process (Thomas & Jajodia, 2004). An extensive conversion plan for *data analysis and conversion* can reduce the risk of reusing existing data. Problems with data can lead to serious delays in the project (Nah & Delgado, 2006).

Project management appears to be important in the data conversion step (step 5). Project management should take measures to ensure that the project schedule is not risked (Chien, Hu, Reimers, & Lin, 2007). It dedicates human forces, ensures timeframe, controls quality, protects security, and provides a contingency approach for data conversion.

Cutover planning (step 6) and go-live assistance (step 8) require large *dedicated resources*. Sufficient resources can reduce potential impacts that cause project fallback. All related resources that supported go-live activities should be readily available in order to ensure that a system goes live.

Vendor support appears to be important in the cutover planning step (step 6). ERP vendors must provide extended technical assistance, emergency maintenance, updates, and even bug fix in the cutover planning step.

Monitoring and evaluation of performance is important in the cutover planning step (step 6). It ensures the cutover timeframe and measures the acceptance of the ERP system. It also provides a key performance indication (KPI) before a system goes live.

It also is recognized widely that a lack of user training is an important factor of failure (Wilder & Davis, 1998). Systemic training is needed for end-user to learn how to use it more effectively (McAdam & Galloway, 2005). End-user training process (step 7) provides adequate hands-on *user training* before an ERP system goes live. End-users can have better understanding of how to use their ERP system for their daily operations.

Organizational culture is significantly important in post-implementation (step 9). It influences user satisfaction at the post-implementation step within ERP implementation models (Thavapragasam, 2003). It is also important in the go-live assistance step (step 8), because it affects the quality of deployment.

In summary, the results of questionnaire survey identified the CSFs of each step within ERP implementation models. The results of personal interviews described the importance of these CSFs for each step within ERP implementation models. Due to the variations between Western and Chinese cultures, ERP consultants acknowledge the difficulties of applying Western ERP implementation models in China.

Five Dimensions of Chinese Culture

Culture can be described as a set of ideas shared by members of a group (Allaire & Firsirotu, 1984). An awareness of cultural differences is critical to ERP success (Yusuf, Gunasekaran, & Wu, 2006). The difference in cultures causes difficulties in employing Western ERP implementation models in China. Kedia and Bhagat (1988) suggested that the five dimensions of national culture influence the cultural background of client organizations. The five culture dimensions are (1) individualism or collectivism, (2) masculinity or feminine, (3) uncertainty avoidance, (4) high or low power distance, and (5) abstractive or associative. Evidence of personal interviews provided the levels of five dimensions in Chinese culture and their causes on those CSFs (Table 5).

Evidence provided that members of implementation teams were acting as members of groups rather than acting as individuals. Low individualism is explained largely by Guanxi. High collectivism affects team members' behaviors and expectations of the ERP implementation project. However, Western countries put more emphasis on individualism. Whilst Western ERP implementation models provide systematic and formal procedures, their designs do not consider the negative impact from high collectivism and do not provide sufficient opportunities for cooperation in order to address this centurial aspect.

Masculinity, which stands for a preference for achievement, heroism, assertiveness, and material success, is opposed to femininity, which stands for a preference for relationships, modesty, caring for the weak, and the quality of life. In a masculine society, even women prefer assertiveness (at least in men); in a feminine society, even men prefer modesty (Hofstede, 1985). Although China has spent the last two decades striving to achieve globalization, its historic national cultures are still very evident. Females are receiving less education than their male counterparts in their early childhood, since they were always expected to sacrifice their opportunities to their brothers due to insufficient family financial resources. Evidence supported that men played a bigger role in the ERP implementation projects, even though most ERP users were females. This study revealed masculinity dimension does not provide much impact on ERP implementation.

Uncertainty avoidance represents how people deal with uncertainty, in particular, by using technology, rules, and rituals (Hofstede, 1980). Members of implementation teams presented a moderate level of anxiety with moderate nervousness, stress, and aggressiveness during ERP implementation process. They rejected BRP and did not want to change their business process with which they were familiar. It was because they were not encouraged to be innovative and to take risks. They believed that less customization was an easier way to success. However, ERP implementation projects emphasize BRP and customization in order to be successful.

The power distance dimension characterizes how individuals behave toward power, concentration of authority, and the differences between less powerful individuals and more powerful ones within the same group (Hofstede, 1980). Chinese culture is a high power distance relationship in which managers exercise benevolence from above and gain employee allegiance from below. Evidence provided that junior team members were looking for strong, committed leadership. They obeyed senior staff commands during the ERP implementation process. Top management does their decision-making autocratically and paternalistically. But top management does not know all the problems related to ground-level daily operations and, therefore, may make wrong decisions that cause the failure of ERP implementation.

Abstractive culture is where the rational cause-effects-relationship thinking process is dominant; associative culture is where associations among people on a less logical basis are dominant (Glenn & Glenn, 1981). Members of

Table 5. Five dimensions of Chinese culture and their causes on CSFs

Dimensions	China	Western	Leads to
Individualism	Low	High	Top management support Steering committee Project champion Project team competence Interdepartmental communication Interdepartmental co-operation
Masculinity or feminine	Masculinity	Balance	
Uncertainty avoidance	Moderate	Low	Minimal customization Reject BRP Less interest on the education on new business processes Monitoring and evaluation of performance
Power distance	High	Low	Top management support Steering committee Project champion Use of consultants Change management Project management Less user involvement Dedicated resources Project team competence Clear goals and objectives
Abstractive or associative	More associative	More abstractive	Company-wide support Management of expectations Interdepartmental communication Interdepartmental co-operation Clear goals and objectives User training

implementation teams were more associative than abstractive where people are associated with similar classes of social circles in the societal ranking. The Western implementation models support abstractive learning. Members of implementation teams with associative thinking need to allocate more effort in the understanding of an ERP system.

Each organization has its unique culture, which develops overtime to reflect organization's identity (Al-Alawi, Al-Marzooqi, & Mohammed, 2007). The organizational culture guides employees' perceptions of ERP implementation project. The results of the personal interviews also showed that Chinese culture has a greater impact than an organizational culture has during ERP implementation. For example, team members of a Japanese-based automobile manufacturer presented the same evidences as did team members of a Hong Kong-based electronics manufacturer during ERP implementation process.

Therefore, Chinese culture overrides Japanese organizational culture and Hong Kong organizational culture.

Due to the small sample size, the evidence remains weak. Undoubtedly, a more complete analysis of the CSFs across ERP implementation models is suggested. However, this study provides the basis for a discussion on the area of ERP implementation models.

Conclusion

Due to the small sample size in the survey, there are some limitations in the generalization of the research results. All interviews were conducted in Chinese and then translated into English. Responses may have lost some of their meaning and intensity in this process. This study is also limited to an area of ERP implementation. This study only concerned in the context of 26 CSFs integrated with FOCUS implementation models. Thus, the study may not be generalizable to all Western ERP implementation models.

Understanding of CSFs across vendor ERP implementation models is a relatively new area; this study demonstrated the importance of CSFs across ERP implementation models. It contributed both theory and practice in examining of the role of CSFs for each step within ERP implementation models. This study also provided implications for practice by helping technical and non-technical practitioners to consider those critical factors at each step within ERP implementation models in order to understand the cultural issues of using Western ERP implementation models in China and in order to improve the results of their ERP implementations.

This study also provides substantial research opportunities in the area of ERP implementation models. Moreover, it is necessary to extend a broad study to uncover the key issues of all Western ERP implementation models in China or other Asian countries. Furthermore, a field study is recommended in order to understand human thought and action in social and organizational contexts in each step of ERP implementation. On the other hand, this study identifies the gap of having Chinese-style ERP implementation models that can address those CSFs of ERP implementation in China. A qualitative research is suggested to examine the use of the Chinese-style ERP implementation models in China.

Acknowledgment

The author is most grateful to anonymous reviewers and the Editor-in-Chief, Professor Angappa Gunasekaran, for their constructive comments that helped to improve the presentation of the chapter considerably. The author also wishes to thank Infor - MAPICS and its alliances in Hong Kong and China for their support in undertaking the study reported in this chapter.

References

Ackroyd, S., & Hughes, J.A. (1992). *Data collection in context.* New York: Longman.

Al-Alawi, A.I., Al-Marzooqi, N.Y., & Mohammed, Y.F. (2007). Organizational culture and knowledge sharing: Critical success factors. *Journal of Knowledge Management, 11*(2), 22-42.

Allaire, Y., & Firsirotu, M.E. (1984). Theories of organizational culture. *Organization Studies, 5*(3), 193-226.

Al-Mashari, M., & Zairi, M. (2000). The effective application of SAP R/3: A proposed model of best practice. *Logistics Information Management, 13*(3), 156-166.

Bacon, A. (2002). *Consultants get high marks for planning ERP upgrades.* AMR Research. Retrieved July 2007, from http://www.amrresearch. com/Content/view.asp?pmillid=1358&docid=8536.

Besson, P., & Rowe, F. (2001). ERP project dynamics and enacted dialogue. *The Database for Advances in Information Systems, 32*(4), 47-66.

Bingi, P., Sharma, M.K., & Godla, J.K. (1999). Critical issues affecting an ERP implementation. *Information Systems Management, 16*(3), 7–14.

Brown, C., & Vessey, I. (1999). ERP implementation approaches: toward a contingency framework. In *Proceedings of the International Conference on Information Systems.* Charlotte, NC. Brown, J. (2001). ERP Doomed By Poor Planning. *Computing Canada, 27*(3), 11.

Bruges, P. (2002). *ERP implementation methodologies.* St. Louis, MO: University of Missouri – St. Louis. Retrieved July 2007, from http://www. umsl.edu/~sauter/analysis/488_f02_papers/erp1.htm

Buckhout, S., Frey, E., & Nemec, J., Jr. (1999). Making ERP succeed: Turning fear into promise. *IEEE Engineering Management Review, 27*(3), 116–123.

Chien, S.W., Hu, C., Reimers, K., & Lin, J.S. (2007). The influence of centrifugal and centripetal forces on ERP project success in small and medium-sized enterprises in China and Taiwan. *International Journal of Production Economics, 107*(2), 380-396.

Chung, A.H., & Snyder, C.A. (2000). ERP adoption: A technological evolution approach. *International Journal Of Agile Management Systems, 2*(1), 24-32.

Computerworld. (2001, September 24). *Never-ending story why ERP projects cause panic attacks.* International Data Corporation. Retrieved May 2006, from http://www.computerworld.com/action/article.do?command=viewArticleBasic&articleID=64064.

Davenport, T.H. (1998). Putting the enterprise into the enterprise system. *Harvard Business Review, 76*, 121-131.

Davenport, T.H. (2000). *Mission critical: Realizing the promise of enterprise systems.* Cambridge, MA: Harvard Business School Press.

Deloitte Consulting. (1999). *ERP's second wave: Maximizing the value of ERP-enabled processes (*Deloitte Consulting Report). New York: Deloitte Consulting. Retrieved May 2006, from http://www.deloitte.com/dtt/cda/doc/content/Erps_second_ware(1).pdf.

Esteves, J.M., & Pastor, A.J. (2001). Enterprise resource planning systems research: An annotated bibliography. *Communications of the Association for Information Systems, 7*(8), 1-51.

Falkowski, G., Pedigo, P., Smith, B., & Swanson, D. (1998, September). A recipe for ERP success. *Beyond Computing,* 44-45.

Ferratt, T.W., Ahire, S., & De, P. (2006). Achieving success in large projects: Implications from a study of ERP implementations. *Interfaces, 36*(5), 458-469.

Ghosh, S. (2002). Challenges on a global implementation of ERP software. In *Proceedings of IEEE International Engineering Management Conference* (Vol. 1, pp. 101-106).

Glenn, E.S., & Glenn, C.G. (1981). *Man and mankind: Conflict and communication between cultures.* Norwood, NJ: Ablex.

Hayes, D., Hunton, J., & Reck, J. (2001). Market reaction to ERP implementation announcements. *Journal of Information Systems, 15*(1), 3-18.

He, X.J. (2004). The ERP challenge in China, a resource-based perspective. *Information Systems Journal, 14*(2), 153-167.

Hofstede, G. (1980). *Culture's consequences: International differences in work-related values.* London: Sage Publications.

Hofstede, G. (1985). The interaction between national and organizational value systems. *Journal of Management Studies, 22*(4), 347–357.

Holland, C.P., & Light, B. (1999). A critical success factors model for ERP implementation. *IEEE Software, 16*(3), 30–36.

Hong, K.K., & Kim, Y.G. (2002). The critical success factors for ERP implementation: An organizational fit perspective. *Information and Management, 40*(1), 25-40.

International Data Corporation. (2004a, May). *World ERP applications 2004-2008 forecast: First look at top 10 vendors* (IDC Research Report Doc#31269). International Data Corporation.

International Data Corporation. (2004b, June). *China enterprise resource planning applications 2004-2008 forecast and analysis*, (IDC Research Report IDC1018477). International Data Corporation.

ITtoolbox. (2004). *2004 ITtoolbox ERP implementation survey.* ITtoolbox. Retrieved September 2005, from http://baan.ittoolbox.com/research/survey.asp?survey=corioerp_survey&p=1.

Jacobs, F.R., & Weston, F.C., Jr. (2007). Enterprise resource planning (ERP) – a brief history. *Journal of Operations Management, 25*(2), 357-363

Kedia, B.L., & Bhagat, R.S. (1988). Cultural constraints on transfer of technology across nations: Implications for research in international and comparative management. *Academy of Management Review, 13*(4), 559-571.

Krumbholz, M., & Maiden, N. (2001). The implementation of enterprise resource planning packages in different organizational and national cultures. *Information Systems, 26*(3), 185-204.

Kumar, K., & van Hillegersberg, J. (2000). ERP experiences and evolution. *Communications of the ACM, 43*(4), 23-26.

Mabert, V., Soni, A., & Venkataramanan, M. (2000). Enterprise resource planning survey of U.S. manufacturing firms. *Production and Inventory Journal, 41*(2), 52–58.

Mahapatra, R.K., & Lai, V.S. (1988). Intranet-based training facilitates on ERP system implementation: A case study. In E.D. Hoadley & I. Benbasat (Eds.), *Proceedings of the Fourth Americas Conference on Information Systems,* Baltimore, MD (pp.1070–1072).

McAdam, R., & Galloway, A. (2005). Enterprise resource planning and organizational innovation: A management perspective. *Industry Management and Data Systems, 105*(3/4), 280-290.

Mendel, B. (1999, July 19). Overcoming ERP project hurdles. *InfoWorld.* Retrieved July 2007, from http://www.infoworld.com/articles/ca/xml/99/07/19/990719caerp.xml.

Motwani, J., Mirchandani, D., Madan, M., & Gunasekaran, A. (2002). Successful implementation of ERP projects: Evidence from two case studies. *International Journal of Production Economics, 75*(1), 83-96.

Nadkarni, S., & Nah, F. (2003). Aggregated causal maps: An approach to elicit and aggregate the knowledge of multiple experts. *Communications of the Association for Information Systems, 12*(25), 406-436.

Nah, F., & Delgado, S. (2006). Critical success factors for enterprises resource planning implementation and upgrade. *The Journal of Computer Information Systems, 46*(5), 99-113.

Nah, F., Lau, J., & Kuang, J. (2001). Critical factors for successful implementation of enterprise systems. *Business Process Management Journal, 7*(3), 285–296.

Nah, F., Zuckweiler, K., & Lau, J. (2003). ERP implementation: Chief information officers' perceptions of critical success factors. *International Journal of Human – Computer Interaction, 16*(1), 5–22.

Nicolaou, A.I. (2004). ERP systems implementation: Drivers of post-implementation success. In *Proceedings of the Decision Support in an Uncertain and Complex World: The IFIP TC8/WG8.3 International Conference.*

PA Consulting Group. (2000). *Unlocking the value in ERP.* Retrieved July 2007, from http://www.paconsulting.com/NR/exeres/582DFEAD-C470-4DBB-A5DB-0C90ACE0B9F6.htm.

Parr, A., Shanks, G., & Darke, P. (1999). The identification of necessary factors for successful implementation of ERP systems. In O. Ngwenyama, L.D. Introna, M.D. Myers, & J.I. DeGross (Eds.), *New information technologies in organizational processes* (pp. 99-119). Boston: Kluwer Academic.

Plant, R., & Willcocks, L. (2007). Critical success factors in international ERP implementations: A case research approach. *Journal of Computer Information Systems, 47*(3), 60-70.

Rajagopal, P. (2002). An innovation–diffusion view of implementation of enterprise resource planning systems and development of a research model. *Information and Management, 40*(2), 87-114.

Roberts, H.J., & Barrar, P.R.N. (1992). MRPII implementation: Key factors for success. *Computer Integrated Manufacturing Systems, 5*(1), 31-38.

Robey, D., Ross, J., & Boudreau, M. (2002). Learning to implement enterprise systems: An exploratory study of the dialectics of change. *Journal of Management Information Systems, 19*(1), 17-46.

Rockart, J.F. (1979). Chief executives define their own data needs. *Harvard Business Review, 57*(2), 81-93.

Rose, J., & Kræmmergaard, P. (2006). ERP systems and technological discourse shift: Managing the implementation journey. *International Journal of Accounting Information Systems, 7*(3), 217-237.

Shang, S., & Seddon, P.B. (2002). Assessing and managing the benefits of enterprise systems: The business manager's perspective. *Information Systems Journal, 12*(4), 271-299.

Shanks, G., Parr, A., Hu, B., Corbitt, B., Thanasankit, T., & Seddon, P. (2000). Differences in critical success factors in ERP systems implementation in Australia and China: A cultural analysis. In *Proceedings of the 8th European Conference on Information Systems,* Vienna, Austria (pp. 537-544).

Soffer, P., Golany, B., & Dori, D. (2003). ERP modeling: A comprehensive approach. *Information Systems, 28*(6), 673-690.

Somers, T.M., & Nelson, K.G. (2001). The impacts of critical success factors across the stages of enterprise resource planning implementations. In *Proceedings of the 34th Hawaii International Conference of System Sciences.* Retrieved September 2005, from http://www.computer.org/proceedings/hicss/0981/volume%208/09818011.pdf.

Somers, T.M., & Nelson, K.G. (2004). A taxonomy of players and activities across the ERP project life cycle. *Information and Management, 41*(3), 257-278

Somers, T.M., Nelson, K.G., & Ragowsky, A. (2000). Enterprise resource planning (ERP) for the next millennium: Development of an integrative framework and implications for research. In *Proceedings of the Americas Conference on Information Systems,* Long Beach, CA (pp. 998–1004).

Standish Group International Inc. (1999). *Chaos: A recipe for success.* The Standish Group International Inc. Retrieved May 2006, from http://www.standishgroup.com/sample_reseach/PDFpages/chaos1999.pdf.

Thavapragasam, X.T. (2003). Cultural influences on ERP implementation success. In *Proceedings of the First Australian Undergraduate Students' Computing Conference*, University of Melbourne, Australia (pp. 93-99).

Thomas, G.A., & Jajodia, S. (2004). Commercial off-the-shelf enterprise resource planning software implementation. *The Journal of Government Financial Management, 53*(2), 2-18.

Tsamantanis, V., & Kogetsidis, H. (2006). Implementation of enterprise resource planning systems in the Cypriot brewing industry. *British Food Journal, 108*(2), 118-126.

Wang, E.T.G., Lin C.C.L., Jiang, J.J., & Klein, G. (2007). Improving enterprise resource planning (ERP) fit to organizational process through knowledge transfer. *International Journal of Information Management, 27*(3), 200-212.

Wilder, C., & Davis, B. (1998). False starts, strong finishes. *Information Week,* 30, 41-53.

Williams, J.J., & Ramaprasad, A. (1996). A taxonomy of critical success factors. *European Journal of Information Systems,* 5(5), 250-260.

Willis, T.H., Willis-Brown, A.H., & McMillan, A. (2001). Cost containment strategies for ERP system implementations. *Production & Inventory Management Journal, 42*(2), 36-42.

Wu, J.H., & Wang, Y.M. (2002). Enterprise resource planning experience in Taiwan: An empirical study and comparative analysis. In *Proceedings of the 36th Hawaii International Conference on System Sciences* (Vol. 8, p. 235.1). Washington, DC: IEEE Computer Society.

Yakovlev, I., & Anderson, M. (2001). Lessons from an ERP implementation. *IEEE IT Professional, 3*(4), 24-29.

Yusuf, Y., Gunasekaran, A., & Wu, C. (2006). Implementation of enterprise resource planning in China. *Technovation, 26*(12), 1324-1336.

Zhang, L., Lee, M.K.O., Zhang. Z., & Banerjee, P. (2003). Critical success factors of enterprise resource planning systems implementation success in China. *In Proceedings of the 36th Annual Hawaii International Conference on System Sciences (HICSS'03)*. Retrieved July 2007, from http://csdl. computer.org/comp/proceedings/hicss/2003/1874/08/187480236.pdf.

Chapter IV

Integrated Design System:
An Information Processing Approach for Knowledge-Based Product Development

Quangang Yang, University of New South Wales, Australia

Carl Reidsema, University of New South Wales, Australia

Abstract

The rapid development of computing technology has facilitated its use in engineering design and manufacturing at an increasing rate. To deliver high quality, low cost products with reduced lead times; companies are focussing their efforts on leveraging this technology through the development of knowledge-based systems such as an integrated design system (IDS). An IDS, which can also be referred to as a design information system, is a part of the overall enterprise information system framework, and plays an important role in improving competitiveness in product development oriented companies. Such a system addresses concurrent engineering (CE) issues by considering downstream aspects of different phases in the product life cycle as early as possible in the design stage. These aspects include production process planning and realisation, manufacturing and assembly resources, maintainability, costing and other factors. Both human expertise and down-stream aspects predominantly consist of information that is descriptive. This chapter discusses the structure and development of a design information system that can convert this descriptive information into forms that are suitable for embedding within decision-making algorithms. Information in such a system is sorted in terms of its nature into three groups: input data information, constraint information and objective information, all having different representations. Information is also mapped to the relevant design objectives and ranked in importance to facilitate the trade-off analysis after a series of processing activities.

Introduction

In today's highly competitive landscape, new product development strategies are imperatives for companies to create and sustain competitive advantages. Concurrent engineering (CE) has become a very attractive and enthusiastically discussed product development approach in recent times. To realize the concurrent design process, a key demand is to find an appropriate way to present life cycle information to the design stage. On the other hand, engineering design is an increasingly complex and information-intensive activity because of higher customer expectations, a multi-disciplinary environment, and many other factors. To enhance the analysis and the solving process of complex design problems, computer-based modelling and simulation technology is being used at an increasing rate. Such technologies as computer aided design/manufacture/engineering (CAD/CAM/CAE) and finite element method (FEM) provide the designer with powerful tools for representing, evaluating and optimising products faster and more effectively than ever before. However, these technologies may focus on distinct aspects and be incompatible in various ways so that designers have to spend considerable time on model and data conversion (Koch, Evans, & Powell, 2002; Lander, Stanley, & Corkill, 1996). To harness the full power of these systems, integration of the design process to realize seamless information transfer and processing within the design environment has become a very important issue.

Knowledge-based engineering (KBE) represents potentially the most significant product development technique to date. It provides a new strategic approach for realizing the concurrent product development process to improve effectiveness in design and manufacturing (Kulon, Broomhead, & Mynors, 2005). Not only does it utilize traditional elements in the design process such as geometric models, it also captures other underlying attributes of design such as experience and expertise. Knowledge, sometimes synonymously referred to as information, is the enabling element in KBE and, therefore, the acquisition and representation of knowledge are two primary tasks in a KBE design system.

The integrated design system (IDS) presented in this research is an integrated environment in which the design problem solving is addressed from the view of information processing. It addresses the "life-cycle" design challenges by incorporating multi-disciplinary knowledge resources into the system to achieve design and manufacturing intent, and other subsequent requirements generated through the product's distribution, use, and disposal. The system can also suggest design alternatives in terms of cost, time, or other critical requirements to enable the creation of a fully engineered design by acquiring, representing, planning, reasoning and then communicating the intent of the design process. Thus, it can provide the necessary degree of intelligent interaction that enhances the designer's own inherent skills and creativity (Cooper, Fan, & Li, 2001).

To implement the IDS, all related product information, including raw numerical input data, physical design and manufacturing constraints, design objectives and various other life-cycle requirements, must be stored in a design information system. The information must be attained and saved in a structured and reusable manner to make it understandable to the user, and capable of being executed by a machine (Gruber, 1989; Clancey, 1992; Szykman, Sriram, Bochenek, Racz, & Senfaute, 2000). With such an information system, the generation and evaluation of new design alternatives can occur quickly and easily by changing and analyzing only the relevant parts of the system within the IDS. This frees the engineer from time-intensive, detailed engineering tasks such as repetitive and unnecessary calculations and allows more time for creative design work.

As a part of the whole enterprise information system (EIS), the IDS can play an important role in a product development-oriented company. Unlike other earlier information systems such as material requirement planning (MRP) and manufacturing resource planning (MRPII), which focus on manufacturing aspects, the IDS is concerned with the product development and the design function of an organisation. It may also interact with other systems, such as CAD, to increase functional integration within a company, and to perform information verification, characterization, development and distribution in the overall perspective of the company.

In this chapter, a brief literature review is first carried out, and the basic requirements for such a design system are summarized. The system configuration and the information classification are then introduced. Following that the information processing activities in the IDS will be described based on the sequential stages.

Literature Review

As an information intensive activity, engineering design is an intellectual, knowledge-based product development process to meet certain design objectives and constraints in the best possible way. Traditionally, the product development cycle occurs in a sequential manner, only allowing a stage to be started after the previous stage has been completed. From the point of view of information flow and processing, the sequential approach has the following shortcomings (Sivaloganathan, Evbuomwan, & Jebb, 1995; Tan, Hayes, & Shaw, 1996):

- The participants of upstream functions have little knowledge of the requirements and constraints of the downstream functions

- Critical design functions occur in relative isolation from each other, restricting the necessary flow of information and ideas.

- Design data is fragmented, and maintaining consistency across various representations is a difficult task.

- Design optimization opportunities are lost because of the lack of communication among functional departments.

- Information is lost as the design progresses and the design intent may not be reflected in the final artefact.

CE is a new strategic product development approach, which can overcome the intrinsic disadvantages of the sequential approach. It is a process in which multiple disciplines work together to perform product development. The essence of CE is the simultaneous execution of the product development process, indicating that a function can be started before the previous function is finished. For the successful implementation of CE in a complex design problem, a fundamental element is a computer-based framework (Sivaloga-nathan, Evbuomwan, & Jebb, 1995; Tomiyama, 1997) because it creates and integrate environment to address the other essential issues, including (Coates, Hills, Whitfield, & Duffy, 1999; Vergeest & Horváth, 1999):

- coordination,
- cooperation,
- communication,
- information sharing, and
- knowledge transfer.

As a promising approach for addressing CE issues, KBE is an enabling tech-nology that allows organizations to capture, structure, and reuse knowledge about a design and its design process (Calkins, 1996). KBE complements traditional CAD/CAM systems by providing a strategic approach for im-proving effectiveness in design and manufacturing (Kulon, Broomhead, & Mynors, 2005). KBE is also a "methodology that bridges the gap between knowledge management and design automation" (Prasad, 2005). By means of incorporating the engineering knowledge that drives the product design process, KBE enables the computer to assist in generating design variants of a product and to automate repetitive design tasks, thus reducing both time and cost in product development (Shikarpur, 2003).

Knowledge acquisition and representation is a critical part of problem solv-ing process in a KBE system (Newell, 1982). It converts the problem solv-ing expertise from some knowledge sources to a program in a way that the computer would be able to use the expertise to draw appropriate conclusions (Buchanan, Barstow, Bechtel, Bennett, Clancey, Kulikowski, Mitchell, & Waterman, 1983; Malhotra, 2001). Gardan and Gardan (2003) proposed to capture knowledge from experts in the form of scripts that can then be in-voked within CAD software. Such design scripts can separate the knowledge from the implementation, and effectively bridge the gap between design and knowledge management. Pokojski et al. (2002) proposed an approach that involves solving new design problems on the basis of similar solutions from previous problems. Matthews et al. (2002) introduced a method for analysing conceptual design data through the identification of the relationships between design components within the database of previous design. These relationships are also transformed into explicit design knowledge, which is used to generate a heuristic-based model for use at the conceptual stage. Myers et al. (2000) proposed an experimental framework to acquire rationale information for the detailed design process by monitoring designer interactions with a commercial CAD tool. The information is then interpreted and structured that enable explanation of certain aspects of the design process.

KBE has already found a large number of applications in product and process design. Chau and Albermani (2002) have developed a system prototype to assist in the preliminary design of liquid retaining structures by providing expert advice to the designer in selection of design criteria, design parameters and optimum structural section based on the minimum cost. Reidsema and Szczerbicki (2001) discussed the development of a general knowledge-based system for the design planning process in concurrent engineering by utilizing the Blackboard Database Architecture. There are also some commercial KBE systems, such as ICAD (Sandberg, 2003), iSIGHT (Koch, Evans, & Powell, 2002), and LS-OPT (Stander, Eggleston, Craig, & Roux, 2003). A common feature of these commercial systems is the use of multiple sophisticated optimization algorithms for design-space searches (Ong & Keane, 2002). The algorithms are used to gain an insight into the variations of a design and the related trade-offs by taking into account all the possible design options that meet the design requirements. But the availability of a large number of optimization algorithms places a large burden of expertise on the designer and particularly so for novices.

In summary, a KBE system must be easy to access, maintain and be documented, and most importantly, is able to solve a design problem correctly and efficiently. Some basic requirements include:

- **Correctness and efficiency:** It must ensure that a design problem can be solved efficiently and accurately.
- **Maintainability:** The model must be flexible so that it is easy to add/remove or modify knowledge.
- **Compatibility:** The model must be easily associated with other commercial software tools to improve its accuracy and efficiency, and broaden its use.
- **Communicability:** It should be easy for a designer to access and communicate with the model, and monitor and intervene in its progress.

- **Reusability:** It must be structured in a reusable manner so that it can be retained as generic design knowledge.

Configuration of the Integrated Design System

A window snapshot of the IDS is shown in Figure 1. Five command bars are located on the top used to perform corresponding information processing activities. The geometrical model is located on the left of the window, while the right-hand side is used to display information to, and accept inputs from, the user. At the bottom, it is a small window for the system to give prompts to the user. Visual Basic (VB) is chosen to code the IDS because of its advantages over the other languages, such as its simplicity and graphical development environment.

As an integrated system to incorporate available computer resources, the physical structure of the IDS is shown in Figure 2. The centre is a module-based platform used to integrate other applications. It is the core of the IDS, and consists of (Yang & Reidsema, 2006):

Figure 1. IDS user interface

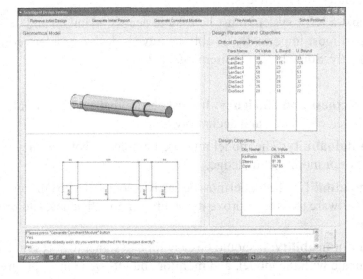

Figure 2. Integrated structure of IDS for computer resources

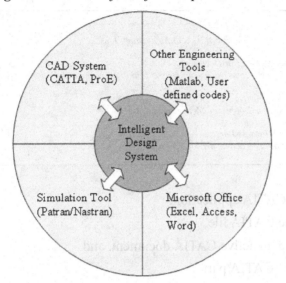

- A database, which includes all the design information such as input design parameters, design knowledge appeared as constraints; and target values of output design objectives.

- A control module, which is an inference engine in the solving process. It makes the run-time decisions by selecting the right design parameter at right time with a right value, under the guidance of design constraints.

- Objective modules, which are used to evaluate the design objectives. Each design objective has a corresponding module used to compute the value of this objective.

The CAD system is used to build the geometrical model. Currently the IDS is configured to integrate only CATIA and Pro/E because they are two of the most widely used CAD systems. It is very easy to link CAD applications with the IDS. Using CATIA as an example, the process of loading a CATIA part consists of four simple steps:

Figure 3. Pseudo code for loading a CATIA part into the IDS

```
Dim catia As Object
Set catia = CreateObject("CATIA.Application")

Dim partDoc As PartDocument
Set partDoc = catia.Documents.Open("Catia Part Name with Full Path")

Dim activePartDoc As Document
Set activePartDoc = catia.ActiveDocument

Dim catiaPart As Part
Set catiaPart = activePartDoc.Part
```

1.   Creating a CATIA application,

2.   Opening the CATIA file,

3.   Establishing an active CATIA document, and

4.   Defining the CATIA part.

The code for realizing this process is shown in Figure 3.

The finite element method has now become a ubiquitous simulation tool in product development. Among the various FEM packages, MSC Patran/Nastran is one of the most popular systems in industry. For the demonstration purpose, the current IDS only includes MSC Patran/Nastran as the simulation tool. The biggest advantage of Patran is that it has a programming language called Patran Command Language (PCL). PCL can be used to write application to perform iterative, variational modelling automatically. The Patran/Nastran simulation is realized in the IDS by running a PCL program. This simulation can be divided into three steps as shown in Figure 4. After exporting the geometrical model from CATIA into a STEP file, a MSC Patran PCL file is called up to run finite element analysis (FEA). Following that a result reading procedure is called to search for the analysis results from the FEA output text file (i.e., .f06 file).

Microsoft Office is also included in the IDS. Microsoft Office is a suite of applications such as Word and Excel, to implement word processing, spreadsheet, and other general office activities. It is very convenient to automate Microsoft Office applications in the IDS since VB, the programming language of the IDS, is also a Microsoft product. Currently, Excel is used as a database framework in the IDS. All the information related to the design problem is saved in spreadsheets. Excel also provides accommodation for

Figure 4. The process to run FEA simulation in the IDS

the intermediate analytical results, such as FEA results and artificial neural network analysis results. In addition, the built-in functions of Excel are used to help process the results of the design space characterization.

Within such a system, we assume that a project library have been established in a company. The library contains all existing products that a company has developed, and is saved in an information model that contains such attributes as geometry, decomposition scheme, information matrices and characterization results. As shown in Figure 5, for a new design, an initial design model can be established based on previous similar design examples. This model will be distributed to the other design personnel who are involved in the new design task in order to acquire new design inputs. All information related to this model is then structured in a manner so that it can be presented to the information pre-processing stage. The processed information will be finally integrated to facilitate the problem solving. In the fifth section, the detail activities related to these information processing stages will be described.

Figure 5. Information process configuration of the IDS

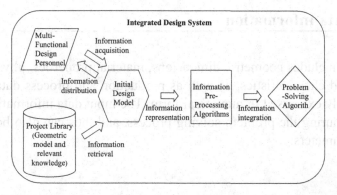

Figure 6. Information sorting wheel

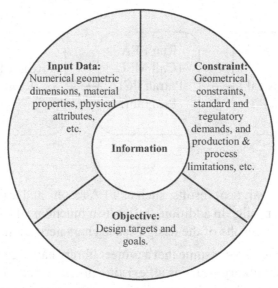

Information Classification in the Integrated Design System

In the IDS, all gathered information is sorted into three groups in terms of its nature: input data information, constraint information and objective information, as shown in the information wheel in Figure 6. These three types of information have different roles in the problem solving process, and also have different expressions.

Input Data Information

Input data includes geometric dimensions, material properties, physical attributes and characteristics, as well as production and process data. They are normally expressed in numerical form. The input data information will be varied during the problem solving process, and thus can also be called design parameters.

Constraint Information

Constraint information includes geometrical constraints, standard and regulatory demands, and manufacturing and process limitations. There are two kinds of geometrical constraints: numerical constraints such as distance and angle, and symbolic constraints such as coincidence and parallel (Wang, 2003). For instance, in the design of a slot it is required that its width should not be less than a certain value and its two edges must be parallel. Here, the width requirement is a numerical constraint while the parallel condition is a symbolic constraint. However, most of the symbolic constraints can be converted into numerical constraints. For example, a perpendicular constraint between two lines can be expressed as a numerical constraint by defining a 90-degree angle between them. Therefore, in the IDS, only numerical geometrical constraints are considered.

Constraints must be observed in the design process, and are ultimately reflected in parameter selection. They may generally be classified into two types in terms of their influences on the design parameters: the first defines the relationships between the different parameters, and the second type represents limitations on only a single parameter. The first type of constraint informa-

Figure 7. Classification of constraint expression

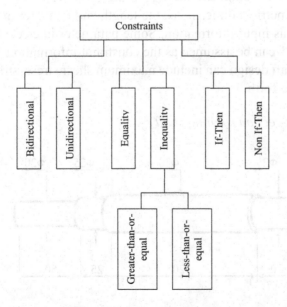

tion is extremely important in a knowledge-based system, as it constitutes a critical component of the knowledge. In this chapter, the term constraint will generally mean the first type of constraint.

Constraints are normally described in different forms, as shown in Figure 7. It should be noted that for an inequality constraint, a greater-then (>) or less-than (<) expression is not acceptable because such an expression is discrete. In addition, a bidirectional constraint means that all parameters involved in this constraint affect each other. Conversely, a unidirectional constraint has a dependent parameter, and the other parameters in the constraint will have an effect on this dependent but they will not affect each other. In an "if-then" constraint, however, parameter(s) in the "then" statement will not affect the parameter(s) in the "if" statement, even for a bidirectional constraint.

Objective Information

Objective information includes certain targets and goals that the design is expected to achieve. Design objectives suggest the primary problem solving focus, and are used as indicators to evaluate design performance. Objectives should be clearly stated and uncomplicated. An ambiguous or ill-defined design objective can easily result in either a failure to arrive at a solution or an excellent, but incorrect recommendation.

Using a common 4-section shaft design as an example, as shown in Figure 8, the eight geometrical dimensions, the length and diameter of 4 sections, can be selected as input information. Some parameter interrelationships as shown in Table 1 can be assumed as the constraint information. The objective of such a shaft design can include maximum shear stress, stiffness/mass ratio, cost and so forth.

Figure 8. A four-section rotating shaft

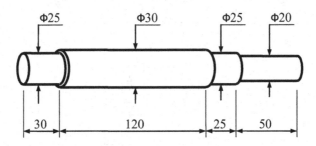

Table 1. Constraints in the shaft design

	Expression	Dir. Type
1	DiaSec1=DiaSec3	Bidirectional
2	LenSec1+LenSec2+LenSec3 <= 180	Bidirectional
3	LenSec1>=LenSec3+3	Bidirectional
4	VarDiaSec2=2*VarDiaSec1	Unidirectional
5	VarLenSec4= - VarLenSec3	Bidirectional
6	*If LenSec4 >= 49 **Then*** *DiaSec4 >=20*	Bidirectional

Dia=Diameter, Len=Length, Sec=Section, Var=Variation.

Figure 9. Information processing tower

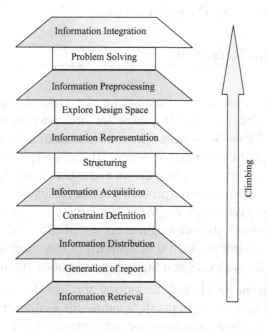

Information Flow and Processing

The information flow in the IDS can be described by the information processing tower in Figure 9. Climbing up to the top of the tower, the information processing is completed. The activities from information retrieval to representation are actually the information preparation for the design problem solving. After the preparation, the information is processed to explore the design space. The design space is normally characterized on the basis of sub-problems, especially for large and complex design problems. Therefore, problem decomposition is also a major activity in this stage. Finally, the problem will be solved as a whole by taking all information into consideration.

Information Preparation

Information preparation includes information retrieval, distribution, acquisition and representation. These four stages have been described in detail in our previous research (Yang & Reidsema, 2007).

Information Retrieval

Design information retrieval mainly involves introduction of a new initial geometrical model. In the IDS, there are three ways to introduce an initial design model into the system. The first is to search for a previous similar design example from the project library. The second is to browse for an existing model. The last option is to create a new trial geometrical model for the design problem. Most design problems can be retrieved from previous design problems that have a high degree of similarity since approximately 75% of design work in industry is thought to consist of either the adaptive or variant type (Singh, 1996). As such it is assumed in this discussion that a similar design case always exists and the last two methods are not discussed.

In the IDS, the project library for storing previous design cases is organized and indexed using the Microsoft Window file system. In the organization of the project library, the name of the directory must be meaningful and descriptive to describe the nature of the model clearly so that the user can quickly pinpoint the target directory for saving and searching. For example, with the previous shaft example, a good directory name can be defined as *OutstretchingDriveShaft_ FourSection_Twogears,* meaning that all shafts in this directory are out-stretching drive shafts with four sections, and can have two gears mounted.

Another important aspect, which affects the efficiency and accuracy of the searching process, is how to name the stored file. A name coding protocol is proposed to name the stored design cases. In this coding protocol, the name has a chain structure, consisting of numbered sets. The numbers represent the values of critical factors, which are chosen to represent the component. For the shaft here, if the length and diameter of the second section, which are 120mm and 30mm respectively, and the value of the *stiffness/mass* ratio, saying 1696, are chosen as the naming factors, it will have a name code of 120-30-1696. It should be pointed out that the selected naming factors must reflect the part's intrinsic attributes. For example, the objective *shear stress* cannot be a naming factor because its value depends on the external load applied to the shaft.

A simple searching algorithm, which is used to search for a previous similar design example from the project library, is given following the proposed naming protocol based on the computation of a weighted similarity index. In search, the targeting directory and the name code must be provided, and the weight numbers and the preferred directions of individual factors need also be defined, as shown in *Figure 10*. The weight of a factor indicates the relative emphasis placed on it during the search. As for the direction, "=" implies that a closer value to the target is more desirable, while ">=" or "<=" suggests that a greater or lower value is wanted. For a stored design case, its weighted similarity index is computed by comparing the values of the individual naming factors in its name code with those values in the target code. The relative similarity of an individual factor is:

Figure 10. Window for initial geometrical model retrieval

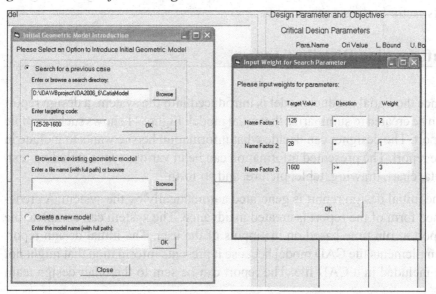

$$s = 1 - \frac{|t - e|}{t},$$
(1)

where s means the similarity, t is the value indicated in the target code, and e is the value indicated in the name code of the stored design case. However, if the preferred direction of this naming factor is ">=" and $e >= t$, or if its direction is "<=" and $e <= t$, s will be assigned value 1 directly, meaning that the target t is already met.

Thus, the weighted similarity index of the stored design case is:

$$S = \sum_i w_i s_i,$$
(2)

where S stands for the similarity index, i is the index of the naming factors, and w_i are the corresponding weight numbers.

After the similarity indices for all stored design cases are computed, the one with the highest index, which means the highest similarity to the target, can be selected. This method is simple and efficient. Another advantage lies in the use of the weighted sum because the user can put different emphases on different factors by giving different weight numbers. If one factor is not of concern to the designer, then a zero weight number can be given to ignore this factor in the search process.

Information Distribution

Once the initial product model is introduced into the system, a design report can be created to summarize the initial model. Figure 11 shows such a sample report. The designer can decide what information he/she wants to include in the report. The presented information can be in various types including text, data, chart, drawing, table, picture, and so forth.

The initial design report is generated automatically by the system. A prede-fined form of the report is created in advance. The system can complete the report at run time based on the inputs of the user. The initial design report complements the CAD model because it presents information that might not be included in a CAD file. The report can be sent to the other design team

Figure 11. Initial design report

members along with the CAD file. With such a report, the other designers can quickly ascertain the design rationale contained within the initial product model, and thus make their contributions or requirements to the initial design. In general, the report must include correct and complete information in order for the other designers to gain a correct and comprehensive understanding of the initial design model.

Information Acquisition

After reviewing the report, the designers can then propose their respective requirements about the initial design model based on their individual information and expertise. Generally, they can define constraints that describe the relationships between design parameters.

A sample constraint definition frame is configured in the IDS, as shown in *Figure 12*. A member of the design team can define his/her requirements using such a window, and send the requirements back to the IDS. He/she needs to input his/her name to identify whom a constraint is defined by. He/she also needs to select the type of the constraint being defined. Depending on the selection of

Figure 12. Constraint definition frame

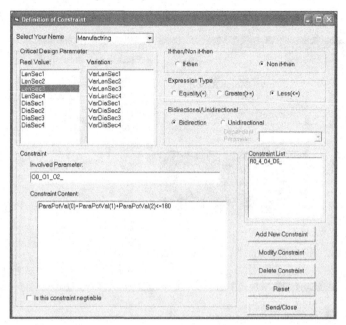

"if-then" or "Non if-then" type, the constraint content window changes correspondingly. During the definition of constraints, once the unidirectional type is selected, a list box for selecting the dependent parameter will be automatically enabled. A constraint can be defined in respect to either the values or the variations of the parameters. However, for a specific parameter, its value and variation cannot be included in the same constraint. This is because the value and variation of a parameter affect each other: the change of one resulting in a change of another. For a constraint, the indices of all its involved parameters will be recorded. In addition, each constraint has a unique name, and this name will appear in a list box once its definition is confirmed. The name of a constraint includes information such as who defines this constraint and which parameters this constraint involves. The user can also modify or delete an existing constraint by selecting it in the name list.

Information Representation

Information representation involves defining explicit descriptions of the acquired facts and relations by organizing information so as to facilitate the decision-making in the system. The information must be structured and stored in a manner such that the system can use it efficiently and correctly. Moreover, the information must be separated from the other parts of the system. Thus, the information can be changed or replaced without altering any other codes, and the system is more compatible to different design problems.

An information matrix is used to represent information in the IDS. Table 2 is such a matrix for the shaft. In this matrix, the design parameters and objectives are listed in both rows and columns. The parameters in the columns are treated as the primary parameters while those in the rows are thought of as dependent parameters. Within the matrix, there are four main parts. The first part includes the original values of all design parameters and the initial results of the objectives. The lower and upper boundaries, which define the variation ranges of the parameters and belong to the second type of constraint, account for the second part. The third part consists of the constraints that indicate how the changes of the column (primary) parameters affect the row (dependent) parameters. The fourth part consists of the dependencies between design parameters and objectives, which are qualitatively indicated by stars.

Embedding the constraints in the information matrix must abide by a few rules. First, all the expressions must be arranged in a way that the involved design parameters must appear on the left of the operators (=, >=, <=), and the right position can only be occupied by a number. For example, the first constraint for the shaft design in Table 1 is expressed as DiaSec1-DiaSec3=0 in Table 2. This rule helps to reduce the variants of an expression dramatically. Second, the proportional relationship between the variations of two parameters is indicated by a number that suggests the proportional strength. For instance, the fourth and fifth constraints in Table 1 are implied by numbers in the information matrix. It is assumed that most of the quantitative relationships among design parameters define how the change of a parameter causes the proportional change of another. A rule in the IDS is thus formulated that if a cell value in the matrix is detected to be a number, this number is explained by default as a proportional strength between the variations of the related row and column parameters. By doing so, the semantic analysis, which will be discussed later, is omitted for this kind of constraints. Third, the expression of an "if-then" constraint must follow the compact one-line syntax of defining "if-then" rules in Microsoft Excel; that is:

IF (Condition, Action_if_true, Action_if_false).

In general, these rules can help make the semantic analysis much easier.

There are a few points worth noting regarding the information matrix. First, for a unidirectional constraint, it is only included in the related cell in the upper triangle, while a bidirectional constraint is embedded in the related cells symmetrical with the diagonal. For instance, the fourth constraint for the shaft is unidirectional, and it is included in upper triangle Cell (DiaSec1, DiaSec2) in Table 2, but not in lower triangle Cell (DiaSec2, DiaSec1). Next, if a constraint involves more than two parameters, it can be placed in all relevant cells. For example, the second constraint for the shaft, which involves three parameters, is placed in all six relevant cells in the information matrix. Last, a cell can accommodate more than one constraint, and they must be separated by a semicolon, as shown in Cell (LenSec1, LenSec3) and (LenSec3, LenSec1) in Table 2.

To understand the meaning of a literal constraint, semantic analysis is performed in the IDS. Semantic analysis is a meaning-finding technique in natural language processing. In the IDS, many predefined standard forms are included in the system to enable this analysis. Each constraint item in the information matrix is compared with these standard forms to determine what constraint it is. During the analysis, the operator (=, >=, <=) is used as a break point in an expression. The analysis is then carried out only on the left hand side expression including the operator, while the right hand side number, which is in the format of text string, is converted to the numeric type directly. The standard forms are written in respect to the primary parameter and the dependent parameter so that they are suitable for different parameters. An example of such a standard form is:

"PriPara - DepPara >=",

where *PriPara* and *DepPara* stand for primary and dependent parameters, corresponding to the column and row parameters as mentioned above.

Information Pre-Processing

Information pre-processing involves two main activities: problem decomposition and relationship characterization. The design problem can be decomposed into smaller and more tractable sub-problems. The quantitative relationships between the design parameters and objectives are also identified in this stage in order to facilitate the final solving of the design problem.

Table 2. Information matrix for the shaft design

Para Name	Ori. Val	Lower B'dary	Upper B'dary	LenSec1	LenSec2	LenSec3	LenSec4	DiaSec1	DiaSec2	DiaSec3	DiaSec4	Shear Stress	K/M Ratio	Cost
LenSec1	30	27	33		LenSec1+LenSec2+LenSec3 <= 180	LenSec1+LenSec2+LenSec3 <= 180; LenSec1-LenSec3 >= 3						*		*
LenSec2	120	115	125	LenSec1+LenSec2+LenSec3 <= 180		LenSec1+LenSec2+LenSec3 <= 180							*	*
LenSec3	25	23	27	LenSec1+LenSec2+LenSec3 <= 180; LenSec1-LenSec3 >= 3	LenSec1+LenSec2+LenSec3 <= 180		-1					*	*	*
LenSec4	50	47	53			-1					If(LenSec4>=49, DiaSec4 >=20)			
DiaSec1	25	23	27							DiaSec1-DiaSec3=0		*	*	*
DiaSec2	30	28	32											*
DiaSec3	25	23	27					DiaSec1-DiaSec3=0						*
DiaSec4	20	18	22				If(LenSec4>=49, DiaSec4 >=20)	2						*
Shear Stress	91.38													
K/M ratio	1696.26													
Cost	167.55													

Problem Decomposition

For large and complex design problem, the divide-and-conquer strategy is often used. The problem is decomposed into smaller tractable sub-problems, which can be solved separately and in parallel. A matrix-based method called a design structure matrix (DSM) has been used to determine the process sequence of interrelated known subtasks of product development and manufacturing (Chen & Li, 2003; Yassine, 2004). Different algorithms, such as the similarity coefficient method (Kusiak & Cho, 1992), branch and bound algorithm (Kusiak & Wang, 1993), and genetic algorithm grouping technology (Falkenauer, 1998) may be employed in order to obtain appropriate decomposition schemes depending on the type of problem under consideration. Instead of focusing on the process sequence, the decomposition in the IDS aims to divide the design problem into subtasks by grouping the information to form subsystems based on the qualitative matrix, such as the one shown in Figure 13 hypothetically.

For a small and simple design problem, an objective-based scheme is used to decompose it by grouping all related design parameters of an objective to form a sub-problem. However, this scheme may not work well for a com-

Figure 13. Information matrix with qualitative relationship indicated by 1

Index	\multicolumn{13}{c}{Design Parameter}													Objective	
	1	2	3	4	5	6	7	8	9	10	11	12	13	14	15
1					1	1							1		
2			1				1				1				1
3										1		1	1		
4		1									1				
5	1					1			1			1			
6	1			1					1			1			
7		1		1											1
8			1							1			1		
9				1	1										
10		1						1				1			
11		1		1											
12		1							1						
13	1				1	1								1	1
14		1						1					1		
15		1					1						1		

plex design problem because the resulting sub-problems may still be too complex and decomposable. To deal with the decomposition of a complex design problem, a diagonal-centered decomposition scheme is developed in the IDS. This scheme is proposed on the basis of an assumption: an optimal decomposition scheme is suggested by that all the 1s in the qualitative information matrix (which indicates the parameters' dependencies) will centre around the diagonal in the closest way.

A genetic algorithm (GA) is employed to implement diagonal-centered decomposition scheme. The chromosome representation is based on the permutation of integers representing the sequence of information items. For example, in the qualitative information matrix shown in Figure 13, a chromosome

12	3	7	15	9	6	2	11	13	1	4	10	5	14	8

represents a permutation in which information item 12 is the first and item 8 is the last. The fitness function in the proposed GA-based decomposition scheme is to compute the total distance of all "1" cells to the diagonal. The distance of a "1" cell in the qualitative matrix is defined as shown in Figure 14. The matrix always has the same dimension of rows and columns since all information items are listed in both rows and columns and with the same sequential order. This means that the horizontal and vertical distances of a cell to the diagonal are the same. Therefore, in the computation of the fitness only the horizontal distance is counted. The fitness function can be expressed as:

$$D = \sum_{i}^{n} \sum_{j}^{n} C_{ij} \times d_{ij} = \sum_{i}^{n} \sum_{j}^{n} C_{ij} \times |(i - j)| \quad (i \neq j) \tag{3}$$

where D is the total distance of "1" cells of the matrix to the diagonal, i and j are row and column index, n is the matrix dimension, C is the cell value, and d is the distance of an individual cell to the diagonal.

To reproduce the next generation chromosomes in the iterative process of GA, four genetic operators are used. In addition to the conventional cyclic crossover and swap mutation, two novel operators, namely unequal position crossover and insertion mutation, are proposed in the IDS:

Figure 14. The distance of a cell to the diagonal

Index	1	2	3	4	5	6	7	8	9	10	11	12	13	14	15
1															
2															
3							$d = 11-4 = 7$								
4											1				
5															
6															
7															
8															
9															
10															
11															
12															
13															
14															
15															

- Cyclic crossover (Oliver, Smith, & Holland, 1987) is employed as the primary operator to deal with the permutation chromosome. The information items up to the crossover point from one parent are retained, and the information items after that point is arranged as it is ordered in the other parent.

- Unequal position crossover is performed based in the comparison between two parents in order to find the positions in which the two chromosomes have the same information items. Then the items in those common positions will remain unchanged in the children chromosomes, while the unequal items are rearranged. The reason behind this crossover operator is that the common items are believed to be in the correct positions, and the two parents have a good performance over the others because of these items.

- Swap mutation is implemented in two ways. First, two information items in a chromosome are selected at random and are simply swapped. Second, similarly as in the unequal position crossover, two chromosomes are compared and then two unequal items in the respective chromosome are randomly selected and swapped.

- Insertion mutation is developed especially for the chromosomes in which only one information item misses its position while all the others are in the correct order. To perform such a mutation, an item in a chromosome is randomly selected and then inserted into another randomly selected position, while all the other items still remain the original sequential order.

Figure 15 shows the resulting matrix in an experiment performing the proposed GA-based decomposition scheme on the matrix shown in *Figure 13*. It can be seen that the three subsystems are clearly indicated, and information item 13 belongs to all subsystems. The final fitness value of this resulting matrix is 75.

An expected decomposition is that each subsystem has no more than one objective. Thus all the information can be mapped to respective objectives after decomposition. In the case where a subsystem doesn't have objective information, it is still acceptable if it has shared items with other subsystems that include objective information. In such a case a shared item can be treated as an objective, such as the item 13 in the first subsystem in Figure

Figure 15. A resulting matrix with fitness of 75

Index	11	4	2	7	15	13	1	5	6	9	14	8	3	10	12
11		1	1												
4	1		1												
2	1	1		1	1										
7		1	1		1										
15		1	1			1									
13						1	1	1	1		1				
1						1		1	1						
5						1	1		1	1					
6						1	1	1		1					
9							1	1							
14						1						1	1		
8											1		1	1	
3											1			1	1
10												1	1		1
12													1	1	

15. Otherwise, such an independent subsystem without an objective can be deleted since it does not affect any objectives.

Design Space Characterization

To improve a design, a widely used approach now is based on the inverse process of first specifying design objectives and constraints and then computing the design parameters (Stander, Eggleston, Craig, & Roux, 2003). A prerequisite for implementing the inverse design approach is that the design space must be characterized so that a design engineer or system can identify the key design parameters in respect to the objectives in a quantitative way.

In the IDS, currently two methods can be used to explore the design space. The gradient-based incremental response method is derived from the conventional response surface method (RSM), but is simplified in order to improve the computational efficiency (Yang & Reidsema, 2006). The evolutionary algorithm artificial neural network (ANN) is a simple back-propagation network, and is coded to be self-evaluated to reduce the objective function evaluations. In this chapter, due to the limitation of length, only IRM is briefly introduced.

The mathematical model of the IRM can be written as (Yang & Reidsema, 2006):

$$Y = \sum_{i=1}^{n} y_i \tag{4}$$

where

$$y_i = \beta_1 x_i + \cdots + \beta_k x_i^k, (i = 1, \cdots, n) \tag{5}$$

Equation 4 indicates the total increase of an objective is the sum of the increases caused by the individual design parameters. Equation 5 is a polynomial used to compute the partial change. In these two equations, Y is the total incremental response of an objective due to the variations of design parameters, y is the partial incremental response, x stands for the variation of the design parameter, β is the coefficient, and i is the index of the parameters.

Figure 16 shows the flow chart of activities in design space characterization. For a design parameter, its range of variation will be equally split into a certain number of intervals. At each interval, the geometrical model is first updated, and the objective modules are then called up to compute respective objective increments. Once all intervals of this parameter are processed, the parameter variation set and the objective variation sets are written to a Microsoft Excel spreadsheet to retrieve the polynomial relationships as expressed in Equation 6.5. Finally, the polynomials are used to replace the stars in the information matrix shown in Table 2, and the parameter is re-

Figure 16. Flow chart of pre-processing

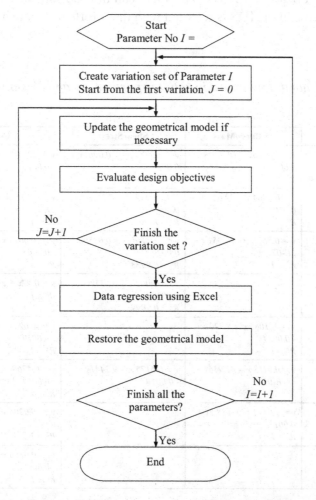

stored to its original value to prepare for processing the next parameter until all parameters are completed.

Table 3 show the exemplary polynomial parameter-objective relationships of the shaft. The R-squared value, which is a number between 0 and 1 used to indicate how accurately the polynomial fits the actual data, is automatically extracted from the regression process using Excel. As shown in the table, the R-squared values for all polynomials are either 1 or very close to 1, meaning the polynomials are very reliable.

Information Integration

After characterization the design problem can then be solved. The problem solving process in the IDS is featured with the information integration. The

Table 3. Polynomial relationship between parameters and objectives of shaft design

Para. Name	Stiffness/Mass	ShearStress	Cost
LenSec1	$y = 0.0676x^2 - 12.35x + 0.001$ $R^2 = 1$	$y = -0.0004 x^2 + 0.0961x + 0.0029$ $R^2 = 0.9998$	$y = -2E\text{-}16 x^2 + 0.7929x - 0.0014$ $R^2 = 1$
LenSec2	$y = 0.2264 x^2 - 22.65x + 0.0005$ $R^2 = 1$	$y = 0.0009 x^2 + 0.267x + 0.001$ $R^2 = 1$	$y = 1E\text{-}16 x^2 + 0.576x + 2E\text{-}15$ $R^2 = 1$
LenSec3	$y = 0.0675 x^2 - 12.35x + 2E\text{-}07$ $R^2 = 1$	$y = -0.0008 x^2 + 0.0359x + 0.0029$ $R^2 = 0.9973$	$y = -0.0013 x^2 + 0.7923x - 0.0005$ $R^2 = 1$
LenSec4	-	$y = 0.0002 x^2 - 0.135x + 0.0019$ $R^2 = 0.9999$	$y = 0.97x + 2E\text{-}15$ $R^2 = 1$
DiaSec1	$y = -0.1085 x^2 - 8.9291x - 0.0014$ $R^2 = 1$	-	$y = -0.023 x^2 - 1.1775x - 0.0019$ $R^2 = 1$
DiaSec2	$y = 0.9113 x^2 - 42.936x + 7E\text{-}07$ $R^2 = 1$	$y = 0.6175 x^2 - 9.2441x - 0.0019$ $R^2 = 1$	$y = 0.1768 x^2 + 12.228x - 0.0029$ $R^2 = 1$
DiaSec3	$y = 2.0184 x^2 + 128.2x + 0.0019$ $R^2 = 1$	-	$y = -0.0206 x^2 - 0.9799x + 0.0024$ $R^2 = 1$
DiaSec4	-	-	$y = -0.0396 x^2 - 1.5697x - 0.001$ $R^2 = 1$

design space characterization discussed in the previous section is normally carried out on the basis of sub-problems. Each sub-problem may concern only a single design objective. To solve a design problem correctly and efficiently, it is necessary to integrate all sub-problems together so that the problem can be solved as a whole by taking all design objectives and constraints into consideration. The shared parameters among sub-problems should be of the most concern in problem solving because they are related to multiple objectives.

The characterized information provides a basis for selecting a parameter to work on among a number of candidates so that there is a greater probability of achieving an objective with the least compromise on other design objectives. A parameter is selected in an iteration of the solving process by performing a sensitivity analysis (SA) that quantifies the relative importance of design parameters (Sudjianto, Du, & Chen, 2005), and identifies which parameter has the largest effect on the objectives. A concept of priority index (PI) is introduced in the IDS to measure the strengths of influence of design parameters on design objectives. On the basis of the instantaneous change rates of the objectives with respect to a design parameter, the PI of this parameter is computed by considering both the positive and negative effects of the parameter on all objectives (Yang & Reidsema, 2006):

$$PI(i) = PosEffect - |NegEffect| \tag{6}$$

The instantaneous change rates of objectives with respect to parameters can be easily computed by differentiating the polynomials obtained in the design space characterization. Whether the effect of a parameter on an objective is positive or negative can also be judged on the basis of the preferred varying direction of the objective and the sign of the instantaneous change rates of the objective with respect to the parameter. It should be pointed out that the effect of a parameter on an objective must be comprehensive, considering not only the parameter itself, but also its possible dependents since the parameters may be interdependent to each other. The constraint information, which defines parameters' interdependencies, is the most difficult part to deal with in this stage. It will not be discussed, however, because of the length limitation.

Failure Recovery

In cases where the desired solutions cannot be achieved, or where conflicts occur in the process preventing the problem solving from continuing, the system is considered to have failed in its efforts to solve the problem. This necessitates consideration of a failure recovery strategy. Failure recovery can concentrate on the following four aspects in accordance with the information processing flow:

- Check where the failure occurs and then examine whether the corresponding sub-problems are correctly characterized.
- Verify the decomposition scheme to see if it is suitable. If necessary, try to decompose the problem using other algorithms.
- Inspect the relationships between the design parameters and objectives to see if any related parameter of an objective is not included. For those relationships that are unsure or unessential, they must be included too. Although this may complicate the characterization stages, it can avoid failure occurring. In fact, the characterization can crosscheck whether a predefined relationship really exists or not. For example, if a parameter is not related to an objective, the objective will show zero response to the parameter changes.
- Review the information gathering and preparation processes, to see if any information is overlooked, and whether constraint and objective information is adequately defined.

Summary

In this chapter, an IDS based on the information processing is presented. As a part of the overall enterprise information system framework, the IDS is a knowledge-based design information system. It can address CE issues in design problem solving, such as integration, cooperation, communication and information sharing. It is easy to access, maintain, able to solve a design problem correctly and efficiently, and has the ability to take a comprehensive consideration of all design objectives. Following the introduction of the configuration, the working principle of the IDS is discussed based on the information handling process. The information is sorted in terms of its nature into three groups: input data, constraint and objective information, all having different representation strategies. All the information must be prepared before they can be used by the system. The information preparation includes retrieval, distribution, acquisition and representation four stages. To explore the design space in the IDS, the problem must be first decomposed. A diagonal-centered decomposition scheme is presented to handle the decomposition of a complex design problem. This scheme employs a genetic algorithm to find an arrangement of information items, such that all the relationship indicators in the qualitative matrix closely locate around the diagonal and the subsystems are thus identified. After decomposing the problem into sub-problems, information is then mapped to the relevant design objectives and processed separately and in parallel to quantitatively characterize the relationships. An incremental response method is proposed to perform the design space characterization. The design problem is finally solved as a whole by taking all design objectives and constraints into consideration. The characterized information enables the parameter selection in the iterative problem solving process. A priority index is introduced to a parameter to measure its strength of influence of on design objectives by considering both its positive and negative effects on all objectives.

The IDS is also an objective-oriented model. By sorting all information, the design objectives are clarified. By decomposing the problem, related information is mapped to respective objectives. By characterizing the strength relationships, the priorities of input data information towards the objectives are quantitatively measured. The success of this system is determined by the adequacy of the information preparation, the accuracy of the relationship identification, and the sufficiency of the problem solving ability.

References

Buchanan, B.G., Barstow, D.K., Bechtel, R., Bennett, J., Clancey, W., Kulikowski, C., Mitchell T., & Waterman D.A. (1983). Constructing an expert system. In F. Hayes-Roth, D.A. Waterman, & D.B. Lenat (Eds.), *Building expert systems* (pp. 127-167). Reading, MA: Addison-Wesley.

Calkins, D. (1996). *Learning all about knowledge-based engineering.* Knowledge Technologies International Ltd. Retrieved July 26, 2006, from http://www.ds-kti.com/pdf/product_design.pdf.

Chau, K.W., & Albermani, F. (2002). Expert system application on preliminary design of water retaining structures. *Expert Systems with Applications, 22,* 169-178.

Chen, S.J., & Lin, L. (2003). Decomposition of interdependent task group for concurrent engineering. *Computer and Industrial Engineering, 44,* 435-459.

Clancey, W.J. (1992). Model construction operators. *Artificial Intelligence, 53,* 1-115.

Coates, G., Hills, W., Whitfield, R.I., & Duffy, A.H.B. (1999). Design coordination for enabling concurrent engineering. In *6th ISPE International Conference on Concurrent Engineering*, Bath, United Kingdom.

Cooper, S., Fan, I-S., & Li, G. (2001). *Achieving competitive advantage through knowledge based engineering – A best practice guide.* Department of Trade and Industry U.K. Retrieved from http://www.ktiworld.com/pdf/kti_dti.pdf.

Falkenauer, E. (1998). *Genetic algorithms for grouping problems.* New York: Wiley.

Gardan, N., & Gardan, Y. (2003). An application of knowledge based modelling using scripts. *Expert Systems with Applications, 25,* 555-568.

Gruber, T.R. (1989). *The acquisition of strategic knowledge.* San Diego: Academic Press, Inc.

Koch, P.N., Evans, J.P., & Powell, D. (2002). Interdigitation for effective design space exploration using iSIGHT. *Journal of Structural and Multidisciplinary Optimization, 23*(2), 111-126.

Kulon, J., Broomhead, P., & Mynors, D.J. (2005). Applying knowledge-based engineering to traditional manufacturing design. *The International Journal of Advanced Manufacturing Technology, 30*(9-10), 945-951.

Kusiak, A., & Cho, M. (1992). Similarity coefficient algorithm for solving the Group Technology Problem. *International Journal of Production Research, 30*(11), 2633-2646.

Kusiak, A., & Wang, J. (1993). Decomposition of the design process. *Journal of Mechanical Design, 115,* 687-695

Lander, S.E., Staley, S.M., & Corkill, D.D. (1996). Designing integrated engineering environments: Blackboard-based integration of design and analysis tools. *Concurrent Engineering: Research and Applications, 4*(1), 59-71.

Malhotra, Y. (2001). Expert systems for knowledge management: Crossing the chasm between information processing and sense making. *Expert Systems with Applications, 20*, 7-16.

Matthews, P.C., Blessing, L.T.M., & Wallace, K.M. (2002). The introduction of a design heuristics extraction method. *Advanced Engineering Informatics, 16*, 3-19.

Myers, K.L., Zumel, N.B., & Garcia. P. (2000). Acquiring design rationale automatically. *AI EDAM, 14*(2), 115-135.

Newell, A. (1982). The knowledge level. *Artificial Intelligence, 18*(1), 87-127.

Oliver, I.M., Smith, D.J., & Holland, J.R.C. (1987). A study of permutation crossover operators on the travelling salesman problem. In *Proceedings of the Second International Conference on Genetic Algorithms and their Applications* (pp. 224-230). Erlbaum.

Ong, Y.S., & Keane, A.J. (2002). A domain knowledge based search advisor for design problem solving environments. *Engineering Applications of Artificial Intelligence, 5*(1), 105-116

Pokojski, J., Okapiec, M., & Witkowski, G. (2002). Knowledge-based engineering, design history storage, and case-based reasoning on the basis of car gear box design. In AI-METH 2002-*Artificial Intelligence Methods*, Gliwice, Poland

Prasad, B. (2005, June). Knowledge technology what distinguishes KBE from automation. *COE NewsNet* (online). Retrieved July 26, 2006, from http://www.coe.org/newsnet/Jun05/knowledge.cfm#1.

Reidsema, C., & Szczerbicki, E. (2001). A blackboard database model of the design planning process in concurrent engineering. *Cybernetics and Systems: An International Journal, 32*(7), 755-774.

Sandberg, M. (2003). *Knowledge based engineering in product development* (Tech. Report). Sweden: Luleå University of Technology.

Shikarpur, D. (2003, February 17). Knowledge-based engineering for effective e-manufacturing. *Express Computer (online)*. Retrieved July 26, 2006, from http://www.expresscomputeronline.com/20030217/opinion3.

shtml. Singh, K. (1996). *Mechanical design principles.* Melbourne: Nantel Publications.

Sivaloganathan, S., Evbuomwan, N.F.O., & Jebb, A. (1995). The development of a design system for concurrent engineering. *Concurrent engineering: Research and applications, 3*(4), 257-270.

Stander, N., Eggleston, T., Craig, K., & Roux, W. (2003). *LS-OPT user's manual.* Livermore, CA: Livermore Software Technology Corporation.

Sudjianto, A., Du, X., & Chen, W. (2005). *Probabilistic sensitivity analysis in engineering design using uniform sampling and saddlepoint approximation.* SAE Transactions (Paper 2005-01-0344). Detroit, MI: SAE Congress.

Szykman, S., Sriram, R.D., Bochenek, C., Racz, J.W., & Senfaute, J. (2000). Design repositories: Next-generation engineering design databases. *IEEE Intelligent Systems, 15*(3), 4855.

Tan, G.W., Hayes, C.C., & Shaw, M. (1996). An intelligent-agent framework for concurrent product design and planning. *IEEE Transactions of Engineering Management, 43*(3), 297-306.

Tomiyama, T. (1997). A note on research directions of design studies. In A. Riitahuhta (Ed.), WDK 25, *Proceedings of the 11th International Conference on Engineering Design* (Vol 3, pp. 29-34). Laboratory of Machine Design, Tampere University of Technology, Tampere, Finland.

Vergeest, J.S.M., & Horváth, I. (1999). Design model sharing in concurrent engineering: Theory and practice. *Journal of Concurrent Engineering Research and Applications, 7*, 105-114.

Wang, Y. (2003). *Constraint-enabled design information representation for mechanical products over the Internet.* Ph.D. Thesis, University of Pittsburgh.

Yang, Q., & Reidsema, C. (2006). An integrated intelligent design advisor in engineering design. *Cybernetics and System, An International Journal, 37*(6), 609-634.

Yang, Q., & Reidsema, C. (2007), Design information handling in a knowledge based intelligent design system. *Cybernetics and System, An International Journal, 38*(5), 549-573.

Yassine, A. (2004). An introduction to modeling and analyzing complex product development processes using the design structure matrix (DSM) method. *Italian Management Review, 9,* 72-88 (in Italian). Retrieved from www.quaderni-di-management.it.

Chapter V

Behavioral Aspects in Strategic Transformation of Organizations

Purnendu Mandal, Lamar University, USA

Abstract

Since behavioral and cultural factors play a major role in organizational transformation, IT managers must understand both the business requirements and human behavioral aspects in implementing large scale IT systems. This chapter stresses on behavioral issues, particularly how human behavior impacts on transforming organizations through implementing large IT systems such as ERP systems. The current business environment is forcing IT managers to use more and more "collective thinking power," generated by team activities, to make strategic decisions, or even to run day-to-day operations. Here we focus on broader issues managed through people's cooperation and efforts.

Introduction

Information technologies (IT), such as the Internet, WWW, EDI, and so forth, have already changed, and are still changing; the way organizations do business today (Mandal & Gunasekaran, 2003; Housel & Skopec, 2001). Significant movement that has occurred relatively recently is the push towards worldwide and national integration of information systems (Dutta, Lanvin, & Paua, 2003; Kumar & van Hillegersberg, 2000; Laughlin, 1999; Palaniswamy & Tyler, 2000) for organizations to achieve competitive advantages. Since it has become critical for businesses to be able to get to relevant data and information quickly and easily, large information systems such as enterprise resource planning (ERP) systems, supply chain management (SCM), enterprise resource/relationship management (ERM), enterprise application integration (EAI), Web services, and customer relationship management (CRM) have grown in importance.

IT systems are helping organizations to deal with increasing competition. Many organizations can no longer compete effectively by themselves; so, they must consider having partners to cope with the competition. For an organization to exploit the benefits of alliances, human factors and information technology (IT) factors must be among the basic components for any analysis and plan. Yet the literature is poor in this regard. Evidences of failure in the implementation of IT systems due to the lack of considerations of human factors have come to light in recent years. The main objective of this chapter is to highlight the human related issues in IT centered organizational transformation.

This chapter is organized around the following topics:

- A review of management fundamentals in managing people. This topic is considered important, as many IT professionals fail to realize that IT management is based on management fundamentals.

- A discussion on coping with change. Change management concepts and how changes could be achieved with ERP are discussed.

- Issues in strategic alliance

- Cultural aspects in strategic alliance

- IT issues in alliance, and

- A case example to illustrate the significance of organizational structure and behavioral issues.

Elements in Managing People

Much of the concepts in IT management are derived from the same basic concepts of management fundamentals. Apart from technology, perhaps *managing people* is the other most important consideration in successfully managing IT organizations. The elements involved in managing people are:

- Designing a **structure of roles** in which individuals perform their activities as per plan,
- **Selecting** staff suitable for these roles,
- Facilitating role playing through **training**, and
- Directing the role players through **motivation** and **leadership**.

Designing a structure, selecting staff, training, motivation and leadership are essential components of management tasks. Human behavior exerts a profound influence on managerial tasks, but managers often neglect or fail to consider **individual and group behavior** while performing their tasks. Personality (behavioral characteristics), which is the manifestation of the combined effect of human factors in an individual, is an important element to consider. Through motivation and leadership it is possible to influence

Figure 1. Elements in managing people

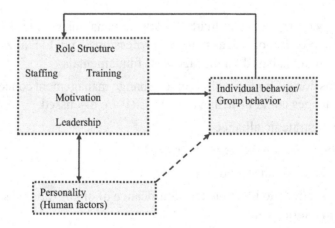

personality and, therefore, the behavior of people in an organization (Figure 1). The behavior of individuals and groups can also influence the managerial tasks of structuring, staffing, training, motivating and leading. Managerial success comes from monitoring individual and group behavior, and obtaining the whole-hearted cooperation of employees.

Behavior of People in Organizations

To be a successful manager, two complementary sources of knowledge are required:

1   technical knowledge (this comes from technical training and experience); and
2   an understanding of the behaviour of people in work situations.

The second requirement comes from observation, reflection and self-insight, aided by the results that others have reached. Not surprisingly, our understanding of the way people behave is not as well developed as our understanding of physical phenomena.

The possible variety of human behavior is enormous. This is due to:

• the variety of situations in which people find themselves;
• the differences between people observing human behaviour; and
• the fact that people's behaviour varies depending on who is watching.

We can identify certain personal preferences that help to characterize the differences between people, including:

• the need for achievement;
• the need for dominance;
• the need for autonomy; and
• the need for affiliation.

Personality is one of the most controversial concepts associated with un-derstanding human behavior. There is no real scientific basis for it, yet it remains one of the key concepts in the management of people. Crouch (1989) defines personality as "a stable and enduring behavioral characteristic of a person which is consistent across situations." So while personality affects the behavior of a person, it has been found that **situational factors** (i.e., the environment a person finds himself in) have a greater influence on behavior than personality.

In understanding the behavior of both individuals and groups it is important to understand that we all perceive things differently, both as individuals and as groups. It is more than a generalization to say that accountants see things differently than engineers, who see things differently than trades people. This selective perception can be the source of much organizational conflict.

Crouch (1989) defines **motivation** as "the human predisposition to act in a particular way." This predisposition is related to personality, but how do we explain differences in personality? Is it hardwired into us at birth or can it be developed? The most recent thinking is that it is a combination of both; we are born with a "reaction range" of possible behavior that is determined by our genes, and the situations we find ourselves in determine our exact behavior at any given time from within our reaction range.

How does a person's job contribute to their motivation and behavior? Just like engineering design, if a person's job is well designed, then it can be performed effectively and efficiently. Two main factors have been identified as important in a well-designed job, these are:

1.   Significance (Does the job make a real and identifiable contribution to the achievement of valued objectives?).

2.   Control (The more control a person has over his or her performance, the higher the potential for enhancing motivation).

If a job is designed to be rewarding, then the worker is likely to be highly involved with the job, and if there are rewards associated with loyalty to the organization (i.e., long-service leave), then we are likely to find a high level of commitment to the organization.

In an organization work is rarely performed independently of other people; we normally work in groups. Whenever people come together to form a group, a predictable pattern of interchange occurs between the group members before any work can be done. We can identify these group development phases as:

- **Forming:** Joining a group means a loss of some freedom and individuality in return for acceptance by the group.
- **Storming:** Issues of power and dominance must be resolved before useful work can be done.
- **Norming:** Accepted patterns of group behaviour ("norms") have to be established.
- **Performing:** The group is now fully functional and can perform its assigned tasks.
- **Adjourning:** When the group's tasks are complete the members separate.

Additionally, there are predictable patterns of behavior and factors that contribute to stabilizing group behavior. These are:

- Group roles;
- Group norms; and
- Group member status.

In most groups we see particular **roles** taken on by group members, and a given person may take on more than one role. The following roles are probably the minimum required for a successful group:

- "Ideas person," who contributes bright ideas as potential solutions to problems;
- "Cynic," who questions the practicality of any new ideas;
- "Task leader," who keeps the group on track toward achieving its assigned objectives; and
- "Social leader," who maintains group harmony and manages conflict between group members.

Group norms are the unwritten agreements between group members about acceptable group behavior; these might include the expected morning start time, the amount of work effort expected, and the amount of chatter permitted while working.

Group norms can be either positive or negative, and hence can be a positive influence on, or detrimental to group performance.

Delegation involves the tasks that can be handed over to subordinates for completion. Effective delegation is essential for managers because managing is by definition concerned with achieving results through the efforts of others. Effective delegation allows managers more time to devote to high-level issues such as planning, and it assists the staff that has been delegated tasks to develop their own skills.

Managers may avoid delegation because they feel they could in fact do the task more efficiently themselves, or because they fear the loss of power if they give up certain tasks to others. But for a manager to be effective, he or she must be effective in their use of delegation. Effective delegation entails:

- Giving the subordinate the required authority to complete the task delegated,
- Setting clear goals and objectives relating to the delegated tasks,
- Providing feedback about the subordinate's performance and progress in completing the delegated tasks, and
- Setting and agreeing on a clear time frame for the completion of the delegated task.

Motivation

Motivation is the process that causes, channels and sustains people's behavior. Motivation does not happen in isolation but depends on all other aspects of management. In particular, the characteristics of the work situation, or the organizational culture, have a strong impact on motivation.

A large part of a manager's task is to get things done through the efforts of others, so an understanding of motivation and what motivates people is essential. People are motivated by their personal needs and by what they perceive as leading to a desirable outcome or reward. To be an effective motivator, a reward must be both worth attaining and actually attainable.

One of the major difficulties for a manager when it comes to motivation is that what one person considers important and worth attaining may have little value to another person.

Abraham Maslow developed a theory of motivation based on a "hierarchy of needs." He believed that people have five basic categories of needs, these being:

1. Physiological needs (food, drink, shelter, warmth)
2. Safety needs (security, safety)
3. Social needs (belonging to a social group, being accepted)
4. Ego needs (self-esteem, respect, recognition for effort)
5. Self-actualisation needs (personal fulfilment)

Maslow believed that the lower level needs had to be at least partially satisfied before higher level needs become activated and, therefore, useful as a motivational tool. For example, we all need food, shelter and security before we worry about whether our job is interesting and fulfilling.

Along similar lines, Frederick Herzberg developed a "two-factor" theory of motivation. Like Maslow, he believed that people have lower and higher level needs. He called the lower level needs "hygiene factors," and the higher level needs "motivating factors." Hygiene factors include things such as salary, working conditions, company policies and supervision style. Motivating factors include things such as opportunities for challenge, achievement, advancement and responsibility in our work.

Herzberg contends that the factors that satisfy hygiene needs are different to those that satisfy motivational needs. If hygiene factors are inadequate, employees quickly become dissatisfied. However, lower level needs are quickly satisfied, and simply adding more of them is generally not an effective motivational tool. Herzberg proposes that the only successful method of motivating people in the long term is to build high-level factors into their jobs.

An important factor in determining motivation of employees is the "culture" of an organization. Organizational culture is the shared beliefs, values and expectations of the organization's employees. There are many factors within an organization that contribute to the culture that exists, including:

- The level of trust between organisational groups;
- The level of stress in the work environment;
- Fear and anxiety;
- The types of social interactions that occur;
- Organisational factions and politics;
- Company policies; and
- Management styles and practices.

The nature and strength of the organizational culture and how it is managed have an important effect on employee motivation. A positive organizational culture assists the manager in that a pre-existing level of motivation and team spirit already exists, and this can then be built upon further. An organization's culture needs to be managed if a positive culture is to be encouraged and sustained, or an inappropriate culture is to be changed. Successful managers can foster a desired culture by:

- Leading by personal example,
- Rewarding and reinforcing positive behaviour,
- Communicating desired behavioural norms, and
- Explaining the importance of organisational culture.

The traditional method of motivating people is based on rewards for good behavior and punishment for undesirable behavior. Obviously this can be effective, but only up to a point. The theories of motivation that we have reviewed above tell us that whatever motivational tools we use; they should be based on the needs of the individual we are trying to motivate.

In an organization there will always be **formal** and **informal groups**. Formal groups are created to fulfil a specific organizational task, and informal groups are usually formed by the members of the group to satisfy some need, be it friendship, affiliation, and so forth.

A group is always more than simply the sum of its parts. This is because the interactions between the group members can create energies and qualities that may not be present in the group members when viewed individually. The energy that groups seem to possess is referred to as "synergy." **Group**

synergy can be positive or negative. Some groups are strong and performance oriented, others are weak, lacking the will to achieve.

Coping with Change

Management is evolutionary. The principles and practices of management are changing with time; new concepts are being written into management literature; old concepts are either being modified or dropped altogether. So it is with the concepts of people management. People management is passing through an era of change. Changes are inevitable, and managers must prepare organizations to embrace these changes. The task of management is to reduce the resistance to change.

It is a truism, but no one can deny that, "one of the few things of real permanence in the world is change." It is also true that we live in an age of ever increasing change, for example:

Over the last 50,000 years of human existence there have been approximately 800 lifetimes and, of these, 650 lifetimes were spent living in caves. Only in the last six have we had the printed word; only in the last four have we been able to accurately measure time; only in the last two have we had electric motors; and the majority of all the material goods we have today have been developed in the last lifetime.

Both academics and practicing managers agree on the need to adapt to change, but the specific skills and attitudes required are still a topic of debate. The term "change" refers to any alteration that occurs in the total environment of an organization. A good analogy for organizational change is a balloon. If your finger pushing on the balloon represents change, then the affects of change are most apparent where you touch the balloon, but areas close by will also be distorted. The change in pressure will be felt throughout the balloon (organization), and repeated applications of pressure (change) may weaken or damage the balloon (organization).

When it comes to implementing organizational change, a manager's objectives should be to gain acceptance for the change, and to restore the group equilibrium that is upset by the change. An organization cannot move forward without making a change, so it needs to be able to withstand the trauma of change. To cope with organizational change an organization requires:

- Enough stability to achieve its current goals;
- Enough continuity to ensure orderly change;
- Enough adaptability to react to demands and opportunities; and
- Enough innovativeness to proactively make changes when appropriate.

Factors that may cause organizational change include:

- Environmental factors, that is, changing government policy, economic conditions, and so forth;
- Changes in customer preferences;
- Changes in technology;
- Organisational restructuring; and
- Changes in the managerial style of the organisation.

If change is one of the few constants in the world, then so is the resistance to change. When an organization attempts to undergo change it may find that people within the organization resist change. Reasons why people may resist change include:

- **Economic factors:** The change may mean they are valued (and hence paid) less by the organisation or made totally redundant.
- **Inconvenience:** A company restructure may mean you have to move your office across the hall or across the country.
- **Uncertainty:** If the reason for change is not properly communicated then those affected may fear ulterior motives.
- **Threats to relationships and power:** Change by definition upsets the balance of power, and loss of power may be strongly resisted.
- **Resentment of control:** Organisational change reminds people that the organisation has the final say, and some people may resent being reminded of this fact.

It is a poor manager who views change as a necessary evil that has to be endured. Better managers realize that it is only through change that the organization can grow and improve. Techniques that can help a manager reduce resistance to organizational change include:

- Recognising and being sympathetic to the social and psychological factors associated with change,
- Encouraging the people affected by the change to participate in the change process (participation brings support),
- Developing trust in management (if management is trusted by the members of the organisation, then implementing change will be easier, as the staff will understand that the management would not propose a change that was bad for the organisation),
- Making only necessary changes (change for no good reason wastes time and effort, and causes unnecessary problems), and
- Force field analysis.

Force field analysis was developed by Kurt Lewin. Its basic principle is that when change is being resisted, we need to analyze the factors (or forces) that are operating for and against the change. From this there are two ways to gain acceptance for a change:

1. Increase the pressure for change, and/or
2. Reduce the resistance to change,

such that the forces for change overcome the resistance to change.

Edgar Schein has developed a model of the change process. It consists of three steps:

1. **Unfreezing:** People have to be made ready and willing to accept new ideas and what they are required.
2. **Changing:** Change will only take place when the new ideas have been accepted and internalised.
3. **Re-freezing:** The final acceptance and integration of the desired new ideas and attitudes.

The model looks simple, however, in reality, unfreezing is difficult to achieve, as it may involve giving up long held beliefs and ways of doing things. It may require a long and slow process of education and convincing of the need for change.

Research shows that the shape of organizational structure is changing continuously and that organizations (and their shapes) in the twenty-first century will be different from those that we currently observe. Traditional organizational structures, such as function-based and product-based structures, are oriented to a relatively stable organizational environment; that is, we are either doing the same things (function-based) or making the same things (product-based). However, newly emerging factors in the environment of modern organizations are coming into direct conflict with rigid organizational structures. These newly emerging factors include:

- **Global markets:** To increase market size, organisations are looking to export to other countries. Likewise, competitors in those countries are likely to be trying to export back into your country.

- **New alliances between the public and private sectors:** Almost every day we hear of another public sector body being privatised or former public service being let out to competitive tender.

- **Collaboration with erstwhile competitors:** In the microelectronics field there are many examples of companies collaborating on joint developments while they continue to compete fiercely in other areas.

- **Social responsibility and ethics:** The community and the law are placing ever-increasing demands on organisations to act responsibly and morally.

- **Individual fulfilment:** Organisations have found that they can no longer consider employees as an expendable labour resource; to get the best from their staff they must balance the needs of the individual with the needs of the organisation.

Most organizations can cope with change if it is gradual, serial, incremental and continual. However, we are finding that even the nature of change has changed. Change is now more likely to be random, episodic and discontinuous. A change is "discontinuous" whenever it does not directly follow the historical logic of the organization's development. One measure of discontinuity is to what extent does the firm depart from the market needs it knows how to serve.

One form of organizational structure that has been proposed (Limerick, 1992) to deal with change, and in particular discontinuous change, is the "network organization." Network organizations come in many different forms and under many different labels. They may incorporate one or more of the following strategic options:

- Internal networking, that is, where the organisation's divisions are set up as independent business units and must compete for work both inside and outside the organisation.

- Sub-contracting. If someone else can do part of a project more efficiently than you, then you should give them that work under a sub-contract arrangement so you can offer the most competitive overall price to your customer.

- Strategic alliances. If you can only perform part of a large project but would like to be able to offer a total project service, you can form a short-term alliance with another organisation that can offer provide the necessary skills to complete the project.

- Franchising. If you have a good idea, but don't have the resources to take it to a mass market, you can license the idea to others and earn royalties on your creativity.

- Strategic networks, that is, collaborations between organisations for mutual benefit.

The common strategic premise of all network organizations is:

If a firm can "farm out" activities to the most efficient supplier, keep for itself those activities in which it has a comparative advantage and lower administrative costs, then a superior form of organization (the network organization) will emerge.

There are two basic types of network organization: internal networks and external networks. The key for internal network organizations is for all the parts of the organization to learn to handle themselves as autonomous business units and to network and collaborate with other resources within the organization. One type of external network organization is the "regional/industry cluster." Here strategic networks between smaller organizations are built, particularly between organizations in the same regional area and/or operating in the same industry. Another type of external network organization is the "global alliance." As organizations realize that the world is now their marketplace, they often look to form strategic alliances with organizations in other countries to give them a presence in global markets.

Network organizations are not a panacea for all of the ills of the modern organizational environment. They are difficult to manage and present a host of inherent complications, but for many organizations they offer new opportunities.

Changing Organization with ERP

ERP implementation is a huge coordinating effort, which involves many teams across all business functions and outside stakeholders such as IT consultants (Mandal & Gunasekaran, 2003). ERP implementation could simply be viewed as IT project management activities or it could also be viewed as an opportunity to change an organization.

From IT perspective, ERP has grown as an integration tool where the aim is to integrate all enterprise applications to a central data repository with easy and discrete access to all relevant parties. By 2000, SAP R/3 was installed in over 20,000 locations in over 107 countries (Bhattacherjee, 2000). Companies such as Geneva Pharmaceuticals, Eastman Kodak, Lucent Technologies, Farmland Industries, Du Pont, Digital Equipment Corporation (Bancroft et al., 1998), Owens Corning, and Dead Sea Works are using SAP R/3 to track cost and resource information, monitor service levels and expenditures, and provide front-line workers with the information needed for better decision-making. By creating a centralized database and standardizing corporate data flow, ERP can make changes and efficiencies take root in a firm.

For successful implementation of ERP three basic requirements should be met: a clear business objective, comprehension of the nature of changes and understanding of the project risk. Strong leadership and constant watch to budget are two other requirements as stressed by Wagle (1998):

For effective implementation of an ERP system, particularly SAP R/3, an organization must take a holistic view of the process (Al-Mashari & Zairi, 2000). Various issues at strategic, managerial, and operational levels should be addressed in order to achieve optimum outcomes from an ERP. Further-

Figure 2. Core competencies in effective implementation of ERP

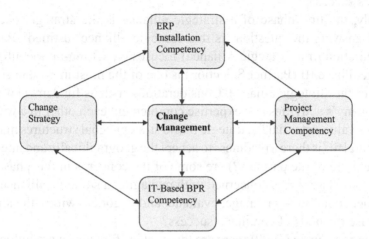

more, *for a successful outcome an organization must have established com-*
petencies in four core areas: change strategy development and deployment,
enterprise-wide project management, BPR integration with IT, and technical
aspects of ERP installation. These competencies will enable managers to ef-
fectively manage the changes and, thereby, move the organization to desired
goals (see Figure 2).

Issues in Strategic Alliance

Strategic alliance focuses on combining resources of various organizations
through acquisition, joint venture, or contracts. The main purpose of an alliance is to create one or more advantages such as product integration, product
distribution, or product extension (Pearlson, 2001). Strategic alliances also
help in utilization of resources even in small organizations (Gunasekaran &
Nagi, 2003). In alliances, information resources of different organizations
require coordination over extended periods of time.
Bronder and Pritzl (1992) suggest a strategic alliance exists when the value
chain between at least two organizations (with compatible goals) are combined for the purpose of sustaining and/or achieving significant competitive
advantage. Four critical phases of strategic alliance are: strategic decision
for an alliance, alliance configuration, partner selection, and alliance management. These four phases provide the basis for a continuous development

and review of the strategic alliance, which increases the likelihood of the venture's success.

Typically, the first phase of a strategic alliance is the strategic decision. Phase I answers the question: Is this strategic alliance justified? Phase II (Configuration of a Strategic Alliance) focuses on setting-up the alliance's structure. Phase III (Partner Selection) is one of the most important success factors of the strategic alliance. Considerations such as fundamental fit (do the company's activities and expertise complement each other in a way that increases value potential?), strategic fit (do strategic goal structures match?), and cultural fit (is there a readiness to accept the geographically and internally grown culture of the partners?) are some of the concerns in this phase. The final phase, Phase IV, is concerned with managing a strategic alliance; how do partners continually manage, evaluate, and negotiate within the alliance to increase the odds of continued success?

According to Currie (2000) there are three major forces that are influencing the formation of alliances between organizations: globalization, deregulation, and consolidation. But, before organizations commit to strategic alliance, they should have a management plan on how to deal with human behavior aspects of the new organizational unit. Once a strategic alliance is a "done deal" the organizations must manage the alliance. Parise and Sasson (2002) discuss the knowledge management practices organizations should follow when dealing with a strategic alliance. They break the creation of a strategic alliance down in to three major phases:

- **Find:** Making alliance strategy decisions and screening and selecting potential partners.
- **Design:** Structuring and negotiating an agreement with the partners.
- **Manage:** Organizations should develop an effective working environment with the partner to facilitate the completion of the actual work. This phase includes collecting data relating to performance and feedback from both partners on how they think the alliance might is progressing. Managing relationships and maintaining trust are particularly critical during the manage phase.

Knowledge management techniques are especially important for a successful alliance (Parise & Sasson, 2002). They discuss the need to develop a systematic approach for capturing, codifying and sharing information and knowledge, a focus on building social capital to enable collaboration among people and communities, an emphasis on learning and training, and a priority on leveraging knowledge and expertise in work practices. They also state their study indicates easy access to information, and knowledge is a recurring theme in successful alliances.

Parise and Sasson (2002) provide a list of the building blocks of alliance management. Four of their building blocks relating specifically to human behavior factors are:

- **Social capital:** Building trust and effective communication with the partner are necessary ingredients for an effective relationship.

- **Communities:** Communities of practice allow for the sharing of personal experiences and tacit knowledge based on a common interest or practice. Communities can be realized using electronic meeting rooms and forums or more formal alliance committees.

- **Training:** Companies that rely heavily on strategic alliances should have formal training for managers and team members.

- **Formal processes and programs:** Alliance know-how should be institutionalized. An example of this is Eli Lilly, a leading pharmaceutical firm, which created a dedicated organization, called the Office of Alliance Management, responsible for alliance management.

Companies that use alliance management techniques that stress knowledge management are more successful than those who do not. Leveraging knowledge management across a company's strategic alliance is a critical success factor for partnering companies. Strategic alliance is a management issue. Both cultural and information technology aspects play a significant role in strategic alliance.

The number of strategic alliances formed between organizations has increased dramatically and is projected to continue to increase in the future. Strategic alliances are a mutual agreement between two or more independent firms to serve a common strategic (business) objective (Bronder & Pritzel, 1992). Alliances have had a growth rate of 25 percent and are projected to have a value of $40 trillion by the year 2004 (Parise & Sasson, 2002). The "make versus buy" decision is becoming the "make versus buy versus partner decision." Through empirical analysis, Yasuda (2005) shows that the primary motivation of strategic alliances is the access to resources, followed by the shortening of time required for development or marketing.

A successful alliance should not imply an imposition of one organization's culture over another. Rather, it should create a new culture that brings together the best elements of each. Unfortunately, "creation of a new culture" is rarely practiced as alliances are often viewed solely from a financial perspective, leaving the human resource issues as something to be dealt with later and without a great deal of effort. The creation of a new culture involves operations, sales, human resources management, technology, and structure among other issues. It is undoubtedly expensive and time consuming to create a new culture, but, in the end, employees become contented and productive.

Cultural Aspects in Alliances

As discussed in the preceding sections, alliance among firms naturally would result in many organizational changes. Leavitt (1965) concluded there are four types of interacting variables to consider when dealing with organizational change, especially in large industrial organizations: task variables, structural variables, technological variables, and human variables. He proposed structural, technological, and people approaches to organizational changes, which derive from interactions among the four types of variables mentioned above.

The above-mentioned four variables are highly interdependent so that a change in any one variable usually results in compensatory changes in other variables. The introduction of new technological tools – computers, for example -- may cause changes in structure (communication system), changes in people (their skills and attitudes), and changes in performance and tasks. Therefore, it is imperative to consider all areas that might be affected when a company plans to introduce change to an organization.

Pre-existing people-related problems at a target company often cause many alliances to fail to reach their full financial and strategic potential. Numerous case studies report failure of alliances due to lack of consideration for the potential impact of behavioral and structural aspects (Brower, 2001; Numerof & Abrams, 2000). To build an effective alliance, institutions must pay particularly close attention to cultural, personality and structural incompatibilities. Leaders from alliance institutions need to recognize the personality differences in their managers as well as the demands required by the life cycle stage of their organizations (Segil, 2000). It has also been demonstrated that successful alliance partners share many strong similarities regarding performance and relationships (e.g., people skills) (Whipple &

Frankel, 2000). Understanding potential incompatibilities gives institutions contemplating alliances a solid foundation on which to explore the feasibility of joint projects. It also increases the likelihood the alliance will operate successfully (Whipple & Frankel, 2000).

Successful alliances are impeded when the culture of one or both associations highly differ in value. "High control value" is inconsistent with the toleration for ambiguity and the "willingness to compromise" often required for strategic alliances. Maron and VanBremen (1999) suggests the use of William Bridges' Organizational Character Index (OCI), which can be a useful tool for analyzing the cultural differences between two associations to determine how well they might work together. It promotes better understanding between two associations, fosters an appreciation for what both partners could bring to an alliance, and identifies underdeveloped qualities in both associations that could inhibit the success of an alliance.

IT Issues in Alliances

Long term IT considerations, such as IT architecture, are major considerations. A strategic consideration, such as new alliances, would require visioning of a different IT architecture. Applegate, McFarlan, and McKenney (1999) view IT architecture as an overall picture of the range of technical options as well as business options. "Just as the blueprint of a building's architecture indicates not only the structure's design but how everything – from plumbing and heating systems, to the flow of traffic within the building – fits and works together, the blueprint of a firm's IT architecture defines the technical computing, information management and communications platform" (p. 209).

Figure 3 brings out the dynamic nature of the IT architecture development process. The technology part, shown by dotted oval, is concerned with design, deployment and how it is used. This part is the core of IT architecture and a huge proportion of IT professionals' time is devoted to these activities. Consideration of business options, which feed to various technology options, is higher-level activities in the IT architecture development process. Business options, such as strategic alliances, mergers and acquisitions, outsourcing, diversification, and so forth, are influenced by major internal as well as external factors, such as current business practices, business opportunities, and organizational strategy. There is a direct link between technology and organizational strategy. The technology (with its operational and technical settings) exerts a strong influence on the organization's future strategic direction. Thus, one can observe (as shown in Figure 3 through connecting lines), a close link between technical and other business factors, and, like ever changing business, the IT architecture is a dynamically evolving phenomena.

An alliance can exist between any types of organization. For example, a telecommunication organization could form an alliance for international joint ventures, or an alliance can be established between a banking organization and an IT supplier. The notion of developing a strategic alliance suggests an organization's performance can be significantly improved through joint, mutually dependent action. For a strategic alliance to be successful, business partners must follow a structured approach to developing their alliances and should include, as part of this process, strategic planning, communication, efficient and effective decision-making, performance evaluation, relationship structure, and education and training.

Strategists have often suggested that organizations should consider entering into similar or somewhat related markets sectors to broaden their product/service portfolios (Henderson & Clark, 1990; Markides & Williamson, 1997). Both the dimensions of market (customer and product) in a related market can easily be identified and strategies formulated for deployment. The main advantage of adopting such a strategy is that an organization can easily use its competencies and strategic assets in generating a strategic competitive

Figure 3. Forces affecting overall IT architecture

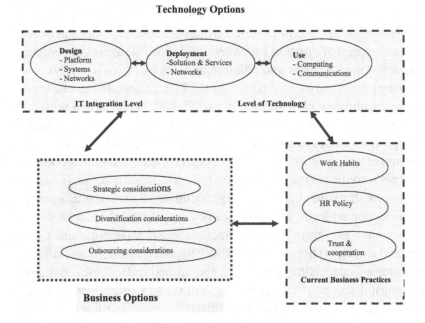

advantage (Markides & Williamson, 1997). Determining the design and the requirements of a new information system (IS) is a relatively simple task. In contrast, diversification into a significantly different market for an IT/IS organization is a very challenging task, which needs considerable evaluation of IT infrastructure and human relations.

A Case Example

To illustrate how important the behavioral aspects are in strategic transformation the case of a telecommunication organization (TEL) is presented here. TEL provides services to its customers through its own telecommunications network and would like to improve its customer base by forming a strategic alliance with the retail electricity distribution organizations. TEL is a Fortune 500 company with annual revenue over $14.5 billion. TEL provides a full range of services in telecommunication markets to more than 10 million fixed line and 6 million mobile subscribers. Many experts believe that a handful of global power companies will soon provide the majority of the world's energy needs (Brower, 2001), and TEL aspires to be one amongst them. As large telecommunication organizations exhibit structural inertia, generating a competitive advantage in a new market poses an enormous challenge (Henderson & Clark, 1990). An organization must make a distinction between a new product and the means to achieve that new product. The recent merger between America Online and Warner Publishing clearly demonstrates that it is not too difficult for an IT organization to offer new products in an existing market. Considering this point, strategic alliances and partnership could be a way out for an IT organization to enter into a completely new product market. From a systems development perspective, alliances may result in the development of new interfaces to the existing ISs or, alternatively, a new integrated IS.

As per the deregulation rules, a retail distributor must make financial settlement with other suppliers of the electricity industry supply chain. This needs to cover the cost of electricity from the wholesale electricity market, tariffs for distribution of the same by the transmission and distribution service providers, and meter data collection from meter providers (MPs) and meter data agents (MDAs). The processes and systems therein must be able to interface with retail energy distributors accounting and billing, service activation and service assurance processes and systems.

To conduct business as a market participant TEL must purchase wholesale electricity and services for the physical delivery and metering to the customer. There are two clear options available to TEL to purchase electricity:

- **By direct participation and trading in the national electricity market (NEM):** This means that TEL would perform all electricity trader functions, including the act to bid and settle wholesale purchases in the national electricity market from its own resources and carry all market and prudential risks and responsibilities.

- **By engaging an existing specialist energy trader:** This means that TEL would form a close and long-term relationship with one (or more) existing trader(s) who would operate all market trader functions and processes on TEL's behalf. This would be an outsourced supply arrangement. The sharing of risk and responsibilities is a matter for specific agreement with the trader.

TEL performed a strategic analysis to find out significant differences with its potential partners. The analysis required a careful evaluation of the strengths and weaknesses of each firm, and detailed planning of what the reorganized alliance would look like. The IT architectural planning would not only present the overview of future challenges, but would also provide the chief information officers (CIOs) a summary of the nature of human related activities they would be faced with once the alliance became a reality. Table 1 shows significant differences between TEL and the other partners.

The cultural differences between TEL and potential industry partners are so high, as evident from Table 1, that one might suggest the proposed alliance is a recipe for disaster. Unless there is a higher authority to ensure compliance this alliance is likely to head for a failure. The perception of relational risks plays a dominant role in strategic alliance. As uncertainty regarding a partner's future behavior and the presence/absence of a higher authority to ensure compliance dominate strategic alliance considerations, it seems to be that the relational risks are very high in this case. Delerue (2004) suggests that informal contextual factors have more influence on relational risks than the formal contextual factors. There are three important reasons related to human behavior factors that might lead to partnership failure in this situation. The reasons are (as per Dixon & Marks, 1999): inattention to the human resources issues; failure to plan for other human resources issues such as benefits, loyalty, identity, and so forth; and poor communication. In addition, it would be necessary to build a new culture and learning environment.

Table 1. Structural and behavioral differences

Factors	TEL	Partners
Company organizational structure/size	Very complex and large in sales volume (Annual revenue $14.5 billion, Assets $24.9 billion)	Small to medium size, relatively simple structure (revenue in the order of million $)
Employee work habit	Flexible work hours	Relatively rigid work hours
Customer relations	Good relations with existing customers – excellent customer services	Indifferent to customer complaints
Employee training	Good opportunity for skill upgrading (formal training department)	Reasonable opportunity for technical skill development
IT system compatibility	Highly developed IT system	Manual or primitive IT systems
Employee satisfaction	Highly motivated, well-paid work force.	Competent, but low paid work force.
Employee turnover	High turnover	Relatively low employee turnover.

Conclusion

In today's competitive business environment, new methods of evolution from independence to interdependence are continuing to unfold – strategic alliance is one of those methods that can transform organizations. In the process for preparing an organization for a change, IT infrastructure and human factors play important roles. IT planning highlights major weaknesses and incompatibilities with information systems of various parties within an organization; those incompatibilities, however, can intensify further due to operational and work practices in partner organizations. The development of an IT system and the serious consideration of human issues would lead to practical improvements in the way most organizations approach strategic alliance development planning.

Effective teamwork, based on sound management principles, is another overarching requirement for successful transformation of organizations. But, the tasks the teams are asked to perform may differ from company to company, from national to global situation. Even, how the teams are formed differs from situation to situation. Are there culture factors that would prevent or alter the historical frame of forming, norming, joining, storming, and belonging by teams in differing countries? Are there perspectives of teams that violate cultural, ethnic, and gender rubrics? When are teams appropriate in a global context, and when do they get in the way?

One should understand that ineffective teams diminish organizational productivity, yet such teams are created by purpose. Team building is also related to individual's self-esteem need. The effective manager must realize this issue when managing teams. Thus, factors of psychology, sociology, anthropology, and ethics influence the development of systemic teams and systemic work within the organization.

References

Al-Mashari, M., & Zairi, M. (2000). The effective application of SAP R/3: A proposed model of best practice. *Logistics Information Management*, *13*(3), 156-166.

Applegate, L.M., McFarlan, F.W., & McKenney, J.L. (1999). *Corporate information systems management: Text and cases*. Boston: Irwin McGraw-Hill.

Bancroft, N., Seip, H., & Sprengel, A. (1998). *Implementing SAP R/3: How to introduce a large system into a large organization*. Greenwich, CT: Manning Publications.

Bhattacherjee, A. (2000). Beginning SAP R/3 implementation at Geneva Pharmaceuticals. *Communications of the Association for Information Systems*, 4, Article 2. Retrieved from http://cais.isworld.org/articles/4-2/article.htm.

Bronder, C., & Pritzel, R. (1992). Developing strategic alliance: A successful framework for co-operation. *European Management Journal*, *10*(4), 412-20.

Brower, D. (2001). Sizing up the power sector. *Petroleum Economist*, *68*(10), 26-28.

Crouch, A. (1989). Behaviour of people in organisations. In D. Samson (Ed.), *Management for engineers* (pp. 155–78). Melbourne: Longman Cheshire.

Currie, W. (2000). *Global information society*. Chichester: John Wiley & Sons.

Delerue, H. (2004). Relational risks perception in European bio-technology alliances: The effects of contextual factors. *European Management Journal*, *22*(5), 546.

Dixon, D., & Marks, M. (1999, November/December). Making mergers, acquisitions & alliances work. *Health Forum Journal*, pp. 30-33.

Dutta, S., Lanvin, B., & Paua, F. (2003). *The global information technology report 2002-2003: Readiness for the networked world*. New York: Oxford University Press.

Gunasekaran, A., & Ngai, E.W.T. (2003). The successful management of a small logistics company. *International Journal of Physical Distribution & Logistics Management, 33*(9/10), 825.

Henderson, R., & Clark, K. (1990). Architectural innovation: The reconfiguration of existing product technologies and the failure of established firms. *Administrative Science Quarterly, 35*, 9-30.

Housel, T.J., & Skopec, E.W. (2001). Global telecommunications revolution: The business perspective. Boston, MA: McGraw-Hill/Irwin.

Kumar, K., & Van Hillegersberg, J. (2000). ERP experiences and evolution. *Communications of the ACM, 43*(4), 23-26.

Laughlin, S. (1999). An ERP game plan. *Journal of Business Strategy, J20*(1), 32-37.

Leavitt, H.J. (1965). Applied organizational change in industry: Structural, technological and humanistic approaches. In J. March, (Ed.), *Handbook of Organizations* (pp. 1144 – 1170). Rand, McNally & Company.

Limerick, D. (1992). The shape of the new organisation: Implications for human resource management. *Asia Pacific Journal of Human Resources, 30*(1), 38–52.

Mandal, P., & Gunasekaran, A. (2003). Issues in implementing ERP: A case study. *European Journal of Operational Research, 146*, 274-283.

Markides, C.C., & Williamson, P.J. (1997). Related diversification, core competencies and corporate performance. In A. Cambell & K. Sommer Luchs (Eds.), *Core competency-based strategy* (pp. 96-122). London: International Thomson Business Press.

Maron, R.M., & VanBremen, L. (1999). The influence of organizational culture on strategic alliances. *Association Management, 51*(4), 86-92.

Numerof, R.E., & Abrams, M.N. (2000). Subtle conflicts that wreck merger visions. *Mergers and Acquisitions, 35*(3), 28-30.

Palaniswamy, R., & Tyler, F. (2000). Enhancing manufacturing performance with ERP systems. *Information Systems Management, 17*(3), 43-55.

Parise, S., & Sasson, L. (2002, March/April). Leveraging knowledge management across strategic alliances. *Ivey Business Journal*, pp. 41-47.

Pearlson, K.E. (2001). *Managing and using information systems*. New York: John Wiley & Sons.

Segil, L. (2000). Understanding life cycle differences. *Association Management*, 52(8), 32-33.

Wagle, D. (1998). The case for ERP Systems. *The McKinsey Quarterly*, (2), 130-138.

Whipple, J., & Frankel, R. (2000, Summer). Strategic alliance success factors. *Journal of Supply Chain Management: A Global Review of Purchasing and Supply*, 21-28.

Yasuda, H. (2005). Formation of strategic alliances in high-technology industries: Comparative study of the resource-based theory and the transaction-cost theory. *Technovation*, 25(7), 763.

Chapter VI

Decisional DNA and the Smart Knowledge Management System:
A Process of Transforming Information into Knowledge

Cesar Sanin, University of Newcastle, Australia

Edward Szczerbicki, University of Newcastle, Australia

Abstract

Some of the most complicated issues about knowledge are its acquisition and its conversion into explicit knowledge. Nevertheless, among all knowledge forms, storing formal decision events in a knowledge-explicit way becomes an important advance. The smart knowledge management system (SKMS) is a hybrid knowledge-based decision support system that takes information and sends it through four macro-processes: diagnosis, prognosis, solution, and knowledge, in order to build the Decisional DNA of an organization. The SKMS implements a model for transforming information into knowledge by using sets of experience knowledge structure. The purpose of this chapter is to show how decisional DNA is constructed through the implementation of the SKMS. Fully developed, the SKMS certainly would improve the quality of decision-making, and could advance the notion of administering knowledge in the current decision making environment.

Introduction

In a world plagued with competitiveness at all levels, any possible strategy or asset that could offer advantages would be, with no doubt, the aim to achieve. Knowledge seems to be one of these assets and it has been considered as the only true source of a nation's economic and military strength (Becerra-Fernandez et al., 2004). Knowledge seems to be an especially strategic advantage (Drucker, 1995) that lately has been converted into the final aim. Consequently, humankind is now immersed in what is called the "knowledge society." Businesses are not the exception, and managers have tried to turn knowledge into one of their assets. Thus, the focus of managers has turned to knowledge administration and many companies have invested huge quantities of money to explore technologies that facilitate control of all forms of knowledge, looking for it as the key that can make the difference between the success and failure of a company in the competitive environment of global economy and knowledge society (Sanin & Szczerbicki, 2004, 2005a).

Lin et al. (2002) explain knowledge as an organized mixture of data, integrated with a set of rules, operations, and procedures, which can be only acquired through experience and practice. How knowledge is acquired and how knowledge is transformed to explicit knowledge is determined by using representations [for explicit knowledge see Nonaka & Takeuchi (1995)]. Knowledge must be obtained and represented in an understandable and shareable form for the agents that experienced it, and once it is acquired, it can be reuse for different agents, therefore they can practice it. Subsequently, knowledge representation and acquisition are considered as the most complicated issues about knowledge.

However, the knowledge society arrived and brought with it all the difficulties that information faces. Characteristics such as unstructured, disintegrated, not shareable, incomplete, and uncertain information represent an enormous problem for information technologies (IT) (Ferruci & Lally, 2004; Deveau, 2002). Under these circumstances, the process of transforming information into knowledge is critical and difficult, because, unfortunately, knowledge depends upon information (Sanin & Szczerbicki, 2004). Moreover, Awad and Ghaziri (2004) give acknowledgement of another difficulty when they affirm that up to 95 percent of information is preserved as tacit knowledge. Hence, it is obvious that some kind of technology is necessary to transform information into not just knowledge, but explicit knowledge.

One theory proposes that experienced decision-makers base most of their decisions on situation assessments (Noble, 1998). In other words, decision-makers principally use experience for their decisions; that is, when a decision event emerges, managers select actions that previously have worked well in similar situations. They extract the most significant characteristics from the current circumstances, and relate them to similar situations and actions that have worked well in the past. Thus, it is very important to keep a record of earlier decisions events and turn them into explicit knowledge. A formal decision event is a decision occurrence that was performed under specific circumstances—that is, under strict established conditions – and was carried out by an agent experiencing some type of knowledge (Sanin & Szczerbicki, 2006c).

Many technologies, such as knowledge management systems (KMS), data mining (DM) and knowledge-based systems (KbS), are currently working with different types of knowledge. Moreover, although these technologies work with decision-making in some approaches, they do not keep structured knowledge of the formal decision events they participate on. For us, any technology able to capture and store formal decision events as explicit knowledge will improve the decision-making process, reducing decision time, as well as avoiding repetition and duplication in the process.

Unfortunately, computers are not as clever to form internal representations of the world, and even simpler, representations of just formal decision events. Instead of gathering knowledge for themselves, computers must rely on people to place knowledge directly into their memories. This problem suggests deciding on ways to represent information and knowledge inside computers. Set of experience knowledge structure (SOEKS or shortly SOE) is a combination of filtered information obtained from formal decision events. It is a structure that facilitates representation of formal decision events taken by different technologies (i.e., it acquires knowledge from technologies that take structured decisions). Nevertheless, despite the fact that the SOEKS is already developed, the ways for acquiring its knowledge are supported on the confidence of every technology that performs formal decisions. Because different technologies can be both a source and a target of set of experience, it must be possible to construct them in a wide-reaching language. Therefore, the SOEKS can be worldwide understandable and shareable.

The SOEKS is utilized in the operation of the smart knowledge management system (SKMS). The SKMS performs by manipulating sets of experience to keep formal decision events and to help managers in the daily operation of decision-making. Moreover, the SOEKS comprises variables, functions, constraints and rules associated in a DNA shape allowing the construction of decisional DNA. Fully developed, the SKMS certainly would improve the quality of decision-making, and could advance the notion of administering knowledge in the current decision making environment.

The purpose of this chapter is to show the application of implementation of the SOEKS in the SKMS in order to produce decisional DNA.

Background

An organization is a consequence of relations among technologies, techniques and people; these associations create an exclusive way of decision-making, which is not easy to replicate (Sanin & Szczerbicki, 2005a). Such fingerprint can be catalogued as the decisional DNA of a company. Set of experience knowledge structure allows keeping and replicating these exclusive forms of decision-making, and it has been implemented to preserve explicit knowledge representation of formal decision events while helping with the construction of decisional DNA. The SKMS is a platform that has been developed to administer explicit knowledge of formal decision events and performs by using decisional DNA. Once a decisional DNA is constructed as explicit experiential knowledge, the possibilities of sharing it among different technologies, areas and firms are open. In the following sections, backgrounds of the platform and the concepts it comprises are briefly described.

Set of Experience Knowledge Structure
and the Decisional DNA

Arnold and Bowie (1985) argue that:

the mind's mechanism for storing and retrieving knowledge is transparent to us. When we 'memorize' an orange, we simply examine it, think about it for a while, and perhaps eat it. Somehow, during this process, all the essential qualities of the orange are stored. Later, when someone mentions the word 'orange', our senses are activated from within, and we see, smell, touch, and taste the orange all over again. (p. 46)

Computers, on their side, must depend on human beings to enter knowledge directly into them. Thus, the problem is how to adequately, efficiently, and effectively represent information and knowledge inside a computer.

The SOEKS has been developed to keep formal decision events in an explicit way (Sanin & Szczerbicki, 2005a). It is a model based upon existing and available knowledge, which must adjust to the decision event it is built from (i.e., it is a dynamic structure that relies on the information offered by a formal decision event); besides, it can be expressed in XML or OWL as way to make it shareable and transportable (Sanin & Szczerbicki, 2005b, 2006a; Sanin et al., 2007a). Four basic components surround decision-making events, and are stored in a combined dynamic structure that comprises the SOE. These four components are *variables, functions, constraints,* and *rules* (see Figure 1).

Variables usually involve representing knowledge using an attribute-value language (i.e., by a vector of variables and values) (Lloyd, 2003). This is a traditional approach from the origin of knowledge representation, and is the starting point for set of experience. Variables that intervene in the process of decision-making are the first component of the set of experience.

These variables are the centre root of the structure, because they are the source of the other components.

Based on the idea of Malhotra (2000, p.51) who states that, "to grasp the meaning of a thing, an event, or a situation is to see it in its relations to other things," variables are related among them in the shape of functions. Functions describe associations between a dependent variable and a set of input

Figure 1. Structure of the set of experience

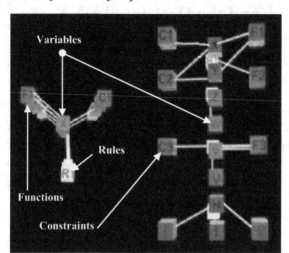

variables; moreover, functions can be applied for reasoning optimal states, because they come out from the goals of the decision event. Therefore, set of experience uses functions, its second component, and establishes links among the variables constructing multiobjective goals, that is, multiple functions that restrict experience on decision-making by the elements of a universe of relationships.

According to theory of constraints (TOC), Goldratt (1986) maintains that any system has at least one constraint; otherwise, its performance would be infinite. Thus, constraints are another way of relationships among the variables; in fact, they are functions as well, but they have a different purpose. A constraint, as the third component of set of experience, is a limitation of possibilities, a restriction of the feasible solutions in a decision problem, and a factor that limits the performance of a system with respect to its goals.

Finally, rules are suitable for representing inferences, or for associating actions with conditions under which the actions should be done. Rules, the fourth component of set of experience are another form of expressing relationships among variables. They are conditional relationships that operate in the universe of variables. Rules are relationships between a condition and a consequence connected by the statements IF-THEN-ELSE.

Following the description of the SOE's components, its structure is organized taking into account some important features of DNA. Firstly, the combination of the four nucleotides of DNA gives uniqueness to itself, just as the combination of the four components of SOE offer distinctiveness. Moreover, the elements of the structure are connected among themselves imitating part of a long strand of DNA, that is, a gene. Thus, a gene can be assimilated to a SOE, and, in the same way as a gene produces a phenotype, a SOE produces a value of decision in terms of its objective functions. Such value of decision can be called the efficiency or the phenotype value of the SOE. The efficiency or phenotype value is a combination of the objective functions and the effect value of the variables (Sanin & Szczerbicki, 2005a). Additionally, it is possible to group several SOE by category; that is, by their objective functions. Each SOE can be categorized, and acts as a gene in DNA. A gene guides hereditary responses in living organisms. As an analogy, a SOE guides the responses of certain areas of the company.

A unique SOE cannot rule a whole system, even in a specific area or category. Therefore, more sets of experience should be acquired and constructed. The day-to-day operation provides many decisions, and the result of this is a collection of many different sets of experience. Hence, it is possible to group several SOE by category; that is, by their objective functions. A group of SOE of the same category comprise a kind of decisional chromosome, as DNA does with genes. These decisional chromosomes of SOE could make a "strategy" for a category. In this case, each module of chromosomes forms an entire inference tool, and provides a schematic view for knowledge inside a company. Subsequently, having a diverse group of SOE chromosomes is like having the decisional DNA of a company, because what has been collected is a series of inference strategies of the company (see Figure 2).

A generic mechanism for expressing machine-readable semantics of data is required, as well as providing the possibility of presenting simple and complex structures of any kind of information or knowledge in a standardized syntax. XML proves being a strong language for those requirements (Sanin & Szczerbicki, 2005b). XML permits the representation of structured, hierarchical data, capable of representing not just the values of individual information and knowledge items, but also the relationships among them. The SOEKS is not the exception to be implemented in XML, opening the possibilities of being shared among multiple technologies.

In conclusion, SOEKS is a compound of variables, functions, constraint and rules, which are uniquely combined to represent a formal decision event. Multiple sets of experience can be collected, classified, and organized according to their efficiency, grouping them into chromosomes. Chromosomes are groups of sets of experience that can comprise a decision strategy for a

Figure 2. Decisional DNA

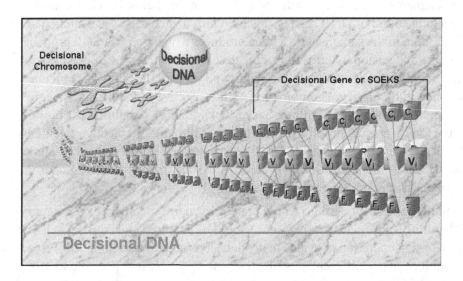

specific area of the company. Finally, sets of chromosomes comprise what is called the decisional DNA of a company. Moreover, it can be expressed in XML as way to make it shareable and transportable. Furthermore, the decisional DNA can be used in platforms to support decision-making, and new decisions can be made based on it. In this text a concise idea of the SOEKS and the decisional DNA was offered, for further information Sanin and Szczerbicki (2005a; 2006b) should be reviewed.

The Smart Knowledge Management System (SKMS)

On each company's daily operation, decision-making is executed several times producing multiple forms of knowledge. Most of this knowledge is acquired for the managers that intervene on the operation of the company. The SKMS is a platform that participates on the decision-making processes of a company, and as managers do, it takes knowledge from it. The SKMS acquires, stores, and administers knowledge produced for formal decision events, and constructs decisional DNA. Moreover, SKMS facilitates sharing knowledge among different areas of a company or different companies aiming to help managers on future decision-making processes (Sanin & Szczerbicki, 2004).

Initially, the SKMS is supported by many applications that provide relationships among variables, human expertise, empirical knowledge from scientific research, and elaborated calculations of large amounts of numerical and qualitative data; that is, the system is based upon several applications that supply information, a condition that is considered an advantage. These applications working together confront a problem or query and perform formal decision events. Subsequently, the SKMS constructs sets of experience based on this information and guides them through a process of transformation into knowledge through four macro-processes (see Figure 3) (Sanin & Szczerbicki, 2004).

The platform takes information and sends it through four macro-processes: *diagnosis, prognosis, solution,* and *knowledge*. Each macro-process is a compound of layers or creators. In essence, the first layer takes information and adds value to it, making a sub-output, which is introduced in another layer producing a new sub-output, and so on. The sub-outputs can be utilised by the user according to the stage at which information is being processed, even if it is not yet a decision. Finally, the information is transformed into knowledge by rules and models of operation in the knowledge macro-process, building up the decisional DNA (see Figure 4).

Diagnosis: The macro-process of diagnosis consolidates and integrates information provided by multiple applications. The diagnosis macro-process gets the characteristics and objectives of the company at a particular moment. Two layers comprise this macro-process in the platform. The first layer, the *knowledge-base layer*, takes in different ways isolated solutions from diverse applications; some could be qualitative and alphanumeric, others quantitative and numeric. The second layer, the *integration layer*, is in charge of unifying

Figure 3. Macro-processes, layers and creators

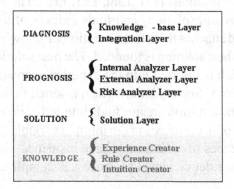

the information into a unique language and structure that can be understood by the whole platform.

Prognosis: Once the diagnosis is reached, the prognosis must produce a set of proposed solutions or management strategies. This is achieved by providing several models to simulate the effect of different variables in the company, not only internally, but also externally. Moreover, each solved model offers a scenario that produces measurements for uncertainty, incompleteness or imprecision.

Three layers comprise this macro-process in the platform. The *internal analyser layer* is able to analyse the factors that affect the internal situation of the company. It evaluates the models focusing on those variables that can be controlled and modified for the company. The internal analyser takes the models, optimises them, and offers a set of scenarios and solutions with the variables that can be transformed internally. The *external analyser layer* is capable of analysing the situation of the company according to external variables. It estimates the models focusing on those variables that cannot be modified for the company. The external analyser takes the models, optimises them, and offers a set of scenarios with the variables that cannot be transformed, acting as a sensitivity analyser. The *risk analyser layer* is able to receive sub-solutions already produced by the previous layers, and cope with the analysis of uncertainty, imprecision and incompleteness of the scenarios.

Process of Constructing the Decisional DNA (see Figure 4): The process starts at diagnosis where multiple applications, performed by users, produce sub-solutions and information (knowledge-base layer). Then, the integrator layer transforms that information into a unified language. Later, at the prognosis, the information is mixed; constructing possible models of decision (M1..Mn). These models pass through the external and internal analyser layers, which establish scenarios according to their contexts (Si1..Sim, Se1.. Sen), and find their solutions (Li1..Lim, Le1..Ler). The risk analyser layer takes this scenarios and solutions and finds indexes of uncertainty (ρ) and imprecision (φ) and attaches them to the solutions. Following, using the user's priorities filter, the best solution is founded. The best solution comprises a set of experience, which is inserted into the experience creator and makes part of the decisional DNA. Such solution is also inserted in the intuition creator to be processed. The intuition creator finds intuited variables, creates a rule, and adds a counter of occurrences to the intuited variable (λ). When a certain number of occurrences of an intuition have happened, this is considered a rule and goes to the ruler creator. The process is complete.

Figure 4. Process of constructing the decisional DNA using the SKMS

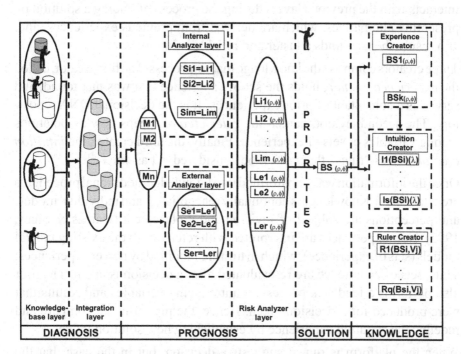

Solution: Choices derive from pre-defined goals (Gerwin & Tuggle, 1977), as a definite solution can only emanate from pre-established priorities. Hence, this macro-process takes the scenarios of the previous layers, and according to priorities established by the user, chooses the best possible solution under those priorities. It comprises the *solution layer*, which is in charge of filtering the solutions, and allowing the user to define parameters for choosing the best one. As the outcome, the system presents the values of the variables that should be modified, the model, and its results. This is the optimal solution for the platform, but in reality, it can always be modified by the user or manager. Finally, it passes the model to the next macro-process.

Knowledge: The platform perceives its environment through a set of applications, makes a decision or solution that is conceived for the platform, and posits a model of the world in which it must function; this is the model the knowledge macro-process receives. The model is a set of experience, which was originated in a defined moment or event grasping the meaning of the situation. The knowledge macro-process starts once the platform established the ultimate set of experience. This macro-process captures the experience acquired during the last decision-making process by a group of applications, named creators, capable of obtaining knowledge. Additionally, this layer interacts with the previous layers during the process of finding a solution by presenting alternatives, which are derived from previous experiences, and, as a result, the user finds a faster and reliable solution.

Three creators comprise the knowledge macro-process. The first creator, called the *experience creator*, holds the set of experience that was just found, and serves as a consultant of prior experiences. It is the decisional DNA repository. The second creator, named the *ruler creator*, keeps new associations among variables or sets of experience. Finally, the third creator, the *intuition creator*, seizes "rules" that cannot be considered yet as one.

Once the information was transformed into knowledge, additional procedures are established. Knowledge is continually renegotiated, and individual models and perceptions are subject of revision and replacement (Gaines & Shaw, 1992). New experiences are interpreted with reference to the existing mental models (sets of experience), which in turn are modified by newer experiences. Thus, sets of experience are re-evaluated after a decision is taken. The user also performs a feedback process by introducing variables and results that were produced for a decision taken. Hence, the platform can compare and redefine the acquired experience by establishing new solution values.

When the platform is run, it suggests a decision, but in the case that the decision is made and performed in a different way by the manager, the differences concerning the solution and reality should be administered to the platform by the users. Moreover, providing the platform with real values allows it to improve its sets of experience, complementing the knowledge process. Hence, the platform experiences a growing knowledge cycle simulating a spiral effect. It grows because of its own processes, and because of the users' feedback.

In addition, the systems should be examined from time to time, which means that the rules and sets of experience already established can be re-evaluated or adjusted. These actions keep the system fresh or improve it. As it can be imagined, most of these activities depend on human intervention. It is important that the system applies intelligent retention of experiences to store knowledge, but human intervention is required to ensure that experiences governing the agent's behaviour are current. Without maintenance, the SKMS is at risk of becoming irrelevant and obsolete.

Because information communication technology (ICT) has increased the possibilities of running and supporting businesses, new technologies allow businesses to transfer information among each other, joining suppliers, producers, and customers in one network. Thus, based on the notion that new knowledge is created by social interactive processes, and continuous dialogues (Senge, 1990), it is said that technology must permit sharing not just information, but also knowledge. Hence, the KSCS, placed inside a group of agents with similar characteristics, acts as a member of a community of practice (CoP) or community of learners. This CoP shares decisional DNAs produced by the members of the community and facilitates companies to share, improve and create knowledge, resulting in efficiency and effectiveness. Such CoP is a society formed by autonomous agents integrated to solve common decision-making problems. It is connected through Internet, and incorporates an electronic society called the e-decisional community that shares experience among its members, and along with this interaction, the e-decisional community would grow and improve itself making available each time more and more decisional DNA.

Integration

Organizations no longer act in isolation; instead, they are integrated into distributed production networks, pursuing the production process in cooperation with other areas or firms. Nevertheless, deficiency of information integration across applications, departments and companies is perhaps the biggest barrier to effective use of information technology in the modern society (Woods, 2004). Thus, new technologies should be developed to consolidate organizations' operations to facilitate business processes and support communications across companies and different systems.

Even though information society had not solved the information integration problem (Calì et al., 2002; Ives et al., 1999), knowledge society arrived. Unfortunately, as well as information, most knowledge is hardly universally shared in any format (Chiang, Trappey, & Ku, 2004), and the knowledge society inherited the same integration difficulties. Then, both information and knowledge technologies are looking for tools that allow their participants to share, distribute, and use information and knowledge to improve strategic and operational efficiency and effectiveness.

Exchanging information and knowledge quickly and securely between applications and systems is an increasingly important requirement. The enterprises involved need to pass relevant information and knowledge along processes; nevertheless, different formats and structures are an obstacle to the continuous flow of information and knowledge. Data integration comes out as an alternative for solving this problem. Data integration allows data used by one tool to be available for other tools, in the same organization or other organizations. It makes possible to assemble new functionalities from small software components into old or new systems.

One of the data integration requirements is data transformation capability. Sometimes the form of source data is not ideal for the requesting system; hence, transformation capabilities are used to convert data and make it more useful by the requesting application. Then, a transformation is a computational way of generating representations from other representations, not necessarily in the same language. In addition, transformations are used for generating specific representations for a particular need or putting representations together. Therefore, in the context of transformation, it is proper to talk about filters. Filters are, generally, simple transformation tools implemented over only one specific interaction type. Filters aim at contributing to the proper understanding of the information and knowledge. For instance, knowledge developed for a user in a system is suited to the use of the same user in the same system, and it is expected that this user interprets in a coherent way the terms used. However, when several users communicate, this understanding becomes problematic. Making filters to transform information or knowledge from one format to a different one allows exchange of information and knowledge.

Figure 5. Traditional deployment of an ETL

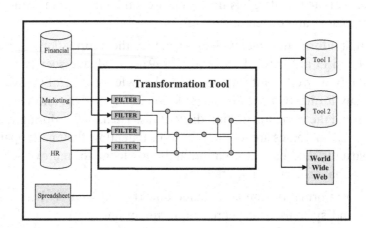

This idea is related to the ETL concept (extraction, transformation and load). ETL processes and technology arose from the business need to extract information from disparate data systems and either moves it to a central storage area or creates load files that feed into other systems. Figure 5 depicts a traditional ETL deployment.

In the process developed by an ETL tool, one or more files are created containing the extracted information or knowledge produced for multiple applications. Specific information or knowledge needed is identified by the filters and recorded into files or temporary databases. These files and/or databases are then fed into a group of processes that perform the transformation activities, such as data validation, creating aggregated or derived values, and unit transformations. Load files containing valid information are created during the transformation process. As the transformation process has performed, load files with information or knowledge can now proceed to the applications that required them.

In that order of ideas, transformation capabilities and filters are based upon a common language. Having a common language to which every technology should translate its information and knowledge seems to be a form of helping to gain integration. Web technologies have developed tools necessary for accessing information from disparate systems and integration of distributed applications. These technologies include the development of standards and protocols that have led to the creation of hundreds of different "languages" (we call them languages for easy understanding) and protocols. To date, we have found almost 390 different languages. Most of these languages are based upon XML, and each one was developed for a different purpose. These languages present defined vocabulary, structure and constraints for expressing information and knowledge in a specific scientific or technological field.

Thus, eXtensible Markup Language (XML) emerges as one of the most important alternatives of integration (Singh, 2003). XML is an efficient information exchange language, which works transparently across internal networks, business-to-business supply chain networks and different computing platforms, showing that implementations based on XML facilitates integration.

Exchanging Information and Knowledge

Researchers and companies have been trying to reach a way of transmitting information and meaning at the same time. Under the sponsorship of the World Wide Web Consortium (W3C), eXtensible Markup Language (XML) has grown into a family of standards integrating key technologies, which was developed under the basis of simplicity, and communicating not just format, but also meaningful information (meta-data) using tags. XML allows to structure information and knowledge as labeled trees, where labels can be chosen by the user to reflect as much of the document meanings require. The XML attribute-value mechanism allows encoding graphs as XML trees, even though its structure remains as a tree. It is easy to understand, easy to read, and easy to author (Sanin & Szczerbicki, 2004).

Now, in a more deep way, knowledge representation for software agent communication has also adopted the XML platform (Grosof, 2001). The W3C (2004) defends XML and agrees in terms of its use on knowledge representation saying: "XML provides a universal storage and interchange format for distributed knowledge representation. XML offers new general possibilities from which AI [Artificial Intelligence] knowledge representation (KR) can profit." For instance, specialized languages for the use of knowledge have been developed based upon XML. Even though these languages are originated on XML, they are excessively specialized and are not worldwide used. Hence, XML remains as the preferred worldwide option for exchanging information and knowledge in a simple and not specialized form.

In conclusion, XML is chosen as the appropriate tool for exchanging knowledge, and it has emerged as the leading method for application integration (Singh, 2003). XML acts as a uniform standard for exchanging business data, through which heterogeneous applications can communicate with others over uniform interfaces and in a language that everyone involved can understand. Its simplicity, transportability, and applicability make it a suitable language for our purposes.

Flow Process of the Set of Experience through the SKMS

Once a brief understanding of the SKMS, the SOEKS, and information and knowledge exchange is done, the flow mechanism of the set of experience through the platform using integration techniques will be easier to explain.

The flow process commences with an ETL structure in the diagnosis macro-process (see Figure 6). The knowledge-base layer is a compilation of many types of applications that provide information, and it is responsible for communicating with the applications in terms of acquiring the results they produce (Sanin & Szczerbicki, 2004). These applications operate by helping in decision-making processes executing formal decision events.

Each computing application produces one document or file in which specific information about a formal decision event is identified by the filters. At this

Figure 6. ETL and SKMS

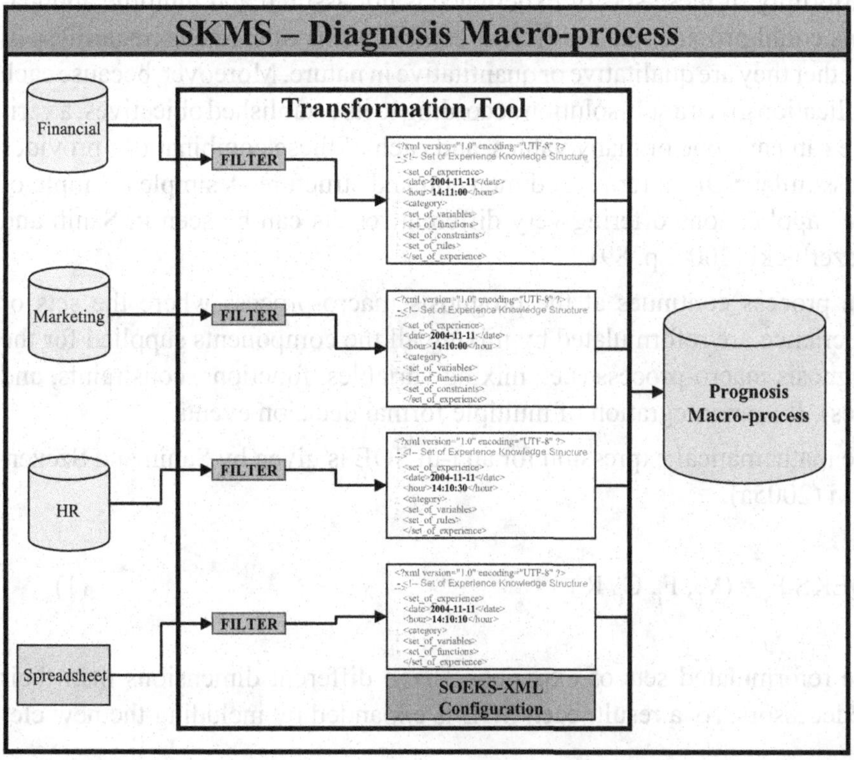

stage it is important to understand the role of the filters. It is indispensable to build up a filter for each application linked in the knowledge-base layer. Subsequently, each filter takes its corresponding document, and according to its content, separates the information into the elements of the SOEKS—that is, variables, functions, constraints, and rules—and assembles a SOEKS. During this process, variables are unified into a unique system of names, and values are unified into a unique system of measurement. Therefore, the filters operate as builders and converters. Then, these documents, translated by the integrator layer into SOE XML-configuration according to the format established by Sanin and Szczerbicki (2005b), provide variables, functions, rules, and constraints to the platform. Thus, this layer is a translator and converter (Sanin & Szczerbicki, 2004). In that way, all the results are in the same language and can be understood, used, and processed by the other layers.

Once all the results are in the same language (XML-configuration), multiple sets of experience are built up, one for each formal decision event, following the structure associated to equation (1), and the structure of SOE by Sanin and Szczerbicki (2005a).

Uniformity of these sets of experience is not assured and multiple applications could provide many different combinations of elements regardless of whether they are qualitative or quantitative in nature. Moreover, because each application gives a sub-solution according to its established objectives, a variable can have one or many values, and each of these combinations provides a dissimilar SOE in terms of dimension and structure. A simple example of three applications offering very different results can be seen in Sanin and Szczerbicki (2004, p. 89).

The process continues at the prognosis macro-process where the sets of experience are reformulated by mixing all the components supplied for the diagnosis macro-process (i.e., mixing variables, functions, constraints, and rules). It is an integration of multiple formal decision events.

The mathematical expression for an i-th SOE is given by Sanin and Szczerbicki (2005a):

$$\text{SOEKS } E_i = (V_{ij}, F_i, C_i, R_i) \tag{1}$$

The reformulated sets of experience have different dimensions than their predecessors. As a result, each SOE is expanded by including the new elements. It is done in the prognosis macro-process. The resulting collection of sets of experience can be expressed as:

$$\text{Sets of Experience } E_{1...n} = (V_{\text{Total \# VBLES}}, F_{\text{Total \# FNS}}, C_{\text{Total \# CTNS}}, R_{\text{Total \# RLES}}) \quad (2)$$

Where $V_{\text{Total \# VBLES}}$ is the union of the variables that belong to the collection of sets of experience. Similarly, the rest of the components in equation (2) are defined.

The number of elements of the collection of sets of experience resulting of this reformulation is expressed by the number of total changing values of each changing field (i.e., fields like a variable or a function or a constraint or a rule that show multiples values):

c is the total of changing fields.

The number of sets of experience resulting can be reduced according to the contradictions among variables, constraints, and rules, suggesting that a process of debugging has to be done.

$$\text{\# of Sets of Experience} = \prod_{k=1}^{c} \text{\# Changing values of the changing field } k.$$

Malhotra (2000, p. 12) argues that "dynamic environments not only require multiple perspectives of solutions to a given problem, but also diverse interpretations of the problem based upon multiple views of future."

As an illustration, in the example given by Sanin and Szczerbicki (2004, p. 89, Table 1), the changing fields are variable X_1, variable H_1, constraint X_1, and constraint H_1, each one with two changing values; therefore, the resulting number of sets of experience is sixteen. Examples of the sixteen resulting sets of experience can be seen in Sanin and Szczerbicki (2004, p. 89, Table 2).

Once the models are built up and debugged, they can proceed to the analysers to be solved according to their principles (Sanin & Szczerbicki, 2004, 2007b, 2007c).

Sets of experience, when they are manipulated by the internal and external analyser layers do not change its structure. They are solved by the analysers,

Figure 7. Value of truth associated to sets of experience

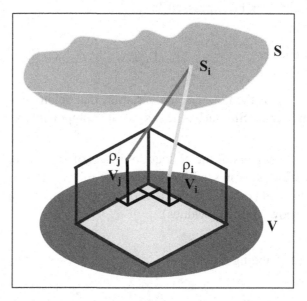

but solved sets of experience essentially change only the effect values of the variables [for cause and effect value of set of experience see Sanin and Szczerbicki (2005a, 2005b)]. The new solved sets of experience can now advance to the risk analyser layer.

Sanin and Szczerbicki (2005a) point out that due to the impossibility of controlling the whole universe of variables, it is necessary to reduce the possibilities of duality in finding an optimal unique set of experience. The key factor here is to find more elements of decision-making that reduce the possibilities of duality, while facilitating knowledge elicitation.

Relationships appear as one element that provides uniqueness while reducing ambiguity. Something will make sense only if it can be associated with the existing schemas: "To grasp the meaning of a thing, an event, or a situation is to see it in its relations to other things..." (Malhotra, 2000, p. 23). Then, variables are connected by meaningful relationships such as functions of certainty and preciseness. The risk analyser layer adds two new values to the SOE, which are meaningful relationships that will help on finding the best solution among all the solved sets of experience playing a very important role in the performance of the SKMS.

For easy understanding, the following operations will be explained using Sanin and Szczerbicki (2005a, 2005b) conventions, one SOE, and using equation (1) as the base.

The first function, function of certainty χ, is applied to the set of variables in equation (1), and it is defined as:

$$\chi : V \rightarrow \mathfrak{R} \mid \chi(V_i) = \rho_i$$

ρ_i is defined as the value of truth (i.e., the certainty value) of the i-th SOE that contain V_i. The value of truth and the function χ are designated according to the ideas established by Sanin and Szczerbicki (2004, p. 91). The value of truth is added to the SOEKS as one of its characteristics to help in the reduction of ambiguity. Hence, the equation (1) is redefined as:

$$\text{SOEKS } E_i = (V_{ij}, F_i, C_i, R_i, \rho_i) \tag{2}$$

Given multiple sets of experience that lead to the same state Si, different values of truth reduce the possibilities of duality when selecting the best solution. For instance, given two set of experience, Vj and Vi, with their corresponding values of truth, ρj and ρi, that lead to same desired state Si, the best solution is chosen according to the best value of truth, that is, the SOE with higher certainty value (see Figure 7).

The second function used for reducing possibilities of duality is related to the concept of preciseness. Having ω as the function of preciseness and R_g as a set of ranges associated to the preciseness of each variable, the index of preciseness is defined as:

$$\omega : (V, R_g) \rightarrow \mathfrak{R} \mid \omega(V_i, R_g) = \phi_i$$

$R_g = \{r_1, r_2, r_3, \ldots, r_n, r_{n+1}\}$ is a set of values related to the corresponding variables $V_{i=1\ldots n}$, and r_{n+1} is a range value of preciseness associated to ρ_i.

ϕ_i is defined as the index of preciseness of the i-th SOE, and the preciseness value of the equivalent formal decision event. The value of preciseness and the function ω are assigned according to the ideas established by Sanin and Szczerbicki (2004, p.90). The index of preciseness, as well as the value of truth, is added to the SOE as one of its characteristics. Accordingly, the equation (2) is redefined as:

Figure 8. Index of preciseness associated to sets of experience

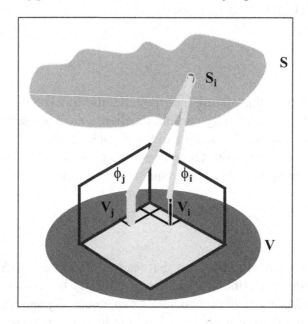

$$\text{SOEKS } E_i = (V_{ij}, F_i, C_i, R_i, \rho_i, \phi_i) \tag{3}$$

Given multiple sets of experience that guide to the same state S_i, different index of preciseness reduce the possibilities of duality when selecting the best solution. For instance, given two SOE, V_j and V_i, with their corresponding index of preciseness, ϕ_j and ϕ_i, that lead to the same desired state S_i, the best solution is chosen according to the best index of preciseness, that is, the SOE with the higher index of preciseness (see Figure 8).

Subsequently, each SOE is formed according to equation (3) and they can proceed to the solution macro-process.

The solution macro-process filters the collection of sets of experience choosing one as the best solution to the integrated formal decision events formulated. For a conditional selection of the best solution, a set of priorities should be posited by the user. This set of priorities is called P and is defined as:

$$P= \{p_1, p_2, p_3, \ldots, p_n, p_{n+1}, p_{n+2}\}$$

Each p_i is related to the corresponding variables $V_{i=1...n}$, p_{n+1} is a priority value associated to ρ_i, and r_{n+2} is a priority value associated to ϕ_i.

Finally, defining E as the collection of sets of experience that arrive into the solution macro-process, the function α chooses the best solution and it is defined as:

$$\alpha{:}E{\rightarrow}E \mid \alpha(E, P_i) = E_i$$

The set of priorities is also added to the SOE as one of its characteristics because it particularizes the decision just taken. Therefore, the equation (3) is redefined as:

$$\text{SOEKS } E_i = (V_{ij}, F_i, C_i, R_i, \rho_i, \phi_i, P_i) \tag{4}$$

If E_i is defined as the final SOE and the best solution for the integrated formal decision events, it will advance to be stored as a gene of decisional DNA and be analyzed for the creators in the knowledge macro-process. This final structure defined in equation (4) is the last modification to the SOE, and finishes its large trajectory trough the SKMS converting it into experiential knowledge (see Figure 9).

The knowledge macro-process stores the SOE E_i in the experience creator to be used to help managers on future decisions responding to new formal decision events. Further processes are performed by the knowledge macro-process that leads to the use of the repository of SOEKS as explicit knowledge in the form of decisional DNA.

The SKMS perceives its environment through a set of applications, makes a decision or solution that is conceived within itself, and posits a model of the world in which it must function; this is the model the knowledge macro-process receives. It is the unique optimal SOEKS, which was originated in a defined query or event grasping the meaning of the situation. The knowledge macro-process starts once the SKMS established the ultimate SOE Ei. This macro-process captures the experience acquired during the last decision-making process by a group of applications, named creators, capable of obtaining knowledge. Additionally, this layer interacts with the previous layers during the process of finding a solution by presenting alternatives, which are

Figure 9. The solution macro-process

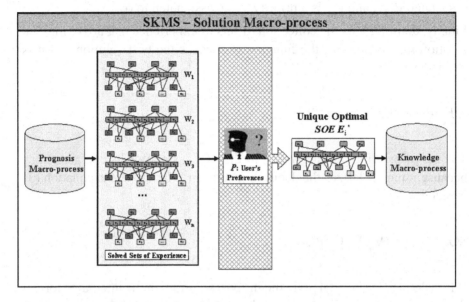

derived from previous experiences, and, as a result, the user finds a faster and reliable solution.

Three creators comprise the knowledge macro-process. The first creator, called the experience creator, holds the SOEKS that was just found, and serves as a consultant of prior experiences. The second creator, named the rule creator, keeps new associations among variables contained by the sets of experience. Finally, the third creator, the intuition creator, seizes "rules" that cannot be considered yet as one.

Once the information was transformed into knowledge, additional procedures are established. Further processes are performed by the knowledge macro-process that lead to the use of SOEKS as explicit knowledge in the shape of Decisional DNA.

Conclusion

Marvin Minsky (2005), creator of the Frame concept, referring to knowledge representation says: "each particular kind of data structure has its own virtues and deficiencies, and none by itself would seem adequate for all the different functions involved." Set of experience knowledge structure is a suitable representation for formal decision events. Additionally, when it is applied in the SKMS and collecting enterprises' decisional DNA, the notion of administering knowledge in the current decision-making environment certainly will advance. Decisional DNA in the way it is stored by the SKMS can explore new ways to put explicit knowledge in the hands of employees, customers, suppliers, and partners.

References

Arnold, W., & Bowie, J. (1985). *Artificial intelligence: A personal commonsense journey.* New Jersey: Prentice Hall.

Awad, E., & Ghaziri, H. (2004). *Knowledge management.* New Jersey: Pearson Education Inc., Prentice Hall.

Becerra-Fernandez I., Gonzalez A., & Sabherwal, R. (2004). *Knowledge management.* New Jersey: Pearson Education Inc., Prentice Hall.

Calì, A., Calvanese, D., Giacomo, G.D., & Lenzerini, M. (2002). On the expressive power of data integration systems. In *Proceedings 21st International Conference on Conceptual Modelling,* Tampere, Finland (LNAI 2503, pp. 338-350). Berlin: Springer-Verlag.

Chiang, A.T.A., Trappey, A., & Ku, C.C. (2004). Using knowledge-based intelligent reasoning to support dynamic collaborative design. In E. Kozan (Ed.), *Proceedings of the Fifth Asia Pacific Industrial Engineering and Management Systems Conference* (p. 334). Gold Coast: QUT.

Deveau, D. (2002). No brain, no gain: Knowledge management. *Computing Canada, 28,* 14-15.

Drucker, P. (1995). *The post-capitalist executive, managing in a time of great change.* New York: Penguin.

Ferruci, D., & Lally, A. (2004). Building an example application with the unstructured I information management architecture. *IBM Systems Journal, 43*(2), 455-475.

Gaines, B., & Shaw, M. (1992, October). Kelly's "geometry of psychological space" and its significance for cognitive modelling. *The New Psychologist,* 23-31.

Gerwin, D., & Tuggle, F. (1978, October). Modelling organizational decisions using the human problem solving paradigm. *Academy of Management Review*, 762-773.

Goldratt, E.M., & Cox, J. (1986). *The goal*. Aldershot, Hants: Grover.

Grosof, N. (2001, August). Standardizing XML rules: Rules for e-business on the Semantic Web (invited talk). *Workshop on E-Business and the Intelligent Web at the International Joint Conference on Artificial Intelligence*, Seattle.

Ives, Z.G., Florescu, D., Friedman, M., Levy, A., & Weld, D.S. (1999). An adaptive query execution system for data integration. In *Proceedings 1999 ACM SIGMOD International Conference on Management of Data*, Pennsylvania (pp. 299 – 310).

Lin, B., Lin C., Hung H.C., & Wu, J.Y. (2002). A knowledge management architecture in collaborative supply chain. *Journal of Computer Information Systems*, *42*(5), 83–94.

Lloyd, J.W. (2003). *Logic for learning: Learning comprehensible theories from structure data*. Berlin: Springer.

Malhotra, Y. (2000). From information management to knowledge management: Beyond the 'hi-tech hidebound' systems. In K. Srikantaiah & M.E.D. Koening (Eds.), *Knowledge management for the information professional* (pp. 37-61). New Jersey: Information Today Inc.

Minsky, M. (2005). *AI topics*. Retrieved December 2, 2005, from http://www.aaai.org/AITopics/html/#minsky.

Noble, D. (1998). Distributed situation assessment. In P.H.R. Arabnia (Ed.), *Proceedings of FUSION '98 International Conference*, Las Vegas (pp. 960). The University of Georgia.

Nonaka, I., & Takeuchi, H. (1995). The knowledge-creating company: How Japanese companies create the dynamics of innovation. New York: Oxford University Press.

Sanin, C., & Szczerbicki, E. (2004). Knowledge supply chain system: A conceptual model. In A. Szuwarzynski (Ed.), *Knowledge management: Selected issues* (pp.79-97). Gdansk: Gdansk University Press.

Sanin, C., & Szczerbicki, E. (2005a). Set of experience: A knowledge structure for formal decision events. *Foundations of Control and Management Sciences*, *3*, 95-113.

Sanin, C., & Szczerbicki, E. (2005b, September 14-16). Using XML for implementing set of experience knowledge structure. In R. Koshla, R. Howlett, & L. Jain (Eds.), *Proceedings on International Conference on Knowledge-Based and Intelligent Information and Engineering Systems – KES2005,* Melbourne, Australia (LNAI 3681, pp. 946-952). Berlin, Heidelberg: Springer-Verlag.

Sanin, C., & Szczerbicki, E. (2006a). Extending set of experience knowledge structure into a transportable language extensible markup language. *Cybernetics and Systems, 37*(2-3), 97-117.

Sanin, C., & Szczerbicki, E. (2006b). Using set of experience in the process of transforming information into knowledge. *International Journal of Enterprise Information Systems, 2,* 45-62.

Sanin, C., & Szczerbicki, E. (2006c). Using heterogeneous similarity metrics on an ontology based knowledge structure. In A. Szuwarzynski (Ed.), *Knowledge management: Selected issues* (pp. 33-49). Gdansk: Gdansk University Press.

Sanin, C., Szczerbicki, E., & Toro, C. (2007). An OWL ontology of set of experience knowledge structure. *Journal of Universal Computer Science, 13*(2), 209-223.

Sanin, C., & Szczerbicki, E. (2007a). Dissimilar sets of experience knowledge structure: A negotiation process for decisional DNA. *Cybernetics and Systems: An International Journal, 38*(5), 455-473.

Sanin, C., & Szczerbicki, E. (2007b). Genetic algorithms for decisional DNA: Solving sets of experience knowledge structure. *Cybernetics and Systems: An International Journal, 38*(5), 475-494.

Senge, P. (1990). *The fifth discipline: The art and practice of learning organization.* New York: Doubleday.

Singh, S. (2003). Business-to-manufacturing integration using XML. *Hydrocarbon processing, 82*(3), 62-65.

W3C. (2004). *XML.* Retrieved April 20, 2004, from http://www.w3.org/XML/.

Woods, E. (2004). KM past and future - changing the rules of the game. *KMWorld, 13*(1), 12-26.

Chapter VII

Organizational Readiness to Adopt ERP:
An Evaluation Model for Manufacturing SMEs

Louis Raymond, Université du Québec à Trois-Rivières, Canada

Suzanne Rivard, HEC Montréal, Canada

Danie Jutras, Université du Québec à Trois-Rivières, Canada

Abstract

Enterprise resource planning (ERP) systems are now being implemented in small and medium-sized enterprises (SMEs). This chapter presents the results of a study that proposes and validates a framework for evaluating the level of readiness for ERP adoption in manufacturing SMEs. The framework conceptualizes readiness to adopt an ERP as including four dimensions: the organizational context, external forces, perception of ERP, and business processes. A field study of eleven manufacturing SMEs was conducted. The framework led to the classification of these firms in three clusters: "committed adopters" (4 firms), "uncommitted adopters" (5 firms), and "late adopters" (2 firms).

Introduction

Until recently, enterprise resource planning (ERP) technology had only been used by large-scale organizations. Over the last few years, however, ERP applications have begun appearing in small and medium-size enterprises (SMEs), and in particular, in SMEs in the manufacturing sector (Everdingen, Hillegersberg, & Waarts, 2000; Palaniswamy & Frank, 2000). Since this technology is particularly complex, applications often present significant risks—as has been demonstrated by many failed attempts at implementation in large firms (Konicki, 2001; Songini, 2002). In this regard, White (1999) has characterized ERP as "the big company solution for small companies" and Pender (2001) suggests that the challenge for SMEs is to deploy large enterprise technology without incurring large enterprise costs.

There is a growing interest by SMEs and ERP providers in the development of enterprise systems that are better adapted to this type of organizations (Gable & Stewart, 1999; Stewart, Milford, Jewels, Hunter, & Hunter, 2000; Muscatello, Small, & Chen, 2003). Yet, past experience has shown that the sole availability of an information technology, as well adapted as it may be, is not sufficient to ensure that it will be successfully implemented and appropriately used in the organization. Indeed, several studies on ERP implementation projects in large firms have shown that these projects are often fraught with difficulties and that their failure rate is high. Studies have also shown that, often times, firms do not reap the benefits that they expected from implementing an ERP (Saint-Léger, 2004). Given significant differences between SMEs and large enterprises with regard to the objectives and constraints of ERP adoption (Laukkanen, Sarpola, & Hallikainen, 2007), determining if a small company will be able to adopt the technology, that is, if it is ready for implementing it, becomes a critical issue.

To address this issue, this study attempts to answer the following questions: What constitutes the readiness for ERP adoption in manufacturing SMEs? And how can firms be characterized in terms of their readiness to adopt an ERP? The study has both a descriptive and a prescriptive aim. First, the paper proposes a conceptual framework of the readiness for ERP adoption in small manufacturing firms. After examining its appropriateness with data gathered from 11 manufacturing SMEs, the paper describes how managers can use the framework, both to assess the level of readiness for ERP adoption of their firm and, when required, to identify the areas that ought to be improved for the firm to reach an appropriate degree of readiness.

Conceptual Framework

What can motivate an organization such as a manufacturing SME to adopt an ERP system, knowing the high cost and high risk of facing complex implementation problems? As shown in Figure 1, ERP adoption motivations can be typified in three basic categories: 1) technological motivations, 2) operational motivations, and 3) strategic motivations (Parr & Shanks, 2000; Ross & Vitale, 2000). Technological motivations have to do with infrastructure. Operational motivations concern the improvement of processes. Motivations of a strategic order are linked to a change in orientation in the design and delivery of services, and are contingent on the will to improve results, both quantitative and qualitative. These motivations emanate from—or are conditioned by—the technological, organizational and environmental context that determines the extent to which a SME is ready and able to proceed with the complex undertaking that is the adoption and implementation of an ERP system, and a context that may differ markedly from that of a large enterprise (Buonanno et al., 2005).

Figure 1. Motivation and contextualization of ERP adoption in SMEs (adapted from Raymond & Uwizeyemungu, 2006)

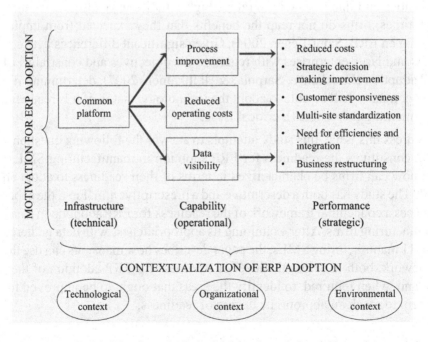

A number of studies have in fact successfully used Tornatsky and Fleischer's (1993) technology-organization-environment (TOE) framework to explain the adoption of information technology, emphasizing three groups of determinants or predictors: 1) characteristics of the environmental context, such as external pressures from the firm's business partners, 2) characteristics of the organisational context, such as the firm's strategy, resources and processes, and 3) characteristics of the technological context, including the advanced manufacturing technologies and applications already implemented by the firm (Raymond, Bergeron, & Blili, 2005). Also drawing on diffusion of innovation theory (Rogers, 1995) as well as on Raymond and Blili's (1997) model of the potential for EDI adoption in SMEs, the framework illustrated in Figure 2 conceptualizes readiness for ERP adoption as having four underlying dimensions: the organization's predisposition to adoption, pressures exerted by the external environment, perceptions about ERP, and the nature of business processes.

Organizational Context

A number of organizational attributes contribute to explain a firm's ability to enter information technology related endeavours (Teng, Fiedler, & Grover, 1998). In the context of ERP adoption, the firm's strategy itself—for instance, a cost leadership strategy—could call for implementing such a system (Banker et al., 2000). The degree of IT sophistication of the firm, that is, the extent to which it currently takes advantage of IT in both operational and managerial applications, is also thought to be an indicator of the firm's capacity to implement an ERP. Operational methods may have an influence; indeed, in a firm with just-in-time production, integrating production planning—a feature common to several ERPs—is likely to improve the production cycle. Also, acquiring an ERP involves relatively sophisticated procurement methods; if such methods are not into place in the organization, the firm may encounter serious difficulties during implementation (Bernard, Rivard, & Aubert, 2003). ERP is a significant investment, which entails three types of costs (Banker et al., 2000): the software package itself, the human resources required for implementation (Laughlin, 1999), and the cost of adapting business practices. Hence, for a firm to be ready for adoption, it must have the necessary resources.

Figure 2. Evaluation model of an SME's readiness for ERP adoption

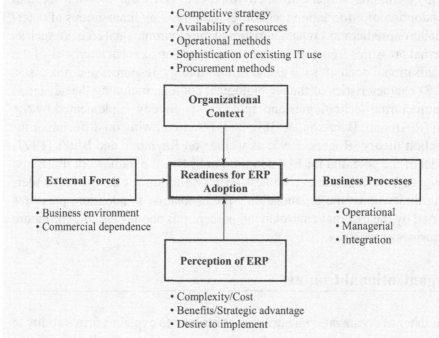

External Forces

Uncertainty about the organization's environment has been identified as a determinant of adoption (Julien, 1998), and being able to maintain the integration of subsystems is a prerequisite to performance in organizations that operate in environments characterized by uncertainty and heterogeneity (Lawrence & Lorsch, 1969). Organizations confronting great uncertainty could show a marked interest in adopting an ERP system, because it would enable them to achieve greater integration of both their information management and operational processes (Banker et al., 2000). In addition, an organization may bow to competitive and institutional pressures, and is thus more likely to adopt a technology such as ERP if its competitors have a similar technology (Benders, Batenburg, & van der Blonk, 2006). SMEs, and more specifically manufacturing SMEs, tend to be dependent on large clients or a prime manufacturer, and this type of relationship is becoming more demanding in terms of the quality needed and the integration required in inter-organizational processes (Raymond & St-Pierre, 2004). Undertaking these types of processes effectively imposes the adoption of technologies like ERP or EDI on SMEs (Raymond & Blili, 1997).

Perceptions About ERP

An SME is usually very "organic," inasmuch as it tends to reflect the beliefs, attitudes and behaviour of an entrepreneur (Julien, 1998). This is particularly true when it comes to decisions concerning the adoption, implementation and use of IT (Raymond & Blili, 1997). A positive perception on the owner/manager's part of the benefits or strategic value that this type of technology can afford is critical for a firm becoming to be ready to implement an ERP (Abdinnour-Helm, Lengnick-Hall & Lengnick-Hall, 2003). This positive perception takes the form of high expectations of the types of benefits to be derived from access to superior-quality information, support for business growth and improvements in decision-making when better information is delivered in real time. Furthermore, concerns may be raised about the complexity or cost of implementing and using ERP. Having management willing to dedicate some of their time and to be actively involved in the project is an important component of readiness.

Business Processes

For an ERP to generate the desired benefits, the business processes of the implementing firm must be aligned with those embedded in the ERP (Somers & Nelson, 2001; Nah & Lau, 2001). If there is no alignment, the organization will have to adapt its processes to those of the ERP (Holland et al., 1999; Chen, 2001). Such an adaptation often entails important risks (Bernard et al., 2004; Brehm, Heinzl, & Markus, 2001). Because processes embedded in an ERP are highly integrated, the degree of integration of a firm's operational and managerial processes contributes to its readiness to implement this type of system. Many SMEs have only achieved limited integration of their business processes. In fact, these firms often use several unintegrated applications to support various functions, creating redundancy in the capture of data and increasing the risk of error, since information is not entered in real time but according to need (Markus & Tanis, 2000; Palaniswamy & Frank, 2000).

While they are not included as overt variables in the evaluation model, size and industry may yet be relevant as antecedents or covariates of the manufacturing SMEs' readiness for ERP adoption. Greater size has been associated with a greater availability of resources and a greater level of information and manufacturing technology sophistication (Swamidass & Kotha, 1998; Gupta & Whitehouse, 2001; Bajwa & Lewis, 2003), thus potentially impacting the organization's predisposition to adopt an ERP. Firms in more technologically intensive industries are seen to have more complex business processes and require greater process integration, thus influencing their core strategies such as technology (Mauri & Michaels, 1998) and rendering them more prone to use advanced manufacturing systems such as computer-integrated manufacturing and ERP (Ellram & Zsidisin, 2002; Boykin & Martz, 2004). Also, in certain medium-high or high technology sectors such as the motor vehicle and aircraft industries where SMEs often act as subcontractors to large firms, external forces such as the power of a few large customers or the need to cooperate within a network of organizations could render SMEs more ready to adopt technologies such as ERP and e-business that increase both internal integration and external integration (Raymond & Blili, 1997; van den Ende & Wijnberg, 2001; Hanna & Walsh, 2002).

Returning to the evaluation model presented in Figure 2, one can define the "ideal" SME, that is, the firm most ready to adopt ERP. Such a firm operates in an industry characterized by a high level of uncertainty or turbulence, where implementing an ERP system becomes a strategic necessity in the face of intense competition or pressure from large customers. Its leaders have correctly evaluated the risks linked to the intrinsic complexity of this technology and to the human, technological and financial resources that are required to successfully implement it. They have also correctly estimated the operational, managerial, and strategic benefits that an ERP can provide in terms of their firm's efficiency, effectiveness, and competitiveness. The ideal SME has formulated a strategy and objectives to which an ERP system can be aligned or upon which the business case for ERP implementation can be based. It already disposes of the necessary resources and competencies, either internally or externally through partnerships and outsourcing, and shows sophistication in its existing use of IT in general and advanced manufacturing technology in particular. Finally, an "ERP-ready" SME is characterized by business processes that are sufficiently integrated already, and can be aligned with the "best practices" embedded within ERP software.

Research Method

In order to perform a preliminary test of the proposed research model, we conducted a field study of 11 manufacturing SMEs. The firms were selected on the basis of convenience, that is, their relative proximity to the researchers' university location and their willingness to participate in the study. Another criterion was the complexity of their organization and business processes, such that the adoption of ERP would be possible a priori. In each firm, the senior officers (owner/managers, operations managers, general managers or other members of management) were interviewed with a semi-structured questionnaire. All interviews were recorded on tape and transcribed with an analysis table to structure the resulting data while preserving its richness and detail. The interview data was complemented with the interviewees later responding to a survey instrument that provided data on the company, such as the types of information systems and technologies used.

As presented in Table 1, the firms ranged in size from 17 to 245 employees, with an average of 124. For the study's purposes, given that there is no internationally-agreed upon definition of manufacturing firms based on size, an SME is defined as an enterprise with more than 10 employees and less than 249, to be included within both North American and European definitions. Whereas in North American research, small and medium-sized enterprises are generally defined as having respectively less than 100 and 500 employees [see Mittelstaedt, Harben, & Ward (2003, p. 71), for instance], in the European Union, the definition is rather based on 50 and 250 employees [see Kalantaridis (2004, p. 249), for instance]. The eleven firms operated in various industries such as metal components, furniture, and plastics, and were classified by their technological intensity as being low-tech (3 firms), medium-tech (5 firms) or high-tech (3 firms).

Given the definition of ERP systems as "comprehensive packaged software solutions which aim for total integration of all business processes and functions," and as modular systems that can be implemented module-by-module (Parr & Shanks, 2000), one SME out of the eleven (firm J) has already adopted this technology (having implemented the production management module of an ERP software package). The data collected were synthesized in matrices based on the components of the conceptual model, as presented in Appendices A and B.

Table 1. Profile of the sampled SMEs

SME	No. of Employees	Size Category	Manufacturing Sector	Technological Intensity[a]
A	100	medium-sized	Steel components	medium-tech
B	140	medium-sized	Industrial equipment	high-tech
C	170	medium-sized	Treatment of surfaces	medium-tech
D	49	small	Plastics	high-tech
E	160	medium-sized	Steel machining	high-tech
F	17	small	Packaging products	medium-tech
G	65	small[b]	Steel transformation	low-tech
H	100	medium-sized	Aluminium components	medium-tech
I	245	medium-sized	Furniture	low-tech
J	150	medium-sized	Transmissions	medium-tech
K	160	medium-sized	Composites moulding	low-tech

[a]based on manufacturing technology used

[b]based on the North American definition (firm G would be medium-sized under the European definition)

Results

The data collected were used to evaluate the sampled enterprises along the four dimensions of the conceptual model.

Evaluation of the SMEs' Readiness for ERP Adoption

Organizational Context

All the firms in the sample had an independent management unit. Most were engaged in subcontracting, which accounted for anywhere between 10% and 99% of revenues, and over half of them manufactured or modified their products in response to client needs. The operational cycle was a function of their principal business, be it product development, manufacturing, machining, assembly or services. Some were active in several of these activities, if not all.

Some of the participating firms, partners of the same prime manufacturer, received a single annual order with a calendar of dates of delivery and the quantities required on each date. This calendar was constantly updated, which could have a significant impact on the operational cycle. Operating in this manner can be problematic without a production planning or work-scheduling tool. Nine of the companies had ISO certification, a requirement imposed by their clients. All agreed that this standard is necessary and believed that they had derived benefits from it. Nine of the companies were engaged in just-in-time production, and some offered customers the capacity to produce one-off items, make a very short production run, or introduce changes in the midst of production. These services require very flexible production management.

In terms of IT resources, nine of the 11 firms were using an MRP or MRP II system upgraded with tools that had been developed in parallel. One firm had already implemented an ERP. At the operational level, advanced installations were being used, but all the respondents reported some dissatisfaction, particularly in terms of software flexibility. All firms had implemented accounting software whose prime use was invoicing, but that was also used for producing financial information. Most of the firms used quite complex technologies, inasmuch as they were using several tools such as spreadsheets and MRP II; some used tools that had been developed in parallel in order to extract information required for financial decision-making. Several respondents mentioned that they lacked information for decision-making, and wanted to find more effective solutions or tools to meet this need. Each of the companies in the sample had an installed base of relatively new equipment, since several of them had updated their equipment for 2000. Few, however, have all their data in one database, so their systems are updated either by request or daily, or data is captured twice, leading to delays or errors. Some of the executives were irritated by the fact that they could not have real time access to data.

The firms engaged in no medium- or long-term planning of their technological infrastructures. Funds for IT were attributed as need arose, not through strategic planning. Three firms had an IT department or someone with formal responsibility for their computing needs, relying on this function or person to foresee or possibly respond to needs. Most of the respondents were able to identify individuals with some knowledge or having a strong interest in information technologies. Half of the firms mentioned that they had a small group of internal resources who provide support to computerization efforts and the management of IT. Two of the firms relied on the support of an external IT services supplier. Over a third of the respondents said that if they were to create an ERP selection committee, they would not call on the services of a consulting firm for fear that the solution would not fully meet their needs. Some of them mentioned that, rather than go directly to a software vendor or a consulting firm, they would seek advice from firms that had lived through an ERP implementation to discover the types of problems that can be expected.

Most of the participating firms operated under several competitive strategies at the same time. Responding to the pressures of globalization requires ingenuity solely to maintain one's market position. The most common competitive strategies were innovating, increasing production capacity, moving into new markets, offering new services (such as assembly or delivery), and forming strategic alliances.

External Forces

Among most of the participating companies, 20% of clients accounted for 80% of revenues. Several firms were trying to avoid having a single client that played too large a role in their business, even if they were not already in a dependent position. One firm, however, was very dependent on a single client, and keenly aware of it. Its executives were striving to develop new markets and grow the customer base. Two companies had experienced difficulties over the preceding two years because they were in a position of dependence. In each case their prime manufacturer had suddenly stopped awarding them contracts, and this put their businesses at risk. They had since rebounded, the result of a careful review of business practices. The end result was a fundamental shift in their attitudes toward their clients; they would no longer allow themselves to have a major customer. At the time of data collection, their strategies included a diversified customer base in order to avoid facing the same sort of problem in the future. All the respondents indicated that they were under no pressure from business partners to implement an ERP. It is worth mentioning that ISO accreditation was quite a different matter; they would not have been able to maintain their clients if they had not attained ISO accreditation.

Perceptions of ERP

The adoption of an ERP system is first and foremost an economic decision. Acquiring, implementing and maintaining the technology represents a major investment, but it enables a firm to reduce production costs and improve performance. The managers were not overly concerned about the cost of an

ERP and the time it takes to implement one. Seven of the eleven firms did not consider cost a major hurdle; other considerations such as the need to review business processes weighed in the balance. Nevertheless, all agreed that implementing an ERP system is a complex undertaking. Some respondents thought that once an ERP was installed, it would be relatively simple to use, although others thought that an ERP would be difficult to use.

Among the various benefits to be derived from an ERP, it is interesting to note that the highest expectations are related to improved management and operations. The interviews revealed that our respondents were most interested in improving production, the product, and the quality of information. They had relatively few expectations concerning improvements in strategic capacity, organizational issues or technological infrastructures.

Participating firms were aware that their technological infrastructure must continually improve if they are to maintain or improve their competitive position. Six of them intended to implement an ERP to improve their technological infrastructure. It is important to mention that the respondents are the people who would initiate an ERP implementation.

Business Processes

Most of the firms were increasing their research of markets (commercial intelligence). It was noted, however, that the scope of this research substantially varied from one firm to the next. For some, the process was informal, and a handful of people were involved. Diffusion of information was by word of mouth. Others had a more formal process that included the use of IT; these firms felt the need for information on their business environment and had acquired the tools required to achieve this goal. The Web was used to gather information on clients, competitors, and suppliers. Managers from these firms indicated that the Internet was being used more and more in their quest for information. It was not, however, the only data gathering tool; exchanges with clients, suppliers and sometimes even competitors were important sources of information, as were industry conventions and trade shows.

Developing a corporate vision and strategy first arose as a requirement to be fulfilled for ISO compliance. Half of the firms had not reviewed either their vision or strategy since that time, and they would appear to use an intuitive approach to corporate strategy. In fact, in these firms the process for developing strategy would appear to be relatively neglected and unfamiliar. The other half of the firms was engaged in a continuous process of gathering intelligence on technology, an exercise that is practiced on an almost daily basis. Their executives stated that it is important to be aware of changes in the environment. This type of vigilance, which focuses mainly on competitors and technological innovation, was their approach to reformulating corporate strategy.

All the firms used tools for product improvement or design. They placed great importance on this process, since it allows them to maintain or improve the firm's market position. The pursuit of continuous process improvement is integral to everything they do. In fact, the executives rely heavily on the process of quality improvement because it provides added value to the products and processes that are the essence of their business.

While the design process was computerized, in most firms it was not fully integrated. There was a trend toward, and a need for, integration of the tools used (CAD and CAM), or at least compatibility between the various programs used, particularly as concerns exchanges with customers. Between 1% and 10% of sales were spent on updating software and maintaining the installed base of IT.

Most of the firms took orders over the telephone, by fax, by e-mail and through formal documents. Only three firms had integrated the process from order taking to delivery. In the other firms, data were entered several times; respondents from these firms nevertheless believed that full integration of the operational chain would save time and money and reduce the number of errors.

The most computerized functions in these firms are production and delivery. Each SME had an MRP, an MRP II; one had an ERP (company J). Most of them were not satisfied with the results. They said to be frustrated by the rigidity of these systems, and their inappropriateness to the company's needs or business processes. All went through difficult installation, adaptation and customization periods and had to deal with resistance to change and lost productivity. There was a fear that adopting an ERP would involve investing as much energy and time and provoke another cycle of resistance.

Although all the firms have computerized invoicing, only one has integrated it into production systems. For some, this separation served a purpose, as it must be verified that the order is complete before an invoice is produced. The delivery function, though, had not been computerized in most of the companies surveyed. Often the customer took delivery where the good was produced at an agreed-upon and confirmed date. Delivery was not integrated, and the process was generally based on the use of Excel spreadsheets.

Half of the firms keep data on products sold in order to conduct after-sales follow-up. Here again, various systems were used, and each would have to be consulted before warranty information can be obtained.

The respondents put more emphasis on organizational development and human resource management. In fact, everything related to HR appeared to require more attention. Training, evaluation, accident prevention, and personnel security were just some of the elements requiring better management and, hence, better information. Respondents had a greater need to have this process computerized so that it is easier to obtain information on employees. At the time of data collection, two of the companies had computerized this function and appeared to be satisfied with the results. The others still operated entirely with manual systems, whether the process was very structured or unstructured, particularly where it concerned professional development. One of the firms had begun to computerize some of its training programs.

A third of the companies in the sample had tools for evaluating both productivity and financial performance. Continuous improvement was an integral part of day-to-day activities, but few firms used tools such as trend charts to follow organizational activities. Respondents acknowledged that these tools can inform the decision-making process, but indicated that the limitations on their time tended to create situations where their decisions were more often based on reacting than on planning. One of the managers pointed out that he had access to the information, but that *"It's all very fine to have documents that describe where we are, but we also have to have the time to read, analyze and interpret the information."*

In most of the firms, operations were more or less integrated. The managers had a good understanding of operational processes, and tools were available that integrated part of these processes. For example, an Excel spreadsheet is used to set production schedules, whereas an MRP system is used to actually plan production. Three of the firms could be qualified as having strongly integrated systems, inasmuch as they had MRP II systems.

Seven of the firms could be qualified as having achieved an intermediate level of integration of their management systems. Most of these types of processes had been developed in a limited way, due to a lack of resources. Information was usually shared on an informal basis. Since most tools were not integrated, either because the systems were incompatible or for lack of gateways, they did not contribute to information sharing, which affects the quality of available information. Most of the executives interviewed could not relate very well to managerial issues, which explains why these processes were relatively simple and some only occasionally used. This observation may be explained by the fact that an SME requires flexibility and an ability to react quickly and often lacks resources. For executives of this type of firm, the focus is on following revenue and expense reports, either on a weekly or monthly basis, and using the information in these reports to make administrative decisions. They have limited awareness of the importance of these processes, because the focus is on production.

Cluster Analysis

We conducted a cluster analysis to group participating companies on the basis of similarities according to variables in the conceptual model. This approach aims to group organizations into clusters such that each cluster's membership is highly homogeneous with respect to certain characteristics. Here, the characteristics (or clustering variables) are the four components of the SMEs' readiness for ERP adoption. A second aim is that each group differs from other groups with respect to these same characteristics. We used SPSS software (mean nearest neighbour algorithm, Euclidean distance). The grouping represented by the dendogram in Figure 3 was obtained for the following variables: presence of resources, operational methods, operational business processes, managerial process, integration of processes, business environment, dependence on a single customer, complexity/cost and benefits/strategic values, because these variables best discriminated members of the groups.

Figure 3. Euclidean distance between the groups

```
               0         5        10        15        20        25
  SME    GR    +---------+---------+---------+---------+---------+

  C      II    -+---+
  G      II    -+   +----------------------+
  E      II    -+   |                      |
  I      II    -+---+                      |
  D      II    -+                          +--------------------+
                                           |                    |
  B      I     ---------------+-------+     |                    |
  J      I     ---------------+       +-+   |                    |
  H      I     ---------------------+ +---+                      |
  F      I     ---------------------+                            |
                                                                 |
  A      III   -------------------------------------------+-----+
  K      III   -------------------------------------------+
```

Table 2. Three profiles of the readiness for ERP adoption

	Group I Committed adopters (B, F, H, J)	Group II Uncommitted adopters (C, D, E, G, I)	Group III Late adopters (A, K)
External forces: Pressure to adopt an ERP	Low	Low	Low
Organizational context: Advanced use of IT	High	Moderate	Low
Perception of ERP: Benefits	High	Moderate to High	Moderate
Business processes: Integration	Moderate to High	Moderate	Low to Moderate
Size: Number of employees	17 to 150	49 to 245	100 to 160
Industry: Technological intensity	Medium to High-tech	Low to High-tech	Low to Medium-tech

A three-cluster solution was found to be most parsimonious in identifying groups of firms that could be clearly distinguished from one another, based on a meaningful pattern of relationships among the clustering variables. The three distinct groups obtained are described below. The salient characteristics of each group with respect to their potential for adoption of an ERP system (high, moderate and low) are synthesized in Table 2. The determining factors for each of the dimensions of the evaluation model were identified through quantitative analysis of the data.

Group I: Committed Adopters

The firms in Group I are SMEs that have already committed or are likely to commit to commencing an ERP adoption process. This commitment is largely explained by their concern for continuous improvement, the search for better management practices, and a desire to improve the quality, quantity and accessibility of information. As opposed to members of the two other groups, their readiness to adopt the technology arises spontaneously from a need for information. They are increasingly preoccupied with the idea of obtaining data in real time in order to make better decisions, and this requires greater integration of the systems used. The firms in Group I believe that their competitors have deployed ERP systems, and this provides an additional incentive to adopt an ERP-type system. As far as potential benefits are concerned, the executives have high expectations. Expectations are not as high, however, when it comes to the strategic value of ERP systems.

Business processes in this group are more complex, most are computerized and they are better controlled by management. All the respondents believed that a greater integration of their systems would improve performance as well as business processes, since an ERP creates better management practices only when the firm decides to minimize customization. The firms in Group I identified individuals from within the organization who would participate in a team or a steering committee during adoption and implementation. In a project of this magnitude, senior management tends to feel that it should get directly involved as leaders and champions, and that users must actively participate, at whatever level. In view of the scope, the complexity and the cost of this type of project, the role played by senior management is critical. Members must be directly involved as motivators in order to minimize resistance to change.

Group II: Uncommitted Adopters

The firms that make up this group are in an intermediate state, inasmuch as questions are being raised about the need to improve their technological infrastructure, and significant changes will need to be made relatively soon. Inconsistencies are apparent in operational methods, and there is little concern shown for improving management processes. These firms seek to become more competitive by growing and increasing production capacity, by distinguishing themselves with product improvements and innovative, improved processes, by developing new products and by finding new market niches. Their managerial approach favours operational processes and information flows as they relate to production. In fact, technological infrastructures for operational processes are much more advanced than those used for managing. Furthermore, at the management level, only accounting functions are computerized and payroll services are outsourced. New applications for the integration and computerization of HR management would appear to generate interest in this group.

Firms in Group II generally have a positive perception of integrated management systems. Members of Firm E, however, did not see the advantages of adopting such a system. Its respondents believed that they would be best served by the technology already in place, as well as the different tools that were developed over the years and continue to be upgraded on a regular basis. But overall, all the companies in the group are interested in more advanced technologies than what is presently being used. They recognize the importance of adopting and implementing IT that will bring improvements to how they work and that will give them access to a wealth of information for decision-making. There are a variety of ways to implement IT, but the key to succeeding is to consult employees and get them to participate in the process. Nevertheless, the technological development of these firms faces a serious handicap: a lack of resources, and in particular financial resources, within the organization. This lack of resources limits their access to IT.

Group III: Late Adopters

The two firms in Group III have been classified as late adopters. In Firm A, managers did not feel the need to adopt a technological infrastructure like ERP. Existing technologies were considered effective enough to meet the firm's needs. Executives also considered the investment too great, given the size of their business and the potential return on investment. They remained reticent about taking on this type of project. The organization's approach to strategic issues is reactive. Since they were not facing pressure from their partners to adopt an ERP system, and since they only have a small share of the market, the firm's management was not considering deploying an ERP package in the short or medium term.

Firm K is governed by a board of directors that oversees an entire group. The first issue to be confronted therefore concerns the group as a whole; should it operate in a centralized or decentralized manner? This question will require considerable reflection. This firm must also review most of its operational and managerial processes before making the transition to ERP-type technology. Finally, the firm is still using traditional methods, few of which are computerized. Last year, top management studied the idea of adopting an ERP system. The project was launched by an executive who had limited information about ERP systems. After a few meetings and getting a better understanding of the implementation process, the company decided to put the project on hold. The committee in charge concluded that the group was not ready to undertake the project. Even so, the project remains on hold, and the executive interviewed hoped that it would be re-evaluated in the short or medium term.

Given the potential effect of size and industry mentioned previously, the three groups were examined to determine if differences exist among them in this regard. As indicated at the bottom of Table 2, there does not appear to be any significant relationship between the SMEs' size and their readiness to adopt ERP. There is also no clear trend in regard to manufacturing industry in which these firms operate. Noting however that there are no low-tech firms among the "committed adopters" and no high-tech ones among the "late adopters," a link between more technologically intensive industries and more advanced use of IT might eventually come into play.

Implications and Conclusion

The conceptual model proved useful to draw profiles of SMEs as to their readiness for adopting ERP. While the model posits that four types of variables play an important role in explaining an SME's predisposition to adopt an ERP, the results show that three of these indeed play such a role. In the study, it was not possible to assess the role played by external pressures, since little variance existed among the firms with respect to this type of variable. Two explanations can be provided for this result. First, it is possible that the external environment of the 11 firms studied was quite similar in that owner-managers perceived no pressure from their clients to adopt an ERP. Second, it may be that other industry forces such as competitive rivalry and power of suppliers come into play. Further research would be needed to better characterize these forces' influence upon SMEs' readiness to adopt ERP.

The practical relevance of the research findings lies in facilitating the successful adoption of ERP within the context of manufacturing SMEs. As illustrated in Figure 4, the evaluation model can become the methodological core of an ERP implementation project, including third parties involved (providers of ERP consulting services and software, industry associations). In light of the factors and profiles of ERP readiness identified in this study, a three-phase methodological framework for the adoption of ERP is proposed.

First, one must look at the organizational context to identify the firm's strategic orientation and objectives and to align the ERP system's objectives (e.g., level of integration) and functions, as this system will constitute the informational and technological infrastructure of the manufacturing SME. One must also assess external forces and respond to environmental influences, competitive rivalry, and especially the pressures from major clients and prime contractors to increase product quality and supply chain integration in light of globalization. The business case for an ERP implementation is thus

Figure 4. Using the evaluation model to implement ERP in SMEs

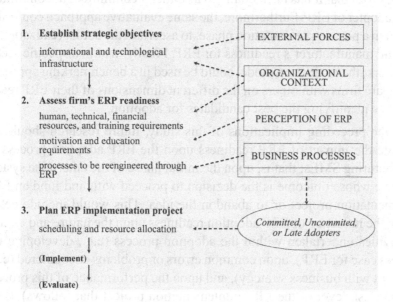

founded and the immediate environment of the eventual ERP implementation project is determined.

In the second phase, the SME's ERP readiness is evaluated in terms of the organizational context, the perception of ERP, and the business processes. The first assessment, focussing on the firm's manufacturing systems sophistication, determines the human, financial and financial resources, and the training required to attain sufficient ERP readiness. By determining opportunities, risks, and benefits perceived by owner-managers, the second assessment orients the motivational and educational efforts that must be made to insure the ERP project will receive the full support and involvement of both management and employees. The third assessment outlines the project's objectives (e.g., initial ERP modules to be implemented) by identifying those business processes that show the most required reengineering, in alignment with the firm's strategic objective.

The third phase involves planning the ERP implementation. It is here that third parties can be solicited to provide external resources such as information, expertise, products and services that fulfil requirements identified in the preceding phase. Here, the organizational context comes mainly into play in regard to resource availability and procurement method. The scheduling and resource allocation parameters would be set in accordance with the SME's profile, given that it has been qualified as either a committed, uncommitted, or late adopter of ERP. Furthermore, the same evaluative approach could also be used in a post-implementation phase, to ascertain the actual realization of the small manufacturer's readiness for ERP. Finally, within a specific sector or network, the evaluation model could be used in a benchmarking approach to compare firms with others on the different dimensions of their ERP readiness, thus identifying the best candidates for adoption.

Given the preceding implications of this study, future research should investigate the impact of ERP readiness upon the ERP adoption process of manufacturing SMEs; that is, upon the initial phase of the enterprise system life cycle whose outcome is the decision to proceed with and fund an ERP implementation project or to abandon the idea. This would include determining the influence of ERP adoption readiness upon the nature and quality of activities undertaken within the adoption process (e.g., developing the business case for ERP), upon common errors or problems encountered (e.g., lack of fit with business strategy), and upon the performance of this process (e.g., the risk level of the ERP implementation project that follows). Such research could be best served by first using a qualitative approach based on in-depth case studies.

SMEs are recognized for their flexibility and adaptability in the face of environmental, operational and technological changes. These firms are increasingly the site of complex and cutting-edge manufacturing systems, and are looking to integrate these systems in order to improve performance. It is still uncertain, however, if SMEs have the will or even the capacity to formalize business processes. This would be a critical asset if the firm decides to undertake the implementation of an integrated management system. If an ERP system is to deliver all the benefits promised by its publisher, the new technologies must completely integrate all corporate functions.

References

Abdinnour-Helm, S., Lengnick-Hall, M.L., & Lengnick-Hall, C.A. (2003). Pre-implementation attitudes and organizational readiness for implementing an enterprise resource planning system. *European Journal of Operational Research, 146*, 258-273.

Bajwa, D.S., & Lewis, L.F. (2003). Does size matter? An investigation of collaborative information technology adoption by U.S. firms. *Journal of Information Technology Theory and Application*, 5(1) 29-46.

Banker, R.D., Janakiraman, S.N., Donstans, C., & Slaughter, S.A. (2000). *Determinants of ERP adoption: An empirical analysis*. Paper presented at the Workshop on Information Systems & Economics, Brisbane, Australia.

Benders, J., Batenburg, R., & van der Blonk, H. (2006). Sticking to standards: Technical and other isomorphic pressures in deploying ERP-systems. *Information & Management*, 43(2), 194-203.

Bernard, J.-G., Rivard, S., & Aubert, B.A. (2004). L'exposition au risque d'implantation de ERP: Eléments de mesure et d'atténuation. *Systèmes d'Information et Management*, 9(2), 25-50.

Bingi, P., Sharma, M.K., & Godla, J. (1999). Critical issues affecting an ERP implementation. *Information Systems Management*, 16(3) 7-14.

Boykin, R.F., & Martz, W.B., Jr. (2004). The integration of ERP into a logistics curriculum: Applying a systems approach. *Journal of Enterprise Information Management*, 17(1), 45-55.

Brehm, L., Heinzl, A., & Markus, L.M. (2001). Tailoring ERP systems: A spectrum of choices and their implications. In *Proceedings of the 34th Hawaii International Conference on System Sciences* (Vol. 8, pp. 1-9). Washington, DC: IEEE Computer Society.

Buonanno, G., Faverio, P., Pigni, F., Ravarini, A., Sciuto, D., & Tagliavini, M. (2005). Factors affecting ERP system adoption: A comparative analysis between SMEs and large companies. *Journal of Enterprise Information Management*, 18(4), 384-426.

Chen, I.J. (2001). Planning for ERP systems: Analysis and future trends. *Business Process Management Journal*, 7(5), 374-386.

Ellram, L.M., & Zsidisin, G.A. (2002). Factors that drive purchasing and supply management's use of information technology. *IEEE Transactions on Engineering Management*, 49(3), 269-281.

Everdingen, Y.V., Hillegersberg, J.V., & Waarts, E. (2000). ERP adoption by European midsize companies. *Communications of the ACM*, 43(4) 27-31.

Gable, G., & Stewart, G. (1999). SAP R/3 implementation issues for small to medium enterprises. In *Proceedings of the 5th Americas Conference on Information Systems*, Milwaukee (pp. 779-781).

Gupta, A., & Whitehouse, F.R. (2001). Firms using advanced manufacturing technology management: An empirical analysis based on size. *Integrated Manufacturing Systems*, *12*(5), 346-350.

Hanna, V., & Walsh, K. (2002). Small firm networks: A successful approach to innovation? *R&D Management*, *32*(3), 201-207.

Holland, C., Light, B., & Gibson, N. (1999). A critical success factors model for enterprise resources planning implementation. In *Proceedings of the 7ᵗʰ European Conference on Information Systems*, Copenhagen (pp. 273-287).

Julien, P-A. (Ed.). (1998). *The state of the art in small business and entrepreneurship*. Aldershot, UK: Ashgate Publishing.

Kalantaridis, C. (2004). Internationalization, strategic behavior, and the small firm: A comparative investigation. *Journal of Small Business Management*, *42*(3), 245-262.

Konicki, S. (2001, March 5). Nike just didn't do it right, says I2 technologies. *Information Week*. Retrieved from http://www.informationweek.com/827/nike.htm.

Laughlin, S.P. (1999, January-February). An ERP game plan. *Information Technology*, 23-26.

Laukkanen, S., Sarpola, S., & Hallikainen, P. (2007). Enterprise size matters: Objectives and constraints of ERP adoption. *Journal of Enterprise Information Management*, *20*(3), 319-334.

Lawrence, P.R., & Lorsch, J.W. (1969). *Organization and environment*. Homewood, IL: Richard D. Irwin Inc.

Markus, L., & Tanis, C. (2000). The enterprise system experience: From adoption to success. In R.W. Zmud (Ed.), *Framing the domains of IT management, projecting the future...through the past* (pp. 173-207, 436-438). Cincinnati, OH: Pinnaflex Educational Resources.

Mauri, A.J., & Michaels, M.P. (1998). Firm and industry effects within strategic management: An empirical examination. *Strategic Management Journal*, *19*(3), 211-219.

Mittelstaedt, J.D., Harben, G.N., & Ward, W.A. (2003). How small is too small? Firm size as a barrier to exporting from the United States. *Journal of Small Business Management*, *41*(1), 68-84.

Muscatello, J.R., Small, M.H., & Chen, I.J. (2003). Implementing enterprise resource planning (ERP) systems in small and midsize manufacturing firms. *International Journal of Operations & Production Management*, *23*(8) 850-871.

Nah, F.F-H., & Lau, J.L-S. (2001). Critical factors for successful implementaion of enterprise systems. *Business Process Management Journal*, *7*(3) 285-296.

Palaniswamy, R., & Frank T. (2000, Summer). Enhancing manufacturing performance with ERP systems. *Information Systems Management*, 43-69.

Parr, A.N., & Shanks, G. (2000). A taxonomy of ERP implementation approaches. In *Proceedings of the 33rd Hawaii International Conference on System Sciences*, Maui, Hawaii (Vol. 7, pp. 1-10). Washington, DC: IEEE Computer Society.

Pender, L. (2001, May 15). Faster, cheaper ERP. *CIO Magazine*.

Raymond, L., Bergeron, F., & Blili, S. (2005). The assimilation of e-business in manufacturing SMEs: Determinants and effects on growth and internationalization. *Electronic Markets*, 15(2), 106-118.

Raymond, L., & Blili, S. (1997). Adopting EDI in a network organization: The case of subcontracting SMEs. *European Journal of Purchasing and Supply Management*, *3*(3), 165-175.

Raymond, L., & St-Pierre, J. (2004). Customer dependency in manufacturing SMEs: Implications for R&D and performance. *Journal of Small Business and Enterprise Development*, *11*(1), pp. 23-33.

Raymond, L., Uwizeyemungu, S., & Bergeron, F. (2006). Motivations to implement ERP in e-government: An analysis from success stories. *Electronic Government, an International Journal*, *3*(3) 225-240.

Rogers, E.M. (1995). *Diffusion of innovations* (4th Ed.). New York: The Free Press.

Ross, J.W., & Vitale, M.R. (2000). The ERP revolution: Surviving vs. thriving. *Information Systems Frontiers*, *2*(2), 233-241.

Saint-Léger, G. (2004). L'après-projet ERP: Retour d'expérience sur un changement qui n'a pas eu lieu. *Systèmes d'Information et Management*, *9*(2) 77-108.

Somers, T., & Nelson, K. (2001). The impact of critical success factors across the stages of enterprises resources planning implementations. In *Proceedings of the 34th Hawaii International Conference on System Sciences* (Vol. 8, p. 8016). Washington, DC: IEEE Computer Society.

Songini, M.L. (2002, February 11). GM locomotive unit put ERP rollout back on track. *Computer World*.

Stewart, G., Milford, T., Jewels, T., Hunter, T., & Hunter, D. (2000). Organizational readiness for ERP implementation. In *Proceedings of the 6th Americas Conference on Information Systems*, Long Beach (pp. 966-971).

Swamidass, P.M., & Kotha, S. (1998). Explaining manufacturing technology use, firm size and performance using a multidimensional view of technology. *Journal of Operations Management, 17*(1) 23-37.

Tornatsky, L.G., & Fleischer, M. (1993). *The process of technological innovation*. Lexington, MA: Lexington Books.

van den Ende, J., & Wijnberg, N. (2001). The organization of innovation in the presence of networks and bandwagons in the new economy. *International Studies of Management and Organization, 31*(1), 30-45.

White, P. (1999). ERP: The big company solution for small companies. *Accountancy Ireland, 31*(4), 36-38.

Appendix A: Process Data Synthesis Form
for Enterprise A

Enterprise A

Name of the firm :

Operational Processes

OP1 Understand the market and consumers	OP2 Develop a vision and a strategy	OP3 Design products	OP4 Market segments & sales	OP5 Produce and deliver	OP6 Post-sales service
The firm has a very specific market - answers the demands of customers - specific products with a long life cycle - reactive in its market because of its small size	A vision and strategy have been defined - a strategic plan has been developed with the arrival of the new CEO - the strategic plan is regularly updated	No design activities	Frequent contacts with customers and suppliers - commercial scanning	Production based on last year's deliveries - updated monthly - very important function for management	Not developed as high quality production is stressed and few products are returned - the firm listens to customers

Managerial Processes

MP1 — Development and management of human resources
No HR department and no HR development plan. Personnel turnover is low. Production employees are unionized. A workers' coop holds 15 % of the firm's shares. Payroll is outsourced.

MP2 — Information management
Management constantly scans the environment (considers itself proactive). Organisational data base. New technology only if it can improve production. No specific plan for data preservation and security.

MP3 — Accounting and financial management
Use the Fortune 1000 accounting package. This process is not very elaborate as documents provided by the existing system seem to satisfy the needs.

MP4 — Management of environmental programs
The firm is a potential polluter due to its effluents and residues, but respects industry standards. It has included non-pollution as one component of its strategic plan and seeks to remain a good corporate citizen.

MP5 — Management of public relations
President and member of the Chamber of Commerce, but nothing more.

MP6 — Performance and change management
No real measures of performance. CEO mentions that one must be prudent when major changes are made due to the risk involved. "Reviewing processes and modifying ways at the same time is bound to fail".

Appendix B: Data Synthesis Matrix

SME	A	B	C	D	E	F	G	H	I	J	K
Variable ORGANIZATIONAL CONTEXT											
Competitive strategy	alliance	innovation/growth/alliance	innovation/growth	innovation/growth	innovation/growth/alliance	innovation/growth	differentiation	innovation/growth/differentiation	differentiation/growth	innovation/growth/differentiation	innovation/alliance
Availability of resources											
Human	yes	yes	yes	yes	yes	yes	yes	yes	yes	yes	yes
Financial	no	yes	yes	yes	no	no	no	yes	no	yes	no
Operational methods											
Production system	MRP	MRP	MRP	MRP II	MRP	in-house system	MRP	MRP	MRP II	ERP	none
Just-in-time	yes	yes	yes	yes	yes	no	yes	yes	yes	yes	no
Transmission of proposals/orders	phone/fax	fax/e-mail/Internet/phone	fax/e-mail	fax/e-mail	fax/e-mail	fax/e-mail	e-mail/fax	fax/e-mail/extranet	fax/official documents	fax/e-mail/official documents	fax/annual planning by OM
Sophistication of existing IT use											
Operational	relatively complex	complex	relatively complex	relatively complex	relatively complex	relatively complex	relatively complex	relatively complex	complex	very complex	simple
Managerial	simple	complex	simple	simple	relatively complex	simple	relatively complex	relatively complex	relatively complex	very complex	simple
Hardware	simple	complex	simple	complex	complex	simple	complex	complex	complex	complex	simple
Level of systems integration	high	high	high	high	high	moderate	high	high	high	high	low
Procurement methods	outsourcing	partnership	partnership	partnership	partnership	outsourcing	partnership	partnership	partnership	partnership	partnership

continued on following page

Appendix B: Data Synthesis Matrix (continued)

SME	A	B	C	D	E	F	G	H	I	J	K
EXTERNAL FORCES											
Business Environment	not very competitive	not very competitive	competitive	competitive	competitive	not very competitive	not very competitive	not very competitive	competitive	competitive	competitive
Competitors have implemented ERP	does not know	possibly	no	possibly	possibly	does not know	does not know	yes	no	yes	yes
Commercial dependency	no	no	no	no	yes	no	no	no	no	no	yes (99 % of sales to one client)
PERCEPTION OF ERP											
Complexity/Cost											
Implementation	yes	no	yes	yes	yes	yes	yes	yes	yes	n/a	yes
Utilisation	no	no	yes	no	no	does not know	no	no	yes	n/a	does not know
Cost	yes	no	yes	no	yes	low	no	no	no	n/a	no
Benefits/Strategic value											
Operational	high	high	high	high	high	high	high	moderate	moderate	high	high
Managerial	moderate	high	moderate	high	moderate	moderate	moderate	high	high	high	high
Strategic	low	low	low	low	low	low	moderate	low	low	moderate	high
IT infrastructure	high	high	low	low	high	low	moderate	moderate	moderate	low	moderate
Desire to implement	does not know	yes	no	yes	no	no	yes	yes	no	n/a	yes

Chapter VIII

Design and Development of ISO 9001:2000-Based Quality Management Information System

M. Sakthivel, Government College of Technology, India

S.R. Devadasan, PSG College of Technology, India

S. Vinodh, PSG College of Technology, India

S. Ragu Raman, R.V.S. College of Engineering & Technology, India

S. Sriram, Arulmigu Kalasalingam College of Engineering, India

Abstract

Among all quality strategies, quality information system (QIS) is the one that finds comparatively little recognition among the quality engineering professionals. The situation is different in the general management arena, where management professionals are striving to attain core competence

of organizations through the implementation of management information systems (MIS). On realizing this trend and anticipating tremendous benefits, a research project has been started with the objective of developing a QIS compatible to ISO 9001:2000. In this chapter, the quality management information system (QMIS) that has been designed by referring to clause 4 of ISO 9001:2000 has been reported. After designing this QMIS, its development in a real time environment was examined by conducting a study at an ISO 9001:2000 certified high technology oriented company. Also, a validation study was conducted by gathering the opinions and assessment of the managing partner of the company on QMIS. These studies revealed the feasibility and possibility of implementing QMIS in ISO 9001:2000 certified companies. The details of this work are presented in this paper.

Introduction

Due to the evolution of globalization, modern companies have been striving to compete with their competitors who are operating from different parts of the world (Prajogo et al., 2007). One of the methods adopted by them for attaining this objective is the installation of quality systems by implementing ISO 9001:2000 standard (Magd, 2006; Singh, 2006). Since the introduction of this standard among the international community (Chin et al., 2004), the companies implementing it enjoy reputation in the global market (Thaver & Wilcock, 2006; Aggelogiannopoulos et al., 2007). It is widely reported that the majority of the customers insist that companies install ISO 9001:2000 compatible quality systems (Singh & Feng, 2006; Bayati & Taghavi, 2007). Because of this trend, till the year 2005, more than 6,00,000 modern companies of different sizes and nature have installed ISO 9000-based quality systems (Boiral & Roy, 2007; Zaramdini, 2007). While this is an appreciable trend, it is to be noted that mere implementation of ISO 9001:2000 standard does not enable the companies to acquire core competencies (Koc, 2007). Hence, despite their effectiveness, suitable leveraging mechanisms are yet to be incorporated with ISO 9001:2000 compatible quality systems (Gotzamani & Tsiotras, 2001; Williams, 2004). One of the additional leverages to be included is the information system component (Tan et al., 2003; Terlaak & King, 2006). Hence, it is high time that information system elements were incorporated with ISO 9001:2000-based quality systems. Presumably on realizing the information requirements, ISO 9001:2000 is incorporated with more information elements (Lari, 2002) than its previous version ISO 9001:1994 (Devadasan et al., 2003). However, careful studies reveal that those information elements are not sufficient to install and manage quality information system (QIS) compatible to ISO 9001:2000. Considering this requirement, the research project reported in this chapter has been carried out. The scope of this module of work was limited to the design and development of information system pertaining to clause 4 of ISO 9001:2000 quality system. This information system is titled as quality management information system (QMIS). Subsequently, a validation study was carried out in a high technology oriented job shop company to assess the penetration of QMIS. After noting the existing gap, the QMIS was developed in this company. The details of this work are presented in this chapter.

Management Information Systems and Quality Information Systems

Management professionals have been using information systems for more than five decades. Managers in particular started to use computer-based information systems, which are today known as management information systems (MIS). Since then the scope of MIS has been increasing and widening (Oz, 2002; O'Brien, 2002; Laudon & Laudon, 2004). In coincidence to MIS development, the world has been toiling to achieve continuous quality improvement in organizations. Yet, there has been no concrete effort by management professionals towards integrating continuous quality improvement projects with information systems (Forza, 1995). In fact, no major discussions have taken place in managerial conferences and seminars about extending support to enhance the effectiveness of continuous quality improvement projects through the application of MIS concepts (Peppard, 1995). At this juncture, it should be noted that a large number of companies have been benefited by implementing total quality management (TQM) (Pearson et al., 1995) and enterprise resource planning (ERP) systems (Themistocleous et al., 2001; Pozzebon & Titah, 2006). ERP projects are incorporated with MIS elements (Subramanian & Hoffer, 2005). Presumably, due to lack of proper guidance, not many companies have invested on developing information systems for enhancing the efficiency of TQM projects. Some experts and researchers in TQM field have advocated the need of developing information systems to support continuous quality improvement projects. The most noticeable is the contribution of Juran and Gryna (1995), who coined the term "quality information system (QIS)" (p. 548). After they advocated the use of QIS, some researchers worked in the direction of developing QIS during 1980s (Forza, 1995). After that the importance of QIS was not much felt by both theoreticians and practitioners (Pearson et al., 1995). This is probably due to the reason that, from late 1980s, companies began to view ISO 9000 series as an essential ingredient for implementing TQM (Ho, 1994: Martinez-Lorente & Martinez-Costa, 2004). Hence, it is projected that the efforts directed towards bridging MIS and TQM principles would be yielding solutions for enhancing the performance quality of companies (Pearson et al., 1995).

The fundamental tenets of MIS envisage the processing of data to evolve useful information to the target users (Adeoti-Adekeye, 1997), whereas the research in QIS has addressed its development features in a different way. The difference in approaches will make it difficult or impossible to integrate MIS principles with TQM projects. Hence, QIS should be developed in accordance to the stipulations of MIS principles. Meanwhile, it is prudent to note that TQM field has grown to a very large extent to encompass a number of new models, techniques, tools and approaches (Tari, 2005). If the scope of QIS includes all the above components of TQM, then managing it will become a cumbersome task. Hence QIS should be coupled with only the vital elements of TQM. However, such elements of QIS should not discord the other elements. Particularly such elements should facilitate in integrating the resources of the organizations for the purpose of attaining continuous quality improvement. In this regard, the discussion in literature on the contribution of ISO 9000 series quality systems standards-based models in organizations is to be recognized (Vouzas & Gotzamani, 2005). Moreover, during recent times, the credibility of ISO 9001:2000 quality system standard is being appraised (Kunnanatt, 2007). Hence, it will be an effective work if QIS is developed by integrating it with ISO 9001:2000 quality system based-model. Hence, if a QIS compatible to ISO 9001:2000 standard is implemented in a company, it will leverage the performance of ISO 9001:2000 standard and offer very powerful solutions towards achieving continuous quality improvement.

Description of Clause 4 of ISO 9001:2000

ISO 9001:2000 encompasses eight major clauses (ISO, 2000). Out of these, the first three are primitive and required only for referral and clarifying purposes. While installing ISO 9001:2000-based quality system, clauses 4 to 8 are required to be adopted. Out of these, clause 4, which is titled as "Quality management system" (ISO, 2000, p. 2) is the foundation of all other clauses of ISO 9001:2000. This clause is considered foundational because it stipulates all the instruments, which are required to build the quality management system (QMS). These instruments are quality manual, procedures, quality policy, and quality objectives. Further this clause specifies the most important activity of managing ISO 9001:2000-based quality system, namely documentation (Besterfield et al., 2004).

Clause 4 of ISO 9001:2000 consists of two sub-clauses. The first sub-clause is given a code number 4.1 and titled as "General requirements" (ISO, 2000, p. 2). As the title implies, this sub-clause stipulates the requirements that the organization shall adhere to manage the quality system and continually improve it. This sub-clause also specifies the processes, which shall have to be managed according to the stipulations of ISO 9001:2000 standard. This particular sub-clause is very specific in stipulating the general requirement of achieving continual improvement of QMS. The second sub-clause is given a code name 4.2 and titled as "Documentation requirements" (ISO, 2000, p. 2). This sub-clause further consists of four sub-clauses. As the title implies, this sub-clause deals with documents that are required to be developed for building the QMS. Further, this sub-clause specifies the requirements for controlling the records. The filled-in documents are called records and clause 4.2 specifies the requirements for controlling them. A distinct difference of sub-clause 4.2 from 4.1 is the absence of specific stipulation on continual improvement of QMS. But the stipulations of sub-clause 4.2 are vital for effecting continual improvement of QMS.

Organizations installing ISO 9001:2000-based quality systems without fulfilling either partially or fully the requirements of QMS specified by clause 4 of ISO 9001:2000 are prone to fail in achieving continual quality improvement in spite of their adherence to the remaining clauses of ISO 9001:2000. This aspect is depicted in the figure given in ISO 9001:2000, which is titled as "Model of a process based quality management system" (ISO, 2000, p. vi). The slightly modified version of this model is shown in Figure 1. This figure stipulates that the clauses 5-8 in sequence act to achieve continual

Figure 1. Continual quality improvement journey through ISO 9001:2000

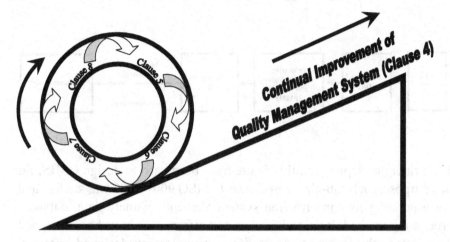

improvement of the QMS. This implies that any leveraging action that is intended to be applied through ISO 9001:2000 must have to begin from clause 4. Accordingly in the module of the research project being reported in this paper, the leveraging action through information system management has been applied through clause 4 of ISO 9001:2000. In order to carry out this leveraging action, clause 4 was searched to locate any stipulation about the information system management. Though there is no mentioning about MIS in clause 4, the listing d) given under sub-clause 4.1 specifies the need of the availability of information necessary to support the operation and monitoring of the processes included in QMS. This kind of monitoring information is inadequate to develop leveraging action and hence an exclusive design of QIS by referring to clause 4 is necessitated.

Quality Management Information System

In order to design QMIS, the traditional MIS principles were referred. This is due to the reason that traditional MIS principles have been found to offer powerful information system management solutions in organizations of all types. The fundamental tenet of MIS is that the collected data shall be processed using appropriate models to provide information to the target users (Laudon & Laudon, 2004; Stair & Reynolds, 2004; O'Brien, 2003). This methodology is depicted in Figure 2.

Figure 2. Traditional MIS methodology

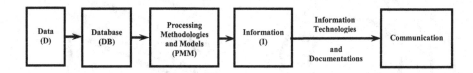

The principles depicted in this figure have been used to design QMIS. For this purpose, each sub-clause of clause 4 of ISO 9001:2000 was studied and, corresponding four information system elements, namely data, database, processing methodology, and models and information have been designed. As a sample, the design of information system elements designed pertaining to sub-clause 4.1 of ISO 9001:2000 is described in this section.

Sub-Clause 4.1 General Requirements

The contents of sub-clause 4.1 of ISO 9001:2000 (ISO, 2000, p. 2) are re-produced here: "The organization shall establish, document, implement and maintain a quality management system and continually improve its effectiveness in accordance with the requirements of this International standard.

The organization shall:

a. identify the processes needed for the quality management system and their application throughout the organization

b. Determine the sequence and interaction of these processes

c. Determine criteria and methods needed to ensure that both the operation and control of these processes are effective

d. Ensure the availability of resources and information necessary to support the operation and monitoring of these processes

e. Monitor, measure and analyze these processes, and

f. Implement actions necessary to achieve planned results and continual improvement of these processes."

Table 1. Data pertaining to the stipulations of sub-clause 4.1

Element Number	Data
D-1	ISO 9001:2000 standard.
D-2	List of processes needed for the QMS.
D-3	List of sequence and interaction required for the listed processes.
D-4	List of criteria and methods required for ensuring the effective operation and control of the listed processes.
D-5	List of locations indicating the availability of resources and information necessary to support the operation and monitoring of these processes.
D-6	List of methods to measure, monitor and analyze these processes and required actions for implementation.
D-7	List of planned results required for the QMS.
D-8	Data on continual improvement measures.

The data pertaining to the stipulations of sub-clause 4.1 have been identified and listed in Table 1.

The database requirements pertaining to the "data" of sub-clause 4.1 have been identified and are enumerated in Table 2.

The methods and models recommended for processing the data are presented in Table 3.

The information elements designed pertaining to clause 4.1 of ISO 9001:2000 standard are presented in Table 4.

The texts are italicized in Tables 1-4 to indicate that the stipulations are pertaining to QMIS. All the elements indicated in these tables are designed using the MIS process indicated in Figure 1. As a sample, the design of the first element indicated in the above tables is illustrated. As shown in Table 1, the data element denoted as D-1 (D stands for Data) pertaining to the first element is ISO 9001:2000 standard itself. As shown in Table 2, the database of this element deals with its electronic posting and deposition of its hard copy with the section head. This is denoted as DB-1 (DB stands for Database). As shown in Table 3, the indexing methodology and FAQs are stipulated as the processing methodologies and models of the sub-clause 4.1. This is denoted as PMM-1 (PMM stands for Processing Methodology and Models). Finally as indicated in Table 4, dissemination of the information is envisaged through physical disseminations and display in electronic environments. Thus a scientific approach incorporated with the principles of MIS (as indicated in Figure 2) was adopted to design QMIS.

Table 2. Database pertaining to the stipulations of sub-clause 4.1

Element Number	Database
DB-1	Posting of ISO 9001:2000 standard in an electronic environment with the provision for retrieving the data based upon the clause number, product, processes and procedures, and so forth. The hard copy of this standard may also be given to all employees or shall be deposited with section heads.
DB-2	Preparation of a handbook containing the processes needed for the QMS with proper chronological ordering and indexing procedures.
DB-3	Preparation of a handbook containing the sequence and interaction needed for the execution of the listed processes with proper chronological ordering and indexing procedures.
DB-4	Preparation of a handbook containing the criteria and methods needed for the execution of the listed processes with proper chronological ordering and indexing procedures.
DB-5	Preparation of a handbook containing the availability of resources and information with proper chronological ordering and indexing procedures
DB-6	Preparation of a handbook containing the methods to measure, monitor and analyze these processes with proper chronological ordering and indexing procedures.
DB-7	Preparing a pamphlet on planned results and posting it on strategic locations of the company. Electronic devices shall be chosen to accommodate the above database elements, which should enable easy retrieval of the required data within a fraction of second.
DB-8	Preparing a pamphlet containing data on continual improvement measures and posting it at strategic locations of the company.

Table 3. Processing methodology and models pertaining to the stipulations of sub-clause 4.1

Element Number	Processing Methodology and Models
PMM-1	An index of the keywords may be prepared with page numbers of ISO 9001:2000 standard, which should enable the user to obtain the right information. Besides, a list of frequently asked questions (FAQs) may be prepared to guide the users to get appropriate information from the standard. Display boards may be designed to paint the appropriate contents of ISO 9001: 2000 standard as required by the user.
PMM-2	An index of the keywords may be prepared with page numbers of handbook containing processes needed, which should enable the user to obtain the right information. Besides, a list of FAQs may be prepared to guide the users to get appropriate information from the handbook.
PMM-3	An index of the keywords may be prepared with page numbers of handbook containing sequences and interaction of the listed processes, which should enable the user to obtain the right information. Besides, a list of FAQs may be prepared to guide the users to get appropriate information from the handbook.
PMM-4	An index of the keywords may be prepared with page numbers of handbook containing criteria and methods needed for the execution of the listed processes, which should enable the user to obtain the right information. Besides, a list of FAQs may be prepared to guide the users to get appropriate information from the handbook.
PMM-5	An index of the keywords may be prepared with page numbers of handbook containing the availability of resources and information, which should enable the user to obtain the right information. Besides, a list of FAQs may be prepared to guide the users to get appropriate information from the handbook.

continued on following page

Table 3. continued

Element Number	Processing Methodology and Models
PMM-6	An index of the keywords may be prepared with page numbers of handbook containing the methods to measure, monitor and analyze, which should enable the user to obtain the right information. Besides, a list of FAQs may be prepared to guide the users to get appropriate information from the handbook.
PMM-7	Impressive font sizes and colors of the letters should be chosen for displaying planned results, which should enable the user to obtain information.
PMM-8	An impressive font size and color of the letters should be chosen for displaying data on continual improvement measures, which should enable the user to obtain right information.

Table 4. Information pertaining to the stipulations of sub-clause 4.1

Element Number	Information
I-1	Circulation of the stipulations of ISO 9001:2000 standard to the target users using circulars and display of the same through electronic media.
I-2	Circulation of the stipulations of processes needed for QMS to the target users using circulars and display of the same through electronic media
I-3	Circulation of the stipulations of sequence and interaction of the listed processes to the target users using circulars and display of the same through electronic media
I-4	Circulation of the stipulations of criteria and methods required for the execution of the listed processes to the target users using circulars and display of the same through electronic media
I-5	Circulation of the stipulations of availability of resources and information to the target users using circulars and display of the same through electronic media
I-6	Circulation of stipulations concerning the methods to measure, monitor and analyze the listed processes to the target users using circulars and display of the same through electronic media.
I-7	Pasting of the planned results in the locations where the target users are working and displaying the same through electronic media.
I-8	Posting of the continual improvement measures in the locations where the target users are working and displaying the same through electronic media.

Penetration of QMIS in Practice

Due to the economical availability of software and information technologies, modern companies have been incorporated with various elements of information systems (Bourlakis & Bourlakis, 2006; Ahmed et al., 2006). Hence it is expected that even without explicit enunciation, modern companies are likely to have been incorporated with a few or many elements of QMIS. Considering this probability, it was decided to estimate the penetration of ISO 9001:2000-based QMIS in a real time environment. For this purpose, a company involved in machining metal alloy components using a high technology-based machining system, namely CNC machining center, was approached. This company is situated in Coimbatore city of India. Large size companies place job orders with this company. The machined components are received by large size companies, which in turn are exported by them to the companies located in various parts of the world. Two reasons prompted the company to install ISO 9001:2000-based quality system and obtain certification from TUV. First reason is that, the customers from different parts of the world insisted on installing ISO 9001:2000-based quality system in the company. This is coinciding with the observation of Arauz and Suzuki (2004) who claim that the ISO 9000 certification provides opportunities for today's companies to obtain international recognition and establishment of the trade. The second reason was due to the desire of the managing partners for continually improving the quality of performance. Due to the personal acquaintance of first and second authors with one of the managerial partners, it was possible to obtain permission to estimate the penetration of QMIS in the company. In order to carry out this estimation process, a workbook containing the design specifications of ISO 9001:2000-based QMIS was prepared. In total there were 24 elements included in the workbook. The manager who is taking care of ISO 9001:2000 quality system maintenance was approached with this workbook.

The data to the questions of the workbook were collected by interviewing the manager as well as by referring to the records and through personal observation. After completion of data collection, the data were analyzed. The results indicated that the data pertaining to QMIS exist to the extent of 87% against the actual requirement. In the case of database, it is 50% against the requirements. However, it was understood that no activities pertaining to processing data and information have been carried out. These findings are depicted in Figures 3 and 4. These quantified results indicate that already the data and database have been created by the company while installing and managing ISO 9001:2000-based quality system implementation. This observation very much tallies with the stipulation of clause 4.1 of ISO 9001:2000. That is, in this clause, the word information is specified only once. Accordingly, the company has developed data and database to a good extent whereas the information is fully missed. It is understood that, despite the economical availability of Internet, intranet and extranet technologies, they are yet to be appropriately used by the company to leverage clause 4 of ISO 9001:2000 standard to create QMIS.

Figure 3. Analysis of responses under data

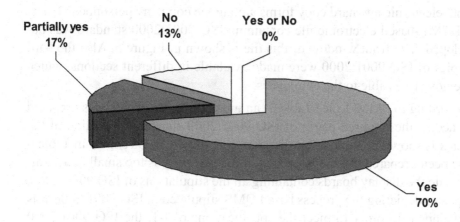

Figure 4. Analysis of responses under database

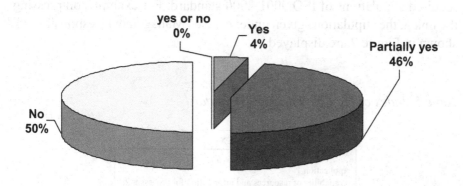

Development of QMIS

As the study on the penetration of QMIS revealed the existence of only the data and database, the remaining stipulations under the titles "Processing Methodology and Models" and "Information" had to be developed in the company. As a sample, the development of first and second elements listed under the QMIS is briefly presented here. The development of QMIS was started by referring to D-1 (see Table 1). According to its stipulation, the availability of ISO 9001:2000 standard was examined. Since this was not available, a copy of it was made available in the company. While referring to DB-1 (see Table 2), it was noted that ISO 9001:2000 was not available in both electronic and hard copy forms among the company personnel. Hence, a HTML-based electronic file containing ISO 9001:2000 standard was developed. The front window of this file is shown in Figure 5. Also the hard copies of ISO 9001:2000 were made available in different sections, which are now accessible to the employees.

According to PMM-1 (see Table 3) an index of the keywords was prepared to access the required pages of ISO 9001:2000 standard. A portion of the index is shown in Table 5. Further a sample of two FAQs shown in Table 6 has been prepared. As the floor area of the company is too small to accommodate the display boards containing all the stipulations of ISO 9001:2000, a poster depicting the process based QMS stipulated in ISO 9001:2000 was developed. In order to meet the specifications of I-1, the ISO 9001:2000 standard has been circulated among the target users, namely employees. Further, the HTML file shown in Figure 6 would enable the display of the required stipulations of ISO 9001:2000 standard. For example, on pressing the link 5, the stipulations given under clause "Management Responsibility" shown in Figure 7 are displayed.

Table 5. Index of the ISO 9001:2000 standard

INDEX
Application 1
Availability of resources and information for processes 2
Continual improvement 2
Control of documents 3
Criteria and methods for processes 2
Documentation requirements 2
Monitor, measure and analyze of processes 2
Normative reference 1
Planned results 2
Process for QMS 2
Quality management systems 2
Quality manual 2, 3
Quality objectives 2, 3
Quality policy 2, 3, 4
Records 2
Scope 1
Scope of QMS 3
Sequence and interaction of processes 2
Terms and definitions 1
Approved documents 3

Figure 5. Front window of HTML file containing ISO 9001:2000 standard

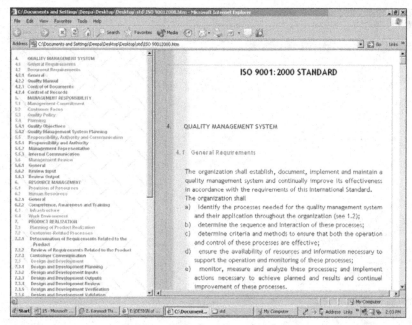

Figure 6. Display of the ISO 9001:2000 standard

Figure 7. Display of the contents of clause 5

Table 6. FAQs of the ISO 9001:2000 standard

1.	**From where I can get the hard and soft copies of the ISO 9001:2000 standard?**
	It is available on the PC and management representative's table.
2.	**What are the processes that take place in our company?**
	Refer pages 46 and 47 of quality system manual.

Table 7. List of processes needed for the QMS (arranged in the order of process numbers and clause numbers.)

Process Number	ISO 9001:2000 Clause Number	Process Description	Responsibility	Interacting Process
P01	4.2.3	Control of Documents	Management Representative	All Business Processes
P02	4.2.4	Control of Records	Management Representative	All Business Processes
P03	5.3	Quality Policy	Managing Partner	All Business Processes
P04	5.4.1	Quality Objectives		All Business Processes

continued on following page

Table 7. continued

Process Number	ISO 9001:2000 Clause Number	Process Description	Responsibility	Interacting Process
P05	5.4.2	Quality Management System Planning	Managing Partner	All Business Processes
P06	5.5.3	Internal Communication		All Business Processes
P07	5.6	Management Review	Managing Partner	All Business Processes
P08	6.1	Provision of Resources		P07, P11, P12, P15, P18, P21
P09	6.2.1	Human Resources		P11, P12, P15, P17, P18
P10	6.2.2	Training	Managing Partner	P03, P04, P11, P15, P17, P18, P21, P22
P11	7.1	Planning for Product Realization (Refer Annexure-I and Process Flow Chart PFC Series for Process Description/ Sequence in Detail)	Supervisor	P01, P02, P04, P08, P12, P13, P14, P15, P16, P18
P12	7.2	Determination & Review of Requirements Related to Product (Refer Process Flow Chart PFC-01)	Managing Partner	P11, P13, P14, P15, P16, P20
P13	7.2.3	Customer Communication		P02, P11, P12, P14, P15, P16, P19
P14	7.4	Purchasing Process (Refer Process Flow Chart PFC-02)		P11, P12, P13, P20
P15	7.5,	Production/Service Provision Process (Refer process Flow Chart PFC-03)	Managing Partner Supervisor	P06, P08, P11, P12, P14, P18, P20
	7.6	Control of Monitoring & Measuring Devices		
P16	8.2.1	Customer Satisfaction	Managing Partner	P03, P04, P11, P12, P13, P20
P17	8.2.2	Internal Audit	MR	All Business Processes
P18	8.2.3	Monitoring & Measurement of Product/Processes		P11, P15, P20
P19	8.3	Control of Non-Conforming Product	Managing Partner Supervisor	P13, P16, P17, P18, P20, P22
P20	8.4	Analysis of Data		P07, P12, P14, P15, P16, P18, P19, P21, P22
P21	8.5.1	Continual Improvement	All employees	All Business Processes
P22	8.5.2 & 8.5.3	Corrective Action & Preventive Action	Managing Partner Supervisor	All Business Processes

Table 8. List of processes needed for the QMS (arranged in the order of process description)

Process Number	ISO 9001:2000 Clause Number	Process Description	Responsibility	Interacting Process
P20	8.4	Analysis of data	Managing Partner Supervisor	P07, P12, P14, P15, P16, P18, P19, P21, P22
P21	8.5.1	Continual Improvement	All employees	All Business Processes
P01	4.2.3	Control of Documents	Management Representative	All Business Processes
P15	7.6	Control of monitoring & measuring devices	Managing Partner Supervisor	P06, P08, P11, P12, P14, P18, P20
P19	8.3	Control of Non conforming product	Managing Partner Supervisor	P13, P16, P17, P18, P20, P22
P02	4.2.4	Control of Records	Management Representative	All Business Processes
P22	8.5.2 & 8.5.3	Corrective action & Preventive action	Managing Partner Supervisor	All Business Processes
P13	7.2.3	Customer Communication	Managing Partner	P02, P11, P12, P14, P15, P16, P19
P16	8.2.1	Customer Satisfaction	Managing Partner	P03, P04, P11, P12, P13, P20
P12	7.2	Determination & Review of requirements related to Product (Refer Process flow chart PFC-01)	Managing Partner	P11, P13, P14, P15, P16, P20
P09	6.2.1	Human Resources	Managing Partner	P11, P12, P15, P17, P18
P17	8.2.2	Internal Audit	MR	All Business Processes
P06	5.5.3	Internal Communication	Managing Partner	All Business Processes
P07	5.6	Management Review	Managing Partner	All Business Processes
P18	8.2.3	Monitoring & Measurement of Product/Processes	Managing Partner Supervisor	P11, P15, P20
P11	7.1	Planning for Product Realization (Refer Annexure-I and Process flow chart PFC Series for process description/Sequence in detail)	Supervisor	P01, P02, P04, P08, P12, P13, P14, P15, P16, P18
P15	7.5,	Production/Service Provision Process (Refer process Flow Chart PFC-03)	Managing Partner Supervisor	P06, P08, P11, P12, P14, P18, P20
P08	6.1	Provision of Resources	Managing Partner	P07, P11, P12, P15, P18, P21
P14	7.4	Purchasing Process (Refer Process Flow Chart PFC-02)	Managing Partner	P11, P12, P13, P20
P05	5.4.2	Quality Management System Planning	Managing Partner	All Business Processes

continued on following page

Table 8. continued

Process Number	ISO 9001:2000 Clause Number	Process Description	Responsibility	Interacting Process
P04	5.4.1	Quality Objectives	Managing Partner	All Business Processes
P03	5.3	Quality Policy	Managing Partner	All Business Processes
P10	6.2.2	Training	Managing Partner	P03, P04, P11, P15, P17, P18, P21, P22

Table 9. Index of the QMIS handbook

INDEX
Controls needed to ensure changes, the current revision status of documents, relevant versions of applicable documents 2
Control of documents 9
Controls needed for approving documents 10
Controls needed to review, update and re-approve documents 11.
Controls needed for documents of external region 12.
Controls needed to prevent the unintended use of obsolete documents 12.
List of processes (Annexure II) 46
Interactions of processes 45
Quality policy 14
Quality objectives 14
Documents containing the procedure 51
Quality Manual 8
Scope of the QMS 51

While referring to D-2 (see Table 2), it became necessary to list the processes needed for the QMS. Unlike in the case of D-1, it was possible to extract immediately and easily the list of processes shown in Table 7 from the quality manual of the company. After this, the task of preparing QMIS handbook was started. According to the stipulations of DB-2 (see Table 2) the list of processes has been arranged according to the alphabetical ascending order of the process titles. This chronological ordering of the list of processes is shown in Table 8.

According to PMM-2, an index of titles of processes has been appended in the QMIS handbook. A portion of the page containing the index of titles is given Table 9. According to I-2, the stipulation of processes has been circulated among the employees using circulars. Besides, a poster facing the entry point of the company containing the list of processes was posted. The photograph showing the posted poster is presented in Figure 7. Further, the HTML file has been developed to portray the "sequence and interaction of the process."

Figure 8. Photograph showing the list of processes

Figure 9. Sequence and interaction of the processes

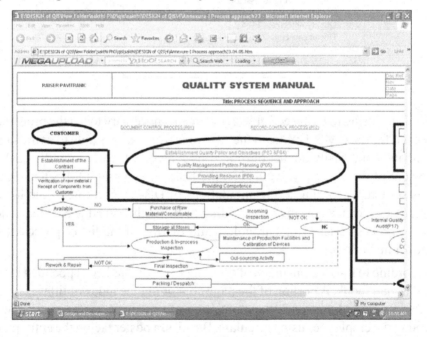

The front page of this HTML file is shown in Figure 8. In a similar way, the QMIS has been developed according to its design specifications.

Validation

In order to validate the QMIS, the managing partner was approached with a questionnaire. The questions asked and his responses in a Likert's scale of range from 0 to 10 are indicated in Table 10. As shown, the questions aimed to gather his assessment of the QMIS in achieving the requirements of the clause 4 of ISO 9001:2000. Since his reactions ranged between 6 and 8, it is inferred that the QMIS is practically compatible. Further he was asked an open question to write about his opinion on QMIS developed in his company. He reacted by writing the statement, "QMIS has improved the performance of the quality management system of my company." Thus the QMIS developed was validated for checking its effectiveness in a real time environment.

Results and Discussions

The advantages of developing QMIS are described here by referring to its two elements 1 and 2. As mentioned earlier, it was not even possible to locate ISO

Table 10. Validation questionnaire and results

Question Number	Question	Managing partner's reactions in a Likert's scale of range 0-10. (0 - Not at all; 5 - Partially; 10 - Fully)
1	To what extent has QMIS leveraged in meeting the general requirements of QMS (as specified in sub-clause 4.1 of ISO 9001:2000)?	8
2	To what extent has QMIS leveraged in meeting the general documentation requirements of QMS (as specified in sub-clause 4.2.1 of ISO 9001:2000)?	7
3	To what extent has QMIS leveraged in meeting the objectives of developing quality manual in QMS (as specified in sub-clause 4.2.2 of ISO 9001:2000)?	8
4	To what extent has QMIS leveraged in meeting the objectives of controlling documents in QMS (as specified in sub-clause 4.2.3 of ISO 9001:2000)?	6
5	To what extent has QMIS leveraged in meeting the objectives of controlling records in QMS (as specified in sub-clause 4.2.4 of ISO 9001:2000)?	7

9001:2000 standard in the company before the development of QMIS. This indicates that there existed a danger that the quality system of the company would be dragged away from ISO 9001:2000 standard. This means that the company was at the threshold of losing the benefits of implementing ISO 9001:2000. As mentioned earlier, after the development of QMIS, the copies of ISO 9001:2000 standard are made available to all the employees and a soft copy is posted electronically using a HTML file. Likewise, before developing QMIS pertaining to element 2, the list of processes was only available in the manual, which was not accessible to all employees. After the development of QMIS, the list of processes is made available in both document and electronic form. This activity enables the employees to be aware of the processes that take place in the company and thereby orients them towards attaining higher degree of quality in totality and continually. Further the validation study conducted after developing QMIS indicated its practical viability. As a whole, the development of QMIS in company led to an indication that QIS would be a leveraging mechanism to enhance the performance of clause 4 of ISO 9001:2000.

Conclusion

In order to face the ever-increasing degree of competition, companies have been striving to enhance the effectiveness of their working by adopting various approaches (Kaye & Anderson, 1999; Rho et al., 2001). When they are prescribed with completely new strategies, implementing them poses harder challenges. Moreover, the benefits of the heavy investment on strategies cannot be reaped back within the lifespan of the concerned projects. Hence it is preferable that companies adopt leveraging actions by adopting the existing and proven strategies. In this direction, the leveraging action of information system management by adopting the widely installed ISO 9001:2000-based quality system draws the attention. In order to examine this proposal, a research project has been carried out in which the QMIS in accordance with clause 4 of ISO 9001:2000 has been designed. This QMIS has been taken to an ISO 9001:2000 certified export-oriented high technology machining-based company. After getting the permission the relevant data were collected. The analysis of the data indicated that this company has progressed towards data elements of QMIS to a good extent and database elements to a reasonably satisfactory extent. However, the company has failed to incorporate the processing methodology and models and information elements of QMIS. In order to fill this gap, the QMIS elements missed in this company were developed. Finally QMIS was validated by gathering its assessment from the point of view of the company's managing partner. The experience of conducting the research project reported in this chapter instigates us to postulate that QMIS can be implemented without any difficulty in companies in which ISO 9001:2000-based quality system is installed. Since this company is aspiring to move forward in international market, the above postulation may hold true for most of the modern companies situated in different parts of the world. Hence, it is a reasonable proposal that modern companies adopt the QMIS presented in this paper and gain the synergic benefits of information systems and ISO 9001:2000 standard.

Acknowledgment

The authors gratefully acknowledge the help rendered by Mr. D. Edwin Joseph Raj, Assistant Professor, English Department, Government College of Technology, Coimbatore, India, toward enhancing the presentation quality of this article. The authors acknowledge with thanks the service rendered by Professor Angappa Gunasekaran, the editor of *International Journal of Enterprise Information Systems* and anonymous referees, toward reviewing this article.

References

Adeoti-Adekeye, W.B. (1997). The importance of management information systems. *Library Review, 46*(5), 318-327.

Aggelogiannopoulos, D., Drosinos, E.H., & Athanasopoulos, P. (2007). Implementation of a quality management system (QMS) according to the ISO 9000 family in a Greek small-sized winery: A case study. *Food Control, 18*, 1077–1085.

Ahmed, A.M., Zairi, M., & Alwabel, S.A. (2006). Global benchmarking for Internet and e-commerce applications. *Benchmarking: An International Journal, 13*(1/2), 68-80.

Arauz, R., & Suzuki, H. (2004). ISO 9000 performance in Japanese industries. *Total Quality Management, 15*(1), 3-33.

Bayati, A., & Taghavi, A. (2007). The impacts of acquiring ISO 9000 certification on the performance of SMEs in Tehran. *The TQM Magazine, 19*(2), 140-149.

Besterfield, D.H., Besterfield-Michna, C., Besterfield, G.H., & Besterfield-Sacre, M. (2004). *Total quality management*. India: Pearson Education.

Boiral, O., & Roy, M-J. (2007). ISO 9000: Integration rationales and organizational impacts. *International Journal of Operations & Production Management, 27*(2), 2007.

Bourlakis, M., & Bourlakis, C. (2006). Integrating logistics and information technology strategies for sustainable competitive advantage. *Journal of Enterprise Information Management, 19*(4), 389-402.

Chin, S., Kim, K., & Kim, Y-S. (2004). A process-based quality management information system. *Automation in Construction, 13*, 241-259.

Devadasan, S.R., Kathiravan, N., Sakthivel, M., Kulandaivelu, K., & Sundararaj, G. (2003). Financial accounting of ISO 9001:1994 based on quality information system. *The TQM Magazine, 15*(4), 275-285.

Forza, C. (1995). Quality information systems and quality management: A reference model and associated measures for empirical research. *Industrial Management & Data Systems, 95*(2), 6-14.

Gotzamani, K.D., & Tsiotras, G.D. (2001). An empirical study of the ISO 9000 standards' contribution towards total quality management. *International Journal of Operations and Production Management, 21*(10), 1326-1342.

Ho, S.K.M. (1999). Change for the better via ISO 9000 and TQM. *Management Decision, 37*(4), 381-385.

International Organization for Standardization (ISO). (2000). *Quality management systems—requirements*. Switzerland: International Organization for Standardization.

Juran, J.M., & Gryna, F.M. (1995). *Quality planning and analysis*. New Delhi: Tata McGraw – Hill Publishing Company Limited.

Kaye, M., & Anderson, R. (1999). Continuous improvement: The ten essential criteria. *International Journal of Quality & Reliability Management, 16*(5), 485-506.

Koc, T. (2007). The impact of ISO 9000 quality management systems on manufacturing. *Journal of Materials Processing Technology, 186*, 207–213

Kunnanatt, J.T. (2007). Impact of ISO 9000 on organizational climate: Strategic change management experience of an Indian organization. *International Journal of Manpower, 28*(2), 175-192

Lari, A. (2002). An integrated information system for quality management. *Business Process Management, 8*(2), 169-182.

Laudon, J.P., & Laudon, K.C. (2002). *Management information systems.* New Jersey: Prentice-Hall, Inc.

Magd, H.A.E. (2006). An investigation of ISO 9000 adoption in Saudi Arabia. *Managerial Auditing Journal, 21*(2), 132-147.

Mortinez-Lorente, A.R., & Martinez-Costa, M. (2004). ISO 9000 and TQM: Substitutes or Complementaries? An empirical study in industrial companies. *International Journal of Quality & Reliability Management, 21*(3), 260-276.

O'Brien, J.A. (2003). *Management information systems – managing information technology in the e-business enterprise.* India: Tata McGraw-Hill.

Oz, E. (2002). *Management information systems.* Singapore: Thomson Asia Pvt. Ltd.

Pearson, J.M., McCahon, C.S., & Hightower, R.T. (1995). Total quality management: Are information systems managers ready? *Information & Management, 29*, 251-263.

Peppard, J. (1995). Management challenges in information systems. *Journal of Information Technology, 10*, 127-130.

Pozzebon, M., & Titah, R. (2006). Combining social shaping of technology and communicative action theory for understanding rhetorical closure in IT. *Information Technology & People, 19*(3), 244-271.

Prajogo, D.I., Laosirihongthong, T., Sohal, A., & Boon-itt, S. (2007). Manufacturing strategies and innovation performance in newly industrialized countries. *Industrial Management & Data Systems, 107*(1), 52-68.

Rho, B-H., Park, K., & Yu, Y-M. (2001). An international comparison of the effect of manufacturing strategy – implementation gap on business performance. *International Journal of Production Economics, 70*, 89-97.

Singh, P.J., & Feng, M. (2006). ISO 9000 series of standards: Comparison of manufacturing and service organizations. *International Journal of Quality & Reliability Management, 23*(2), 122-142.

Singh, P.J. (2006). ISO 9000 in the public sector: A successful case from Australia. *The TQM Magazine, 18*(2), 131-142.

Stair, R.M., & Reynolds, G.W. (2001). *Principles of information systems – a managerial Approach* (5th Ed.). Singapore: Thomson Learning.

Subramanian, G.H., & Hoffer, C.S. (2005). An exploratory case study of enterprise resource planning implementation. *International Journal of Enterprise Information Systems, 1*(1), 23-38.

Tan, B., Lin, C., & Hung H-C. (2003). An ISO 9001:2000 quality information system in e-commerce environment. *Industrial Management and Data Systems, 103*(9), 666-676

Tari, J.J. (2005). Components of successful total quality management. *The TQM Magazine, 17*(2), 182-194.

Terlaak, A., & King, A.A. (2006). The effect of certification with the ISO 9000 quality management standard: A signaling approach. *Journal of Economic Behavior & Organization, 60*, 579–602.

Thaver, I., & Wilcock, A. (2006). Identification of overseas vendor selection criteria used by Canadian apparel buyers: Is ISO 9000 relevant? *Journal of Fashion Marketing and Management, 10*(1), 56070.

Themistocleous, M., Irani, Z., & O'Keefe, R.M. (2001). ERP and application integration – exploratory survey. *Business Process Management, 7*(3), 195-204.

Vouzas, F.K., & Gotzamani, K.D. (2005). Best practices of selected Greek organizations on their road to business excellence – the contribution of the new ISO 9000:2000 series of standards. *The TQM Magazine, 17*(3), 259-266.

Williams, J.A. (2004). The impact of motivating factors on implementation of ISO 9001:2000 registration process. *Management Research News, 27*(1/2), 74-84.

Zaramdini, W. (2007). An empirical study of the motives and benefits of ISO 9000 certification: The UAE experience. *International Journal of Quality & Reliability Management, 24*(5), 472-491

Chapter IX

Motivational Aspects of Legitimate Internet File Sharing and Piracy

Alan D. Smith, Robert Morris University, USA

Abstract

This chapter examines potential and active customers' intrinsic and extrinsic values associated with selected legal, ethical, and economic impacts of file sharing, especially in relationship to potential impacts on customer relationship management (CRM). The pros and cons of file sharing are highlighted in a conceptual model and empirically tested through graphical and statistical analysis through hypothesis testing, via factor analysis and principal component analysis (PCA) techniques. Recommendations on the potential growth of file-sharing industry, through the lens of price, competition, increased selection, and regulation, are included. These file sharing topics, issues, and concerns will have a variety of impact on potential and active customers, businesses, and strategic leveraging of CRM. The success of the P2P industry will depend on several important issues: copyright protection, communications infrastructure, and innovative pricing and payments strategies.

Introduction

File Sharing and the Emergence of MP3

With broadband Internet service becoming more accessible and affordable, there is an ever-growing group of users who are looking to exchange files with other users of similar interests. The concept of peer-to-peer (P2P) file sharing initially became popular when the digital music revolution hit in 1999 and Napster was introduced to the public. MP3s (MPEG Audio Layer 3) have revolutionized the music industry, and are considered the global ex facto standard for digital music. MP3s have CD quality sound but are relatively small in size because they are in digital format. Since they are a small file size it makes them easy to transfer over the Internet. These small files are transferred over two main types of servers and networks. They include pay Web sites where the user pays for each song downloaded and free sites where there is no cost to the user (Healy, 2002; *MP3 information*, 2004; Saroiu, Gummad, & Gribble, 2002). The ease and accessibility of these cost free files makes P2P file sharing very popular. Perhaps, the general public does not realize that P2P file sharing has moved past the exchange of digital music and into other entertainment mediums. Along with MP3 files, movies, video games and books are also readily available to download for free or a reasonable fee on the Internet.

All of these media types and more can be found through a variety of easy to use file sharing programs. A consumer can now find movies even before they are released in the theater. It is possible to download episodes of your favorite television shows, books, and audio books in MP3 formats. Magazines, video games and computer software are also available through such file-sharing programs (Clark & Tsiaparas, 2002). Unfortunately, due to the current copyright laws, these files can be considered by some to be illegal in nature.

Roots of File Sharing

One model of P2P file sharing is based around the use of a central server system, which directs traffic between individual registered users. The central servers maintain directories of the shared files stored on the respective PCs of registered users of the network. These directories are updated every time a user logs on or off the network. Each time a user of a centralized P2P file-sharing system submits a request for a particular file, the central server creates a list of files matching the search request by crosschecking the request with the server's database of files that are currently connected to the network. This is the model used by Napster and certain other P2P networks. This has also been the most successful model employed because it gave users fast, direct connections to each other (Aberer, Hauswirth, & Schmidt, 2002).

Napster, a peer-to-peer file-sharing program for MP3 files, experienced legal problems in just six short months of being in service. The lawsuit brought on by the Recording Industry Association of America caused Napster to change its method and philosophy of doing business (Heidmiller, 2002). Although Napster is no longer a free site, over 180 other file-sharing services entered the market to ease the distribution of files by providing a free network (Schwartz, 2004). These file-sharing services have grown rapidly in popularity mainly by word of mouth and via the Internet.

File-sharing programs work by making a connection to a network's central computer and automatically uploading a digital file that is currently on the user's hard drive and computer. These networks collect a master list of all the digital files from every user connected to its server (Schwartz, 2003). When looking for music, an individual can type in a name of a song or artist in a network's search engine. The network then will check its collective database obtained from every logged in user. Once a search is complete, it will display a list of songs from various users. After the user finds the desired file, he/she downloads and will be automatically sent the file thus completing the P2P file-sharing exchange. When connected to file-sharing program, one must also allow others to download music off their personal files and computer. These file-sharing networks are used most frequently for exchanging MP3 files, which most commonly is music (Schwartz, 2003). However, there are wide varieties of entertainment files currently available and there are other services to assist in the course of action of file sharing. Gnutella is a similar file-sharing program. Nullsoft, a subsidiary of America Online, originally designed Gnutella. AOL management halted Nullsoft's development of the Gnutella protocol shortly after the protocol was made available to the public (Aberer, Hauswirth, & Schmidt, 2002). Gnutella was only up on the Nullsoft for a few hours before it was taken down, but during that time several thousand downloads occurred. Using these downloads; programmers reverse-engineered the software and created their own unique Gnutella software packages.

However there are some unique qualities and differences. For one, Gnutella supports every type of file ranging from entertainment files to informational sources (Aberer, Hauswirth, & Schmidt, 2002). Secondly, there is no centralized computer like Napster. Therefore, it is very difficult for the legal process to take action against Gnutella file-sharing programs. The user connects to numerous peers, which serves as their connection to the network. These peers are then searched for the user's requested file. This process takes longer than a peer-to-peer file-sharing program and can take up to five minutes for a complete and thorough search. Gnutella programs have the capability to connect to one another allowing for a greater search and larger file library. Gnutella programs seem to be growing in popularity very rapidly. Gnutella is one of the most successful file-sharing networks today. It is undoubted that new file-sharing programs will be developed in the near future and as technology continues to rapidly change.

Overview of the Problem

File-sharing activities are easing the transfer of information from user to user (U2U) or P2P without much interaction from the affected industries. A major question is how the entertainment industry will adapt to this possible threat to their business and livelihood. There is the possibility for laws to be enacted or changed to accommodate this new and growing technology, with mixed results. Some in the music industry say that there should be payment by the individual obtaining the files, such as a monthly fee or "pay per download" (Kovacs, 2001). Current companies are testing this new business venture to see if this is a legitimate, profitable, and worthwhile option.

Since technology is rapidly changing, current laws cannot keep up with this continuing technology transformation. The actual laws may create a gray area for society. File sharing is becoming increasingly popular, breaking cultural and language barriers and allowing users to share files with one another around the world. However, there are issues that need to be addressed including ethical, economical, and legal concerns. Although the exact future of file sharing is unknown, its impact on customer relationship management (CRM) will be great. Some areas will include regulation, price and competition and increased selection, as reflected in the conceptual model presented in Figure 1.

Figure 1. Model of file sharing and its factors on how it will affect various industries and the public in the future

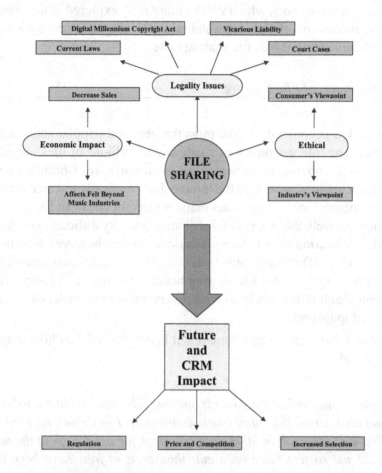

File Sharing and its Stimulants

Overview of Stimulants

File sharing is becoming an increasingly popular online activity and involves many elements of intrinsic and extrinsic motivation on behalf of both customers and businesses alike. The interaction of these factors may, in turn, cause numerous cause and effect relationships on business, consumers, and CRM implementations. Internet-based file-sharing activities are having a direct short-term economic impact on the entertainment industry; its full effect remains to be seen and felt. There are at least two very opinionated ethical arguments and viewpoints, which will be more fully explored in the coming sections. Government officials are watching, analyzing, and starting to react because of the legality issues file sharing raises.

Financial Impacts of File Sharing

File sharing has become one of the most frequent and popular activities on the Internet. The Internet serves as a gateway to millions of files including pictures, songs, movies, documents, and even software. Continuous and improving technology as well as the Internet has drastically lowered the cost of copying information and provides many outlets for cheap and almost free distribution. As well, these ways of distribution are very difficult to track and be traced. File sharing does have an economic impact, however, how much remains to be seen (Declining music sales ..., 2004). There has been research to support both sides – that file sharing benefits the music industry, while others argue that it is drastically and negatively impacting music, movie, and other related industries.

Jay Berman, Chairman of the International Federation of the Phonographic Industry stated:

Internet piracy means lost livelihoods and lost jobs, not just in record companies but also across the entire music community. For those who think the 10.9% first half sales fall in 2003 does not speak for itself, look at the other evidence. Artist rosters have been cut; thousands of jobs have been lost, from retailers to sound engineers, from truck drivers to music journalists. (Berman, 2003, p. 3)

From this quote it is clear that file sharing can definitely impact more than just the recording companies and the artists. According to recent statistics by the Recording Industry Association of America (RIAA), the number of CDs shipped in the U.S. fell from 940 million to 800 million (http://www.riaa.com), which is approximately 15% decline between 2000 and 2002 (*The Recording Industry Association of America's 2002 yearend statistics*, 2002; *Recording industry in numbers 2003*, 2003). The record industry has claimed this steady decline is due to file sharing. They view file sharing as stealing their products, and in some aspects consider it virtual shoplifting. Top-level managers in the entertainment industry feel their livelihood is at stake if file sharing is not stopped. This is why they are heavily lobbying the U.S. Congress to ensure their rights are protected and that their bottom line will not be impacted as significantly.

The other side of file sharing is that it is not having a negative economic impact. It cannot be argued that music sales have declined. However, it is more likely a lack of adaptation on managements' end rather than on technology. It is a basic fact that most products follow the product life cycle. It is important to note that a similar drop in record sales occurred in the late 1970s and early 1980s, and that record sales in the 1990s may have been abnormally high as individuals replaced records with compact disks (*Declining music sales ...*, 2004). The decrease in music sales can be attributed to many things. For instance, fewer and fewer albums are being produced and released. In addition, music is facing growing competition—as well as the entertainment industry—because of the growing focus on video games and digital-video disks (DVD). Both the video game industry and movie industry understand the importance of price (*Declining music sales ...*, 2004). Consequently these industries have increased promotions and significantly decreased their prices. They believe that by keeping prices in line with new technology it will not hurt or affect their sales significantly. Some consumers are turning to more independent labels as a backlash against record industry tactics and are tired of their monotonous music.

The many applications of file sharing are here to stay and the entertainment industry, as well as other industries, will need to adapt. Although regulation may eventually get in place, there are going to be legal loopholes and improving technology. File sharing is allowing information to get from one user to another user and this is only going to continue to get faster, quicker, and cheaper. The entertainment industry needs to concentrate on how they can incorporate file sharing into their business model. Some companies are and are having great success. The future of file sharing and how companies can possibly benefit from such technologies will be discussed further in this chapter.

Ethics and File Sharing

It used to be that when a person wanted to obtain the hot new artist or the hit blockbuster he or she would go to the mall to purchase the newly released album or movie. Today however, with the advent of file sharing networks such as Kazaa and Napster, there is a much simpler, and not to mention cheaper, method of obtaining the latest releases. Although these new techniques are effortless and essentially free, a new dilemma has arisen—is file sharing ethical? More specifically, do the people who participate in this practice maintain a different view of ethical standards?

Basically, the term ethical may be defined as conforming to acceptable professional standards of conduct. In general terms, it is unacceptable to steal or commit fraud and laws are enacted that prohibit these types of actions. If a person was to steal a car, someone's wallet, or expensive jewelry he or she would more than likely be sent to jail. In all of those situations it is easy to see that the person committing the crime had no recognition of or willingness to adhere to common ethical standards.

Thus, people need to take a long hard look at the practice of file sharing from two different points of view. First, the general public must put themselves in the shoes of the music and entertainment industries, such as television and film. Money and the ability to make a profit, as with many other facets of life, drive the aforementioned industries for without it they would not succeed. But what happens when the lifeblood of these industries, such as ticket and compact disc sales, are cut off? What are these companies and organizations to do? This may be due to the fact that file-sharing activities are a direct consequence of these industries' barriers that must now maneuver around.

As a result, many people in the music and entertainment industries would view the pirating of illegal music and videos as unethical. People are putting hundreds of man-hours into producing, directing, and editing music videos, television shows, and movies. Consequently, money must be paid to compensate these persons for their hard work. Companies then present their numerous products to the general public and expect a significant and large return. Nowadays, file sharing has made it possible to obtain songs before they are released, or even films prior to their debut in theaters. Thus, people are able listen to and view new material without paying a cent for any of it. The various industries are experiencing lost revenue and profits as a result. In their minds then, they feel that people are stealing directly and blatantly from them. An assortment of legal battles have been posed by the music and entertainment industries against a variety of P2P file sharing networks, which will be examined later on in the text.

The general public though has a different perspective. As will be found in the present research effort, the vast majority of professionals and semi-professionals surveyed saw nothing illegal or unethical about file sharing. Generally speaking, the consuming public may believe they are being fed the same repetitive music and lack sufficient music product choices. As Grimm (2003) suggested, "they [the music industry] fail to see that the revolution in music delivery occurred in reaction to the industry's mismanagement, not to mention its complicity in force-feeding the public a flavorless diet of sonic pabulum" (p. 1). Consequently, people across the nation were forced to go elsewhere for the music they crave.

Thus, persons all across America believe they are not the unethical ones, but rather the music recording industry is. Recording labels pay millions of dollars each year to radio stations across the country to play their packaged and refined artists. As a result, the public is dictated as to what the music selection they listen to (Grimm, 2003). In many instances, people across America believe that they have no say and are being controlled by a monopoly. Consequently, the general public turns to file sharing as an ethical practice to combat the entertainment industry control.

Legalities

Copyright Laws

The legal issues behind file sharing are very controversial. Many feel that sharing files is against the law, and in violation of many copyright laws. Meanwhile others feel that it is something that makes listening to their favorite recording artist, seeing a new movie or even looking at pictures from a recently printed magazine quick, easy and cost efficient. The copyright law is a federal law that protects owners of copyrighted materials. Owners of these materials are protected from unauthorized reproduction or distribution of the protected works through a license. Infringing on such rights differ in civil and criminal cases.

It is possible for a person to be prosecuted, even if the person had no prior knowledge of the infringement. Criminal penalties are available for international acts undertaken for purpose of private gain. The penalties apply whether there is a financial loss of the copyrighted or a gain by the defendant. Sound recording infringements can be punishable by up to five years in prison and $250,000 worth of fines (Recording Industry of America,

2004). Copyright laws ran for fourteen years with an equally long possible renewal. However, over the last 40+ years, the U.S. Congress has extended these laws approximately 11 different times. To the date of this research, the law extends copyrighting to about 70 years after the artist or creator's death and 95 years for those held by large and highly centralized corporations (An abuse of copyright, 2002). Approximately six years ago, the U.S. Congress extended copyrights by 20 years. This extension of copyright protection may directly restrict access to a large amount of copyrighted items, which also limits new talents from borrowing ideas and sampling songs.

Digital Millennium Copyright Act of 1998

The Digital Millennium Copyright Act of 1998 (DMCA) was enacted in response to the potential for a massive copyright infringement. This was due to the file sharing programs being established on the Internet. This law would protect the digital music industry and provide some form of flexibility in order for the Internet business and technologies to remain competitive (Heidmiller, 2002; Smith, 2004, 2005, 2006, 2007; Smith & Offodile, 2007).

Anti-Booting Law

The federal Anti-Booting Statute is punishable by five years in prison and large and substantial fines. This act covers the unauthorized recording and distribution of sound or video of artists. This practice is known as trafficking. Two of the most important legal concepts pertaining to the Internet are contributory infringement and the vicarious liability laws (Smith, 2002; Smith & Clark, 2005; Smith & Rupp, 2002a, 2002b).

Contributory Infringement and Vicarious Liability

Contributory infringement is the act of a person who induces or materially contributes to the infringing conduct of another and is usually done with the knowledge of the infringing acts. Vicarious liability laws may be enforced when a person has the right and the ability to control the actions of the person infringing upon the copyrighted material. In addition, they are receiving financial benefits from the infringement (Recording Industry of America, 2004; Smith, 2004).

The NET Act

To address the growing concerns digitally, legislation passed the No Electronic Theft Act (NET). The NET Act describes in detail the copyright laws that focus on the infringement occurring on the Internet. An encroachment of a copyright occurs when a song is made available to the public by uploading it to an Internet site. Consequently, other people are capable of downloading and sharing files through e-mail. This includes reproduction without authorization. The NET Act states that infringement can occur whether or not money has been or will be exchanged. In a criminal case, if a financial loss by the copyright holder or a financial gain by the infringing party can be proven, there can be legal consequences (Recording Industry of America, 2004).

P2P Piracy Prevention Act

The major recording labels have requested legal support to put an end to file-sharing networks. A bill is being revised by U.S. Congress to help provide copyright holders with various methods to combat piracy, which is referred to as the P2P Piracy Prevention Act. This act refers to basically all Internet open networks, which are file-sharing networks in which Internet users can send and receive files. If the P2P Piracy Prevention Act were to get passed by U.S. Congress in its entirety, copyright holders will be able to block and disable P2P distribution of music without permission of the copyright holder. Copyright holders will not be allowed to completely remove files from personal computer hard drives, but the users will not be able to sue copyright holders if the files get accidentally deleted (Recording Industry of America, 2004).

Kazaa

Kazaa, a strong successor of Napster, is creating a difficult situation for the U.S. Supreme Court. It is unclear whether or not the U.S. government has jurisdiction over Kazaa. Sharman Networks Inc. currently distributes this file-sharing program. Kazaa is incorporated in the South Pacific Island nation of Vanuatu. Kazaa is managed in Australia (Winstein, 2003). As a result of their international location, U.S. governmental agencies may find it to be a difficult dilemma when using regulation in the file sharing industry.

Recording and motion picture companies asked for the creators and inno-
vators of Kazaa to be liable for copyright infringement. Furthermore these
companies are trying to prove that they are being hurt financially from the
service. Another reason why the U.S. court is having trouble shutting down
Kazaa is because they have no copyrighted material. All of the files transferred from Kazaa go from computer to computer, so essentially, there is no
central server.

Non-Entertainment

File sharing is expandable beyond the entertainment industry, as well as its
legal ramifications. More specifically, CoStar sued LoopNet, stating that the
company used copyrighted pictures to post real estate listings on its Web
site. LoopNet argued that there was no knowledge of infringements and
that they should not be held liable. However, according to the law, even if
the company did not have prior knowledge, they are still held accountable
(Heidmiller, 2002).

As another non-entertainment example, Hendrickson sued eBay. Hendrickson stated that eBay was participating in the unlawful sale of pirated digital
videodisk movies. Hendrickson argued that eBay was involved in the piracy
and that they should be held accountable. However, eBay is a site that allows
users to sell goods and services, and they have no direct connection with the
items auctioned, sold, or purchased (Heidmiller, 2002).

Methodology and Statistical Analysis

Purposes and Statistical Techniques

Some of the more important aspects of Internet file sharing have been discussed, including economic impact, ethical issues, and the legality of file
sharing. A variety of perspectives have been explored as to portray some of
the major views on file sharing. However, there is a need to empirically explore selected intrinsic and extrinsic motivations on the part of the potential
and active P2P file-sharing user in terms of music products and/or services,
especially in relation to CRM concepts. Regulation of file sharing, price and

competition in the entertainment industries, and increased music selection were all recognized as potential future results of the current file sharing practices and habits.

However, to support the various research propositions inherent in the model presented in Figure 1, a number of statistical techniques used to test specific hypotheses that deal with the elements in the model are made. As a result, a total of 60 fully employed professional and semi-professional service management and Internet users, representing a college-educated and knowledge-based sample, was derived from the metropolitan section of Pittsburgh, PA. Three companies in the service sector were selected due to time and convenience factors and 60 out of a possible 116 individuals were successfully interviewed for the purposes of this study, representing an assortment of backgrounds, age groups, and gender distributions.

The initial personal survey conducted focused on a wide variety of aspects dealing with the entertainment industry and file sharing, with questions ranged from how many compact discs do you currently purchase per month to how ethical do you feel file sharing is and why do you engage in Internet file sharing? The personal survey that was interviewed and collected can be found in Appendix A. From these inquiries and questions, a relatively interesting and revealing body of knowledge was gathered, especially in terms of the importance of CRM concepts on potential and active participants' views on Internet file-sharing motivations, both intrinsic and extrinsic in nature. In order to accomplish testing the validity of the model previously presented in Figure 1, a variety of data reduction techniques [factor analysis and principle components analysis (PCA)], multiple regression, graphical analyses, and cross-tabulation procedures were employed. However, principal components and factor analyses techniques will be the dominant multivariate statistical procedures to be used in this research effort.

Principal component analysis (PCA) is a classical linear transform statistical method, which has been widely used in data analysis and compression (Bishop, 1995; Cumming, 1993). The technique is based on the statistical representation of a random variable X (Oja, 1989). For p such random variables,

$$X' = [X_1, X_2, ..., X_p] \tag{1}$$

The objective of PCA is to make p linear combinations of these variables in such a way that each captures as much of the variation in X as possible. In doing so though, each of the principal components must be linearly independent of the others. Thus, the linear combination of a principal component Y_j, of p variables with unknown coefficients $\hat{\beta}_1, \hat{\beta}_2, ... \hat{\beta}_p$ is given by,

$$Y_j = \hat{\beta}_1, X_{1j} + \hat{\beta}_2 X_{2j} + ... + \hat{\beta}_p X_{pj}, \quad \text{for} \quad j = 1, 2, ..., n \quad (2)$$

Equation (2) can be represented using a matrix notation of the form,

$$\hat{\beta} = \begin{bmatrix} \hat{\beta}_1 \\ \hat{\beta}_2 \\ \cdot \\ \cdot \\ \cdot \\ \hat{\beta}_p \end{bmatrix}, \quad Y = \begin{bmatrix} Y_1 \\ Y_2 \\ \cdot \\ \cdot \\ \cdot \\ Y_p \end{bmatrix}, \quad \text{and} \quad X = \begin{bmatrix} X_{11} & X_{21} & \cdot & \cdot & \cdot & X_{p1} \\ X_{12} & X_{22} & \cdot & \cdot & \cdot & X_{p2} \\ \cdot & \cdot & & & & \cdot \\ \cdot & \cdot & & & & \cdot \\ \cdot & \cdot & & & & \cdot \\ X_{1n} & X_{2n} & \cdot & \cdot & \cdot & X_{pn} \end{bmatrix}.$$

With this matrix representation, the principal component can be written as,

$$Y = X\hat{\beta} \quad (3)$$

In general, if the data are concentrated in a linear subspace, this provides a way to compress data without losing much information and simplifying the representation. Hence, by picking the eigenvectors having the largest eigenvalues, as little information as possible in the mean-square sense is lost. Therefore, by choosing a fixed number of eigenvectors and their respective eigenvalues hopefully a consistent representation or abstraction of the data will emerge. This procedure preserves a varying amount of energy of the original data. Alternatively, we can choose approximately the same amount of energy and a varying amount of eigenvectors and their respective eigenvalues.

This would, in turn, give approximately consistent amount of information at the expense of varying representations with regard to the dimension of the subspace. Unfortunately, when using principal conpoments anaylsis, there are contradictory goals. On one-hand, we should simplify the problem by reducing the dimension of the representation. The other choice is to preserve as much of the original information content as possible. PCA offers a convenient way to control the trade-off between loosing information and simplifying the problem at hand. Thus, it may be possible to create piecewise linear models by dividing the input data to smaller regions and fitting linear models locally to the data. However, PCA is only a transformation process.

The factor analysis process is a representation of the general case with no regard to which components of the input vector are either composed of independent or dependent variables. This arrangement will have not committed the reseacher to a certain relationship between the vector components or named any components as the inputs or the outputs of the researched relationships of consumer behavior towards file sharing activities. Therefore, through these statistical procedures, the ability to constrain any component of the input vector to be constant and to fetch the rest of the vector values with the aid of known values will be possible. Suppose that as in (4) p is the set of responses for the multivariate system of interest. Then, the general factor analysis model is:

$$Y_j = \hat{\beta}_1 X_{1j} + \hat{\beta}_2 X_{2j} + \ldots + \hat{\beta}_m X_{mj} + d_j U_j, \quad \text{for} \quad j = 1, 2, \ldots, n \quad (4)$$

Each of the m terms in (4) represents factor contributions to the linear composite while the last is the error term.

Basic Analysis and Results

Economically, Internet file sharing has become a pitfall for the music, film, and entertainment industries. No longer are people who currently or have file shared willing to purchase as many compact discs or pay as much for them as they would prior to the file sharing revolution. These phenomena can be witnessed as one compares the graphs of active Internet P2P user versus the major questions or items on the personal survey, as demonstrated in the various components in Figure 2.

It is important to research the ethical beliefs of people when it comes to file-sharing programs on the Internet. As evident from the plots in Figure 2, is a wide view of ethical standards when it comes to file sharing, but out of the entire sample, only five males and females felt file sharing is a very unethi-

Figure 2. Cross-tabulation of an active user of P2P sharing versus the major components of the personal survey

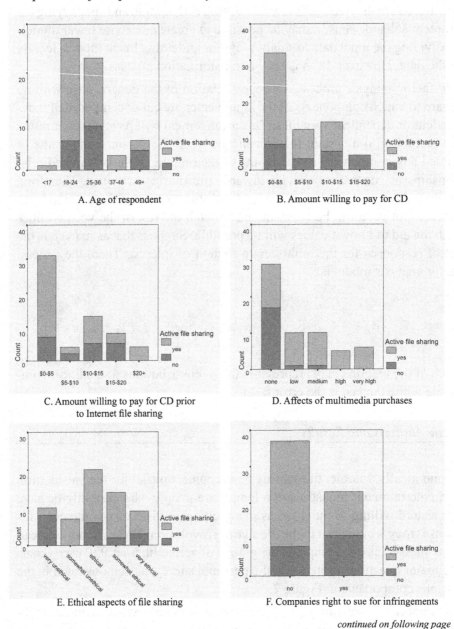

A. Age of respondent

B. Amount willing to pay for CD

C. Amount willing to pay for CD prior
to Internet file sharing

D. Affects of multimedia purchases

E. Ethical aspects of file sharing

F. Companies right to sue for infringements

continued on following page

Figure 2. continued

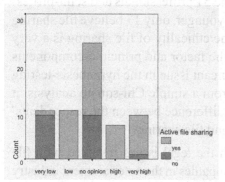

G. Perceived survey level in file-sharing activities

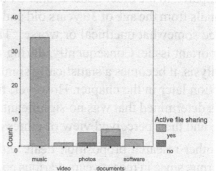

H. Type of file sharing categories

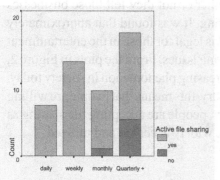

I. Frequency of participation in file sharing

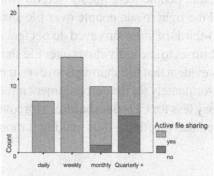

J. Place of participation in file sharing

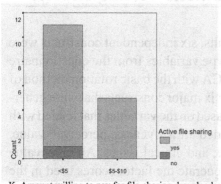

K. Amount willing to pay for file-sharing downloads

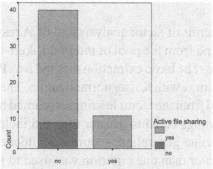

L. Willingness to pay for file sharing

cal practice. Also, a basic intuitive research proposition is that the younger generations would be more apt to perceive file sharing as an ethical practice compared to the older generations. Of the 51 professionals and semi-professionals from the age of 36 years old and younger, only 13 believe file sharing to be somewhat unethical or worse. The ethicality of file sharing is a very important issue. Consequently, during the factor and principle-components analysis, it becomes a statistically significant issue in the hypothesis-testing section later in the chapter. However, from a simple Chi-square analysis, it was determined that was no significant difference between the respondents' age and their perceived view of ethics and file sharing.

Another research proposition dealt with the legal issues involved with file sharing, since in recent years, various companies in the entertainment industry have filed numerous lawsuits against those who have pirated their material. As a result, people were questioned on whether or not they felt those businesses had the right to sue people over file sharing. It was found that approximately two-thirds of those surveyed do not feel it is legal for those in the entertainment industries to sue individuals over file sharing issues. From the plots in Figure 2, it is evident that file sharing is an ever-increasing phenomenon in society today. Unfortunately for the entertainment industry, this means that people are willing to pay less for CDs than before. Moreover, people are accepting file sharing as an ethical practice—thus making it more widely accepted and utilized.

Factor Analysis and Hypothesis-Testing Results

In terms of factor analysis and PCA results, six independent constructs were found from the pool of interval Likert-type variables from the questionnaire data. The basic extraction method was PCA with the basic rotation method of varimax with Kaiser normalization. The six major constructs that were generated from the factor loadings, renamed based on the variables that loaded with loadings equal to greater than 0.5 included attractiveness, perceived value, revenue generation, security confidence, and ethical issues. An eigenvalue greater than one criterion was used to generate the factor scores used in the analysis. The dependent variable chosen to be regressed against these major independent factor-based constructs was being an active Internet P2P user, as illustrated in Figure 2. Tables 3 and 4 present the hypothesis-testing results of regressing the six independent factor-based scores or constructs against being an active Internet P2P user.

As evident from the statistics displayed in Tables 3 and 4, the basic tenets of attractiveness, perceived value, revenue generation, security confidence, and ethical issues accounted for 64.5% (adjusted 46.7%) of the explained variance in active Internet P2P users and were statistically significance (F=3.626, P=0.039). In terms of the most important independent variable constructs (Table 4) were ethical issues (i.e., not an ethical problem when dealing with Internet-based file sharing activities) and increased security confidence in filing sharing among active users.

Discussion

Future and CRM Impacts

As evident from the model in Figure 1 and the hypothesis-testing results (Table 1 through 4), consumers typically benefit from maximizing or directly increasing their value-added payoffs when using file-sharing options over the

Table 1. Total variance explained on the six independent factor-based constructs

Factor	Initial Eigenvalues			Extraction Sums of Squared Loadings			Rotation Sums of Squared Loadings		
	Total	% of Variance	Cumulative %	Total	% of Variance	Cumulative %	Total	% of Variance	Cumulative %
Attractiveness	3.467	28.894	28.894	3.467	28.894	28.894	2.515	20.957	20.957
Perceived Value	2.286	19.051	47.944	2.286	19.051	47.944	2.181	18.172	39.129
Revenue Generation	1.845	15.376	63.321	1.845	15.376	63.321	2.058	17.146	56.275
Security Confidence	1.468	12.232	75.552	1.468	12.232	75.552	1.842	15.352	71.627
Ethical Issues	1.218	10.154	85.706	1.218	10.154	85.706	1.689	14.079	85.706

Extraction Method: Principal Component Analysis

Table 2. Varimax rotated-component matrix displaying the factor loadings into each major independent construct, in decreased order of importance

	Attractiveness	Perceived Value	Revenue Generation	Security Confidence	Ethical Issues
What is your age?	.341	.168	-.808	.154	2.810E-02
How many CDs do you purchase per month?	.594	-.195	.308	-.271	.498
Prior to filing sharing how much were you willing to pay for a CD?	.840	.277	-.264	.238	.152
How much are you currently willing to pay for a CD?	.803	-5.979E-02	-.106	-.103	.104
Has file sharing affected you multi-media purchases?	.595	.569	-8.402E-02	.252	-.120
Do you feel that file sharing is ethical?	.161	-4.632E-02	-4.043E-02	.204	.933
Do you think that companies have the right to sue individuals who participate in file sharing of their products/services?	3.242E-02	.830	.183	-.291	-9.738E-02
What level of security do you have in file sharing?	.198	4.776E-02	-.113	.936	7.823E-02
How often do you participate in file sharing?	.524	9.648E-02	-.305	-.739	-1.826E-02
Would you pay for a file sharing service?	3.342E-02	.887	-7.878E-02	.158	.104
If yes, how much would you be willing to pay per month?	-7.253E-03	.435	.820	.120	-5.721E-02
What is your gender?	-2.435E-03	-.177	.635	.162	-.701

Extraction Method: Principal Component Analysis

Rotation Method: Varimax with Kaiser normalization

Note: Rotation converged in 14 iterations

Table 3. ANOVA results of testing active Internet P2P user as predicted by the factor-based constructs

A. Model summary

R	R Square	Adjusted R Square	Std. Error of the Estimate
.803	.645	.467	.18

B. ANOVA table

	Sum of Squares	df	Mean Square	F	Sig.
Regression	.604	5	.121	3.626	.039
Residual	.333	10	3.333E-02		
Total	.937	15			

Note, Predictors: (Constant), REGR factor score 5 for analysis, REGR factor score 4 for analysis, REGR factor score 3 for analysis, REGR factor score 2 for analysis, REGR factor score 1 for analysis

Table 4. Statistical results of individual coefficients in the factor-based hypothesis test

	Un-Standardized Coefficients		Standardized Coefficients	t	Sig.
	B	Std. Error	Beta		
(Constant)	1.938	.046		42.452	.000
REGR factor score 1 for analysis (Attractiveness)	2.734E-02	.047	.109	.580	.575
REGR factor score 2 for analysis (Perceived Value)	8.186E-02	.047	.327	1.737	.113
REGR factor score 3 for analysis (Revenue Generation)	-4.843E-02	.047	-.194	-1.027	.328
REGR factor score 4 for analysis (Security Confidence)	.104	.047	.416	2.205	.052
REGR factor score 5 for analysis (Ethical Issues)	-.140	.047	-.561	-2.976	.014

Note, Dependent Variable: Active file sharing

Web. However, technology is rapidly changing and businesses are recognizing this untapped market and revenue. This section will discuss future aspects of file sharing and P2P networks and how it is affecting basic principles of CRM. More specifically, the three main CRM issues of price and competition, increased selection, and regulation are examined.

Price and Competition

The current forces shaping the future file sharing will continue to break down the fixed-pricing cartel of the profitable and large music labels and create increased competition, as evident by the lack of moral or ethical dilemmas associated with downloading music and other products over the Web. The breakdown in this monopoly began with free file-sharing services. These file-sharing services have led to severe price competition in the industry, both on the Internet and in the retail stores. According to Fattah (2002), file-sharing activities have contributed to lower suggested retail prices, aggressive discounting, and the creation of new legitimate online music stores. For example, Apple has introduced a music site called iTunes, Roxio has revived Napster as a legitimate site, Microsoft created MSN Music, and many other companies have recently created legitimate music Web sites. Prices for downloading music files, movies, games, and software legally start as low as $0.49 per month for unlimited downloading at some non-mainstream Web sites (Fattah, 2002), as compared to iTunes, which charges $0.99 per song downloaded. Meanwhile the business giant Wal-Mart retail chain charges $0.88 per song downloaded on its company Web site (*Wal-Mart music downloads*, 2004). These prices are well below what is the music industries' suggested retail price to purchase a CD in the retail marketplace.

Although the free version of Napster was shut down a few years ago, free file-sharing sites still exist and are gaining popularity. Some of the current free P2P Web sites in operation include BearShare, LimeWire, Kazaa, Morpheus, OpenNap, Aimster, Freenet, DirectConnect, eDonkey2000, and Mojo Nation (Fattah, 2002; Smith, 2004). Each Web site operates differently and has a different degree of visibility. BearShare and LimeWire provide free access to an array of multimedia files. Kazaa and Morpheus provide targeted searches and information about the files. OpenNap is an underground version of Napster. Aimster incorporated instant messaging technology into its file-sharing program. Freenet claims to keep its users' information anonymous so that users cannot be prosecuted for piracy. DirectConnect and Mojo Nation provided service based on how many files a user contributes to their network. Edonkey2000 is noted primarily for downloading movies. These free services can provide an overview to businesses of what customer demands are present in the marketplace.

Free file-sharing services appear to be in existence only to hurt the entertainment industry, but they do serve a purpose. Free Web sites allow users to find and try out music before they purchase it. This function eliminates the consumer's reliance on the music industry to find and promote new artists. However, some in the entertainment industry argue that free file-sharing Web sites are lowering the perceived price of music, movies, games, and software. Prices are also falling based on the changing of the basic economics of the music industry. In the past, music labels would take on market risk in exchange for a potential profit. The market risk included the search, development, and distribution of artist's music (Fattah, 2002). The music labels in return would be compensated by consumers for the risk they took by paying a high price for the music they bought. File sharing takes out a large portion of the risk that the music labels took because consumers can find the artists themselves. Lower risk leads to a lower return, thus lower prices for music and other entertainment goods.

It is the author's opinion that the entertainment industry should work in cooperation with file-sharing sites to get free research about the popularity of artists and their music prior to the promotion and distribution of their music. This cooperation would lower the cost of promotion because the industry would only be promoting and distributing music that has also been proven to be popular with the consuming public. This enhanced cooperation between the music industry and file-sharing services will also help to keep customers satisfied with the variety of music that they promote.

Increase Selection

File sharing is often mostly associated with music. However, file-sharing activities are growing rapidly and integrating into every facet for many consumers. The movie industry is fearful of file sharing. In fact, some movies are even being available on the Internet via file-sharing options before the movie is even released to the normal retail outlets. Although this begs the question of legality issues and concerns, it is undoubtedly a reality that most consumers have, as the results of the present study show, no problem in accepting as status quo. If the entertainment industry can adopt file sharing and strategically leverage the new technology, they may truly benefit their consumers. There would be an increased selection in many facets, including the types of media available via file sharing and an increase in the number of sites and services. In addition, there are many other industries that can benefit from file sharing, and this will indeed benefit the consumer and business CRM techniques.

One industry that is already adopting file-sharing options is the financial industry. P2P technologies and file sharing has be used as an integral collaboration tool for financial companies. These P2P technologies are possible because of standards in common messaging formats and also the move to Internet-friendly languages, most notably XML (Bielski, 2001; Smith, 2004). This language allows the possibility to exchange files, programs, and even how computer power is deployed. P2P technology has many benefits including the ease of retrieving data but also the possibility for Web collaboration. This will allow e-banking institutions, as well as traditional banking and financial services, have a greater profit with more options for consumers. The file-sharing process will allow the distribution of reports that contain information from various sources and is able to be compiled using the peer-to-peer technologies (Bielski, 2001). This process will continue to become increasingly automated, and will greatly simplify the process for the both the business and the consumer. This will also allow banks and other financial institutions to serve their customers in enhanced and extended modes, such as being able to process special requests sooner. Furthermore, additional information will be more readily available to the consumer because of file-sharing options. Most of this new information will be concerned with researching new securities and other investment options (Bielski, 2001). Not only will their CRM techniques improve but it will also improve their bottom line greatly.

Another industry that is being affected by file sharing is the electronic book industry. E-books are growing in popularity as an alternative to printed materials. An e-book is essentially a book that is a collection of bits of data that can be stored on a hard drive, CD-Rom or a network (Van Hoorebeek, 2003). In order to read these books a user does need a specialized reader program. Probably the main industry that is bringing attention to this is the academic book industry. Academic e-books typically do not need a specialized reader, which is a growing concern. Academic e-books' legitimate and illegal file sharing sites are one of the fastest growing sectors in this industry (Van Hoorebeek, 2003). The book industry is one of the few industries that are trying to profit by adapting file-sharing techniques. Most book publishers are including discounts if a customer buys an e-book rather than the hard copy. This is allowing the customer to have the information to be portable in nature.

File-sharing options will continue to integrate Internet-based technologies into the routine decision-making of active Web-enabled users, as well as millions of other potential P2P users that adapt to the openness and convenience of use of the widespread connectivity that is so characteristic of the Web. As Web sites that link friends and family, such as facebook.com and friendster. com, continue to grow in popularity, file sharing could be included on them. This will allow families and friends to exchange photos, home videos, and much more (Schwartz, 2004). Many industries recognize these important business opportunities and are adapting to file-sharing technology by increasing selection and product offerings because they have another affordable and alternative outlet of distribution.

Regulations

The whole issue of Internet-based file sharing has led to the development of a new industry. Copyright holders have been hiring companies to use new technologies and create programs to prevent piracy. The implementation of controls can help regulate this phenomenon and possibly help to bridge a gap between those for and those against file sharing. Altnet is based out of Los Angeles and it delivers files from copyright holders safely to the P2P program, Kazaa. Altnet offers very reasonably priced distribution and, in the meantime, controls piracy. Both Altnet and Kazaa receive a fee for each file downloaded (Healy, 2002).

Many companies are deciding whether or not to sue individuals using P2P networks. To find out exactly who is sharing files and downloading music, the companies get information from Internet Service Providers such as America Online, Comcast, and Net Zero. Lawsuits have already been filed against Kazaa, Morpheus and other online file sharing companies in a strong effort to close them down in a permanent fashion.

Many music executives are very reluctant to acknowledge the fact that they cannot stop the Internet file sharing, but they are trying to influence consumers in a way that stops them. The major companies along with the Recording Industry Association of America (RIAA) have enlisted popular recording artists to take a stand against file sharing (Healy, 2002). Some of these artists include U2 and Metallica. Most of the record companies have invented anti-copying compact discs that make it impossible to play or download without causing the computer to crash. These examples are typical strategies used by the music industry to help regulate file-sharing activities. Most of these regulatory strategies were initially designed to stop file sharing, but have only served to temporarily slow down the adoption process. However, no matter what preventative strategies are in place, technology is ever-changing and computer users and P2P users will continue to find way to circumnavigate the regulatory system in place and continue their Internet-based file-sharing activities.

General Conclusion and Implications

A major component in the CRM process that is driving the increased use of Internet-based file sharing is the mode of communication. The Internet allows users to have instantaneous access to an immeasurable wealth of knowledge and information. Businesses must adapt to this ever growing and emerging practice of file sharing or risk losing out on opportunities that these changes in the entertainment industry may bring. Although there will continue to be free file-sharing services, it is possible for business and the entertainment industry to have successful CRM. Companies such as Apple with their iPod are adapting to the benefits of this technology and are experiencing revenues from increased user traffic and music downloads. While Apple is utilizing a high marketing campaign to make the public aware of this technology and their product, it will be customer relationship management that will make this practice lucrative for such companies. The legal and governmental polices are continuing to change as technology changes but there is a slight lag.

Even though file sharing is extremely popular, one must look back at the product life cycle of compact disks and wonder if file sharing will have similar results. The success of the P2P industry will depend on several important issues: copyright protection, communications infrastructure, and pricing and payments strategies, whether it is per song or by subscription. There is an obvious need for low-priced distribution of music, along with convenient methods of purchase. Music should be sold inexpensively over the Internet so the consumers do not resort to pirating. They will need to persuade their consumers to pay for a service that was once free. Many will be willing to subscribe to a reasonably priced service that offers fast, convenient, accurate downloads for music that is freely available elsewhere, regardless of convenience of use, as evident in the empirical section of the present study.

File-sharing options will continue to bring about new technological break-throughs. It is vital to remember that file sharing is expanding beyond the perimeter of entertainment industry. File sharing will continue to impact society as well as various other industries, and most active users of such materials, as evident from the statistical results of the present study, see value-added and have essentially no ethical issues in using filing sharing. It is only when these industries recognize file sharing and its correlation with CRM that success will be possible.

References

Aberer, K., Hauswirth, M., & Schmidt, R. (2002, January-February). Improving data access in P2P Systems. *IEEE Internet Computing* [Online]. Retrieved from http://computer.org/internet/.

An abuse of copyright. (2002, October 11). *The New York Times.*

Berman, J. (2003, December). *IFPI Network Newsletter* [Online]. Retrieved from www.ifpi.org/site-content/library/newsletter9.pdf.

Bielski, L. (2001, June). Peer-to-peer technology. *American Bankers Association Journal*, 56-62.

Bishop, C.M. (1995). *Neural networks for pattern recognition*. Oxford, UK: Oxford University Press.

Clark, J.A., & Tsiaparas, A. (2002, January). Bandwidth-on-demand networks – a solution peer-to-peer file sharing. *BT Technology Journal*, *20*(1), 53-61.

Cumming, S. (1993). Neural networks for monitoring of engine condition data. *Neural Computing and Applications, 1*(1), 96-102.

Declining music sales: it's not all digital downloading. (2004, April 3). NPD Group, Inc.Retrieved from http://www.npd.com/press/releases/press_030605.htm.

Fattah, H. (2002). *P2P: How peer-to-peer technology is revolutionizing the way we do business*. Chicago, IL: Dearborn Trade Publishing.

Grimm, M. (2003). … 'bout your g-g-generation.' *American Demographics*, *25*(7). 38.

Healy, M. (2002, October 17). Don't steal my music! *Rolling Stone*, p. 24.

Heidmiller, S. (2002, April). Digital copying and file sharing on trial. *Intellectual Property and Technology Law Journal*, 14(4), 1-8.

Kovacs, A.Z. (2001). Quieting the virtual prison riot: Why the Internet's spirit of "sharing" must be broken. *Duke Law Journal, 51,* 753-785.

MP3 information. (2004). Random House. Retrieved from http://www.booksontape.com/mp3help.cfm.

Oja, E. (1989). Neural networks, principal components, and subspaces. *International Journal of Neural Systems, 1*(1), 61-68.

Recording industry in numbers 2003. (2003). IFPI. Retrieved from www.ifpi.org.

Recording Industry Association of America. (2004). Retrieved from http://www.riaa.com.

Saroiu, S.P., Gummad, P.K., & Gribble, S.D. (2002). A measurement study of peer-to-peer file sharing systems. University of Washington, Technical Report.

Schwartz, J. (2003, November 4). Licensing concerns shut MIT music library. *International Herald Tribune,* p. 11.

Schwartz, J. (2004 April 5). A heretical view of file sharing. *New York Times.*

Smith, A.D. (2002). Loyalty and e-marketing issues: Customer retention on the Web. *Quarterly Journal of E-Commerce, 3*(2), 149-161.

Smith, A.D. (2004). Potential for growth and security in Internet file-sharing: The VPN concept of Gnutella. *Journal of Internet Commerce, 3*(2), 1-19.

Smith, A.D. (2005). Reverse logistics and their affects on CRM and online behavior. *VINE: The Journal of Information and Knowledge Management, 35*(3), 166-181.

Smith, A.D. (2006). Exploring security and comfort issues associated with online banking. *International Journal of Electronic Finance, 1*(1), 18-48.

Smith, A.D. (2007). Collaborative commerce through Web-based information integration technologies. *International Journal of Learning and Innovation, 4*(2), 127-144.

Smith, A.D., & Offodile, O.F. (2007). Exploring forecasting and project management characteristics of supply chain management. *International Journal of Logistics and Supply Management, 3*(2), 174-214.

Smith, A.D., & Clark, J.S. (2005). Revolutionizing the voting process through online strategies. *Online Information Review, 29*(5), 513-530.

Smith, A.D., & Rupp, W.T. (2002a). Application service providers (ASP): Moving downstream to enhance competitive advantage. *Information Management and Computer Security, 10*(2), 64-72.

Smith, A.D., & Rupp, W.T. (2002b). Issues in cybersecurity: Understanding the potential risks associated with hackers/crackers. *Information Management and Computer Security, 10*(4), 178-183.

The Recording Industry Association of America's 2002 yearend statistics. (2002). RIAA. Retrieved from http://www.riaa.com.

Wal-Mart music downloads. (2004). Walmart.com. Retrieved from http://www. walmart.com/music_downloads/introToServices.do.

Winstein, K.J. (2003, May 26). *Engineering an accessible music library: Technical and legal challenges.* Retrieved from http://lamp.mit.edu/lamp-aup.pdf.

Van Hoorebeek, M. (2003). Napster clones turn their attention to academic e-books. *New Library World, 104*(4/5), 142-149.

Chapter X

The Next Generation of Customer Relationship Management (CRM) Metrics[1]

Timothy Shea, University of Massachusetts Dartmouth, USA

Ahern Brown, HDR Inc., USA

D. Steven White, University of Massachusetts Dartmouth, USA

Catharine Curran, University of Massachusetts Dartmouth, USA

Michael Griffin, University of Massachusetts Dartmouth, USA

Abstract

Adopting a focus on CRM has been an industry standard for nearly two decades. While evidence exists that a majority of the attempts to implement CRM systems fail, there is a surprising lack of understanding as to why. The

authors contend that the limitations of mostly internally-focused, marketing-based, efficiency-oriented CRM metrics has hindered both the understanding of why CRM systems often fail as well as led to the perception of failed CRM implementations. Only through the development, application and use of CRM metrics can organizations hope to better understand CRM implementations or achieve their CRM goals. To make matters more difficult, the growing capabilities of CRM applications over the past few years has been raising the expectations and sophistication of customers. A new generation of CRM metrics is needed—a generation of relevant, enterprise-wide, and customer-centric metrics. This next generation of CRM metrics is discussed in detail.

Introduction

For nearly two decades, businesses worldwide have sought a means of connecting meaningfully with their customers. For many, the integration of information technology and marketing has provided a platform on which to build this connection. Thus, customer relationship management (CRM) has emerged as the strategic bridge between information technology and marketing strategy (Wehmeyer, 2005). CRM is a customer-centric business strategy in which an organization seeks to increase customer satisfaction and loyalty by offering customer-specific services (Kristoffersen & Singh, 2004). CRM allows companies to collect and analyze data on customer patterns, interpret customer behavior, develop predictive models, respond with timely and effective customized communications and deliver product and service value to individual customers (Chen & Popovich, 2003). Recent research by Sin et al. (2005) suggests that CRM is a multidimensional construct consisting of four components: key-customer focus, CRM organization, knowledge management and technology-based CRM (see Figure 1). The four interact to provide businesses with a competitive advantage by allowing them to better understand their customers. Acquiring a better understanding of existing customers allows companies to interact, respond and communicate more effectively with them to improve retention rates, among other things. The goal is to return to the feeling of yesteryear when small business owners and customers knew each other intimately and shared a sense of community (Chen & Popovich, 2003).

Figure 1. Sin, Tse, and Yim (2005): Four components of CRM

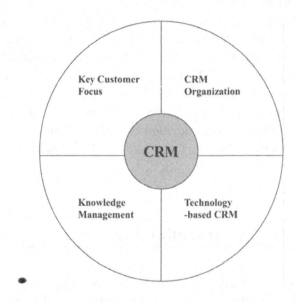

Since CRM requires an integration of information technology and marketing, cross-functional cooperation becomes mandatory for success (Nairn, 2002). But this cooperation isn't the only prerequisite for success. Two other critical success factors have been identified: 1) a customer-centric business model (Chen & Popovich, 2003), and 2) appropriate business processes and integrated systems (Bull, 2003). In addition, resource constraints impact CRM implementation. It is estimated that the average investment in CRM applications per company is $2.2 million (Chen & Popovich, 2003). And estimates of 2004 global corporate expenditures on CRM range from U.S. $23.5 billion (Bull, 2003) to U.S. $125 billion (Adebanjo, 2003; Winer, 2001). Finally, customer expectations are changing—for example, an expectation for more personalized and more sophisticated service—which means the metrics to measure CRM success need to continue to evolve.

The next sections review CRMs today, the potential benefits and pitfalls of CRMs, the current status of CRM metrics, and the need for a new generation of CRM metrics.

Overlap Between Enterprise Resource Planning (ERP) and Customer Relationship Management (CRM)

Many CRM packages were developed or purchased by legacy systems vendors, such as ERP vendors Oracle and SAP, to be seamless additions or modules (Adebanjo, 2003). ERP systems are thought of as back-office systems, whereas CRM systems are thought of as front-office systems (Corner & Hinton, 2002). ERP systems address fragmented information systems while CRM systems address fragmented customer data. The two systems should work together interactively to produce data on which managers are able to use to increase competitiveness by reducing costs and increasing sales. One of the problems hindering the smooth interface between ERP and CRM is that many companies use multiple ERP systems (Maurizio et al., 2007). Regardless, the goal of CRM technology is to link front office (i.e., sales, marketing and customer service) and back office (i.e., financial, operations, logistics and human resource) functions with the company's customers (Chen & Popovich, 2003). And, according to Kymal (2006), on the horizon are enterprise integrated management systems (EIMS). These systems, focusing primarily on quality management, need to fully integrate with both ERP and CRM systems in order to provide managers with a full picture of their operations.

Thus, the importance of integrated corporate applications such as ERP and CRM is increasing despite reports of negative experiences and failed implementations (Huang et al., 2003). But prior to focusing on the pitfalls of CRM implementation, the following section offers the potential benefits sought by businesses that pursue CRM as an active business strategy.

Potential Benefits of CRM

There are many potential benefits from integrating ERP and CRM systems (Huang et al., 2003). Some of the possible outcomes of successful CRM implementation include increased competitiveness through higher revenues and lower operating costs, increased customer satisfaction and retention rates, increased customer value, potential to assess customer loyalty and profitability, and ability to measure repeat purchase, dollars spent and customer longevity (Ling & Yen, 2001; Chen & Popovich, 2003).

Company-wide, CRM systems provide each employee with a tool to manage contacts, activities, documents and the information necessary for personalizing or customizing marketing efforts to meet individual consumer needs (Bygstad, 2003). The most frequently cited critical success factors for implementation includes defining a CRM strategy that is consistent with corporate strategy and determining the scope and scale of the cross-departmental infrastructure changes needed (Kotorov, 2003). Finally, all businesses seeking to develop and implement a CRM system would be wise to realize that the goal of developing a perfect CRM system is unattainable (Corner & Rogers, 2005).

The Dark Side of CRM

CRM implementation is hard work (Bygstad, 2003) and many firms have not obtained the expected results after implementation (Gonzalez Alvarez, 2006). By some estimates, 75-85 percent of the CRM systems implementations either are outright failures (Bygstad, 2003; Earley, 2002; Tafti, 2002) or disappoint to the level that CRM has frequently come to mean "Can't Recover Money." In a recent study of Australian businesses that had adopted CRM systems, 60 percent were less than satisfied with the results achieved to date (Ang & Buttle, 2005).

Therefore, it's safe to say that many of the companies who have implemented CRM systems have failed to realize the potential benefits sought (Kristoffersen & Singh, 2004). The question is why? Many companies underestimate the complexities of CRM, lack clear business objectives and tend to invest inadequately in implementation (Bull, 2003). Others fail because they assume that the same methodologies used for implementing ERP systems are suitable implementing for CRM systems (Corner & Rogers, 2005). And still others fail because they fail to successfully integrate with ERP systems (Chan, 2005). To be fair, the CRM failure rate mirrors the implementation success rates of other enterprise information systems such as ERP systems because business process and integration issues that haunt ERP implementations are also leading causes of failure for CRM implementations (Chan, 2005).

On the other hand, is there something we can point at to try to improve the situation? One interesting area we would like to focus in on for a moment is the use—or lack of use—of CRM metrics. Chan (2005) contends that the inability to align the correct metrics across business activities is a critical reason for CRM failure.

The Current Status of CRM Metrics

In a sample drawn from Fortune 1000 companies, 39 percent had no CRM metrics, 48 percent had internal metrics and only 12 percent had external goals and metrics (Rogers, 2003). The need for valid and reliable metrics is clear. In order to optimize CRM performance, metrics need to be enterprise-wide and customer-centric (Chan, 2005) and relevant (Rogers, 2003). Metrics from sales, marketing, customer service and operations should be unified to drive measures of customer profitability, customer satisfaction and market share (Chan, 2005). The disconnect between CRM and CRM metrics negatively impacts marketing effectiveness, customer retention and loyalty (Chan, 2005)

The problem with CRM metrics today is that they are mostly internally focused, measuring items such as increase in sales revenue, improved sales productivity, reduction in marketing waste, reduction in costs in call centers, reduction in sales cycle time, increase in campaign response and decrease in cost of response. To be useful, metrics are needed that focus on the customer's experience, measuring items such as improvement in first contact resolution or improved speed of order fulfillment (Rogers, 2003).

Building the Case for the Development of CRM Metrics

The emergence of the quality movement in the 1980s in the United States—spurred on by Edward Demming's mantra "You can't manage what you can't measure"—helped energize the push for performance management, benchmarking, metrics, and the like. While initially focused on financial and non-financial measures for manufacturing, performance measures have evolved to include the full range of activities within a company, including service activities and even strategic activities. The Metrus Group is one of many to document the effectiveness of performance management.

At the same time, as addressed above, there is also considerable evidence that CRM implementations today are not very good at measuring their impact or their benefit to the company and the company often lacks in even having an approach to metrics or analytics. Granted, like other new technology waves, the CRM wave began with too many vendors promoting flash over substance. However, now that we are about ten years into the wave and have the benefit

Table 1. Benefits of strategic performance management (© Metrus Group, 2002)

Measure of Success	Measurement-Managed Organizations	Non-Measurement Managed Organizations
Industry leader over the past 3 years	74%	44%
Three-year return on investment (ROI)	80%	45%
Success in last major change effort	97%	55%
Clear agreement on strategy among senior management	93%	37%
Effective communication of strategy to organization	60%	8%

of thousands of ERP and CRM implementations, what is the holdup? Why are we still fumbling with metrics?

It is true that metrics can not simply be slapped onto the front bumper and be expected to provide value. A company needs to know what they are trying to accomplish with their CRM before developing metrics. That is, a company first needs to have an overall strategic plan as well as an enterprise-wide CRM strategy that integrates information needs, technology needs and alignment with company processes and goals. The CRM should have organizational goals, technology goals, and goals for customer offerings (Sawhney, 2001). And yes, a company with many legacy systems that make it difficult to integrate across various information silos will have a slow start.

Others have suggested that people, culture, and processes are also factors that can inhibit a company from adding value across its customer value chain from the integrated information that a CRM can provide. Put a slightly different way, we suggest it is not the technology anymore—be it data communications issues or application maturity—it is people and culture and change. A simple example is the new CRM system that identifies problem areas. Who wants to be the "messenger" to deliver the bad news in a corporate culture that does not support such activities?

Distance learning technology was at a similar point seven or eight years ago. For a number of years people had plenty of legitimate complaints about distance learning technology— "it doesn't work," "the server is down too often," "the connection is too slow," "the software is too frustrating and doesn't do what I need it to do," "it takes too much time," and so forth. Over a few short years connection speeds—even to the home—became fast and reliable, the learning management software matured, and adequate infrastructure, such as servers, were in place. Seemingly in a flash, the discussions moved from technology to pedagogy and assessment. Likewise, we believe the maturity of CRM applications available today and the experience of companies using CRM applications are now permitting companies to move from a technology focus to an application focus as well as the evaluation of its performance and benefits.

We believe it is time to revisit and re-invigorate efforts to develop, implement, and research CRM metrics. Some CRM metrics, such as developing useful measures to support return-on-investment (ROI) or using the balanced scorecard technique, can take time to learn and implement. One such metric proposed is the customer value scorecard (CVS). The CVS is a customer performance metric that looks at transition rates from stages and segments that affect the value of the customer base (Hansotia, 2002). However, many current CRM metrics exist today that can be applied quite readily to help demonstrate value and profitability. Metrics such as relative customer satisfaction, customer retention, and customer lifetime value provide valuable benchmarks for managers (Rogers, 2003). The following suggested metrics assume a full CRM implementation, integration with ERP reporting, and data mining capabilities. CRM metrics include:

- **Changes in conversion or sales rate:** An increase in the number of "opportunities" versus the number of "wins" can show growth. Data mining techniques can show conversion results in specific markets or within a range of customers.

- **Changes in cross-selling rate for existing customers:** Silos are often built in organizations between diverse product offerings. The ability to show an increase in cross-selling to existing customers provides many intrinsic returns in an organization's ability to maximize their share of customer's wallets.

- **Evaluating marketing campaigns:** The ability to measure the productivity of a campaign with hard numbers and trend data is especially important to organizations where larger individual investments in marketing are needed to produce a "win."

- **Predicting future sales:** Over time, an integrated CRM system can provide more information about future sales and more accurate probabilities about potential "wins."

- **Evaluating the CRM system:** The data documenting the effectiveness of the customer life cycle for customers—including order and supply process improvements, customer support, sales, sales and marketing expenses, and customer satisfaction—can document the value of the CRM system.

- **Bringing new marketing and sales personnel up to speed:** Staff transition is a fact of doing business, especially in today's dynamic environment. CRM systems metrics as well as the valuable history of past and present interactions with customers can significantly speed up a new employee's productivity learning curve.

The following do not even require an integrated, full CRM implementation—just some time and—for most of them—just an Excel spreadsheet:

- **Cost per acquisition:** Customer acquisition cost is the costs associated with convincing a consumer to buy your product or service, including marketing, research, advertising costs, and Web content. It is calculated by dividing the costs by the number of acquisitions. Customer acquisition cost should be considered along with other data, especially the value of the customer to the company and the resulting return on investment (ROI) of acquisition.

- **Customer lifetime value:** Loyal customers mean future revenues. Customer lifetime value (CLV) is the present value of the future revenue generated from a customer for as long as you retain that customer. If CLV is an indication of the value of a relationship, companies must find ways of maximizing CLV by utilizing strategies that maximize incremental sales and by launching effective customer loyalty programs. The formula for CLV is: customer lifetime value = revenue from initial purchase + present value of future revenues over the projected lifetime—the acquisition cost of the customer.

- **Changes in customer satisfaction:** While satisfaction measures may not provide verifiable results as quickly as other metrics, they provide important, overall, long-term trends as well as valuable feedback on the organization's most important customers.

- **E-mail effectiveness:** E-mail effectiveness can be measured a number of ways. The return on investment (ROI) of a particular e-mail campaign can be calculated by dividing the total cost of the mailing into the net income produced. A monthly e-mail churn rate (number of undeliverable e-mail names plus the names deleted from the list during the month divided by the total number of e-mail names on your list at the end of the month) measures how much your customer base "rolls" over every month.

- **Web traffic analysis:** There are a number Web traffic analysis packages available, many of which are very affordable—for example, ClickTracks, Hitslink, and FastCounter Pro. They can support Web marketing through ROI analysis, detailed visitor analysis, content performance, and ad tracking.

Summary

To be useful, CRM results must be measured, controlled and benchmarked (Curry & Kkolou, 2004). For some, the development and use of CRM metrics is a case of too little too late and can only confirm for you that the organization is already in trouble (Rogers, 2003). But this should not dissuade organizations from the pursuit of the development of well-defined CRM metrics. Metrics provide actionable data, either positive or negative, and have the ability to help demonstrate the value and profit attributable to a CRM implementation.

The next generation of CRM metrics needs to be cross-functional in nature and customer-focused. In addition, efficiency metrics need to be supplemented with effectiveness metrics that are flexible enough to evolve with rapidly changing marketplaces and the ever-growing demands of customers. Implemented correctly, CRM systems, with appropriate metrics, can fulfill the promise of CRM—that is, becoming an area of strategic advantage (Sin et al., 2005).

References

Adebanjo, D. (2003). Classifying and selecting e-CRM applications: An analysis-based proposal. *Management Decision, 41*(5/6), 570-577.

Ang, L., & Buttle, F. (2005). CRM software, applications and profitability. In *Proceedings of the 2005 Academy of Marketing Annual Conference* (pp. 1-11). Dublin, Ireland: Dublin Institute of Technology Press.

Bull, C. (2003). Strategic issues in customer relationship management (CRM) implementation. *Business Process Management Journal, 9*(5), 592-602.

Bygstad, B. (2003). The implementation puzzle of CRM systems in knowledge-based organizations. *Information Resources Management Journal, 16*(4), 33-45.

Chan, J.O. (2005). Toward a unified view of customer relationship management. *Journal of American Academy of Business, 6*(1), 32-38.

Chen, I.J., & Popovich, K. (2003). Understanding customer relationship management (CRM): People, process and technology. *Business Process Management Journal, 9*(5), 672-688.

Corner, I., & Hinton, M. (2002). Customer relationship management systems: Implementation risks and relationship dynamics. *Qualitative Market Research, 5*(4), 239-251.

Corner, I., & Rogers, B. (2005). Monitoring qualitative aspects of CRM implementation: The essential dimension of management responsibility for employee involvement and acceptance. *Journal of Targeting, Measurement and Analysis for Marketing, 13*(3), 267-274.

Curry, A., & Kkolou, E. (2004). Evaluating CRM to contribute to TQM improvement: A cross-case comparison. *The TQM Magazine, 16*(5), 314-324.

Earley, R. (2002). How to avoid the CRM graveyard. *Customer Interaction Solutions, 20*(12), 26-30.

Gonzalez Alvarez, J., Raeside, R., & Jones, W.B. (2006). The importance of analysis and planning in customer relationship marketing: Verification of the need for customer intelligence and modeling. *Journal of Database Marketing & Customer Strategy Management, 13*(3), 222-230.

Greenyer, A. (2006). Measurable marketing: A review of developments in marketing's measurability. *Journal of Business & Industrial Marketing, 21*(4), 239-242.

Hansotia, B. (2002). Gearing up for CRM: Antecedents to successful implementation. *Journal of Database Management, 10*(2), 121-132.

Huang, A., Yen, D., Chou, D., & Xu, Y. (2003). Corporate applications integration: Challenges, opportunities, and implementation strategies. *Journal of Business and Management, 9*(2), 137-150.

Kotorov, R. (2003). Customer relationship management: Strategic lessons and future directions. *Business Process Management Journal, 9*(5), 566-571.

Kristoffersen, L., & Singh, S. (2004). Successful application of a customer relationship management program in a non-profit organization. *Journal of Marketing Theory and Practice, 12*(2), 28-42.

Kymal, C. (2006). Enterprise quality management evolves. *Quality, 45*(11), 36-39.

Ling, R., & Yen, D. (2001). Customer relationship management: An analysis framework and implementation strategies. *The Journal of Computer Information Systems, 41*(3), 82-97.

Maurizio, A., Girolami, L., & Jones, P. (2007). EAI and SOA: Factors and methods influencing the integration of multiple EPR Systems (in an SAP environment) to comply with the Sarbanes-Oxley Act. *Journal of Enterprise Information Management, 20*(1), 14-31.

Metrus Group. (2002). Measurement-managed organizations. Retrieved from http://www.metrus.com.

Nairn, A. (2002). CRM: Helpful or full of hype? *Journal of Database Marketing, 9*(4), 376-382.

Rogers, B. (2003). What gets measured gets better. *Journal of Targeting, Measurement and Analysis for Marketing, 12*(1), 20-26.

Sawhney, M. (2001). Don't homogenize, synchronize. *Harvard Business Review, 79*(7), 100-108.

Sin, L.Y.M., Tse, A.C.B., & Yim, F.H.K. (2005). CRM: Conceptualization and scale development. *European Journal of Marketing, 39*(11/12), 1264-1290.

Tafti, M.H.A. (2002). Analysis of factors affecting implementation of customer relationship management systems. In *Proceedings of IRMA 2002 Annual Conference*. Hershey, PA: Idea Group Publishing.

Wehmeyer, K. (2005). Aligning IT and marketing—the impact of database marketing and CRM. *Journal of Database Marketing and Customer Strategy Management, 12*(3), 243-256.

Winer, R.S. (2001). A framework for customer relationship management. *California Management Review, 43*(4), 89-105.

Endnote

[1]   An earlier version of this paper was published as:

Shea, T., Brown, A., White, D. Steven, Curran-Kelly, C., & Griffin, M. (2006). Customer relationship management (CRM) metrics—what's the holdup? *International Journal of Enterprise Information Systems*, 2(3), 1-9.

Chapter XI

Development of Intelligent Equipment Diagnosis and Maintenance System using JESS:
Java Expert System Shell Technology

Yin-Ho Yao, Ta Hwa Institute of Technology, Taiwan, ROC

Gilbert Y.P. Lin, National Tsing Hua University, Taiwan, ROC

Amy J.C. Trappey, National Tsing Hua University and
National Taipei University of Technology, Taiwan, ROC

Abstract

In modern manufacturing organizations, tasks of equipment and facility maintenance are complex and often geographically dispersed due to enterprise globalization. Diagnosing modern equipment breakdown requires considerable expertise and collaboration among equipment users and technical experts. Therefore, an intelligent diagnosis and maintenance system is necessary to support agile production and collaborative equipment maintenance in real time. This chapter focuses on describing the development of a rule-based intelligent equipment trouble-shooting and maintenance platform using JAVA Expert System Shell (JESS) technology. A prototype system is designed and developed combining rule-based knowledge system and inference engine to support real time collaborative equipment maintenance across geographical boundary. The main modules of the system include diagnosis knowledge management, project or case management and system administration. The knowledge management module consists of key functions such as knowledge type definition, knowledge component definition, document definition, mathematical model definition, rule and rule-set management. The project management module has key functions such as project definition, project's role management, project's function management and project's rule-set execution. Further, a thin-film transistor liquid-crystal display (TFT-LCD) production equipment diagnosis and maintenance system is designed and implemented to demonstrate the intelligent maintenance capability. The prototype system enhances agility of TFT-LCD collaborative manufacturing processes with real time equipment diagnosis and maintenance.

Introduction

In modern factories, production equipment maintenance represents a very significant and important task to ensure that equipment continues to function properly. Research has shown that up to 20% of the cost is wasted in non-realized revenue due to poor maintenance decisions (Bengtsson, 2003) and good maintenance often extends 30-40% capital equipment life. Hence, there is an urgent need to develop intelligent diagnosis and maintenance systems to prevent equipment failures and reduce the chances of breakdowns. Intelligent maintenance and diagnosis systems have been developed for a variety of domains, such as trouble shootings of electrical and mechanical equipment, identification of software/hardware problems and integrated circuit failures, and fault-detection in nuclear power systems (Abou-Ali & Khamis, 2003; Balakrishnan & Honavar, 2003; Chan, 2005; Liu & Liu, 2003; Rong et al., 2005). It is desirable for the intelligent system to identify the possible causes that could explain the symptoms and propose suitable solutions. In order to perform the tasks, an intelligent system must collect adequate domain knowledge constantly (Balakrishnan & Honavar, 2003) and dynamically emulate human reasoning and decision-making based on the most updated knowledge. The system must also support collaborative maintenance in real time and remote locations. The development of Web technology has changed the way the intelligent system is being designed and implemented. Web-based intelligent systems use the Web interface to deliver services online. Developing Web-based intelligent or expert systems faces a greater challenge than traditional standalone systems (Duan et al., 2005). The challenges include knowledge representation, validation, inferencing and results explanation. In this research, an intelligent equipment maintenance system platform, applying cyber-enabled Java Expert System Shell (JESS) technology, is designed and developed to demonstrate how the tasks can be implemented effectively in the maintenance domain and related applications.

Literature Review

This section provides a brief overview of JESS technology and rule-based expert system. The challenges of developing an intelligent equipment maintenance system and some related research literatures are reviewed.

Rule-Based Expert System

Based on the advances in artificial intelligence and information technology, expert system (ES), also called knowledge-based system (KBS), has been widely applied in a variety of domains to solve problems and support decision-making (Cai & Xu, 2000; Lamma et al., 2001). Turban et al. (2004) classified expert systems into the following generic categories including diagnostic systems, repair systems, design systems, interpretation systems, prediction systems, planning systems, monitoring systems, debugging systems, instruction systems, and control systems. The expert systems address many different applications. For example, Cakir and Cavdar (2006) developed a knowledge-based expert system for solving metal cutting problems. Duan, Edwards, and Xu discussed three Web-based ES for e-business strategy development, fish disease diagnosis and intelligent interviews (Duan et al., 2005). Batanov, Nagarur, and Nitikhunkasem (1994) have proposed using a knowledge-based system (KBS) to support the maintenance management activities. Chiang, Trappey, and Ku (2004) have developed a mechanical design intelligent system using JESS knowledge platform for collaborative design. Tor, Britton, and Zhang (2005) presented a knowledge-based blackboard framework for stamping process planning. Ngai and Cheng (2001) proposed expert system application for performance measurement of advanced manufacturing technology projects. Rao, Miller, and Lin (2005) presented an expert system for productivity analysis. Trappey, Chiang, and Ke (2006) developed an intelligent workflow management system to manage project processes with dynamic resource control. Trappey et al. (2007) presented a rule-based knowledge system to address how the engineering knowledge can be dynamically represented and efficiently utilized in the production dispatching.

The rule-based expert system gathers a set of factual data and produces actions (recommendations) by interpreting the data with a set of pre-defined rules that a human expert would follow in diagnosing a problem (Bielawski & Lewand, 1998; TechEncyclopedia, 2007). An architecture of rule-based expert systems including knowledge base, fact base, and inference mechanism is shown in Figure 1. The knowledge base contains domain knowledge useful for problem solving in *IF-THEN* rule formation (Buchanan & Shortliffe, 1984; Roesner, 1988) that combine the condition and the conclusion (action) for handling a specific situation. Rule can represent relations, directives and recommendations. The facts database, that is, the working memory, contains a set of facts, which can be entered by user or created (inferred) automatically by the system. Facts can be created by one rule and used in other rule. Facts must be presented in the working memory in order for a rule to become

Figure 1. The architecture of a rule-based expert system

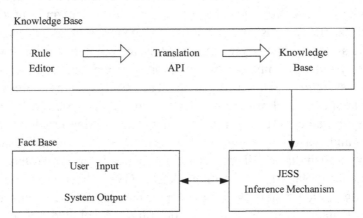

available for activation (Preece, Grossner, & Radhakrishnan, 1996). Inference mechanism, an interpreter of rule-based expert systems, compares rules in knowledge base with fact base, selects rules for firing, and executes the actions associated with the rules. In order to reduce the effort for constructing a rule base, a rule base can be built up with rule-based knowledge system tools, such as JESS (Menken, 2002).

A rule-based system has many advantages, for example, (1) natural knowledge expression, (2) separation of knowledge from its reasoning processing, (3) modularity, which enable easy construction, debugging, maintaining of system, and (4) easiness of explanation (Reichgelt, 1991). The basic operations of a knowledge base are to manipulate facts and rules in the knowledge domain, for example, defining facts and rules, deleting rules, creating rule sets, query of rules, adding and removing facts from working memory.

JESS Technology

JESS, developed at Sandia National Laboratories (Friedman-Hill, 2001), is a powerful tool for building intelligent applications. The major advantage of JESS is its capability to easily integrate with other Java programs through its well-defined API for controlling the reasoning processes using Java language (Eriksson, 2003). JESS is essentially a reimplementation of a subset of the earlier CLIPS shell (CLIPS, 2003) in Java.

The JESS shell provides the basic elements of an expert system including fact-list, knowledge base that contains all the rules, and inference engine, which controls overall execution of rules. Facts are the constructs that define information that is generally acknowledged to be true. In a JESS platform, there are three types of facts, that is, ordered facts, unordered facts, and definstance facts. Ordered facts are facts without a pre-defined structure. Unordered facts are constructed based on using frames or templates. Further, definstance facts are actually instances of user-defined Java classes (Jovanovic et al., 2004).

JESS uses a special algorithm called Rete to match the rules to the facts. The rules are "if-then" statements that have a left-hand side part (IF-portion) and a right-hand side part (THEN-portion) with the "implies" operator in between. Rules are responsible for taking actions based on facts in the knowledge base. Whenever the patterns of the rule match with existing facts, the rule is activated and its right-hand side actions executed (Cabitza, 2005).

Intelligent Equipment Maintenance System

As the pressure of market competition continues to increase, automated equipment maintenance and monitoring are necessary. The online equipment diagnosis and maintenance systems based on latest information technology have gained popularity among equipment providers and users (Byman et al, 2000; Wang & Wang, 1997). Lee (2001) suggests a framework for Web-enabled and Internet-based intelligent maintenance system (IMS), which consists of intelligent machine degradation assessment, e-prognostics, and e-diagnostics to enable near-zero breakdown equipment conditions. A number of useful intelligence tools/systems using information technology have been studied and developed by the research community and industries to assist the equipment diagnosis and maintenances. McArthur et al. (2004) study how multi-agent system technology, combined with intelligent systems, can be used to automate the fault diagnosis activities. Wang, Liu, and Griffin (2000) developed a combination system of neural network and expert system for diagnosis. Shal and Morris (2000) proposed a fuzzy expert system for the equipment fault detection. Balakrishnan and Honavar (2003) examine and compare several different approaches to the design of intelligent systems for diagnosis applications. Bengtsson (2003) discusses the technical components of a complete condition-based maintenance system for industrial robot fault detection and diagnosis. Further, Carreau, Menard, Landry, and Eksioglu (2000) trace the evolution of a collaborative project aimed at the implementation of rules for a diagnostic expert system.

Although many systems and tools have been developed in the maintenance domain, effectively and dynamically designing, implementing, and updating these systems, especially in e-manufacturing maintenance applications, is still a challenging task. The challenges are mainly in the ill-defined nature of the fault symptoms, real time discovering of faults, complexity of knowledge representation, and ever-updating diagnosis and maintaining rules. These factors restrict the efficiency of facilities maintenance and waste more resources and cost, so effective ways to solve these problems are extremely important. This paper addresses how the maintenance knowledge can be expressed dynamically and utilized in various sites using cyber-enabled JESS technology and its application platform to remotely diagnose equipment via the Internet.

Conceptual Architecture of IEMSP

An intelligent equipment maintenance system needs to identify the breakdown components, diagnose the possible causes and recommend suitable remedial actions accurately. In this research, a conceptual architecture of intelligent equipment maintenance system platform (IEMSP) is developed to support collaborative maintenance in real time and multiple locations over Internet. Development methodologies, main functions of the intelligent equipment maintenance system, and conceptual modeling of domain knowledge base are presented in the following sub-sections.

Methodologies for Knowledge-Based System Platform Development

The development methodologies and stages of the IEMSP consist of the following stages, that is, the requirements gathering and analysis stage, the design stage, the development stage, the unit and integration test stage, and, at last, the acceptance test stage. In the requirements gathering and analysis stage, functional specifications are developed in details. The standard use-case and activity diagrams of Unified Modeling Language (UML) are applied to describe these requirements. Figure 2 shows a use case diagram for an overview of system modules including system administration, knowledge management, and project management.

The requirements, obtained during requirements gathering and analysis stage, are defined as an operational system with sub-functional design. In this stage, conceptual architecture of the knowledge base is designed as shown in Figure 3. The database is defined and modeled using entity-relationship diagram. Further, the functional modules of the system are depicted. Further, the specification of each module is defined in details. The conceptual architecture of the system can be divided into three main modules, that is, (1) knowledge building and management module (including definition of knowledge types, knowledge components, mathematical models, knowledge component attributes, mathematical model attributes, documents, and measurement units), (2) rule definition and management module, and (3) project (i.e., case or instance) management and execution module. Those three modules support four roles of participants in the system platform, that is, the knowledge engineer, the domain expert, the project manager, and the end-user.

Figure 2. The UML use-case diagram for an overview of system functions

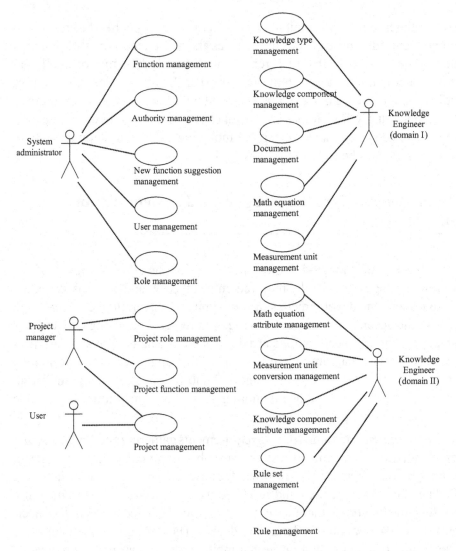

During the development stage, implementation of system requirements and specifications are undertaken and codes are created based on the specifications. In the unit and integration test stage, the operational scenario is defined and the functions of the system are tested against the requirements and specifications. The test case set is developed and all critical functions must be run and tested fully. In the acceptance test stage, the thin-film transistor liquid-crystal display (TFT-LCD) equipment maintenance scenarios are defined and specific rule sets are developed for real case testing.

Figure 3. The conceptual architecture of the knowledge base

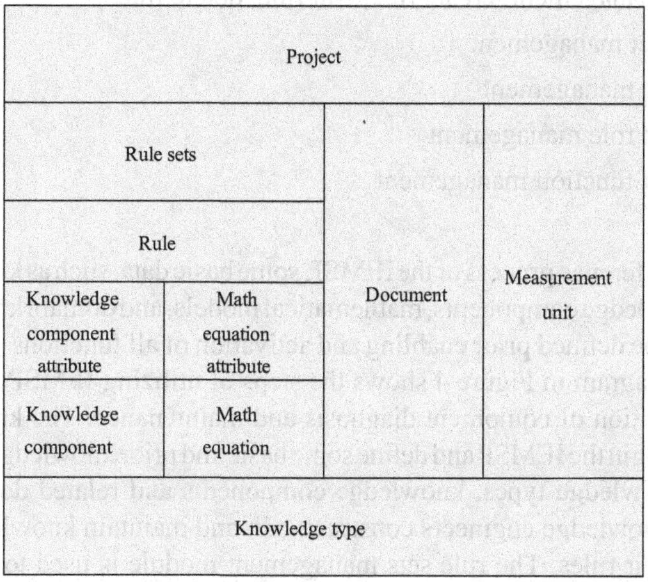

Project			
Rule sets		Document	Measurement unit
Rule			
Knowledge component attribute	Math equation attribute		
Knowledge component	Math equation		
Knowledge type			

Main Functions of IEMSP

The main functions of the intelligent equipment maintenance system platform (IEMSP) developed are outlined as follows:

- System administration and authority management
- New function suggestion management
- User management
- Role management
- Knowledge type management
- Knowledge component management
- Knowledge component attribute management
- Document management
- Mathematical equation definition
- Mathematical equation attribute management
- Measurement unit management

- Measurement unit conversion management
- Rule management: create rule, edit rule, delete rule
- Rule set management
- Project management
- Project role management
- Project function management

In the rule inference process of the IEMSP, some basic data, such as knowledge types, knowledge components, mathematical models, and domain knowledge rules must be defined prior enabling and activation of all functions and rules. The flow diagram in Figure 4 shows the steps of utilizing IEMSP for every case application of equipment diagnosis and maintenance. The knowledge engineers login the IEMSP and define some basic and prior knowledge objects, such as knowledge types, knowledge components and related documents. Then the knowledge engineers construct, edit and maintain knowledge rule sets and their rules. The rule sets management module is used to combine and quote needed knowledge objects and rules in the knowledge repository (Trappey et al., 2007). After rule constructing, a project can be defined by project manager and rule sets can be applied and executed. The inference engine performs the reasoning process and produces the inference results of action.

Conceptual Modeling of Domain Knowledge Base

The development of an intelligent system needs sufficient domain expertise and transfer expertise into rules of the knowledge base. In related equipment diagnosis and maintenance applications, it is desirable for the system to identify the breakdown components, detect the possible causes and match suitable remedial actions (Balakrishnan & Honavar, 2003). The system will take a set of symptoms as input facts. By examining the symptoms, the system must answer critical questions, such as the relationship between the observed symptoms and the consequent diagnosis, the representation of this relationship, and the representation of diagnosis and actions to effectively support equipment maintenance tasks. The above relationships are often expressed as rules in an intelligent system. For complex cases, it is useful to group rules into rule sets with a number of subsidiary rules. Figure 5 shows

Figure 4. The flow diagram and definition steps for using IEMSP

Document management
Login in
Knowledge type definition
Knowledge component management
Rule set management
Rule management
A
Math equation management
A
Project definition
Apply rule sets
I/O definition
Rule inference
Results of inference

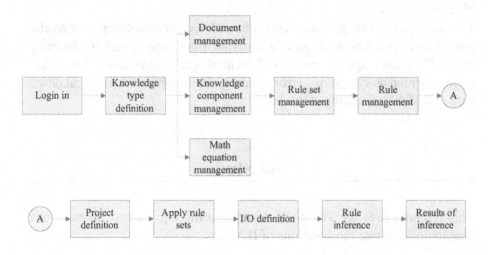

Figure 5. Conceptual modeling of the domain knowledge base

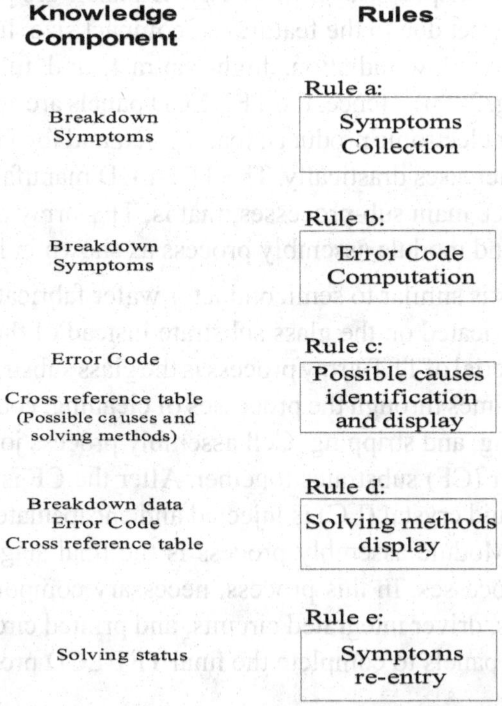

Knowledge Component
Rules
Rule a:
Breakdown Symptoms
Symptoms Collection
Rule b:
Breakdown Symptoms
Error Code Computation
Rule c:
Error Code
Cross reference table (Possible causes and solving methods)
Possible causes identification and display
Rule d:
Breakdown data
Error Code
Cross reference table
Solving methods display
Rule e:
Solving status
Symptoms re-entry

the conceptual modeling of the domain knowledge base represented as a set of rules.

The rule types include symptom collection rules, error code computation rule, causes identification rules, problem-solving rules, and symptoms re-entry rules. The knowledge components of the intelligent maintenance system can be represented as symptoms, error codes, cross reference tables, breakdown data and problem-solving statuses.

Case Study

This research uses the TFT-LCD manufacturing equipments maintenance case to demonstrate the functions of IEMSP.

Overview of the TFT-LCD Manufacturing Process

The display screen devices have gradually evolved from cathode ray tubes (CRTs) to flat panel displays (FPDs). TFT-LCD panels are particularly successful in FPD market due to the features of compact size, lightweight, low power consumption, low-radiation, high-contrast, and full-color display capabilities (Hung, 2006). Hence, the TFT-LCD panels are applied in a wide range of consumer electronic products; that the demand for TFT-LCD panels of various sizes increases drastically. The TFT-LCD manufacturing process is divided into three main sub-processes, that is, TFT-array process, cell assembly process, and module assembly process as shown in Figure 6.

TFT-array process is similar to semiconductor wafer fabrication except that transistors are fabricated on the glass substrate instead of the silicon wafer. The main raw material of TFT-array process is the glass substrate, which must be processed 5-7 times through the processes of cleaning, coating, exposure, developing, etching, and stripping. Cell assembly process joins the TFT-array and color filter (CF) substrates together. After the CF is adhered to the TFT-array, the liquid crystal (LC) is injected and encapsulated between two glass substrates. Module assembly process is the final stage of TFT-LCD manufacturing processes. In this process, necessary components (e.g., polarizer, back lights, driver integrated circuits, and printed circuit boards) are mounted onto the panels to complete the final TFT-LCD production.

Figure 6. Manufacturing processes of the TFT-LCD panel (Lalama, 1994)

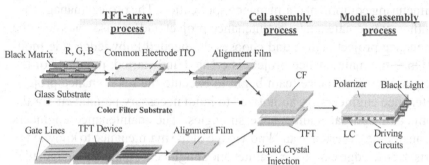

TFT-LCD has been an emerging industry over the past few years in Taiwan. TFT–LCD panel production capacity began to expand rapidly after third- and fourth-generation plants launched production in 1999. In 2006, the production value in Taiwan is expected to reach more than US$ 40 billion (Lin et al., 2006). The TFT-LCD industry is a capital-intensive business and requires highly automated production equipments. A fifth-generation TFT-LCD plant costs at least US$ 1 billion to build (Chen, et al., 2006). The stable quality and high yield are crucial. Therefore, the most challenging tasks during manufacturing processes are to diagnose and analyze the equipment problems and identify proper maintenance and repairing methods effectively. In the past, the trouble shooting analysis is based on the experience and the skill of equipment experts. In this research, a Web-based prototype IEMSP, which combines rule-based knowledge system and inference engine, is designed and developed to support equipment maintenance in the collaborative production environment. Based on a cognitive analysis of maintenance tasks, the rules are developed and maintenance engineers can acquire the knowledge immediately online; context-sensitive feedback on problem solving prior or during equipment breakdown can be achieved using the IEMSP.

Applying IEMSP in TFT-LCD Manufacturing Equipments Maintenance

In this case, IEMSP has four roles of users participating collaboratively in the equipments maintenance. They are the shop floor operators, the maintenance engineers, the knowledge experts, and the project manager of a maintenance department. Figure 7 shows the IEMSP system architecture for TFT-LCD manufacturing equipment maintenance application. The project manager has the authority to create a new maintenance project and/or case, monitors the maintenance project status, and chooses the needed knowledge rule modules. Once the maintenance project is created and started, members of the collaborative maintenance team begin to execute the maintenance project. Maintenance engineers are authorized to input necessary parameters for the reasoning of optimal maintenance strategies. The maintenance engineers will transfer the experience and knowledge of the maintenance to knowledge experts. Knowledge experts or maintenance engineers input knowledge rules into project database and fact database through the interface of knowledge rule management. Project database saves the data about maintenance projects including the definition of maintenance project and the relations. Fact base saves the fact-format data. All messages in the project can be transmitted efficiently through the Internet in real time to manufacturing facilities in different locations.

In this research, a TFT-LCD factory maintenance project is used as a case study. The factory is divided into several assembly lines. The assembly line can be further divided into detailed equipment modules, and the equipment modules contain many manufacturing devices. The inactive or improper functioning of components, machines and systems reflects toward many breakdown indications. It is important to realize the relationship between the possible cause and breakdown indications for accurate diagnoses. The IEMSP has to identify problems arising from a failure of one or more modules and devices. To detect problems effectively, it is necessary to divide the machine or system into many modules and sub-modules that contain individual rules and facts for diagnoses and repair suggestions. The related rules and facts form the complete maintenance knowledge base to assist the maintenance engineers for correct actions. In the case study, we select the magnetic switch and magnetic switch circuit of the power supply system (Figure 8) as the device example to describe the functions of the IEMSP (AUO, 2005).

Figure 9 shows the maintenance inference process of the power supply system maintenance. In this case, the diagnosis/maintenance rules for the TFT-LCD manufacturing equipment breakdown are shown in Table 1. Knowledge rules for each maintenance inference step have been developed, as formulated in Table 2. When IEMSP detects any maintenance indications, it automatically informs the project manager and the related maintenance members and generates some suggestions for solving the maintenance problems.

Figure 7. The IEMSP architecture for TFT-LCD manufacturing equipment maintenance

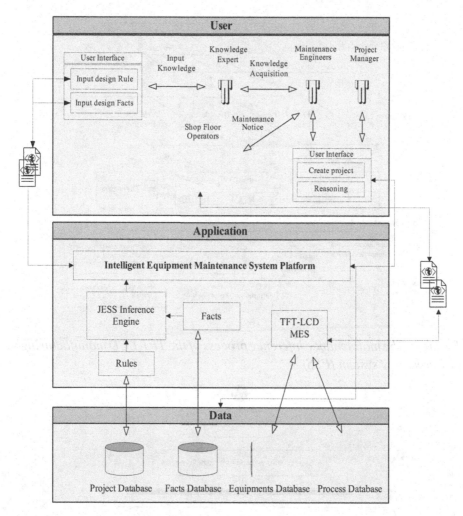

IEMSP provides an integrated collaborative maintenance environment. Maintenance engineers can efficiently conduct and evaluate the diagnosis and maintenance of manufacturing facilities such as the TFT-LCD manufacturing equipments in Figure 10 (AUO, 2005). Knowledge rules of the maintenance can be reused by different projects. Therefore, maintenance know-how and experiences can be accumulated. Maintenance engineers can avoid errors and maintenance conflicts to shorten the time finding the fault reason and the solution.

Figure 8. The breakdown structure of TFT-LCD manufacturing facility as the knowledge reasoning base

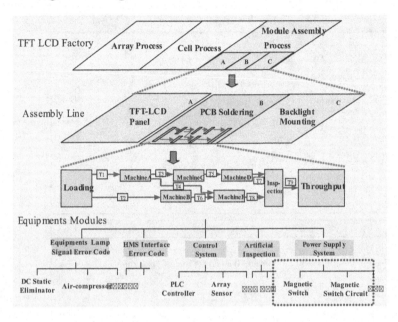

Figure 9. The maintenance inference process of the TFT-LCD manufacturing power supply system (PSS)

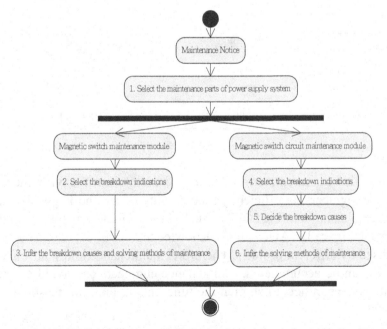

Table 1. Illustrated examples of TFT-LCD manufacturing equipment break-downs and maintenance methods

Maintenance Parts	Breakdown Indication	Possible Causes of Breakdown	Suggested Methods of Maintenance
Magnetic Switch	Screw Rustiness	Damp or use rusty screw	Keep the inside of controller arid
	Magnetic Switch Fatigue	On and off frequently	Avoid on and off magnetic switch frequently and change new magnetic switch
	Burn Down	Overload or short circuit	Change new magnetic switch
Magnetic Switch Circuit	Slack	Shake of machine	Check the reason of shake
		Screw not fastened firmly during setup and maintenance	Fasten screw firmly during set up and maintenance
	Breakage	Circuit pulled and dragged	Re-assemble and fasten screw firmly
		Overload	Change new magnetic switch circuit
		Crushed by a foreign matter	Change new magnetic switch circuit

Table 2. Example rules for the TFT-LCD IEMSP

Rule No.	Rule formulation	
	IF	THEN
1	Maintenance = Yes	Q: Select the maintenance part of PSS A1. Magnetic switch A2. Magnetic switch circuit Insert A1 or A2 to FACT - Maintenance part.
2	(Component failed = Yes) AND (Maintenance part EQ Magnetic switch)	Q: Select the breakdown indication A1. Screw rustiness A2. Magnetic switch fatigued A3. Burn down Insert A1, A2 or A3 to FACT – Breakdown indication.
3	(Breakdown indication EQ Screw rustiness)	Insert "Damp or use rusty screw" to FACT – Breakdown cause.
4	(Breakdown cause EQ Damp or use rusty screw)	Insert "Keep the inside of controller arid" to FACT – Breakdown solving method.
5	(Component failed = Yes) AND (Maintenance part EQ Magnetic switch circuit)	Q: Select the breakdown indication: A1. Slack A2. Breakage Insert A1 or A2 to FACT - Breakdown indication.

continued on following page

Table 2. continued

Rule No.	Rule formulation	
	IF	THEN
6	(Breakdown indications EQ Slack)	Q: Decide the breakdown cause: A1. Shake of machine A2. Screw not fastened firmly Insert A1 or A2 to FACT – Breakdown cause.
7	(Breakdown cause EQ Shake of machine)	Insert "Check the reason of shake" to FACT – Breakdown solving method.
8	(Breakdown indication NEQ Null)	Output message - Breakdown cause AND Breakdown solving method.

Figure 10. Examples of TFT-LCD manufacturing equipments maintained by IEMSP

Conclusion

This chapter depicts that maintenance efforts can be improved through the use of the intelligent equipment maintenance system platform, IEMSP. An IEMSP prototype is developed, which combines rule knowledge base and the inference engine to support collaborative maintenance across time and geographic boundaries. The system platform allows knowledge engineers to construct, manage and maintain rules easily and flexibly to satisfy ever-changing collaborative maintenance requirements. The case study for TFT-LCD manufacturing equipment diagnosis and maintenance has shown the intelligent equipment maintenance system platform at work. Through the rule base, maintenance know-how and experiences can be represented, accumulated, transferred, shared, and reused. Thus, the system can reduce the time required to reach diagnostic decision, increase maintenance efficiency, ensure consistent maintenance quality, and keep maintenance costs under control with Web-based knowledge provision.

Acknowledgment

This research is partially supported by the Industrial Technology Research Institute (ITRI) and the National Science Council (NSC) in Taiwan.

References

Abou-Ali, M.G., & Khamis, M. (2003). TIREDDX: An integrated intelligent defects diagnostic system for tire production and service. *Expert Systems with Applications, 24*, 247-259.

AUO. (2005). *Pollution prevention.* Retrieved January 7, 2005, from http://www.auo.com/auoDEV/about.php?sec=environmentSub.

Balakrishnan, K., & Honavar, V. (2003). *Intelligent diagnosis systems.* Artificial Intelligence Research Group, Department of Computer Research Group, Iowa State University, USA.

Batanov, D., Nagarur, N., & Nitikhunkasem, P. (1994). EXPERT-MM: A knowledge–based system for maintenance management. *Artificial Intelligence in Engineering, 8*(19), 283-291.

Bengtsson, M. (2003). Standardization issues in condition based maintenance. In *Proceedings of the 16th International Congress on Condition Monitoring and Diagnostic Engineering Management,* Vaxjo University, Sweden.

Bielawski, L., & Lewand, R. (1988). *Expert systems development: Building PC-based applications.* Wellesley, MA: QED Information Sciences, Inc.

Buchanan, B.G., & Shortliffe, E.H. (1984). *Rule-based expert systems.* London: Addison-Wesley.

Byman, B., Yarborough, T., Carolefeld, R.S.V., & Gorp, J.V. (2000). Using distributed power quality monitoring for better electrical system management. *IEEE Transactions on Industry Applications, 36*(5), 97-102.

Cabitza, I.F. (2005). Introduction to JESS: The Java expert system shell. Retrieved from http://www.mac.disco.unimib.it.

Cai, Z.X., & Xu, G.Y. (2000). *Artificial intelligence: Principles and applications.* Beijing: Tsinghua University Press.

Cakir, M.C., & Cavdar, K. (2006). Development of a knowledge-based expert system for solving metal cutting problems. *Materials and Design, 27*, 1027-1034.

Carreau, D., Menard, S., Landry, M., & Eksioglu, K.M. (2000, February 22). *Condition monitoring diagnostics expert system: A project roadmap.* EPRI SEDC VIII, New Orleans.

Chan, C.W. (2005). An expert decision support system for monitoring and diagnosis of petroleum production and separation processes. *Expert System with Applications, 29*, 131-143.

Changchien, S.W., & Lin, L. (1996). A knowledge-based design critique system for manufacture and assembly of rotational machined parts in concurrent engineering. Computers in Industry, *32*, 117-140.

Chen, K.S., Wang, C.H., & Chen, H.T. (2006). A MAIC approach to TFT-LCD panel quality improvement. *Microelectronics Reliability, 46*, 1189-1198.

Chiang, A.T.A., Trappey, A.J.C., & Ku, C.C. (2004). Using knowledge-based intelligent reasoning to support dynamic collaborative design. In *Proceedings of the Asia-Pacific Industrial Engineering and Management Systems* (APIEMS), Gold Coast, Queensland, Australia.

Chiang A.T.A, Trappey, A.J.C., & Ku, C.C. (2006). Using knowledge-based intelligent reasoning to support dynamic collaborative design. *International Journal of Advanced Manufacturing Technology, 34*, 421-433.

CLIPS. (2003). *CLIPS, a tool for building expert systems.* Retrieved from http://www.ghg.net/clips/CLIPS.html, last visited September 26th, 2003.

Cooney, J., Mann, D., & Winkless, B. (2003). *Case study: Applying the TRIZ methodology to machine maintenance.* Retrieved from http://www.trizjournal.com/archives/2003/08/f/06.pdf.

Duan, Y., Edwards, J.S., & Xu, M.X. (2005). Web-based expert systems: Benefits and challenges. *Information & Management, 42*, 799-811.

Eriksson, H. (2003). Using JessTab to integrate protégé and JESS. *IEEE Intelligent Systems, 18*(2), 43–50.

Friedman-Hill, E.J. (2001). *JESS, the expert system shell for Java platform.* Sandia National Laboratories, Version 6.

Hung, S.W. (2006). Competitive strategies for Taiwan's thin film transistor-liquid crystal display (TFT-LCD) industry. *Technology in Society, 28*, 349-361.

Jovanovic, J., Gasevic, D., & Devedzic, V. (2004). A GUI for JESS. *Expert Systems With Applications, 26*(4), 625-637.

Lalama, S.J. (1994). Flat panel display manufacturing overview. In *Proceedings of the IEEE Electronics Manufacturing Technology Symposium*, La Jolla, CA, USA (pp. 185-190).

Lamma, E., Maestrami, L., Mello, P., Riguzzi, F. & Storari, S. (2001). Rule-based programming for building expert systems: A comparison in the microbiological data validation and surveillance domain. Paper Presented at the Second International Workshop on Rule-Based Programming Affiliated with PLI 2001, Firenze, Italy.

Lee, J. (2001). *A framework for Web-enabled e-maintenance system*. Wisconsin Distinguished and Rockwell Automation Professor & Director of NSFI / UCRC for Intelligent Maintenance System (IMS), University of Wisconsin-Milwaukee, USA.

Lin, J.T., Wang, F.K., Lo, S.L., Hsu, W.T., & Wang, Y.T. (2006). Analysis of the supply and demand in the TFT–LCD market. *Technological Forecasting & Social Change, 73*, 422-435.

Liu, S.C., & Liu, S.Y., (2003). An efficient expert system for machine fault diagnosis. *The International Journal of Advanced Manufacturing Technology, 21*, 691-698.

McArthur, S.D.J., Davidson, E.M., Hossack, J.A., & McDonald, J.R. (2004). Automating power system fault diagnosis through multi-agent system technology. In Proceedings of the 37th Hawaii International Conference on System Sciences (Vol. 2, p. 20059.1). Washington, DC: IEEE Computer Society.

Menken, M. (2002). *JESS tutorial*. Retrieved from http://www.cs.vu.nl/~ksprac/export/jess-tutorial.pdf.

Ngai, E.W.T., & Cheng T.C.E. (2001). A knowledge-based system for supporting performance measurement of AMT projects: A research agenda. *International Journal of Operations and Production Management, 1*(1-2), 223-234.

Preece, A.D., Grossner, C., & Radhakrishnan, T. (1996). Validating dynamic properties of rule-based systems. *International Journal of Human-Computer Studies, 44*, 145-169.

Rao, M.P., Miller D.M., & Lin, B. (2005). PET: An expert system for productivity analysis. *Expert Systems with Applications, 29*, 300-309.

Reichgelt, H. (1991). *Knowledge representation, an AI perspective.* Norwood, NJ: Ablex Publishing Corporation.

Roesner, H. (1988). Expert systems for commercial use. *Artificial Intelligence and Expert Systems*, 35–59.

Rong, Z., Chen, K., & Ying, B. (2005). Distributed intelligent fault diagnosis for hydraulic motors. *International Journal of Information Technology*, 11(10), 133-139.

Shal, S.M.E., & Morris, A.S. (2000). A fuzzy expert system for fault detection in statistical process control of industrial processes. *IEEE Transactions on Systems, Man, and Cybernetics*, Part C, 30, 281-289.

TechEncyclopedia. (2007). *Rule-based expert system.* Retrieved from http://www.answers.com/topic/rule-based-expert-system.

Tor, S.B., Britton, G.A., & Zhang, W.Y. (2005). A knowledge-based blackboard framework for stamping process planning in progressive die design. *International Journal of Manufacturing Technology, 26*, 774-783.

Trappey, A.J.C., Chiang, T.A., & Ke, S. (2006). Develop an intelligent workflow management system to manage project processes with dynamic resource control. *Journal of the Chinese Institute of Industrial Engineers, 23*(6), 484-493.

Trappey, A.J.C., Ku, C.C., Lin, G.Y.P., & Ho, P.S. (2007). Design and analysis of rule-based knowledge system supporting intelligent dispatching and its application in TFT-LCD industry. The International Journal of Advanced Manufacturing Technology, 35(3-4), 385-393.

Turban, E., Aronson, J.E., Liang, T.P., & Quinnipiac, R.V. (2004). *Decision support systems and intelligent systems* (7th ed.). Prentice Hall.

Wang, H., & Wang, C. (1997). Intelligent agents in the nuclear industry. *IEEE Computer, 30*(11), 28-31.

Wang, Z., Liu, Y., & Griffin, P.J. (2000). Neural net and expert system diagnosis transformer faults. *IEEE Computer Applications in Power, 13*, 50-55.

Chapter XII

Measuring of Web Performance as Perceived by End-Users

Leszek Borzemski, Wroclaw University of Technology, Poland

Abstract

Users perceive good Internet performance as characterized by low latency, high throughput, and high availability. When browsing the Web, users are concerned with the performance of entire pages. Understanding and identifying the sources of the performance problems is a very important issue, especially for e-business. Therefore, there is the need to have a service for testing and measuring e-business Web site performance from the perspective of the end-users. We present our contribution in this area, that is, the Wing free service that has been developed for the purpose of Web transaction visualization. Our Web client that probes a target Web site is a real Web browser (MS IE), so the user can observe how a particular browser uses the network. Such known tools use their own Web browsing methods. Therefore, the solutions can be different from that used by real browsers and the results can be inadequate. Wing helps identify inefficient network usage by the browser and helps to tune Web pages to use the network efficiently. Therefore, Wing can be a good analysis tool for Web page and network application developers. Wing was used in an extensive study of WUTs Web access characteristics using statistical and data mining analysis methods. We also introduce the MWING system, which is based on our experiences from Wing project. MWING is a generic automated distributed multiagent-based measurement framework for running different measurement, testing and diagnosing tasks related to Internet; for example, in Internet topology discovering, Web benchmarking, or Grid services performance studies. One of possible agents can be Wing-like agents downloading different Web pages in periodic experiments from many agent locations.

Introduction

In the past few years, the World Wide Web has grown from a speculative medium to a robust telecommunication infrastructure that handles several mission-critical business as well as research computing traffic. Web users perceive good Internet performance as low latency, high throughput, and high availability. Web quality of service is extremely difficult to study in an integrated way. It is never been easy to determine whether slow responses are due to network problems or end-systems problems on both sides, that is, user and server sides. Moreover, because most of these performance problems are transient and very complex in the relationships between different factors that may influence each other, we therefore cannot exactly diagnose and isolate the issue key sources. Understanding and identifying the sources of the performance problems are very important issues for Internet designers.

There is the need to have a service for testing and measuring e-business Web site performance from the perspective of the end-users. This chapter surveys and compares such services that are available on the Internet. Almost all are commercial. We may also obtain free access to their functions, however, limited in time or functionality. Here, we also present our contribution in this area, that is, the Wing free Internet service that has been developed for the purpose of Web probing, visualization and performance analysis from the user perspective. Wing can be used in instant and periodic measurements of Web sites, including e-commerce solutions.

We also introduce a new Internet measurement platform for distributed measurements called MWING (Borzemski et al., 2007). MWING was developed with the intention to be used for the purpose of the analysis of Web page downloading processes as seen from different users' perspectives. But because the system has been developed based on a multiagent oriented architecture, we can deploy a generic measurement and processing functionality concerning Web and Internet. Agents usually are designed to meet special needs; among them are Wing-like agents, which can be installed in distinct places in the Internet to observe Web page downloading from different geographical and network locations.

The chapter is organized as follows. The next section discusses related work and gives a background. Different tools are compared and discussed. The third section presents the Wing service. The fourth section gives an illustrative example of instant measurement of a Web page. The fifth and sixth sections show the application of the periodic measurements performed by Wing to throughput estimation and Web page "mortality" evaluation study. The seventh section outlines the idea of Web performance mining. The eighth section introduces the MWING framework. Finally, the last section concludes the chapter.

Background and Related Work

Network protocol visualization tools have been developed since the very beginning of computer networks. They are considered as tools for better understanding of a computer network. They can help network administrators or end-users in analysis of network reliability and performance. They can be general tools used for several network protocols or developed specifically to assist some chosen protocol or a suite of protocols. Due to the rapid development of the Internet, there is the need to have such tools for the TCP/IP protocol suite. Nowadays, the most important visualization challenge is HTTP protocol and especially Web page downloading.

Internet uses IP network protocol, and all information is carried in packets. The data transfers are organized under control of TCP transport protocol that provides end-to-end reliable connectivity. Web clients communicate with Web servers using HTTP protocol (Mogul, 2004).

The end-users perceive good Internet performance through Web page downloading. Therefore both end-users and Web site administrators are anxious of the knowledge found in how well the Web pages are downloaded.

To study Web page download time, we can consider the following components, as illustrated in Figure 1: DNS, DNS2SYN, CONNECT, ACK2GET, FIRST_BYTE, and LEFT_BYTES.

In the first phase of a Web transaction, there is the need to determine the IP address based on the symbolic server name. DNS is the time to translate the server name into the IP address. Sometimes, this operation may take much time; therefore, we need to include this component in the measurements of Web page download. Next is the time period to open the TCP connection by the browser. The client downloading a Web page opens the TCP connection using an exchange of SYN packet that initiates the three-way handshake. DNS2SYN is the time spent by the client between DNS resolution event and this SYN packet exchange. The elapsed time between transmitting the SYN to the server and receiving the SYN response is CONNECT time. The connection phase begins when a client initiates connection request SYN, and ends when the connection is established, that is, when the server receives ACK packet from the client. Then the client starts the browsing phase. There can be another delay in browser action, namely ACK2GET time, after which the browser sends GET request for Web page component. The GET request can be for a base page (HTML) or an object embedded in a page. The FIRST_BYTE is the time between the sending of GET request and the reception of the first packet including requested component. The LEFT_BYTES is the time spent for downloading the rest of the requested object. Contrary to other developments in the field of Web page downloading and visualization, we propose to take into account DNS2SYN and ACK2GET time components.

The Web transaction illustrated in Figure 1 is simple. Web transactions are usually much more complex. Web pages have its skeleton and many objects embedded. They can be downloaded from different servers; the redirection occurs during the browsing phase. The browser usually employs more advanced HTTP protocol features such as connection persistency and pipelining. These features are widely used by the browsers to speed up page downloading.

The end-users perceive good Internet quality through Web page download performance. They want to know how their browsers exploit the WWW network, either well or not well. They are especially interested in how leading browsers use the network and download Web pages.

Figure 1. Time diagram of Web transaction

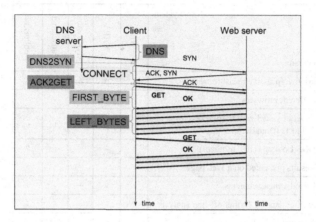

Passive and active measurement techniques can be used in order to achieve visualization of Web transactions (Hall et al., 2003). Most of them are active probing projects that are based on the target Web page measurement performed using a special measurement tool. Some of them are non-intrusive passive measurement techniques (Luckie et al., 2001). The comparison of HTTP measurement and visualization tools, including our Wing service, is given in Table 1.

The Patrick.net (www.patrick.net) is worthy to mention, as it was one of the first non-commercial services for testing Web pages. It was a companion Web page for the book on Web performance tuning (Killelea, 1998), and from October 2000 supported free service for analyzing the performance of any Web site as seen from California, where it was localized. Unfortunately, this service was taken down in the beginning of 2005 and now gives a discussion on the U.S. housing crash. There were no periodic measurements, and the returned information was not too detailed as in current projects but yet useful, especially if included Patrick's comments, which would be used by the user to improve page downloading.

Another approach is presented by NAPA (Network Application Performance Analyzer) project (Yoder, 2002). In this open source project, the user can freely download the NAPA, install it on his/her Windows workstation, and see Web page downloading timelines for all browsers that are installed in this operation system. It is simple and useful, but unfortunately, our experience showed that it has some bugs and it is not stable. We cannot use Unix-based

Table 1. Comparison of http measurement and visualization tools

Feature \ System	Wing	NAPA	MyKeynote	Patrick.net	WebPerf.org
(a)ctive (p)assive measurements	a	p	a	a	a
Different browsers	+	+	–	–	–
Level of visualization: (p)ackets (o)bjects (t)ransactions	o	p	o	t	o
DNS Lookup (UDP protocol)	+	-	+	+	?
Results presented on a Web page	+	-	+	+	+
Periodic measurements	+	-	+	-	+
Storing data for further off-line analysis	+	-	+	-	-
Free instant full page measurements	+	+	+	+	+
Free periodic full page measurements	+	-	-	-	-

browsers or process off-line data because NAPA is only a Windows-based visualization system.

There are also other developments featuring the Web page performance analysis, but unfortunately, without the graphical option showing the diagram how target Web page is downloaded in time (e.g., www.empirix.com; www. paessler.net; www.silktide.com; www.softwareqatest.com; www.webpageanalyzer.com; www.websiteoptimization.com). However, we think that the visualization is a very important in the analysis and decision-making. One picture tells much more than plenty of numbers. In many technology and science fields, that is, in statistical data analysis, data mining, we have taken advantage of visualization tools for several years.

Probably the MyKeynote (www.mykeynote.com) service is the most advanced benchmarking service that measures Web site's performance and availability from a worldwide network of measurement agents. It is a commercial service with some free (demo) functionality. In the demo version, the user can make some measurements of target URL and obtain valuable information on how the target page is seen by MyKeynote. Unfortunately, the MyKeynote agents use HTTP/1.0 protocol that is not still commonly used in the Internet. Leading browsers, such as MS Internet Explorer that is used by about 59% Internet users (www.w3schools.com, 2007), use more advanced HTTP/1.1 protocol. FireFox has become popular for 34% users. Therefore, we need tools running like most common browsers. Nevertheless, MyKeynote presents very valuable information for understanding how the page can be loaded.

Because we are often focused on the continuous observation of Web site, we would like to have the possibility to run periodic measurements. URLs would be measured in this way by loading the base page from the specific measurement sites by the MyKenote, but not by other services.

We are especially interested in MyKeynote as it is one of the distributed performance measurement systems and the MWING framework is our contribution in that area. MyKeynote service has own infrastructure of over 1,000 measurement systems positioned at different Internet Service Providers (ISP) locations. In addition to MyKeynote features discussed before, basically a user cannot freely designate the IP node where from he/her would like to observe the Web. The strong Keynote feature is that it has been designed purely having in mind Web performance measurements. However as a commercial service it is not recommended in open projects, which we want to overview here.

Distributed active performance measurements have been conducted in some open projects, but mostly for the needs of Grids. The comprehensive lists of Internet measurement projects are presented at the SLAC (www.slac.stanford.edu) and CAIDA (www.caida.org) Web sites. They are generally aimed to deal with the performance problem related to whole or a significant part of Internet where large amounts of measured data regarding, for instance, round trip delay among several node pairs over a few hours, days or months, and using specific measurements and data analysis infrastructures are obtained. These projects present the network behavior reports that are mainly focused on the whole Internet or a significant part of it, and they use the measurements mainly performed in the core of Internet. Probably the WAWM (Wide Area Web Measurement) project was the only one developed thinking of the Web in mind, to benchmark a local Web server infrastructure from client distributed across the wide area network (Barford & Crovella, 1999). However, the experiments run only on the specific testbed infrastructure.

One of the most important Grid related projects in the area is the Network Weather Service (NWS) (Wolski, 1998), which is frequently used for forecasting the performance of various resource components, including the network itself by sending out and monitoring lightweight probes through the network to the sink destinations at regular intervals. It is intended to be a lightweight, non-invasive monitoring system. This service operates over a distributed set of performance sensors network monitors from which NWS gathers readings of the instantaneous network conditions. It can also monitor and forecast the performance of computational Unix related resources. Now NWS is used commonly in several Grid projects.

Grid performance is also a topic of current research in DiPerF (diperf. cs.uchicago.edu), which is a distributed performance-testing framework, aimed at simplifying and automating service performance evaluation. DiPerF coordinates a pool of machines that test a target service, collects and aggregates performance metrics, and generates performance statistics. In 2006 DiPerF moved to Globus Incubator/ServMark project, which joins two performance evaluation tools, namely DiPerF and GrenchMark. GrenchMark has been designed, implemented, and deployed also for Grids (grenchmark.st.ewi. tudelft.nl/index.html) as a framework for synthetic workload generation and submission. ServMark is a Grid project that allows testing different parts of the Globus Alliance Toolkit (www.globus.org), and any other new services developed by end-users, and for benchmarking the environments where the Globus Toolkit is deployed (dev.globus.org/wiki/Incubator/ServMark). The applications of ServMark include rapid application and environment benchmarking, functionality testing and system tuning, and building runtime performance databases for Grid schedulers.

The browsers download Web pages in different ways, so the Web page downloading time chart can be different, and, as a result, the actual perceived performance is different. Therefore, it is very important to have the tools that perform in the same manner as the browser under observation. The best is to build-in a tool inside the browser, but this may have a great impact on browsing itself, and on performance especially. Of course, such an approach requires that such functionality be organized on the user side. The related works discussed in this section were partly directed this way with the exception of one thing—they could not work as real browsers. Moreover, we need a service with appropriate functionality for the users from a local domain, not at "higher" ISP level.

Wing Service

The Wing (*Web ping*) Internet free service has been developed for the purpose of Web probing, visualization and performance analysis from the user perspective (Borzemski et al., 2004a). Our service downloads a target page as the real Web browser. Today's implementation is done for MS IE, which is one of the most common Web browsers in the Internet, but the service is developed to monitor activity of any browser.

Using a real Web browser, Wing supports real-life studies and tests of Web-based applications. It is very important to notice that we may observe how a real browser uses the network. We can compare browsers and Web sites; we can compare our design and other designs, as well. Such known services, unfortunately, use their own Web browsing method. Browsing by specially developed browsers (e.g., they use HTTP/1.0 protocol only) is different from that made by the most popular browsers; therefore, the result is inadequate.

Wing downloads a target page to the service location and returns to the user a page showing an HTTP timeline chart and both detailed and aggregated information about Web page downloading. At the moment, Wing is localized in Wroclaw University of Technology (WUT) campus computer network at WASK location. WASK is the Metropolitan Academic Computer Network in Wroclaw, Poland. Our Web client that probes a target Web site is a real Web browser (MS IE), so the user can observe how a real browser uses the network.

Wing measures, visualizes and stores all Web page download time components shown in Figure 1. It supports IP, TCP, and UDP, DNS and HTTP protocols, logging a dozen parameters of HTTP transactions and TCP connections, thus facilitating a much deeper analysis. For example, we used it in the research on the estimation of the HTTP throughput and round-trip time.

Our solution is based on passive monitoring that originated with TCPdump protocol packet capture program (Jacobson, 1994; Ostermann, 1996) that allows recording of all network traffic that flows through a link. This assumption makes it a possibility to take into account both Unix (Linux) and Windows-based browsers. Wing traces all steps performed during browsing. We trace the entire communication between our Web client and target server. Tracing is done on the raw IP packages level. After tracing, the browsing time chart is reconstructed. The result is the same as the user achieves using a browser under consideration. Hence, if for example, the browser features HTTP/1.1 persistent connection, the Wing shows that activity as well. If there is the compressed transmission, then such communication is also shown. Additionally, Wing stores collected data in a local database for further post-processing. This feature was exploited in the analysis of generic Web characteristics from the perspective of the end-user as shown in fifth and sixth sections.

The main emphasis in the Wing project was to develop a system for support-

Figure 2. The Wing architecture

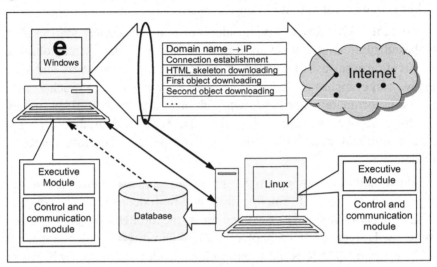

ing real-life usage of different Internet browsers. The most common browser is MS IE running under MS Windows. Therefore, first we built a system in Windows environment. Wing uses P-CAP API. Unfortunately, our initial programming showed that there was disadvantageous effect of the browsing process on the monitoring process. Therefore, we decided to use two computers, one for browsing and one for monitoring the traffic. The third computer is used for collecting data in a database.

The Wing service has a distributed local infrastructure consisting of three components (Figure 2): Linux-based Wing controller, Local Web client, and database server.

Wing is activated by a remote user request sent to Linux-based Wing controller targeting the URL to be tested. As the service is invoked, the Wing controller starts a Web local client that issues GET request to target URL as well as GET requests for all objects that are embedded in the target page.

Wing works like a sonar-location system, sending requests for the target Web page and waiting for the answer. Wing controller monitors and time stamps of all the browser's actions, determines the end of the Web page uploading, and pre-processes gathered data into the format convenient for further statistical and data mining analysis, as well as for visualization. Data is also stored in a database server. The most complex processing is done after collecting the row data from the network. Then, the whole Web transaction must be reconstructed. Transactions usually performed are parallel TCP sessions with an active persistency feature. During the analysis, it is important to remember that the data can be compressed by the Web server; the packets can arrive in another sequence than were sent or can be doubled. We need to identify embedded objects and track all redirections in URL addresses. Also, it is not a commonplace problem to reconstruct HTML documents built from frames. Wing fulfils all requirements in this area. The return page shows HTTP timeline chart and a number of detailed and aggregated data about Web page downloading.

Wing can be used for either instant or periodic measurements. The fourth section presents an example of instant measurement, whereas in the fifth section we discuss the application of periodic measurements in the estimation of the throughput, and latency of network links between user's browser and Web servers in the Internet. In the seventh section a new MWING multi-agent distributed measurement platform is presented where a Wing-like agent can be localized anywhere in the Internet to measure the Web in point-to-point, multi-point or much more complex configurations of agent sites, targeted Web servers, and different agent-to-server probing relationships.

An Illustrative Example of Instant Measurement

To show the issue, consider the following example of Web page downloading. We targeted the home page of the APIEMS2004 Conference. We perform and compare Web page visualizations prepared by MyKeynote (Figure 3) and Wing (Figure 4), respectively.

As we can see, MyKeynote uses an individual TCP connection for every object (there are 17 TCP connections as shown by Connect bars) whereas the real browser (MS IE) stimulated and observed by Wing uses only two connections to download all objects. Moreover, we also used Web Page Analyzer (www.weboptimization.com) and Paessler Site Inspector (PSI) (www.paessler.com), two popular tools for the analysis of Web pages but without a visualization feature. Table 2 shows a comparison of measured components. The mismatches between the results are set in boldface. LE stands for the message sent by MyKeynote: "3004 Byte Limit Exceeded," but this limitation is well justified. N/A is the message displayed by Site Inspector. MyKeynote omits the objects that are really transferred through the network by the real browser and used for improving further navigation (items 4-9). Web Page Analyzer and PSI do not properly recognize items 1 and 2. PSI recognizes item 2, however does not count its size. However, both tools recognize them correctly in case of individual analysis of these objects.

Wing helps identify inefficient network usage by the browser and helps to tune Web pages to use the network efficiently. The comparison shows Wing can be a good analysis tool for Web page and network application developers. The "last but not least" feature is that Wing can process scripts so we can automate the usage of the service and use it in the advanced Internet measurements.

Table 2. Measured components

Item	Wing	Bytes	Keynote	Bytes	Web Page Analyzer	Bytes	PSI	Bytes
0	+	12076	+	12076	+	12062	+	12076
1	+	30737	+	30737	+	30737	+	-
2	+	27400	+	27400	-	-	-	-
3	+	164625	+	LE	+	164625	+	-
4	+	261	-	-	-	-	-	-
5	+	287	-	-	-	-	-	-
6	+	288	-	-	-	-	-	-
7	+	266	-	-	-	-	-	-
8	+	238	-	-	-	-	-	-
9	+	280	-	-	-	-	-	-
10	+	43	+	43	+	43	+	43
11	+	1584	+	1584	+	1584	+	1584
12	+	1281	+	1281	+	1281	+	n/a
13	+	1870	+	1870	+	1870	+	n/a
14	+	1337	+	1337	+	1337	+	n/a
15	+	1919	+	1919	+	1919	+	n/a
16	+	1638	+	1638	+	1638	+	n/a
17	+	1420	+	1420	+	1420	+	n/a
18	+	537055	+	LE	+	537055	+	537055
19	+	465578	+	LE	+	465578	+	465578
20	+	32504	+	LE	+	32504	+	32504
21	+	4167	+	LE	+	4167	+	4167
22	+	41410	+	LE	+	41410	+	41410
		1328264		78038		1299230		1259042

Figure 3. Instant measurement of www.maths.qut.edu.au/apiems2004/ from Frankfurt DTAG performed by MyKeynote on 23-Jul-04 2:26:14 PM EDT (User: Demo)

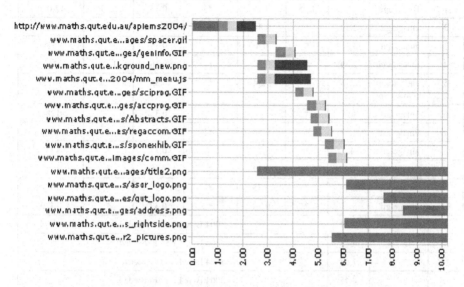

© 1995-2004 Keynote Systems, Inc.

APIEMS2004 Web page breakdown   *Measured Components*

Item	URL
1	http://www.math....au/apiems2004/
2	www.maths.qut.e...ages/spacer.gif
3	www.maths.qut.e...ges/geninfo.GIF
4	www.maths.qut.e...kground_new.png
5	www.maths.qut.e...2004/mm_menu.js
6	www.maths.qut.e...ges/sciprog.GIF
7	www.maths.qut.e...ges/accprog.GIF
8	www.maths.qut.e...s/Abstracts.GIF
9	www.maths.qut.e...es/regaccom.GIF
10	www.maths.qut.e...s/sponexhib.GIF
11	www.maths.qut.e...images/comm.GIF
12	www.maths.qut.e...ages/title2.png
13	www.maths.qut.e...s/asor_logo.png
14	www.maths.qut.e...es/qut_logo.png
15	www.maths.qut.e...ges/address.png
16	www.maths.qut.e...s_rightside.png
17	www.maths.qut.e...r2_pictures.png

Selected Components

- DNS Lookup
- Initial Connection
- Redirection
- First Byte Download
- Content Download
- Error

continued on following page

Figure 3. continued

Item	Type	Start Offset	DNS Sec.	Connect Sec.	Redirect Sec.	FirstByte Sec.	Content DLSec.	Bytes Downloaded
1	Base Page	-	1.05	0.35	*	0.35	0.77	12,076
2	image/gif	2.59	*	0.34	*	0.37	*	43
3	image/gif	3.31	*	0.4	*	0.35	*	1584
4	image/png	2.59	*	0.34	*	0.36	1.28	27400
5	application/ x-javascript	2.58	*	0.34	*	0.35	1.42	30737
6	image/gif	4.09	*	0.34	*	0.35	*	1281
7	image/gif	4.57	*	0.36	*	0.36	*	1870
8	image/gif	4.7	*	0.34	*	0.37	*	1337
9	image/gif	4.8	*	0.34	*	0.38	*	1919
10	image/gif	5.3	*	0.35	*	0.39	*	1638
11	image/gif	5.41	*	0.34	*	0.37	*	1420
12		2.59	3004 Byte Limit Exceeded					
13		6.13	3004 Byte Limit Exceeded					
14		7.64	3004 Byte Limit Exceeded					
15		8.45	3004 Byte Limit Exceeded					
16		6.06	3004 Byte Limit Exceeded					
17		5.55	3004 Byte Limit Exceeded					
Average			0.06	0.36	-	0.37	2.04	78038
Total						18.59		1,326,644

* Either the item was not necessary (such as redirection, where there are no redirects) or the operation took < 0.01 seconds.

Periodic Full Page Measurements: Web Performance Study

Web quality is extremely difficult to study in an integrated way. End-users perceive good Web quality mainly in the context of good performance, availability, security and accessibility. Network, Web site, and Web infrastructure solutions (DNS resolution, caching, traffic shaping, content distribution networks, load balancing, etc.) have deep impact on Web quality. It has never been easy to determine whether bad performance or non-availability of a

Figure 4. Instant measurement of www.maths.qut.edu.au/apiems2004/ from Wroclaw WASK performed by Wing on 23-Jul-04 20:15:46 Europe/Warsaw

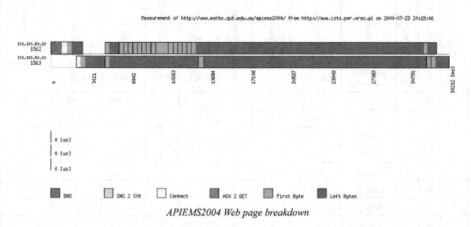

APIEMS2004 Web page breakdown

Item	URL	IP address	Port	Bytes
0	http://www.maths.qut.edu.au/apiems2004/	131.181.53.23	1512	12076
1	http://www.maths.qut.edu.au/apiems2004/mm_menu.js	131.181.53.23	1513	30737
2	http://www.maths.qut.edu.au/apiems2004/images/background_new.png	131.181.53.23	1512	27400
3	http://www.maths.qut.edu.au/apiems2004/images/title2.png	131.181.53.23	1513	164625
4	http://www.maths.qut.edu.au/apiems2004/images/mmmenu6_159x18_up.gif	131.181.53.23	1512	261
5	http://www.maths.qut.edu.au/apiems2004/images/mmmenu5_245x18_up.gif	131.181.53.23	1512	287
6	http://www.maths.qut.edu.au/apiems2004/images/mmmenu4_248x18_up.gif	131.181.53.23	1512	288
7	http://www.maths.qut.edu.au/apiems2004/images/mmmenu3_172x18_up.gif	131.181.53.23	1512	266
8	http://www.maths.qut.edu.au/apiems2004/images/mmmenu2_88x18_up.gif	131.181.53.23	1512	238
9	http://www.maths.qut.edu.au/apiems2004/images/mmmenu1_221x18_up.gif	131.181.53.23	1512	280
10	http://www.maths.qut.edu.au/apiems2004/images/spacer.gif	131.181.53.23	1512	43
11	http://www.maths.qut.edu.au/apiems2004/images/geninfo.GIF	131.181.53.23	1512	1584
12	http://www.maths.qut.edu.au/apiems2004/images/sciprog.GIF	131.181.53.23	1512	1281
13	http://www.maths.qut.edu.au/apiems2004/images/accprog.GIF	131.181.53.23	1512	1870
14	http://www.maths.qut.edu.au/apiems2004/images/Abstracts.GIF	131.181.53.23	1512	1337
15	http://www.maths.qut.edu.au/apiems2004/images/regaccom.GIF	131.181.53.23	1512	1919
16	http://www.maths.qut.edu.au/apiems2004/images/sponexhib.GIF	131.181.53.23	1512	1638
17	http://www.maths.qut.edu.au/apiems2004/images/comm.GIF	131.181.53.23	1512	1420
18	http://www.maths.qut.edu.au/apiems2004/images/ver2_pictures.png	131.181.53.23	1512	537055
19	http://www.maths.qut.edu.au/apiems2004/images/ver2_pictures_rightside.png	131.181.53.23	1513	465578
20	http://www.maths.qut.edu.au/apiems2004/images/asor_logo.png	131.181.53.23	1512	32504
21	http://www.maths.qut.edu.au/apiems2004/images/qut_logo.png	131.181.53.23	1513	4167
22	http://www.maths.qut.edu.au/apiems2004/images/address.png	131.181.53.23	1513	41410

continued on following page

Figure 4. continued

Measured Components

Item	Pkt OK	Pkt NOK	rtype	ctype	DL timesec	DNS	DNS2SYN	Connect	ACK2GET	First	Index	Content
0	9	0	S	text/html	34212368	974006	6294	394020	1220	384273	944950	31507605
1	22	0	C	application/x-javascript	2427324	0	0	379175	939	398459	1648751	0
2	19	0	C	image/png	1207986	0	0	0	0	397849	810137	0
3	113	0	C	image/png	8030071	0	0	0	0	404991	7625080	0
4	1	0	C	image/gif	390086	0	0	0	0	390086	0	0
5	1	0	C	image/gif	381964	0	0	0	0	381964	0	0
6	1	0	C	image/gif	382435	0	0	0	0	382435	0	0
7	1	0	C	image/gif	382188	0	0	0	0	382188	0	0
8	1	0	C	image/gif	381742	0	0	0	0	381742	0	0
9	1	0	C	image/gif	381800	0	0	0	0	381800	0	0
10	1	0	C	image/gif	381365	0	0	0	0	381365	0	0
11	2	0	C	image/gif	386307	0	0	0	0	386307	0	0
12	2	0	C	image/gif	1112084	0	0	0	0	1112084	0	0
13	2	0	C	image/gif	384620	0	0	0	0	384620	0	0
14	2	0	C	image/gif	384107	0	0	0	0	384107	0	0
15	2	0	C	image/gif	384635	0	0	0	0	384635	0	0
16	2	0	C	image/gif	383953	0	0	0	0	383953	0	0
17	2	0	C	image/gif	383837	0	0	0	0	383837	0	0
18	369	0	C	image/png	19868386	0	0	0	0	394812	19473574	0
19	320	0	C	image/png	19543741	0	0	0	0	399137	19144604	0
20	23	0	C	image/png	1179073	0	0	0	0	393571	785502	0
21	4	0	C	image/png	387146	0	0	0	0	384619	2527	0
22	29	0	C	image/png	1572654	0	0	0	0	393183	1179471	0

particular Web site is due to either network problems or end-systems problems, or both. The relationships between different factors that may influence each other are transient and very complex; therefore, we cannot often exactly diagnose, isolate and evaluate key sources of problems.

The evaluation of Web quality using *ad hoc* instant measurements only is not sufficient. We need to measure Web quality in periodic full-page measurements. Wing supports such active periodic full-page measurements mode. Here we show how Wing was used in the empirical study of Web quality. We measured the Web from the Wroclaw University of Technology campus to evaluate how the Web is seen (in the context of perceived quality) from the perspective of users located in our campus (Borzemski & Nowak, 2004b). The users perceive Web quality mostly by latency and throughput. The main goal of our work was to answer the question whether it is possible to develop a general model describing Web performance for the users surfing the Web from some site. Our model takes into account network latency and throughput. We investigated the correlation between latency and throughput to examine whether connections with shorter latency tend to transfer more data.

Almost 60% latency, as perceived by end-users at their microscopic level while accessing the Web server by the browser, refers to the network latency; that is, the delay between sending the request for data and receiving (the first bit of) the reply. The latency is evaluated by the round trip time (RTT), which is a measure of the time it takes for a packet to travel from a computer, across a network to another computer, and back. RTT reflects the Internet path properties, especially the cumulative end-to-end queuing delays. The lower the latency, the faster we can do low-data activities. RTT is commonly used to check whether the target server is reachable. Then RTT samples are taken by sending ICMP messages by Ping or Traceroute tools. Ping-based RTT estimate is not very valuable in Web quality evaluation studies, as ICMP packets do not match usual Web-based traffic. For example, ICMP packets can be blocked by firewalls and the routers often provide different prioritizing for them than for "normal" traffic, which is made of IP packets within TCP sessions used for HTTP transfers. Therefore, we need more suitable the estimation technique of RTT, that is, at the TCP (HTTP) protocol level.

Throughput is the "network bandwidth" metric, which tells about the actual number of bytes transferred over a network path during a fixed amount of time. Throughput determines the "speed" of a network as perceived by the end-user. The higher the throughput (at the HTTP level) of Internet connection, the faster a user can surf the Internet.

Transport protocols like TCP compute an estimate of the current RTT on each connection, but unfortunately the results of such estimation are not available for the user (application program). TCP uses RTT estimate to determine how long to wait for an acknowledgment before retransmitting. We developed exactly the same method as one used by TCP, and RTT was estimated using the technique based on the measurements of time spacing between the SYN packet sent by the client to the server and the ACK-SYN packet sent back in the reply by the server. This is a CONNECT time as shown in Figure 1. Thanks to Wing service, we can perform the same analysis as TCP when estimates RTT.

In order to estimate the average transfer rate of the TCP connection, we measured time spacing between the first byte packet and the last byte packet of the object received by client using that connection. Transfer rate was calculated by dividing a number of bytes transferred by the amount of time taken to transfer them. The throughput measured is the amount of pure data traffic available at the application level, that is, IP, TCP and HTTP headers are not included into the calculations.

We have monitored and traced the HTTP transactions that have been sent periodically by IE client localized within our campus network during 20 weeks. Each time, our Web client requested the same file from a few dozen Web servers all over the world. We chose to download the rfc1945.txt file that was found in several Web sites. Our chosen resource was large enough—it has an original size of 137,582 bytes—to estimate average transfer rate, and still was not too large to overload Internet links and Web servers. The target servers were found by the Google search engine. Among a few hundred links found we have chosen 209 direct links to rfc1945 document. After preliminary tests we have decided to use, for further measurements, only 83 servers, which were fully active during preliminary tests. Wing was programmed to download (and monitor the HTTP transaction and measure) the rfc1945 document from every server 10 times a day. After 20 weeks of measurements, we received the database with 65,428 Web transactions.

We investigated the correlation between a connection's RTT and transfer rate to examine whether shorter-RTT connections tend to transfer more data. Based on the measurements that we had analyzed so far, it was inconclusive to say that we can show such tendency for individual connections, but we can show specific performance behavior in the sense of a global performance characteristics found for the specific location of users in the Internet, such as in our case for the Wroclaw University of Technology location. The presence of such characteristics can be discovered when we plot a graph for the median values for the average transfer rate vs. RTT for all servers in question across the period of 20 weeks. Figure 5 shows such distribution of the median values for the average transfer rate vs. RTT in double logarithmic scale for all servers in question across the period of 20 weeks. We obtained a power-law behavior where the distribution of the average transfer rate vs.

RTT can be described using power law of the form y=kxα with k=46456 and α=-0.8805.

Periodic Full Page Measurements: URL "Mortality" Study

We are now just learning that the Web content is very volatile. Wing has been used in the study on the reliability (availability) of Web servers and the "mortality" of URLs in the sense of their disappearance in time. In our experiment, we wanted to portray the statistics of the disappearance of measured URLs. We have continued the measurements that were introduced in the fifth section for the next 27 weeks, collecting almost 150,000 Web transactions together. These measurements have been analyzed in the context of the "mortality" of URLs. Our measurements discovered the "mortality" process of URL links as presented in Figure 6. We determined the death rate of measured

Figure 5. Distribution of median values of average transfer rate vs. RTT (double logarithmic scale)

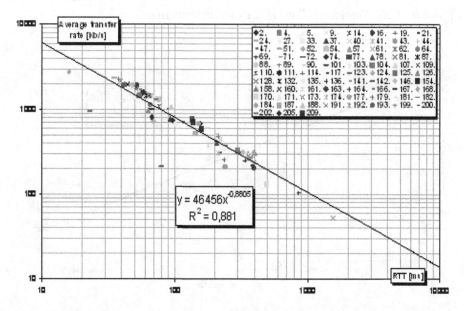

URL links as -0.06. Only about 80% of URLs available in the beginning of measurements were still valid in the end of experiment.

Web Performance Mining

Data mining is a promising and relatively new area of current research and development, which can provide important advantages to the users (Witten & Frank, 2005). It can yield substantial knowledge from data gathered. We can find several data mining applications in science, engineering, business, industry, health care, and medicine.

The ongoing rapid growth of measured data on the Internet and Web has created an immense need for data mining and knowledge discovery methodologies applied to the Internet issues. There are two potential areas of the application of data mining in the case of the Internet, considering it as a technical system. Namely, at first we can study the problems related to the communication network of Internet, that is, issues that can be found at the IP

Figure 6. URL "mortality" vs. day of measurement

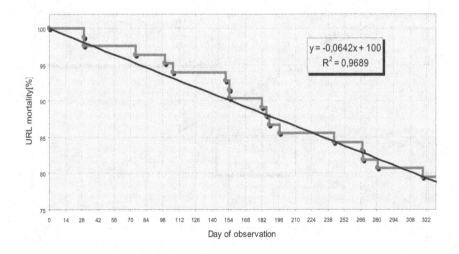

protocol, which constitutes the "bottom" layer of the network. In this sense, we show in Borzemski (2007) the application of data mining to the predictive performance analysis of the communication paths connecting hosts in Internet. The performance is evaluated by the round trip time (RTT). The World Wide Web is constructed as the "upper" layer of Internet and of course has own performance problems.

Nowadays, the data mining on Internet-related datasets is mainly applied to Web layer problems and this area of research is called generally *Web mining* (Chakrabarti, 2003). Web mining focuses mainly on *Web content mining*, *Web usage mining*, *Web structure mining*, and *Web user profile mining*. Typically, in Web mining we analyze such data sources as the content of the Web documents, the Web data logs, the data describing the Web structure and the Web user profile data. Then, for example, Web usage mining concerns the identification of patterns in user navigation through Web pages and is performed for the reasons of service personalization, system improvement, and usage characterization.

In Borzemski (2006), we showed how data mining could be applied to Web performance problems. We introduced a *Web performance mining*—a new Web mining dimension that discovers the knowledge about Web performance issues using data mining. We proposed to use two data mining functions, namely the clustering and the classification in the deployment of the predictive model of the page downloading throughput behavior on the communication path between the Web client and targeted Web site, against the time-of-the-day and day-of-the-week.

For each of the probing Web sites in periodic full-page measurements presented two sections earlier, we mined data individually for each client-to-server connection. The data analysis was performed in two stages. At first, we applied the clustering function to discover the rules of grouping data with similar properties. We used the neural clustering algorithm, which employed a Kohonen Feature Map neural network. Internet seasonal behavior is well evidenced by Web and network event logs. Hellerstein et al. (2001) showed that the time of day explains 53% of the variability in the raw data of HTTP transactions collected over eight months from a production Web server. We must remember that the server type (commercial/non-commercial), server loading, HTTP server type and site design, geographic and AS (autonomous system) locations can also affect ultimate Web performance. For our further exploratory analysis we assumed that weekly and daily period seasonal phenomenon exists. Therefore, we have chosen the day of the week, the hour of the measurement, RTT and throughput as active attributes participating in creation of clusters. One of the disadvantages of cluster models is that there are no explicit rules to define each cluster. The model is thus difficult to implement, and there is no clear understanding of how the model assigns cluster IDs. That's why we applied in the second step the decision tree to classify the cluster IDs, using the output data that was created as a result of the clustering algorithm at the first stage. The resulting decision tree can be used as the decision-making model to predict future Web behavior while transferring Web data from a given server. For example, in Borzemski (2006) we extracted the following prediction model: IF (TIME<4.5) AND (DAY≥3.5) AND (TIME≥ 3.5) AND (DAY<4.5) THEN CLUSTER_ID=4, where RTT is predominantly 47-55 ms and THROUGHPUT is medium (180-260 KB/s). The rule says that, if we want to download Web resources from that server between 00:00 am and 10:40 am (TIME<4.5) on Wednesday, Thursday, Friday or Saturday (DAY≥3.5), and when this is after 8:00 am (TIME≥ 3.5), and on Sunday, Monday, Tuesday or Wednesday (DAY<4.5), then we can expect that the network behavior as described by for the cluster #4.

Our ultimate aim is to develop an Internet intermediary brokering service for measuring network performance, describing Web characteristic and publishing the forecasts of Web behavior, especially for automatic Web resource selection. We focus on performance seen by end-users of some domain at the same geographical localization with the intermediate service that would maintain as many predictive performance models as many Web sites are measured.

Consider a common situation, when the user searches the resource by means of invoking search machines. Typically there are three phases to complete the result: the search made by the search engine, the URL decision making made personally by the user, and the resource downloading from the target server which URL was chosen by the user. Usually, the user receives from the search engine the list of URLs pointing to the relevant resources that match the user query. The relevance of the found Web pages is calculated by the search engine using its specific page rank index storing. Usually, a list of addresses of the Web pages (resources) is in descending order of their relevance to the search query. The user tries to evaluate the quality of found resources during the decision phase and, by clicking on the suitable position on result list, selects the resource that is likely right for him/her. Then the resource downloading starts and the resource gaining process ends.

Many times the page ranks are the same or very similar, so the user would substantially target any page from the result list. Such a situation may exist when we search resources in a duplicated content environment, such as file mirroring system or content distribution network. Then, we are obviously interested in determining URL address from the result list, which is characterized by the least downloading time at the specific time. Generally, the user has no chance to determine a priori which link has the best performance without the measurements of the server-to-client throughput at the moment of the decision-making. Using common browsers we are not able to perform such probing. It is also time consuming to check all links (some of them may be even unavailable using host reachability tools as ping). Also a common user may have no appropriate tool or required skill.

In our approach we propose an automated *best performance* URL selection performed by our intermediary service, which has the throughput knowledge on the selected Web URLs collected through active measurements. Then the result list is not returned to the user but is analyzed by the intermediary service to determine which link characterizes the best-expected downloading performance.

There are two possible situations, either the URL on the user result list matches one of the probed Web sites, or is different. The former case is simple; the latter case is more complex. In the former situation, we can simply use proposed data mining prediction procedure. In the latter case, which by the way is much more probable than the former case, the prediction is more complicated as we have not any measurements related to that URL. We proposed to use a prediction model that probed Web sites that are the nearest neighbor of considered URL. The nearest neighbor choice is based on the minimization of the specific neighborhood index, which is defined on the geographic distance basis (Borzemski & Nowak, 2005). The geographic distance-based selection has been proposed and evaluated using data sets collected from live Internet. We have shown that the geographic distance is accurate and effective.

MWING: A Multi-Agent Measurement Distributed System

The characterization of local access to the Web is essential for planning and future development of Internet (Crovella & Krishnamurthy, 2006). Our periodic measurements with Wing showed that it is possible to discover a power-law like characteristics of local Web access. However, we can do it only for locations where Wing infrastructure is installed and deployed *in situ*. Of course, this cannot be done practically. Therefore, we have developed a new system called MWING (Multi-agent Wing), being some successor of Wing (Borzemski et al., 2007). MWING is based on agent technology. We developed the "headquarters" of MWING, which cooperates with the measurement agents localized anywhere in the Internet. A user who is interested in his/her characteristics of the access to the Web may download and install locally the MWING agent, which is able to make autonomously required measurements based on a given user measurement design plan for user location. The measurements are temporarily stored locally (mainly for operational purposes, but they can be delivered to the user), and sent to the MWING "headquarters" for permanent storing in a database and further processing. MWING collects all measurements in the database where the measurements are stored in a row data format now (XML-based data format), but we plan to deploy a common logical measurement format to make it easy to incorporate MWING database with other Internet measurement databases. CAIDA (www.caida.org) and MOME (www.ist-mome.org) have tried to organize such scalable Internet measurement repositories.

Two basic definitions have introduced agent technology to computer systems area (Maes, 1994; Wooldridge & Jennings, 1995). They have claimed that agents are computational systems that inhabit some complex dynamic environment, sense and act autonomously in this environment and, by doing so, realize a set of goals or tasks for which they are designed. Agents can be also defined as computer systems that are situated in some environments, and that are capable of autonomous action in these environments in order to meet their design objectives. Agent-based approach is a modern system deployment in many current Internet projects in different interest domains and environments (Manvi & Venkataram, 2004; Park & Sugumaran, 2005; Sugawara et al., 2001; Weyns et al., 2005).

Both definitions agree in that the agent technology can be a well-recognized challenge in distributed network measurement and monitoring. Autonomous agent technique taken from the field of artificial intelligence can be used to deploy a style of interaction, which can be referred to as indirect management. Instead of common user-initiated interaction via commands and/or direct manipulation, the user is engaged in a cooperative process in which human and agents initiate communication, monitor events and perform measurement tasks.

Initially, the main goal of our project MWING was to develop a distributed platform for Web active measurements allowing for the integration of current and future measurement applications at the common high-level interface for measurements, data management, data processing and data exploration, including the API-based interface to build own applications to automate this functioning at the level of user programs. However the project has evolved towards a generic system, in the sense of measurement purposes and agent designs. The proposed solution named MWING is a generic multiagent distributed measurement platform for measuring, testing and performance evaluation (Borzemski et al., 2007), which can be used in Internet not only for Web measurements but anything else; for instance, in application to Internet tomography to discover network topology.

The general architecture of the system is shown in Figure 7. MWING consists of four main components: Web Application, System Controller, Database and Agent Set.

Web Application (WebApp) is responsible for communication with the system's administrator and the users. The main component in WebApp is the Measurement Management (MeasureMgmt) unit where all the functionality offered by the system is placed. By the usage of WebApp services the user can control system behavior, add new measurement tasks, define new agents and create measurement programs. This unit has been designed with ease of usage in mind. The Data Browser unit in MeasureMgmt visualizes whole measurement platform functionality. Visualization concerns not only currently performed tasks but also the historic data stored in a database.

The System Controller module is the central component of MWING. It consists of three units: *Server*, *Scheduler* and *Management Controller*.

Server communicates with Database and Measurement Management (MC) units. It is responsible for adding and deleting measurement tasks, registering agents and measurement programs. Scheduler features the activation of tasks at proper date and time. Both units are always up and ready to action. The MC is, contrary to the previous one, not always in action. MC is called by the Scheduler only when a task needs to be done. MC communicates with system's Database, gets task parameters and depending on the task to be executed, calls the proper measurement agent from a proper Agent Set. An Agent Set can be a single agent or a group of agents working together or independently within a single location. The Database is a single or multiple RDBMS configured for the needs of the MWING. Different DBMSs can be

Figure 7. The architecture of MWING

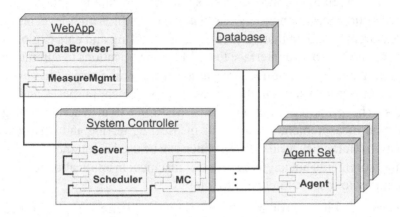

coupled with MWING platform. Agent Set is responsible for execution of custom-built tasks for measurement agents. After completion of agent activity (usually, after making some number of measurement series planned in the measurement design plan), the results are returned to MC. Then the gathered data is sent to the Database, and MC finishes its activity.

The key concept of flexibility of cooperation of agents within and outside the system is an interaction based on XML messages. After the execution of the agent's procedure the result data is sent back to the MC in the form of XML file. XML message containing results gathered by the agent during its activity consists of the following tags: the return value describing the status of execution of the agent, the possible error/warning information, and the data collected by the agent. Such measurement data can be used for any further analysis, for example, in Web performance mining analysis (Borzemski, 2006).

Measurement activity of MWING is programmed by the measurement designer. Any operating system and programming language can be used for the implementation of MWING agent. The requirements of agent construction are not restricting. It is only required that the target operating system platform has to provide the SSH protocol as all communication with agents is performed using that protocol. Generally, each agent can make unlimited in scale, type and amount measurements.

Figure 8. The architecture of Wing agent

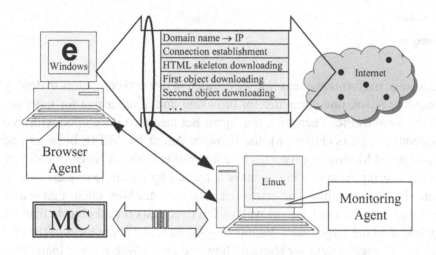

At first, we have developed an agent working as Wing in periodic full-page measurements. The measurement plan included the series of the measurements from different user locations to the same set of given Web servers.

An example of the XML message sent by Wing-like agent to MC is as follows:

```
<?xml version="1.0" encoding="utf-8" ?>
<response xmlns="http://www.w3schools.com">
    <retVal>0</retVal>
    <msg></msg>
    <data>
        <id>'3'</id>
        <slot_id>1</slot_id>
        <agent_id>2</agent_id>
        <datetime>'2007-01-19 15:41:27'</datetime>
        <record_seq>0</record_seq>
        <record_type>'S'</record_type>
        <measurementerror>458962</measurementerror>
        <dns>0</dns>
        <connect>48448</connect>
```

<firstbyte>52800</firstbyte>

...

</data>

</response>

Because of performance reasons, we decided to use two computers to deploy Wing-like agent, one computer for browsing and another one for monitoring the local traffic. Therefore, the Agent Set has been developed with two cooperating agents (Figure 8): the Browser Agent for MS IE browser and Linux-based Monitoring Agent. The cooperation with MC is carried out by the Monitoring Agent. Wing agent is activated by a remote request sent to Linux-based controller. The controller starts a local Web client that issues GET request to target URL, as well as GET requests for all objects that are embedded in the target page. Monitoring Agent looks at the local traffic and collects all needed data for showing how the target Web page is loaded locally. The results of the whole experiment are downloaded by MC to store them into the relational database for further off-line processing.

In preliminary HTTP performance tests Wing agents were placed in three locations: WUT campus network in Wroclaw (PWr), and in two housing computer networks, one in Wroclaw (UPC) and other in Opole (Opole). The aim of experiments was to investigate the correlation between a connection's RTT and transfer rate at specific Internet locations and to develop local models of Web performance. Eighty Web servers were simultaneously measured every two hours from three locations over the period of 76 hours. Figure 9 shows the trendlines for the median throughput vs. median RTT for UPC, PWr, and Opole locations. The coefficient of determination R^2, which is a measure of how well the regression line represents the data, was calculated for all datasets using the least square method. The measurements show that the characteristics of both links in Wroclaw are balanced, in that sense, that the trendlines can be determined rather strongly, whereas Opole has very variable behavior, probably due to the wireless link.

Conclusion

In this paper, we have surveyed the measurement services, which can be used by a user to visualize and analyze how the target Web page is downloaded.

Figure 9. Distribution of median values of average throughput vs. RTT (CONNECT) for three locations: WUT campus network in Wroclaw (PWr), housing cable computer network in Wroclaw (UPS) and housing wireless computer network in Opole (Opole)

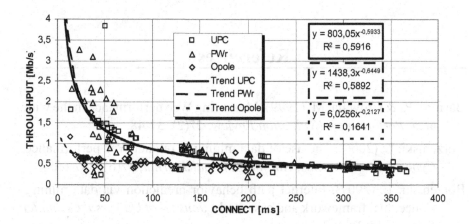

Especially, we present the abilities of Wing and MWING systems, being our contributions in the area. In instant measurement mode, Wing helps to identify inefficient network usage by the browser and server and helps to tune applications and Web pages to use the network efficiently. This is done by precise data collection and exact visualization of instant measurement traffic. Therefore, Wing can be a good analysis tool for Web page and network application developers.

Wing can also be used in periodical measurements. We presented the results of two such experiments. In the first study, the collected data was employed in model building of Web characteristics of WUT location. We obtained a *power-law* behavior where the distribution of the transfer rate versus the round-trip time can be described using power law of the form $y=kx^{\alpha}$ with $k=46456$ and $\alpha=-0.8805$. In the second experiment, we studied URL "mortality" issue and determined URL death rate.

Wing has, in some sense, its successor, the MWING multi-agent system, which is devoted to generic distributed measurements deployed according to given design scenario. In preliminary experiments with Wing-like agents we were able very easily to show how different performance had various Internet locations while accessing simultaneously the same Web resources.

Acknowledgment

This work was supported by the Polish Ministry of Science and Higher Education under Grant No. N516 032 31/3359 (2006-2009).

References

Barford, P., & Crovella, M. (1999). Measuring Web performance in the wide area. *Performance Evaluation Review, 27*(2), 37-48.

Borzemski, L. (2006). The use of data mining to predict Web performance. *Cybernetics & Systems: An International Journal, 37*(6), 587-608.

Borzemski, L. (2007). Internet path behavior prediction via data mining: Conceptual framework and case study. *Journal of Universal Computer Science, 13*(2), 287-316.

Borzemski, L., Cichocki, L., Fras, M., Kliber, M., & Nowak, Z. (2007). MWING: A multiagent system for Web site measurements. In *Proceeding of the First KES International Symposium KES-AMSTA 2007* (LNCS 4496, pp. 278-287). Berlin, Heidelberg: Springer-Verlag.

Borzemski, L., & Nowak Z. (2004a). WING: A Web probing, visualization and performance analysis service, In *Web Engineering: 4th International Conference, ICWE 2004*, Munich, Germany (LNCS 3140, pp. 601-602). Berlin, Heidelberg: Springer-Verlag.

Borzemski, L., & Nowak, Z. (2004b). An empirical study of Web quality: Measuring the Web from Wroclaw University of Technology campus. In M. Matera & S. Comai (Eds.), *Engineering Advanced Web Applications* (pp. 307-320). Princeton, NJ: Rinton Press.

Borzemski, L., & Nowak, Z. (2005). Using the geographic distance for selecting the nearest agent in intermediary-based access to Internet resources. In *Knowledge-Based Intelligent Information and Engineering Systems. 9th International Conference on Knowledge-Based & Intelligent Information & Engineering Systems, KES'2005* (LNCS 3683, pp. 261-267). Berlin, Heidelberg: Springer-Verlag.

Chakrabarti, S. (2003). *Mining the Web: Analysis of hypertext and semi structured data*. San Francisco: Morgan Kaufmann Publishers, Elsevier.

Crovella, M., & Krishnamurthy, B. (2006). *Internet measurement: Infrastructure, traffic, and applications*. Southern Gate, Chichester: John Wiley & Sons Ltd.

Jacobson, V. (1994). *TCPdump, the protocol packet capture and dumper program*. Retrieved from ftp://ftp.ee.lbl.gov/tcpdump.tar.Z

Hall, J., Moore, A., Pratt, I., & Lesli, I. (2003). Multi-protocol visualization. In *Proceedings of the ACM SIGCOMM 2003 Workshop on Models, Methods and Tools for Reproducible Network Research*, Karlsruhe, Germany (pp. 13-22). New York: ACM Press.

Hellerstein, J., Zhang, F., & Shahabuddin, P. (2001). A statistical approach to predictive detection. *Computer Networks*, *35*, 77-95.

Killelea, P. (1998). *Web performance tuning. Speeding up the Web*. Cambridge, MA: O'Reilly & Associates, Inc.

Luckie, M.J., McGregor, A.J., & Braun, H-W. (2001). Towards improving packet probing techniques. *ACM SIGCOMM Internet Measurement Workshop*, San Francisco (pp. 145-150). New York: ACM Press.

Maes, P. (1994). Agents that reduce work and information overload. *Communications of the ACM*, *37*(7), 31-40.

Manvi, S.S., & Venkataram, P. (2004). Applications of agent technology in communications—a review. *Computer Communications*, *27*, 1493-1508.

Mogul, J. (2002). Clarifying the fundamentals of HTTP. In *Proceedings of the Eleventh International Conference on World Wide Web*, Honolulu, Hawaii (pp. 25-36). New York: ACM Press.

Ostermann, S.. (n.d.). *Tcptrace*. Retrieved from http://irg.cs.ohiou.edu/software/tcptrace/index.html.

Park, S., & Sugumaran, V. (2005). Designing multi-agent systems: A framework and application. *Expert Systems with Applications*, *28*, 259-261.

Sugawara, T., Murakami, K., & Goto, S. (2001). A multi-agent monitoring and diagnostic system for TCP IP-based network and its coordination. *Knowledge Based Systems*, *14*, 367-383.

Weyns, D., Parunak, H.V.D., Michel, F., Holvoet, T., & Ferber, J. (2005). *Environments for multiagent systems state-of-the-art and research challenges* (LNCS 3374, pp. 1-47). Berlin, Heidelberg: Springer-Verlag.

Witten, I.H., & Frank, E. (2005). *Data mining. Practical machine learning tools and techniques*. San Francisco: Morgan Kaufmann Publishers, Elsevier.

Wolski, R. (1998). Dynamically forecasting network performance using the Network Weather Service. *Cluster Computing, 1*(1), 119-132.

Wooldridge, M., & Jennings, N.R. (1995). Intelligent agents: Theory and practice. *Knowledge Engineering Review, 10*(2), 115-152.

Yoder, J., (2002, February 27)). *Better end user visible Web browsing performance*. Paper presented at Intel Developer Forum, San Francisco. Retrieved from http://www.intel.com/cd/ software/products/asmona/eng/219852.htm.

Zhi, J. (2001). Web page design and download time. *CMG Journal of Computer Resource Management, 102*, 40-55.

Additional Information

http://dev.globus.org/wiki/Incubator/ServMark

http://diperf.cs.uchicago.edu/

http://grenchmark.st.ewi.tudelft.nl/index.html

http://www.caida.org

http://www.empirix.com

http://www.globus.org

http://www.ist-mome.org

http://www.mykeynote.com

http://www.paessler.com

http://www.patrick.net

http://www.silktide.com

http://www.slac.stanford.edu

http://www.softwareqatest.com

http://www.w3schools.com

http://www.webpageanalyzer.com

http://www.websiteoptimization.com

Chapter XIII

Information System Development:
Using Business Process Simulation as a Requirements Engineering Tool

Tony Elliman, Brunel University, UK

Tally Hatzakis, Brunel University, UK

Alan Serrano, Brunel University, UK

Abstract

This chapter discusses the idea that even though information systems development (ISD) approaches have long advocated the use of integrated organisational views, the modelling techniques used have not been adapted accordingly and remain focused on the automated information system (IS) solution. Existing research provides evidence that business process simulation (BPS) can be used at different points in the ISD process to provide better-integrated organisational views that aid the design of appropriate IS solutions. Despite this fact, research in this area is not extensive; suggesting that the potential of using BPS for the ISD process is not yet well understood. The paper uses the findings from three different case studies to illustrate the ways BPS has been used at different points in the ISD process, especially in the area of requirements engineering. It compares the results against IS modelling techniques, highlighting the advantages and disadvantages that BPS has over the latter. The research necessary to develop appropriate BPS tools and give guidance on their use in the ISD process is discussed.

Introduction

This chapter looks at information systems development (ISD) and examines the potential role of simulation techniques within the information system (IS) developer's toolkit. Since the inception of business data processing in the 1950s, ISD has remained a complex and unreliable process with the research repeatedly reporting high levels of "failed" projects (Standish Group, 1999).

Early approaches to discipline ISD focused on treating it as a production process and gave rise to the linear, or waterfall, systems development life cycle (SDLC). This was perceived to have three advantages: a) it follows a series of specific and sequential phases from the beginning of the project until its end; b) it advocates the use of techniques and tools to formulate, step by step, the detailed design and implement the IS, and c) it introduces the use of project management tools to control the overall process.

Despite the initial success of the linear SDLC, it did not deliver a dramatic reduction in the project failure rate and a number of limitations were identified. For example, it is argued that instead of meeting organisational objectives, the traditional or linear SDLC aims to design an IS to help to solve low-level operational tasks (Avison & Fitzgerald, 2003). In addition, it is claimed that the traditional SDLC focuses on "automating" processes, rather than proposing innovative integrated solutions (Rhodes, 1998). It is important to recognise that in parallel with the adoption of more rigorous ISD techniques there has also been a progressive demand for IS to deal with more complex and wide ranging business processes.

In trying to address some of these limitations, IS practitioners have proposed a wide range of alternative ISD approaches by emphasising different aspects of the development process. For instance, some methodologies claim that organisational objectives can be better met by stressing the analysis of the organisational processes. Examples of these are structured analysis and design of IS (STRADIS), SSADM (OGC, 2000) and Yourdon Systems Method (YSM). Others, such as information engineering (IE), claim that organisational goals can be better addressed by placing more emphasis on the analysis of the data. Finally, there are those approaches, like Merise, that considers both processes and data with equal importance (Vessey & Glass, 1998). Most of the approaches above stress a scientific or functionalist approach by breaking-up a complex system into its constituent parts. However, there are other approaches, like soft systems methodology (SSM) (Checkland & Scholes, 1999), that suggest that the properties of the whole system cannot be explained in terms of the properties of its constituent parts, but can be better understood when looked at from a holistic perspective. A key issue is the dichotomy between methodologies, like SSM, that see the human actors and decision makers as part of "the system" and those that focus on the automated all programmed elements as "the system." The former wider view introduces complex socio-technological issues, which are avoided in the latter narrower perspective.

Even though ISD approaches have long advocated the use of integrated organisational views, appropriate modelling techniques have not been adopted and practice remains focused on the automated IS solution. For example, well defined IS modelling techniques are available to understand the overall function of the system in question, to understand IS data structures, or to model the processes involved in the IS software (see Table 1). There is, however, very little indication of modelling techniques for examining organisational views that explicitly integrate automated software and human activities (Giaglis et al., 2004).

To address this problem it is proposed that business process simulation (BPS) can be used at different points in the ISD process to better integrate the organisational views and thereby to aid the design of appropriate IS solutions. To this end, the chapter is structured in the following way. In order to illustrate the advantages of using BPS for the ISD process, the second section describes the underlying principles behind BPS. To provide a reference point for this critique, the next three sections describe the objectives pursued in the main phases of the linear SDLC. In addition, a critique of the modelling techniques used in these phases is provided together with a description of how BPS has been used in ISD projects to address some of the limitations found in the critique. The linear SDLC paradigm [as described by Avison &

Table 1. Classification of modeling techniques adapted from Avison and Fitzgerald (2003)

Stage/Aspects addressed	Overall	Data	Process
Strategy	Rich Pictures		
Investigation &Analysis	Rich Pictures Objects Martices Strcuture diagrams Use Cases	Entity Modelling Class Diagrams	Data Flow Diagrams Entity Life Cycle Decision Trees Decision Tables Action Diagrams Root Definitions Conceptual Models (UML)
Logical design	Objects Matrices Structure diagrams	Normalisation Entity Modelling Class Diagrams	Decision Trees Decision Tables Action Diagrams
Implementation	Objects Matrices Structure diagrams	Normalisation	Decision Trees Decision Tables Action Diagrams

Fitzgerald (2003)] was chosen as the reference point because it can be seen as a generalisation of the variety of IS methodologies available in the field. Arguably, iterative, star and spiral SDLC models modify rather than escape from this basic linear model. Advocates of specific ISD approaches can all refer back to the linear model, and the way BPS is useable in each phase of a linear SDLC can be related to the corresponding phases of particular ISD approaches. The seventh section is a discussion of the implications of this approach and the research needed to establish the use of BPS within the ISD toolkit. Finally, the last section draws general conclusions from this paper and points at future research in the area.

Business Process Simulation

Business process simulation (BPS) can be defined as:

the process of designing a model of a real system and conducting experiments with this model for the purpose, either of understanding the behaviour of the system or of evaluating various strategies (within the limits imposed by a criterion or set of criteria) for the operation of the system. (Shannon, 1975)

Simulation can be used to understand the behaviour of the existing business system, to identifying problematic tasks and to experiment with alternative scenarios (Hlupic & Robinson, 1998; Vreede, 1998). Business process practitioners have long recognised this advantage and have been using this technique in process innovation projects. In particular BPS has been used to:

- Evaluate process and information systems (Paul et al., 1998)
- Allow multidisciplinary teams to understand the system under investigation and enforce communication amongst the stakeholders (Vreede & Verbraeck, 1996; Paul et al., 1998)
- Understand, analyse, and improve business processes (Pegden et al., 1995).
- Provide quantitative information related to the system performance, hence to take better decisions (Pegden et al., 1995; Sierhuis et al., 2003).
- Evaluate different system alternatives (Levas et al., 1995; Giaglis, 1999).

Subsequent sections of this chapter will use this information to show that BPS is a modelling technique that can, in principle, be used to model many of the aspects needed for different stages of the ISD process. In particular this chapter concentrates to demonstrate that BPS can be used within the feasibility study, system investigation, system analysis and system design phases of the linear SDLC.

Feasibility Study Phase

The purpose of the feasibility study phase is simply to answer the question: "is this system worth building?" A feasibility study will review analysis and design issues in sufficient detail to answer this question but it will not go further. It is therefore a preview of the analysis and design process but conducted at low cost within a short timescale. As soon as the question can be answered the project will go through a full management review and the decision on whether to make the necessary investment is taken.

Because this phase focuses on capturing general aspects of the present system, the modelling techniques used in this phase are mainly holistic and process oriented. Rich pictures, root definitions, conceptual models, and cognitive mapping are some of the techniques used in this phase to help to understand the problem situation being investigated by the analysts. Rich pictures are particularly useful as a way to understanding the general problem situation at the beginning of the project. Root definitions help the analysts to identify the organisational context the system has to deal with, in particular human activity systems. Conceptual models show how the various activities in the human activity system relate to each other.

It can be argued that the aforementioned IS modelling techniques are capable of modelling the information required in this phase with few, if any, limitations. The following section, though, describes the way BPS can be used to obtain other information that these traditional IS techniques cannot expose.

BPS for the Feasibility Study Phase

The different reasons for using simulation in process innovation projects and the information obtained from simulation models (see the second section) does not differ much from the information collected in a feasibility study. Thus, BPS is a technique that could be used to get most of the results needed for the feasibility study.

The major advantage that BPS has is related to its dynamic properties. Traditional techniques can be used to understand the problem situation, to identify the organisational context (people, resources, processes, etc.) and extract system requirements. However, these models are static in the way that they represent a particular moment during the operation of the system. On the other hand, BPS can be used not only as a graphical representation of the system but also to simulate the operation of the system as it evolves over time (Paul et al., 1998). This feature allows practitioners to gain a better understanding of the behaviour of the system because the analyst can observe the way the system operates without the need to interrupt the organisation's operations or the need to be in the organisation's premises. The quantitative data provided by simulation runs, such as queuing times, processing, time, resource utilisation, and so on, can also be used to complement the qualitative information derived from the graphical interface, providing more information to take better decisions (Pegden et al., 1995; Sierhuis et al., 2003). These metrics can also be used for evaluating different system alternatives (Levas et al., 1995; Giaglis, 1999).

Recent research provides evidence that BPS has already successfully been used in IS projects for similar purposes. For example, Eatock et al. (2002) used BPS to assess the impact that the insertion of new IT may have on the organisational process. The authors argue that the performance measurements provided by the BPS model helped them to gain a better understanding of the current system. This in turn allowed IS practitioners to propose alternative IS solutions that better fit the identified problems. The proposed alternatives were also modelled using BPS so performance measurements could be compared.

Similar to this research, Giaglis et al. (2004) used BPS to assess the expected operational benefits of Electronic Data Interchange (EDI) in the textile/clothing sector in Greece. The main purpose of the simulation exercise was to provide quantitative measures of the supposed ability of EDI to facilitate inventory reduction in the organisations that use this technology as part of their ordering and logistics processes. The study showed that the process of developing, validating and using simulation models for the design of BP and IS was a very useful learning exercise for all participants in the study. It generated greater awareness of both the specifications of the proposed system and the conditions of the business operations under which the system can produce the desired results.

Systems Investigation Phase

This phase is an extension of the work performed in the previous phase but in much more detail. This phase usually looks at:

- Functional requirements of the existing system and whether these requirements are being achieved
- The requirements of the new system
- Any constraints imposed
- Range of data types and volumes to be processed
- Exception conditions
- Problems of present working methods

The modelling techniques used in this phase are the same used in the feasibility phase, namely rich pictures, root definitions, conceptual models, and cognitive mapping. The major difference is that the models developed in previous phases are elaborated in much more detail. Thus, there is the need to collect detailed information about the system. This phase, therefore, uses other techniques for gathering information. Amongst the most popular ones are the five-fact finding techniques: observation, interviewing, questionnaires, searching records, and documentation and sampling.

The advantages and disadvantages of IS modelling techniques used in this phase were already discussed in the third section. In relation to the five-fact finding techniques the following disadvantages can be listed (Bennett et al., 1999):

- Written documents do not match reality; for instance company reports can be biased and out of date
- Lack of access to required people
- Interviews are time-consuming and can be the most costly form of data gathering
- The interviewee may be trying to please and saying what they think the interviewer wants to hear
- Most people do not like being observed and are likely to behave differently from the way in which they would normally behave.
- Questionnaires are easier to ignore and hence suffer from low response rates.
- Good questionnaires are difficult to design.

BPS for the Systems Investigation Phase

The main difference between the investigation phase and the feasibility phase is related to the depth in which the system is analysed in the former. Thus, the uses of BPS illustrated in the feasibility phase apply also to the systems investigation phase, where the distinction lies on the depth in which the models are constructed.

Apart from the advantages already described in the third section, Paul and Serrano (2004) provide evidence that BPS can also be used as a requirements gathering technique. Paul and Serrano reported that the analysis of

BPS models had helped IS analysts to identify IS requirements, in particular non-functional requirements, that were overlooked by traditional IS techniques. Based on the results derived from a case study, the authors reported that in order to reduce the time to complete an order (identified as a system requirement) the system depended on one particular factor: the number of backorders produced by the system. Hence, a non-functional requirement that was previously overlooked and that was derived from the analysis of the BPS model is related to the reduction of backorders. Moreover, the results provided by the simulation model suggested that in order to deliver orders within the period of time set by the organisation (24 hours) the system should produce no more than 5% of backorders. This information was obtained because the BPS model produced performance measurements of the whole operational processes including those supported by the proposed IS solution. In this way analysts were able to identify system requirements that were related to performance and also provide specific metrics for those requirements. Therefore, BPS can be used to complement the information derived from traditional gathering techniques.

BPS can also help to overcome some of the limitations found in the five-fact finding techniques. It is argued that a simulation exercise can engage staff in the process because it presents a dynamic and visual impression of the system or process (Hlupic & Vreede, 2004). By engaging staff, problems related to unambiguous or biased information can be reduced.

Systems Analysis Phase

In this phase the efforts concentrate on understanding the information gathered in the previous phase. It seeks to describe all aspects of the present system, the reasons it was developed as it is, and eventually, proposing alternative solutions for the creation of a new system. The analysis of the present system is usually done by asking the following questions:

- Why do the problems exist?
- Why were certain methods of work adopted?
- Are there alternative methods?

Apart from the modelling techniques used in previous stages, in this phase analysts count on other modelling techniques to capture more specific information. For example, to model the data used, produced and manipulated by the system, data techniques such as entity modelling and class diagrams are used. Similarly, process-oriented techniques, such as data flow diagrams, entity life cycle, decision trees, decision tables, and action diagrams, are also employed as basic techniques for functional decomposition. This is, to break down the problem into more and more detail in a disciplined way.

Entity modelling and class diagrams are designed to identify specific issues related to the data that the system uses and manipulates and they have proved very reliable to achieve this aim. Thus little criticism can be made in this respect. This is not the case, though, for process techniques.

Once again, the main disadvantage that traditional IS modelling techniques have is related to their static nature. The main questions posed in this phase, such as identifying the reasons of why problems exists and if there are alternative methods of work, are very difficult to answer with static models (Pidd, 1998; Robinson, 1994). IS analysts rely much on their experience and expertise to answer such questions since these techniques are mainly used to portray the analyst perspective and they rarely provide more information to the analysts to make better decisions.

BPS for the Systems Analysis Phase

BPS has been proved an excellent tool for functional decomposition and systems analysis. It has been said that simulation models can be regarded as problem understanding rather than problem solving tools (Hlupic & Vreede, 2004). Therefore, BPS can be used to answer the questions: *Why do the problems exist?*, and, *Why were certain methods of work adopted?*

A major difference between BPS and traditional IS techniques is that the former is capable of conducting "what if" analysis whereas the latter cannot. Once a BPS model is build and validated, changes to system variables and processes can be done to test alternative scenarios. According to Giaglis (2004), there are two main sets of variables to be studied by decision makers: the configuration of the proposed information system (IS functionality) and the organisational arrangement regarding the structures and operations that surround it (business processes). By measuring the performance of the business processes with and without the use of IT, decision makers can collect the quantitative information needed to conduct further investment appraisal and IS design using established methods (Giaglis et al., 2004).

Paul and Serrano (2004) have used BPS to analyse five different process solutions for the case study reported in their research. The experiments' results provided more information, such as performance measurements, that helped on the selection of the scenario that better matched the organisational needs. More importantly, prior to the experimentation with BPS models, the scenario that included the use of IT was thought to be the most appropriate one for the organisation. The analysis of the simulation results indicated that the scenario that included the insertion of IT did not improve, in a significant manner, the overall system's performance. It was identified that one of the main problems with the system was due to the way processes were organised rather than the lack of adequate IT infrastructure to support them. Similar to this work, Giaglis et al. (2004) have used BPS to assess different solutions in an IS development project. The main objective of the simulation study was specified to provide a measure of the efficiency gains that could be achieved in inventory control within the textile/clothing value chain. The simulation exercise was also aimed to explore the possible benefits of the insertion of EDI in inventory reduction. To this end the authors developed two simulation models, one to portray the organisation's operations as they are and one that included an Electronic Data Interchange (EDI) solution. The results provided evidence that indicated that all inventory levels were reduced after the introduction of EDI. Materials inventory, for example, were reported to be reduced by up to a 46% whereas the product inventory by up to a 27%.

Systems Design Phase

This stage involves the design of the system. To achieve this aim, analysts use the information gathered during previous phases to produce the documentation that portrays the functionality of the new system. Many parts of these documents can be seen in the form of models. Models used in previous phases can be used to derive more detailed models of the way the system will operate. For example, *use cases* is a modelling technique that can be used in the first stages of an ISD process to capture the functionality of the system. At the systems design phase, the information depicted in use cases is commonly used to design collaboration, sequence and activity or state diagrams. These models provide detailed information about how the system will function at particular points in time. For example, they can provide information about how the system will perform a specific transaction and how it will interact with the user to achieve this aim. Traditional IS techniques, however, cannot be used to assess how different workloads may affect the performance of such transactions. More importantly, they cannot be used to assess the impact that this new way of operating will have on the system as a whole.

BPS for the Systems Design Phase

It is argued that misinterpretation of user requirements is one of the main factors that contribute to IS failure (Vessey & Conger, 1994). Therefore, one of the challenges faced by analysts in this phase is to ensure that the functionality proposed for the new system matches, in the best possible way, user requirements. Because misinterpretation of user requirements may cause significant changes on the system's design, hence adding unexpected time delays and/or expenses, validation of requirements should be done prior the implementation phase. Validation of user requirements is frequently done iteratively throughout previous phases of the ISD process. The techniques used to validate requirements are usually those employed to capture user requirements. For example, *use case* is one modelling technique that is commonly used to capture user requirements. Once requirements are captured and translated into use cases, these models are taken to the users to validate that their requirements are well represented in such models.

Traditional IS techniques such as use cases, however, cannot provide information on whether the functionality proposed in such models will improve the performance of the system as a whole or to provide predictive metrics of such performance. Use case models cannot provide information related to what could be the benefits of implementing the functionality described considering the organisational context. In other words, traditional IS techniques cannot be used to answer questions such as: What is the performance of the proposed IS functionality?, or, What would be the impact that the proposed system will have on other processes?

When asked to validate requirements models, users typically focus on items of detail rather than the impact of system on general working practices. The experience of using the system is not the same as reading about using it. Users will be able to perceive the impact of the system on their individual tasks but not know how these effects combine to change the behaviour of the organisation as a whole. Long-term systemic impacts will often remain hidden.

Researchers in this area argue that BPS can be used in this phase to verify that the functionality proposed for the new system matches global or systemic requirements. Paul and Serrano (2004) and Giaglis et al. (2004) have proposed alternative ways of using BPS to simulate the effects that a proposed IS functionality will have on the business processes and vice versa. Paul and Serrano (2004) proposed a BPS modelling approach that uses the specifications derived from IS models, such as use cases, collaboration, and activity diagrams to represent the IS functionality within a BPS model. In this way, analysts can obtain metrics of a) the performance of the IS as it evolves over time (known as non-functional requirements), and b) the impact that the functionality proposed by the IS would have in the business processes. More importantly, Paul and Serrano (2004) report that the use of BPS models helped analysts to identify flaws in system design and thus, redesign the proposed IS functionality. With the aid of the BPS model, the authors observed that the IS functionality proposed for their organisational case study would not improve, in a significant manner, the overall system's performance. They observed that in order to take full advantage of the proposed information system, changes to other processes were also required. This helped them to redesign the system's functionality so it better meets the organisational targets.

Prototyping is a method that has long been used by the IS community to ensure that the proposed IS functionality meets user requirements. Software engineers use the term prototype, or prototyping, to reflect a variety of different activities. In this chapter, we will concentrate on the conventional engineering sense of prototyping. This is the production of a partial system (interface, a key algorithm, etc.) for the purpose of evaluating or selecting an element of the design. Such prototypes are not of adequate quality or sufficiently complete to be regarded as early deliverable versions of the system (Oxford University Press, 2002).

A traditional prototyping process consists of designing and building a scaled-down usable model of the proposed system and then demonstrate the working model to the user with the purpose of obtaining feedback on its suitability and effectiveness. Developers then take the feedback and make corresponding changes on the design. This process is repeated until the users agree that the prototype is satisfactory (Boar, 1984; Arthur, 1992) .

There are some cases, however, where prototypes, all pilot systems, may not be appropriate. Organisational processes and their supporting information system(s) require input from users at different points in time. The time between these points may range from seconds, minutes or hours to days, months or even years depending on the organisational processes. For example, an arbitration process can take more than one year to be completed, having several users' input information at different times during this period. Similarly, insurance processes can take months to be completed. Prototype systems need to wait for the processes and related transactions to be completed in real time to obtain user feedback. Thus, when processes take long periods of time, prototyping methods cannot provide the desired results within acceptable limits.

Ongoing research in the School of Information Systems and Computing at Brunel University (Elliman & Eatock, 2004) claim that BPS can be used to validate user requirements in cases where long term processes are involved. The authors propose a modelling approach that combines prototyping with simulation techniques, specifically with BPS. The approach is composed of two main models: a BPS model that simulates the organisational processes and an IS prototype that simulates the functionality of the proposed information system. The business process simulation will model the behaviour of actors within, or even without, the organisation. It will generate "work" for the organisation and play out the way actors respond to information from the proposed new IS. Thus the link between the two components in this prototyping experiment is:

- Signals of events that are recorded by the information system
- Outputs from the information system that change the behaviour of actors

Note that the level of implementation required is well below that of a completed information system. For example, the system has no user interfaces nor data that affects the state of the information held in such a way as to change the subsequent behaviour of actors. For example, it is not necessary to work out whether a particular arbitration case requires the use of an expert. In the simulation one can simply assign a probability to this necessity and ensure that, at random, an appropriate number of cases are tagged as needing an expert witness. The IS implementation simply carries this tag rather than a full set of name, address, and so on describing the witness. Upon interrogation the IS can confirm the involvement of the expert and provide the tag value as a sufficient identifier.

Because this approach simulates the interactions between the system's components, namely actors, IS and processes, analysts were able to test the way the system would behave without the need to wait for long periods of time. Processes that take long periods of time, for example months, were now simulated by the BPS model in minutes.

Discussion

Previous sections provide evidence that business process simulation (BPS) is a modelling technique that can be used effectively in different phases of the IS development process paradigm and, more importantly, that it can be used to overcome some of the limitations identified in traditional IS modelling techniques. To this end, parts of the third, fourth and fifth section discuss the ability that BPS has to provide the information required for the *feasibility*, *systems investigation* and *systems analysis* phases of the SDLC. More importantly, that it provides other information that traditional IS techniques cannot provide, such as performance metrics of the system as it evolves over time.

Although this suggestion of simulation as an ISD technique has a long history, it has not been developed as a routine tool in the analysts' armoury. To achieve the potential value set out in this chapter two areas of ongoing research are necessary. First, there is the need to develop business process simulation tools and techniques that can be rapidly applied. Second, there is the need to develop awareness and acceptance of the techniques.

The development of a model in the E-Arbitration-T project (Elliman & Eatock, 2004) involved significant technical effort that could have been reduced if appropriate tools were available off the shelf. This project suggested a need for three lines of tool development research. These are explained next:

- **Simulating the interactions between human activity and IS state:** The first area of development is to enhance business process simulation tools so they can model the interactions between human activity (e.g., activities or processes) and the different states of the information system. Information systems have an effect on user behaviour, which is not currently captured by traditional discrete event simulation tools for business process. For example, an office clerk uses the information system to process a purchase order. The system then informs the clerk whether the items chosen are available or not. Depending on the output of this transaction (e.g., available or not) the clerk will choose the process or activity to follow. In the example the possible options could be (a) to proceed with the purchasing order without the products that are not available, (b) cancel the order, or (c) create a backorder for those products that are not available. This example suggests that the IS data about the current transaction state determines user action, which in turn will influence the performance of the processes being modelled. Therefore, this research argues that, in order to model the impact that the system will have on the organisation's processes, existing business process simulation tools should be able to portray the interactions between human activity and the IS state. The most important part in this development is to add a representation of the IS itself and its interface to the already existing discrete event simulation of human activity (e.g., processes). The main objective of adding the IS element to the BPS tool is to show how the business process can be guided (or misguided) by the IS output. Thus if interaction with the IS fails to adequately capture transaction state changes, the simulation reveals the consequential (and potentially incorrect) business process behaviour. For the simulation to be constructed rapidly and effectively this component needs to be easily configured and integrated within the model. The authors argue that the proposed IS component can be achieved if the IS model is state-based (i.e., technical requirements are expressed as entity life history or UML activity state diagrams). These models depict key global IS state rather than specific data, thus they can be built rapidly at a high level of abstraction. They can be constructed early in the development life cycle (including feasibility) and, thus, the time to deliver—given appropriate tools—should be practicable.

- **Pre-built business process elements:** The second area of technical development is the need to provide other pre-built business process elements. Almost all simulation packages provide pre-built elements for modelling manufacturing systems – machine tools, stores, conveyors and transport devices. The availability of business elements is less frequent and more basic. Although packages may have elements like call centres they do not deal with higher levels of knowledge worker behaviour

(Kidd, 1994; Elliman & Hayman, 1999). Research to formulate and develop these components is also necessary (Elliman et al., 2005).

- **Work Generation:** The last area of technical development concerns the generation of "work" for the simulated business. The demands for information or knowledge services are much more variable than those experienced in general manufacturing. Thus there is a need to enhance the case or work generation capabilities of most simulation packages so that they can handle complex case of generation efficiently. With the increasing use of mass customisation and flexible manufacturing improved "work" generation, tools may incidentally have benefits for manufacturing systems simulation.

These three tool development areas are not independent and research is needed not only to develop models for each of these tools but also to establish the relationships between them and the different ISD phases. Given the time and cost limits on a feasibility study, the time and cost of setting up current simulation packages could be inappropriate for most IS projects, at least for this phase. BPS practitioners argue, however, that it is possible to create broad-brush models with only limited detail but with enough information to determine whether the synergies exist to deliver the expected benefits or whether the reorganised system contains negative interactions that could undermine the anticipated benefits. Furthermore, the information captured from models developed during the first phase of the SDLC is frequently used to design models for subsequent phases. This suggests that IS analysts could use the simplified version of the BPS model designed in the first phase and gradually modify the level of detail according to the requirements needed for each phase.

In conventional engineering, simulation is an accepted and standard element of design practice. The use of models in wind tunnels or model ships in wave tanks are examples of tried and trusted simulation techniques. Engineers understand the limitations of these models and their relationship to the final product. Similarly, discrete event simulation of physical production plant is an accepted methodology (Siemer et al., 1995). In ISD these relationships are less well defined and understood, and thus there is a reluctance to accept simulation in this context. Further research is needed to refine the techniques and present them to practitioners. These lines of research are intimately tied up with building a bridge between objective technology and subjective evaluations or perceptions. Developing appropriate guidelines for their use will be important.

The knowledge required to construct adequate BPS models for many elements of the feasibility study, system investigation and system analysis phases is relatively simple. IS developers can refer to the simulation steps found in the literature, such as those suggested by Banks et al. (2000) or Robinson (1994). However, in order to answer deeper questions about performance measurements of both BPS and IS functionality, particularly in the design phase (see the sixth section), developers need significant modifications to the way traditional BPS models are constructed as described above.

Conclusion

This chapter argues that BPS models are able to provide the same and more information than traditional IS modelling techniques, thus, they are suitable to address the modelling needs required at different points in the ISD process. Evidence to sustain this argument has been presented in the following ways:

a. BPS has been successfully used in the business process innovation domain to obtain very similar information to that required in different phases of the SDLC paradigm, and

b. BPS models have already been used within the IS domain for similar purposes.

The main advantage that BPS provides over traditional BPS modelling techniques is its ability to simulate the dynamic behaviour of the system as it evolves over time. In particular it provides models that better integrate the dynamics of human activity and the automated IS. It has been discussed that the quantitative metrics provided by BPS models can be used by IS analysts to:

• Better understand the operation of the current system
• Identify possible system bottlenecks
• Evaluate different system alternatives
• Obtain performance measurements of the system's behaviour for both processes and IS

To justify these arguments, three different case studies that employ BPS in IS projects are used: Paul and Serrano (2004), Giaglis et al. (2004), and Elliman and Eatock (2004).

The evidence presented in this chapter strongly suggests that BPS models are able to provide more information than traditional IS techniques and that this information can be very useful to design better IS solutions. Thus, the authors of this chapter advocate the idea that practitioners in this domain should routinely consider the use of BPS as an alternative tool to support different stages of the ISD process. Moreover, the seventh section argues that BPS models can be used to simulate proposed IS functionality and the effect that it may have on the organisation as a whole. The development of such models, however, is more complicated than the way traditional BPS models are designed. Thus, further research in this area is needed to improve the BPS toolkit and demonstrate its effectiveness in various ISD scenarios.

References

Arthur, L.J. (1992). *Rapid evolutionary development: Requirements; prototyping and software creation.* New York: John Wiley & Sons.

Avison, D.E., & Fitzgerald, G. (2003) *Information systems development: Methodologies, techniques and tools.* London: McGraw-Hill.

Banks, J., Carson, J.S., Nelson, B.L., & Nicol, D.M. (2000). *Discrete-event system simulation.* Upper Saddle River, NJ: Prentice-Hall.

Bennett, S., McRobb, S., & Farmer, R. (1999). *Object-oriented systems analysis and design using UML.* London: McGraw-Hill.

Boar, B.H. (1984). *Applications prototyping: A requirements definition strategy for the 80s.* Chichester, UK: John Wiley & Sons.

Checkland, P., & Scholes, J. (1999). *Soft systems methodology in action.* Chichester, UK: John Wiley & Sons,.

Eatock, J., Paul, R.J., & Serrano, A. (2002). Developing a theory to explain the insights gained concerning information systems and business processes behaviour: The ASSESS-IT project. *Information Systems Frontiers, 4*(3), 303-316.

Elliman, T., & Eatock, J. (2004). Online support for arbitration: Designing software for a flexible business process. *International Journal of Information Technology and Management, 4*(4), 443-460.

Elliman, T., Eatock, J., & Spencer, N. (2005). Modelling knowledge worker behaviour in business process studies. *Journal of Enterprise Information Management, 18*(1), 79-94.

Elliman, T., & Hayman, A. (1999). A comment on Kidd's characterisation of knowledge workers. *Cognition. Technology and Work, 1*(3), 162-168.

Giaglis, G.M. (1999). *Dynamic process modelling for business engineering and information systems.* Unpublished doctoral dissertation, Brunel University, London.

Giaglis, G.M., Hlupic, V., Vreede, G.J., & Verbraeck, A. (2004). Synchronous design of business processes and information systems using dynamic process modelling. *Business Process Management Journal, 11*(5), 488-500.

Hlupic, V., & Robinson, S. (1998). Business process modelling and analysis using discrete-event simulation. In D.J. Medeiros, E.F. Watson, J.S. Carson, & M.S. Manivannan (Eds.), *Proceedings of the 1998 Winter Simulation Conference,* Washington, DC (pp. 1363-1369).

Hlupic, V., & Vreede, G.J. (2005). Business process modelling using discrete-event simulation: Current opportunities and future challenges. *International Journal of Simulation & Process Modelling, 1*(1-2), 72-81.

Kidd, A. (1994). The marks are on the knowledge worker. In J. Olson (Ed.), *CHI'94: Celebrating independence: Proceedings of the Conference of Human Factors in Computer Systems,* Boston (pp. 186-191).

Levas, A., Boyd, S., Jain, P., & Tulskie, W.A. (1995). The role of modelling and simulation in business process reengineering. A. Alexopoulos, K. Kang, W.R. Lilegdon, & D. Goldsman (Eds.), *Proceedings of the Winter Simulation Conference* (pp. 1341-1346).

Office of Government Commerce. (2000). *SSADM Foundation (Office of Government Commerce).* London: The Stationery Office Books.

Paul, R.J., Hlupic, V., & Giaglis, G. (1998). Simulation modeling of business processes. D. Avison & D. Edgar-Neville (Eds.), *Proceedings of the 3rd U.K. Academy of Information Systems Conference,* Lincoln, U.K.

Paul, R.J., & Serrano, A. (2004). Collaborative information systems and business process design using simulation. In *Proceedings of the 37th*

Hawaii International Conference on Systems Sciences (CD/ROM), Big Island, Hawaii (p. 9).

Pegden, C.D., Shannon, R.E., & Sadowski, R.P. (1995). *Introduction to simulation using SIMAN.* London: McGraw-Hill.

Pidd, M. (1998). *Computer simulation in management science.* Chichester, UK: John Wiley & Sons.

Prototype. (2002). *A dictionary of business.* Oxford Reference Online. Retrieved February 27, 2005, from http://www.oxfordreference.com/views/ENTRY.html?subview=Main&entry=t18.e4769

Rhodes, D. (1998). Integration challenge for medium and small companies. In *Proceedings of the 23rd Annual Conference of British Production and Inventory Control Society,* Birmingham (pp. 153-66).

Robinson, S. (1994). *Successful simulation: A practical approach to simulation projects.* Maidenhead, UK: McGraw-Hill.

Shannon, R.E. (1975). *Systems simulation: The art and the science.* Englewood Cliffs, NJ: Prentice Hall.

Siemer, J., Taylor, S.J.E., & Elliman, A.D. (1995). Intelligent tutoring systems for simulation modelling in the manufacturing industry. *International Journal of Manufacturing System Design, 2*(3), 165-175.

Sierhuis, M., Clacey, W.J., Seah, C., Trimble, J.P., & Sims, M.H. (2003). Modeling and simulation for mission operations work system design. *Journal of Management Information Systems, 19*(4), 85-128.

Standish Group. (1999). West Yarmouth, MA: Standish Group International.

Vessey, I., & Conger, S.A. (1994). Requirements specification: Learning object, process, and data methodologies. *Communications of the ACM, 37* (5), 102-113.

Vessey, I., & Glass, R. (1998). Strong vs. weak: Approaches to systems development. *Communications of the ACM, 41*(4), 99-102.

Vreede, G.J. (1998). Collaborative business engineering with animated electronic meetings. *Journal of Management Information Systems, 14* (3), 141-164.

Vreede, G.J., & Verbraeck, A. (1996). Animating organizational processes: Insight eases change. *Journal of Simulation Practice and Theory, 4*(3), 245-263.

Chapter XIV

Selfish Users and Distributed MAC Protocols in Wireless Local Area Networks

Ratan K. Guha, University of Central Florida, USA

Sudipta Rakshit, University of Central Florida, USA

Abstract

In this chapter we consider the effect of "selfishness" on distributed MAC protocols in wireless local area network (WLAN). The inherently contention-based medium access in distributed systems is modelled as a non-cooperative game: "access game." Both quality of service (QoS) and battery power (BP) are incorporated in modelling the game. It is shown that the Nash equilibrium (NE) for incomplete information games is usually inefficient compared to the NE of complete information games. We propose some simple mechanisms to approximate the incomplete information scenario as complete information. For complete information games, we investigate whether fairness can be achieved by selfish users. Different cases are considered and it is shown that the NE does not result in fairness. We next compute the constrained NE (CNE) for the access game. Finally, we analyze the stability of the distributed system.

Notations

G	$\rightarrow$	A formal game
I	$\rightarrow$	Set of players in G
n	$\rightarrow$	Total number of users in G
i	$\rightarrow$	Generic user
$-i$	$\rightarrow$	The system without user i
A_i	$\rightarrow$	Strategy space of user i
p_i	$\rightarrow$	Transmission probability of user i
θ, Θ	$\rightarrow$	Throughput
$u_i, \bar{u}_i, U_i$	$\rightarrow$	Utility function for user i
$c_{1,i}$	$\rightarrow$	Payoff for success for user i
$c_{2,i}$	$\rightarrow$	Payoff for wait for user i
$c_{3,i}$	$\rightarrow$	Payoff for failure for user i
r_i	$\rightarrow$	Payoff ratio $(c_{2,i} - c_{3,i})/(c_{1,i} - c_{3,i})$
g	$\rightarrow$	$\prod_{i=1}^{n}(1 - p_i)$
NE	$\rightarrow$	Nash equilibrium
BNE	$\rightarrow$	Bayesian Nash equilibrium
CNE	$\rightarrow$	Constrained Nash equilibrium
λ	$\rightarrow$	Poisson arrival rate
μ	$\rightarrow$	Exponential service time
ρ	$\rightarrow$	λ / μ

Introduction

In this chapter, we consider the fairness issues in a distributed wireless local area network (WLAN) with a finite but fixed number of selfish users. Bandwidth is one of the primary resources in computer communication networks and quality of service (QoS) is influenced by how bandwidth is shared in a distributed system. In the case of WLANs, battery power (BP) conservation is also an important issue [Jones et al. (2001), and references therein] in addition to the QoS. As access to bandwidth is dependent on medium access control (MAC) protocols [Garcia et al., 2000], the research on bandwidth fairness has focused on devising efficient MAC protocols to achieve fairness. MAC protocols can be broadly classified into two types: centralized and distributed. In centralized MAC protocols, namely HIPERLAN (Kruys, 1992; ETSI, 1996), a central entity arbitrates for a particular user. On the other hand, in distributed protocols, namely carrier sense multiple access (CSMA), users vie with each other for media access. Distributed protocols have several advantages over the centralized protocols, for example, scalability and robustness. Due to their widespread popularity, we discuss and analyse distributed MAC protocols only.

ALOHA (Abramson, 1970) was one of the earliest distributed MAC protocols. ALOHA was attractive because of its simplicity. However, maximum achievable throughput was not very high ($1/2e$). Improvements were suggested in the form of slotted ALOHA (maximum achievable throughput $1/e$). CSMA and carrier sense multiple access/collision detection (CSMA/CD) (Nutt et al., 1982; Exley et al., 1987; Chiao et al., 1987; O'Reilly et al., 1984; Dai, 1982) protocols were introduced to further improve the efficiency of the ALOHA. Today Ethernet, by far the most popular choice for media access in local area networks (LANs), employs CSMA/CD algorithm. At the same time, carrier sense multiple access/collision avoidance (CSMA/CA) algorithm is being widely used for wireless local area networks (WLANs) (Visser et al., 1995; P802.11 IEEE Draft, 1997; IEEE 802.11e Draft/D7.0, 2002). A comprehensive description of these protocols can be found in Garcia et al. (2000, Chapter 6). One of the early works on the throughput and delay characteristics of CSMA protocols can be found in Kleinrock et al. (1975).

Previous Work

Previous work on distributed MAC protocols mostly deals with the stability (Fayolle et al., 1977) and the throughput of the system (Kleinrock et al., 1975). QoS also has been a widely researched topic. In all this work, the focus has been on the global and/or average system performance, simply because system designers are interested in the performance of the system as a whole. However, an acceptable system-level performance can be achieved even when users might not have received their fair share of the system resource(s). With the growing demand for QoS, it is conceivable that users would devise access strategies to maximize their share of the system resource, namely bandwidth. We designate these users as "selfish" users (MacKenzie et al., 2003). Similar notion of "selfishness" has been applied to other areas of computer communication, for example routing (Korilis et al., 1995; Orda et al., 1996; Koutsoupias et al., 1999; Roughgarden et al., 2002) and congestion control (Shenker, 1994; Akella et al., 2002; Papadimitriou, 2001).

Mackenzie et al. introduced the concept of selfishness in MAC design and proved the existence of equilibrium for selfish users in ALOHA. In this chapter, we investigate the feasibility of realistic CSMA protocols where user satisfaction and system performance are well balanced.

Fairness

Fairness in bandwidth sharing is a widely researched topic (Demers et al., 1989; Bharghavan et al., 1997; Choudhury et al., 1985; Sharrock et al., 1989; Vaidya et al., 2000; Qiao et al., 2002). We argue that if selfish users achieve fairness in resource sharing, "selfishness" in users will be justified.

Specifically, we address weighted fairness issues in a distributed local area network (LAN) setting with a finite but fixed number of users with different weightages. For the rest of this chapter, weighted fairness is simply referred to as "fairness." Users with higher resource (bandwidth) requirements should be assigned higher weightages (assuming users are willing to pay according to their resource requirements). Therefore, the question is which user requires more bandwidth? Since we consider the fairness issues for WLAN, we include QoS and BP in our modelling. However, more importance is attached to QoS; and BP is considered a non-negligible factor. As BP is incorporated in the modelling, the fairness is considered per-node as opposed to per-flow.

There are two fundamental problems in achieving fair share of bandwidth in distributed systems:

- **Lack of information:** In a distributed system, users usually do not know about the number of other users.
- **Lack of coordination:** In a distributed system, users cannot possibly coordinate their activities and determine who is going to transmit when.

Lack of coordination is more fundamental in nature. Even if it is assumed that users have complete information about the other users in the network, there is no possible way the network access of users can be coordinated to avoid collision: a user with a packet to transmit does not know (unless it is a deterministic system) if the other user(s) are also trying to access the medium at the same time. Therefore, the medium access scenario in distributed systems is inherently contention-based in nature and there is always a probability of collision.

We model the contention-based medium access scenario as a complete information non-cooperative game (Fudenberg et al., 1991) designated as the "access game." We compute various game-theoretic solutions of this game for various conditions and analyse the results for their "fairness" properties. In order to realize the "access game" as a complete information game, a simple technique is proposed.

Our findings are as follows:

- Nash equilibrium (NE) of the "access game" is usually inefficient.
- Constrained Nash equilibrium solutions (CNE) of the "access game" result in fairness.

Organization

The rest of this chapter is organized as follows: the second section discusses some relevant game-theoretic concepts, the third section models the "access game," the fourth section provides a simple technique to approximate incomplete information game as a complete information game, the next three sections present the main results of the chapter, and the last section concludes the chapter.

Game Theoretic Concepts

Before modelling the contention-based MAC scenario as a non-cooperative game, we discuss some relevant game-theoretic concepts.

Actions and Payoff

Formally, a finite game G consists of a non-empty finite set I of players. A player, say i has a set of possible strategies/actions A_i. In order to play the game, all the players choose an action from the respective strategy sets simultaneously. At the end of the game, there is an outcome or result. Clearly, the outcome space of G can be given by $S = \times_i A_i$. Let $s \in S$ be a generic outcome of the game. Associated with the outcome s is a payoff to each of the players. Let us designate by $u_i = u_i(s)$ the payoff function for the ith user. The payoff function of the game u is given by $u(s) = (u_1(s) \dots u_n(s))$.

Pure Strategy, Mixed Strategy, and Utility Functions

The concept of "mixed strategy" (Nash, 1951) is that instead of deciding for a particular action with certainty (i.e., pure strategy), a user i randomizes its decision and chooses a particular action from A_i with a non-negative probability. Consequently, the elements of the outcome set S also become probabilistic in nature. As the payoffs are associated with the outcome of the game, it follows that in a mixed strategy game there is a non-negative probability attached to the value of the payoff a user receives by playing the game. This entails the formulation of utility function $\bar{u}_i$. Utility function $\bar{u}_i$ is the expected payoff for player i from playing the game.

We consider two solution concepts for non-cooperative game theory: NE and CNE.

Nash Equilibrium

NE is arguably the most important solution concept for non-cooperative game theory. For each finite complete information game (where users have complete information about other users) G, Nash (1951) proved the existence of equilibrium in mixed strategy. For this equilibrium, the action of one user is completely independent of what other users are doing. Formally, NE can be presented as follows:

Let the generic mixed strategy of user i be denoted by π_i. Let π_{-i} denote the collective strategies of all the users other than i, that is, $\pi_{-i} = (\pi_1, \dots, \pi_{i-1}, \pi_{i+1}, \dots, \pi_n)$. For an NE strategy $(\pi^*_1, \dots \pi^*_n)$ of the game, the following holds

$$\overline{u}_i \left(\pi^*_i, \pi^*_{-i} \right) \geq \overline{u}_i \left(\pi_i, \pi^*_{-i} \right) \qquad \forall i$$

We provide a simple example to compute NE using best response correspondence of the users. Consider two users: X and Y. $A_X = \{x_1, x_2\}$ and $A_y = \{y_1, y_2\}$. The payoffs for the game can be represented in a matrix form as follows:

Y \ X	x_1	x_2
y_1	(5, 3)	(4, 6)
y_2	(2, 5)	(10, 7)

Payoff Matrix

As an example, the entry (5, 3) implies that if X plays x_1 and Y plays y_1, the payoff to X is 5 and the payoff to Y is 3.

If X chooses to play x_1 with probability p and Y chooses to play y_1 with probability q, the utility function for X can written as

$$U_X = p \times q \times 5 + p \times (1 - q) \times 2 + (1 - p) \times q \times 4 + (1 - p) \times (1 - q) \times 10$$

Player X's best response correspondence for a value of q is the set of p that would maximize U_X. Let us rewrite U_X as

$$U_X = p[9q - 8] + 10 - 6q$$

In this case, the "best" value of p will depend on q as follows:

if $[9q - 8] > 0$, U_X is maximized by $p = 1$
if $[9q - 8] < 0$, U_X is maximized by $p = 0$
if $[9q - 8] > 0$, U_X is maximized by any value of p in (0, 1)
Similarly, $U_y = q[3p - 6p + 6 - 2p - 7 + 7p] + 2p + 7 - 7p = q[2p - 1] + 7 - 5p$

Therefore,

if $[2p - 1] > 0$, U_Y is maximized by $q = 1$

if $[2p - 1] < 0$, U_Y is maximized by $q = 0$

if $[2p - 1] = 0$, U_Y is maximized by any value of q in $(0, 1)$.

NE is obtained when both U_X and U_Y are maximized simultaneously. From the above discussion, it is clear that it will happen when for a value of (p, q), both U_X and U_Y are maximized. If p is plotted as a function of q and q is plotted as a function of p, the set of NE will be the intersections of these two plots.

The three NE of this game are $(p = 1, q = 1)$, $(p = 0, q = 0)$, and $(p = 1/2, q = 8/9)$.

For the above game theoretic equilibria, it was assumed that players have complete information about the system: the number of other players, their payoffs and utility functions, and so on. This assumption may not hold in many practical situations of interest. Players may have incomplete information about the system. This issue was first addressed in Harsanyi (1967-68). The solution concept for incomplete information games is that of Bayesian Nash equilibrium (BNE). Here we model and analyse an incomplete information game and then complete information game.

Constrained Nash Equilibrium

In Nash's formulation, the actions taken by users are completely independent of each other. Rosen (1965) considered the important case where strategies of users are constrained, that is, some relations exist among the strategies (Azouzi et al., 2003). For such a case, he proved the existence of equilibrium for concave utility functions. We refer to this equilibrium concept as CNE. The solution for CNE is still non-cooperative, as users do not communicate with each other about their actions. CNE provides an interesting tool for analysing situations where NE is inefficient.

With these concepts and tools of the game theory, we now model the medium access scenario in a game theoretic framework.

Modelling

Medium Access

In order to transmit, users first have to access the medium successfully using MAC protocols. CSMA protocols are the protocols of choice for distributed LANs. Consider a MAC protocol using CSMA. When a user has a packet to send, the transmitter senses the medium and if the medium is sensed busy, it can take several actions. Depending on these actions, CSMA protocols can be classified as follows (Garcia et al., 2000):

1. **1-persistent:** Keep on sensing the medium and transmit the packet when the channel becomes idle.
2. **Non-persistent:** Do not sense the medium for some time (i.e., back-off).
3. **p-persistent:** Keep on sensing the medium as long as the medium is busy and when the medium becomes idle transmit with probability p [and wait with probability $(1-p)$].

Figure 1 presents a schematic representation of p-CSMA.

As can be observed from Figure 1, at the end of a transmission period there is a brief idle period after which users contend with each other to access the medium. The idle period essentially signals the end of the previous transmission period. Contention is eventually resolved in one user's favour and that user transmits next. Based on p-CSMA, we present the following MAC protocol.

Figure 1. Successive states of the system in p-CSMA

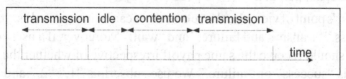

Proposed Protocol

Our proposed MAC strategy is similar to the *p*-CSMA. The significant difference is that the value of "*p*" is not constant in our proposed protocol. Users compute appropriate values of *p*, based on the state of the system. More specifically, users will transmit with different probabilities depending on the number of users present in the system.

Modelling

In order to model the distributed access scenario as a non-cooperative game, it is assumed that users are "selfish" (MacKenzie et al., 2003; Korilis et al., 1995; Orda et al., 1996; Koutsoupias et al., 1999; Roughgarden et al., 2002; Shenker, 1994; Akella et al., 2002; Papadimitriou, 2001; Rakshit et al., 2004] in nature, that is, users are solely interested in maximizing their own utility functions.

Players, Actions and Payoff

Players of the "access game" are the users trying to access the medium. We consider *n* users with user *i* having a weightage of w_i (> 0). All the users use *p*-CSMA type MAC protocol. At the beginning of each contention period, each player has two actions to choose from: "transmit" and "wait." User *i* transmits with probability p_i. If there are *n* users, then strictly speaking outcome space *S* consists of 2^n elements. However, there are essentially three distinct outcomes: "success," "failure," and "waste." If exactly one user transmits, the outcome is "success" and "success" can happen in $\binom{n}{1} = n$ possible ways. If no user transmits, the outcome is "waste" and "waste" can happen in $\binom{n}{n} = 1$ possible ways. If more than one user transmits, the outcome is failure and "failure" can happen in $2^n - n - 1$ possible ways.

From a user's point of view, the above outcomes can be interpreted as: "transmit and success," "transmit and failure," and "wait." Moreover, if a user *i* decides to wait, it should receive the same payoff irrespective of whether the game's outcome is "success" or "failure." We use subscripts "1," "2," and "3" for "transmit and success," "wait," and "transmit and failure" respectively.

The payoffs to users from playing the "access game" are as follows:

1. If only user i transmits, then the outcome of the game is "success." User i receives a payoff of $c_{1,i}$ and user j[$\neq i$] receives a payoff of $c_{2,j}$.
2. If no user transmits, the game's outcome is "waste" and the user i receives a payoff of $c_{2,i}$.
3. If more one user transmits, collision occurs and the outcome of the game is "failure." If user i had transmitted, then user i receives a payoff of $c_{3,i}$. If user i had not transmitted, it receives a payoff of $c_{2,i}$.

We note that the probability that user i "transmits and succeeds" is given by $p_i \times \prod_{j \neq i}^{n}(1 - p_j)$, probability for "transmit and failure" is $1 - p_i \times \prod_{j \neq i}^{n}(1 - p_j)$, and probability of "wait" is $1 - p_i$.

Therefore, the utility function u_i of user i can be written as:

$$\bar{u}_i = p_i \times \prod_{j \neq i}^{n}(1 - p_j) \times c_{1,i} + p_i[1 - \prod_{j \neq i}^{n}(1 - p_j)] \times c_{3,i} + (1 - p_i) \times c_{2,i} \quad (3.1)$$

The NE of the "access game" will be a strategy profile $p^* = (p^*_1 \dots p^*_i \dots p^*_n)$ satisfying the following

$$\bar{u}_i(p^*_i, p^*_{-i}) \geq \bar{u}_i(p_i, p^*_{-i}) \qquad \forall i \qquad\qquad (3.2)$$

Similarly, for the existence of CNE, the following condition should hold:

$$\frac{\partial^2 u_i}{\partial p_i^2} \leq 0 \qquad \forall i \qquad\qquad (3.3)$$

From the expression of the utility function, it can be inferred that the values of payoffs for different outcomes play important roles in the equilibrium of a game. Therefore, we now discuss the nature of the payoffs in the "access game."

Payoff Structure

Payoffs of an outcome underline the physical results of that outcome. There are two components influencing the payoffs of the access game: quality of service (QoS) and battery power (BP). When a user transmits and succeeds in accessing the medium, it is able to transmit a packet over the network. Clearly, this is beneficial for QoS. However in order to transmit the packet, the user spends some BP also. Therefore, the payoff for "success" has a positive QoS component and a negative BP component. On the other hand, if the user waits, then no or minimal BP is expended; however, QoS is adversely affected. Therefore, the payoff for not transmitting has a positive BP component and a negative QoS component. If the outcome is "failure," both the components are adversely affected. Therefore, logically the payoff for "failure" should have negative components of both BP and QoS and should be less than the payoffs for both "success" and "waste."

We consider the case where QoS is relatively more important than BP (although one special case is considered where both are equally important). This clearly reflects the practical reality in LANs. It can be argued that the reverse is true for sensor networks.

Following the above discussion, it can be said that the following relation usually holds between the payoffs for different outcomes:

$$c_{1,i} > c_{2,i} > c_{3,i} \tag{3.4}$$

In order to quantitatively represent the relative importance of QoS and BP in the access game, we define the payoff ratio r_i given as

$$r_i = \frac{(c_{2,i} - c_{3,i})}{(c_{1,i} - c_{3,i})} \tag{3.5}$$

Moreover, generally $r_i < 1$.

Weightage

We assume that the following holds for the weightages.

$$r_i > r_j \Rightarrow w_i > w_j; r_i = r_j \Rightarrow w_i = w_j \qquad (3.6)$$

An intuitive explanation is that higher weightage is given to users that consider both QoS and BP to be more important. However, it should be noted that for equation (6) to hold certain relationship has to hold between QoS and BP components. As this chapter treats these two components in a qualitative fashion, these issues have not been explored.

Assumptions

We conclude this section by outlining the assumptions made for the analysis in the subsequent sections.

A1. The "access game" is a complete information game. In the next section, a simple technique is proposed to approximate incomplete information games as complete information games.

A2. Users always have packets to transmit. This assumption has been made for simplicity and it is quite straightforward to relax this assumption. This is shown in the fourth section.

A3. Packets are of equal length. This assumption is also made for simplicity.

A4. The system is stable.

A5. The number of users playing the game is n and this number does not change. As $n = 1$ presents a trivial case, $n > 1$ is assumed.

Incomplete Information Games

In this section, we first analyse the incomplete information game in some detail and show that the optimal strategy in incomplete information game is inefficient compared to optimal strategy in a complete information game. For a more detailed analysis of access games with incomplete information, refer to Rakshit et al. (2004).

In an access game with incomplete information, users are not aware of the number of other users present in the system. Therefore, from the point of view of an individual user, say player i, all the other users can be combined together in one single player, $-i$. "Transmit" and "wait" for player $-i$ are defined as follows: player $-i$ transmits if one or more of the constituent players transmit. Player $-i$ waits if none of the constituent players transmit.

Formal description of G can be given as follows: G is a game with two players i and $-i$. Strategy spaces of both i and $-i$ are {transmit, wait}. The suitable concept for analysing the incomplete information game is BNE and we compare BNE with the NE for the corresponding complete information game.

Simple Example

We consider a simple system where users arrive according to a Poisson process with average rate λ, the staying time of a user is exponentially distributed with mean $1/\mu$. Let us define throughput as the probability that at least one user succeeds in transmission.

For the incomplete information scenario, the average optimal throughput is given by Rakshit et al. (2004):

$$\overline{\theta}^* = \frac{1-\rho}{4} \tag{4.1}$$

The load factor ρ is given by

$$\rho = \frac{\lambda}{\mu} \tag{4.2}$$

The corresponding average throughput for the complete information case can be given as:

$$\Theta^* = (1-\rho)\sum_{n=1}^{\infty} \rho^n (1-\frac{1}{n})^{n-1} \tag{4.3}$$

Let us designate by δ the difference in optimal throughputs.

$$\therefore \delta = \Theta^* - \overline{\theta}^* = (1-\rho)[\sum_{n=1}^{\infty} \rho^n (1-\frac{1}{n})^{n-1} - \frac{1}{4}]$$

Figure 2 provides an illustration of the relation between δ and ρ.

It is easy to verify that $\delta > 0$ for all values of $\rho \in [0.25, 1]$. For most of the practical scenarios, the value of ρ lies in this region. Therefore, the optimal strategy in incomplete information scenario is inefficient compared to the complete information scenario.

We now propose a simple technique that will make a user aware of the number users in the system and their weightages. This technique would enable us to approximate an incomplete information scenario as a complete information one.

Approximation Scheme

The key to our approximation process is as follows: in most of the distributed systems, there is usually a registration authority R that performs sev-

Figure 2. Illustration of the relation between δ and ρ

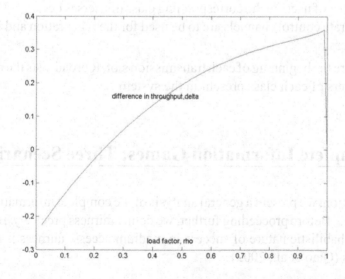

eral accounting functions. We use this authority to gather and disseminate information.

Information Gathering and Dissemination

Let us call the approximation scheme as *appxm*. There are two conceptual steps in *appxm*. Information is sent to R by users (information gathering) and the information accumulated from all the users is broadcast over the network by R (information dissemination). There is a wide body of work dealing with information gathering and dissemination. Our objective is to provide a simple, case-specific mechanism to achieve approximation. The particulars of the mechanism are as follows (Figure 3):

1. Users are divided into C classes. Associated with a class c are two parameters: weightage w_c and the probability of having a packet at the beginning of a transmission slot $p_{p,c} \neq 0$, 1. Users know these parameters a priori.

2. R maintains a table containing the number of different classes of users in the system.

3. When a user enters the system, it is assigned a class and the number of users in the corresponding class is increased by one. Similarly, when a user leaves the system, it informs R about its decision to leave. The number of users in the corresponding class of users is decreased by one. Separate control channels are to be used for the registration and leaving process.

4. Before the beginning of each transmission slot, R broadcasts the number of users of each class present in the system.

Complete Information Games: Three Scenarios

In this section, we present a general analysis of the complete information "access game." Before proceeding further, we define fairness precisely. Because of the probabilistic nature of success in medium access, fairness is defined as follows (Qiao et al., 2002).

Figure 3. Approximation scheme appxm

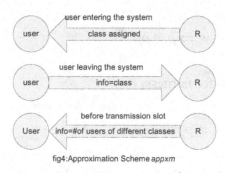

fig4:Approximation Scheme *appxm*

$$\Pr\{success\}_i = p_i \prod_{j \neq i}^{n} (1 - p_j)$$
(5.1)

Hence, fairness can be quantitatively expressed as

$$\frac{p_1 \prod_{j \neq 1}^{n} (1 - p_j)}{w_1} = \dots \frac{p_i \prod_{j \neq i}^{n} (1 - p_j)}{w_i} = \dots \frac{p_n \prod_{j=1}^{n-1} (1 - p_j)}{w_n}$$
(5.2)

It can be observed from (5.2) that if $p_i \in \{0, 1\}$ $\forall i$, the fairness criteria are satisfied but the probability of success is zero for all or some of the users. Clearly, these solutions are of no interest.

For acceptable solutions:

$$p_i \neq 0,1 \qquad \forall_i$$
(5.3)

Equilibrium, Weightages and Fairness

Before presenting the detailed analysis, a discussion is presented on the feasibility of achieving fairness through the "access game."

From (5.1) and (5.13), it can be said that for fairness,

$$w_i > w_j \Rightarrow p_i > p_j; \; w_i = w_j \Rightarrow p_i = p_j$$

Therefore using (3.6) for fairness,

$$r_i > r_j \Rightarrow p_i > p_j; \; r_i = r_j \Rightarrow p_i = p_j \tag{5.4}$$

The equilibrium solution of the "access game" depends solely on the payoffs. Moreover, it will be seen in the following that the solutions of the "access game" are dependent only on the payoff ratios of the users. Let the solutions of the "access game" be denoted by p^*_i, p^*_j and so on; then, if an access game is to achieve the objective of fairness, the following should hold:

$$r_i > r_j \Rightarrow p^*_i > p^*_j; \; r_i = r_j \Rightarrow p^*_i = p^*_j \tag{5.5}$$

The relationships presented in (5.5) are necessary conditions for fairness and will be used in our subsequent analysis.

Nash Equilibrium

From hereon, for the sake of convenience, we drop the "bar" in $\bar{u}_i$ and denote the payoff function of user i as simply u_i.

Rewriting (3.1),

$$u_i = p_i \times [\prod_{\substack{j \neq i}}^{n}(1 - p_j) \times (c_{1,i} - c_{3,i}) - (c_{2,i} - c_{3,i})] + c_{2,i} \tag{5.6}$$

Consequently, for NE

$$[\prod_{\substack{j \neq i}}^{n}(1 - p_j)] \times (c_{1,i} - c_{3,i}) - (c_{2,i} - c_{3,i}) = 0 \tag{5.7}$$

Rewriting (5.7)

$$\prod_{j \neq i}^{n}(1 - p_j) = \frac{(c_{2,i} - c_{3,i})}{(c_{1,i} - c_{3,i})} \tag{5.8}$$

Using (3.5),

$$\prod_{j \neq i}^{n}(1 - p_j) = r_i \tag{5.9}$$

From (5.9) it can be seen that for NE to exist,

$$0 \leq r_i \leq 1 \qquad \forall i \tag{5.10}$$

Therefore, for the existence of NE following relations are permissible amongst the payoff values of a user i

$$c_{3,i} > c_{2,i} > c_{1,i}; \ c_{2,i} = c_{3,i} \neq c_{1,i}; \ c_{1,i} = c_{2,i} \neq c_{3,i}; \ c_{1,i} > c_{2,i} > c_{3,i}$$

It should be noted that although $c_{3,i} > c_{2,i} > c_{1,i}$ presents a mathematical possibility, it does not reflect any physical reality: payoff for failure is more than payoffs for either success or waste. As per our previous discussion, this case is discarded. Therefore, we have the following distinct interesting situations:

Case 1: $c_{2,i} = c_{3,i} \neq c_{1,i}$ (5.11a)

Case 2: $c_{1,i} = c_{2,i} \neq c_{3,i}$ (5.11b)

Case 3: $c_{1,i} > c_{2,i} > c_{3,i}$ (5.11c)

Case 3 corresponds to (3.4), that is, it represents the general case where QoS is more important than power constraints.

Case 1 can represent two distinct scenarios depending on the relationship between $c_{2,i}$ and $c_{1,i}$. If $c_{1,i} > c_{2,i}$, then it can be said that QoS is much more important than BP constraints. If this is true for all the users, then we have the important special case of wired networks. On the other hand, if $c_{2,i} > c_{1,i}$, then the scenario can be thought of as the case where BP is much more important than QoS. This second scenario does not hold any special significance for the purpose of this paper.

Discarding the possibility of $c_{3,i} > c_{1,i}$, $c_{2,i}$, Case 2 can be rewritten as

Case 2: $c_{1,i} = c_{2,i} > c_{3,i}$ (5.11d)

Case 2 as represented in (5.11d) can be interpreted as an interesting special scenario where both QoS and BP are equally important.

Let us introduce the following definition.

Definition 1: *A solution of the access game is acceptable if and only if the probability of success is non-zero for all the users.*

Using Definition 1, we have the following result for Cases 1 and 2.

Theorem 1: *Nash Equilibria for the access game with payoff structures as in (5.11a) and (5.11d) are not acceptable.*

Proof: There are two possible cases.

Case1: Only one user $\underline{i}$ is transmitting with $p_i = 1$. $Pr\{\text{success}\} = 0$ for all the other users.

Case2: More than one user is transmitting with probability "1." Hence, $Pr\{\text{success}\} = 0$ for all the users.

Theorem 1 proves that Cases 1 and 2 have only trivial solution in NE. As we are primarily interested in the general scenario represented by Case 3, we will not investigate these cases any further. In the next section, we provide a detailed analysis for Case 3. Before proceeding to the next section, some preliminary analysis is presented for computing CNE.

Preliminaries for CNE

The rationale behind computing CNE is that if NE is inefficient, then selfish users would be willing to adhere to some set of constraints; more so if the end result is beneficial. Clearly, the fairness constraints of (5.2) and (5.3) are beneficial for the users and can be used for the computation of CNE.

In order to compute CNE, the condition in (3.3) needs to be checked first. From (5.5),

$$\frac{\partial^2 u_i}{\partial p_i^2} = 0 \qquad \forall i \tag{5.12}$$

Hence, (3.3) is satisfied.

The fairness constraints of (5.2) and (5.3) are used as constraints. Combining (5.2) and (5.3), the fairness constraints can be expressed as:

$$[\frac{1}{p_i} - 1] = \frac{w_j}{w_i}[\frac{1}{p_j} - 1] \qquad \forall i,j \tag{5.13}$$

From (5.13), it can be observed that there are an infinite number of ways fairness can be achieved. In order to see this, note that (5.13) can be rewritten as:

$$w_i y_i - w_j y_j = w_i - w_j \quad \forall i,j \text{ where, } 1/p_j = y_j, 1/p_i = y_i.$$

Therefore, there are $n - 1$ independent equations involving n variables. Consequently, the number of possible solutions is infinite. However, CNE gives the solutions that optimize the individual utility functions (i.e., interests) of users with fairness given by (5.13) as constraints. Therefore, the solution given by CNE is efficient in nature.

General Case: Case 3

In this section, the general case represented by Case 3 is analysed.

Nash Equilibrium

From Theorem 1, it can be said that if Case 1 or Case 2 holds for even one user, the Nash equilibrium is not acceptable.

Therefore, for the analysis in this section, the following holds

$$c_{1,i} > c_{2,i} > c_{3,i} \Rightarrow 0 < r_i < 1 \quad \forall i \tag{6.1}$$

Theorem 2: *If an NE exists for the "access game" satisfying (6.1), it is unique.*

Proof: We Use (5.9).

Taking natural logarithm on both sides in (5.9)

$$\ln[\prod^{n}_{j \neq i}(1 - p_j)] = \ln r_i \ \forall i \tag{6.2}$$

For the existence of the NE, the following conditions should hold.

$$\prod_{j=1}^{n} \rho_j < \frac{1}{r_{\min}} \tag{6.3}$$

Where, $r_{\min} = \min\{r_1 \dots r_n\}$ and $\rho_j = \dfrac{r_j}{r_{\min}}$

If (6.3) holds, the unique NE is given by

$$p_i^{NE} = 1 - \frac{\left[\prod_{j=1}^{n} r_j\right]^{\frac{1}{(n-1)}}}{r_i} \qquad \forall i \tag{6.4}$$

Problems with the NE

It is easy to see that for $n = 2$, the existence condition of (6.9) or (6.10) is satisfied for any values of the payoff ratios. However, for higher values of n, the situation becomes problematic. Let us give a few numerical examples. For the first two examples $1/r_{min} = 2.5$ and for the last example, $1/r_{min} = 10$

Example1: Let there be four different users with payoffs of "0.4", "0.5", "0.6", "0.7". In this case, $\prod_{j=1}^{n} \rho_j = 3.1875 > \dfrac{1}{r_{min}}$. Hence, (6.10) is not satisfied

Example2: Consider 11 users. The jth user has a payoff ratio of $r_j = 0.4 + (i - 1)*.01$. In this case, $\prod_{j=1}^{n} \rho_j = 3.5549 > \dfrac{1}{r_{min}}$

Example3: Consider 11 users. The jth user has a payoff ratio of $r_j = 0.1 + (i - 1)*.01$. In this case, $\prod_{j=1}^{n} \rho_j = 67.0443 > \dfrac{1}{r_{min}}$

These examples show that it is difficult to hold the existence condition if the number of users are large. Therefore, CNE is considered for the general case also.

Constrained Nash Equilibrium

For Case 3, the utility function is same as in (3.1). Therefore,

$$u_i = p_i \times \prod_{j \neq i}^{n} (1 - p_j) \times c_{1,i} + p_i [1 - \prod_{j \neq i}^{n} (1 - p_j)] \times c_{3,i} + (1 - p_i) \times c_{2,i} \quad (6.5)$$

For CNE,

$$\frac{\partial u_{i,Case3}}{\partial p_i} = 0 \quad \forall i \qquad\qquad (6.6)$$

subject to (5.13)

$$\therefore g(1 - \sum_{i=1}^{n} p_i) = r_i(1 - p_i)^2 \quad \forall i \tag{6.7}$$

Therefore, for CNE we have

$$\frac{p_i}{w_i / \sqrt{r_i}} = \frac{p_j}{w_j / \sqrt{r_j}} \tag{6.8}$$

Remarks: As the CNE is guaranteed to exist; solution of (6.7) will give transmission probabilities that satisfy fairness. Moreover, these probabilities will satisfy the relationship in (6.8). From (6.8) it can be concluded that equilibrium transmission probability is proportional to the weightage and inversely proportional to the square root of the payoff ratio. This means that as the importance of battery power relative to the importance of QoS increases, equilibrium transmission probability decreases to reduce the probability of collision where battery power is wasted for no benefit. On the other hand, as QoS is more important, equilibrium transmission probability increases with increasing weightage.

Numerical Examples: We provide some simple numerical examples for the CNE of general case.

Example 1: Consider two users with $w_1 = 1$, $w_2 = 2$.
Let, $r_1 = 0.3$ and $r_2 = 0.6$.
The transmission probabilities satisfying fairness are given by $p_1 = 0.3135$, $p_2 = 0.4434$.

Example 2: Consider the previous example with $r_1 = 0.4$ and $r_2 = 0.5$. The transmission probabilities satisfying fairness are given by $p_1 = 0.1841$, $p_2 = 0.3294$.

Example 3: Consider three users with $w_1 = 1$, $w_2 = 2$, $w_3 = 3$ and $r_1 = 0.2$, $r_2 = 0.3$, $r_2 = 0.4$.

The transmission probabilities satisfying fairness can be given by $p_1 = 0.1428$, $p_2 = 0.2332$, $p_3 = 0.3029$

Stabilization Strategy

In the previous sections, we proposed CNE as a solution to the problem of fairness in the "access game." However, there is a problem with the CNE: it is not self-enforcing in nature. CNE is based on a mutual agreement amongst users. If one or more than one users deviate from the mutual agreement for selfish reasons, there is no enforcing mechanism in the system to force the deviating users to the point of mutual agreement, that is, the CNE. This is a drawback of the CNE as a solution concept. In this section, we provide certain mechanisms to provide an effective solution to this problem.

For the rest of this section, the scenario of interest is the general scenario considered in the previous section. It was observed that the solution obtained in the fifth section has certain desirable properties, namely it satisfies fairness and the throughput is maximized. In order to tackle the instability problem of the CNE, we propose that the NE of the general scenario be such that it also satisfies the fairness property and maximize throughput. For this purpose, our objective is to design the "access game" in such a way that the NE of the "access game" will be same as the CNE computed in the fifth section. In this section, we propose two mechanisms to achieve stability: one through choosing suitable weightages for users and the other by incorporating a punishment model for the deviant users.

Computing Weightages

In the fifth section, a simplified scenario was considered and it was observed that the CNEs as computed from $p_i = \dfrac{w_i}{K + w_i}$ $\forall i$ and $\sum_{i=1}^{n} \dfrac{w_i}{K + w_i} = 1$ have the following properties:

1.   They satisfy the fairness.

2.   The throughput of the system is maximized.

For convenience, we reproduce the formula for NE in the general scenario from (6.4)

$$p_i^{NE} = 1 - \frac{[\prod_{j=1}^{n} r_j]^{\frac{1}{(n-1)}}}{r_i} \qquad \forall i \qquad (7.1)$$

From (7.1), it is apparent that the NE is dependent on the payoff ratios. Therefore, it can be argued that by choosing the payoff ratios properly, the NE can have the desirable properties 1 and 2. However, the payoff ratios are strictly user specified and can not modified easily.

On the other hand, the transmission probabilities as computed from

$p_i = \frac{w_i}{K + w_i}$ $\forall i$ and $\sum_{i=1}^{n} \frac{w_i}{K + w_i} = 1$, depend solely on the weightages. These

weightages can be chosen such that the NE satisfies fairness and maximizes throughput subject to satisfying fairness. We ask the following question:

Given a set of payoff ratios $(r_1 ... r_n)$, how should the weightages $(w_1...w_n)$ be chosen so that the NE of the "access game" satisfies fairness and maximize the throughput?

Mathematically, this translates to the following:

$$p_i^{NE} = 1 - \frac{[\prod_{j=1}^{n} r_j]^{\frac{1}{(n-1)}}}{r_i} = \frac{w_i}{K + w_i} \qquad \forall i$$

where K is computed from $\sum_{i=1}^{n} \frac{w_i}{K + w_i} = 1$. We have the following result:

Theorem 3: *If:*

$$w_i = \frac{r_i - \dfrac{n-1}{\sum\limits_{j=1}^{n} 1/r_j}}{r_1 - \dfrac{n-1}{\sum\limits_{j=1}^{n} 1/r_j}}$$

$\forall i \neq 1$ *exists and* $w_1 = 1$, *then NE as given (7.1) satisfies fairness and maximizes the throughput.*

Proof: For NE, we have from (7.1)

$$r_i = \prod_{j \neq i}^{n} (1 - p_j^{NE})$$

$$\therefore r_i (1 - p_i^{NE}) = r_j (1 - p_j^{NE}) \qquad \forall i, j$$

Let $r_i (1 - p_i^{NE}) = \lambda$

(7.2)

Now we have,

$$\sum_{j=1}^{n} p_j^{NE} = 1$$

$$or, \sum_{j=1}^{n} 1 - p_j^{NE} = n - 1$$

Using (7.2),

$$\lambda = \frac{n-1}{\sum\limits_{j=1}^{n} 1/r_j}$$

(7.3)

Using (7.2) and (7.3),

$$r_i(1 - p_i^{NE}) = \lambda$$

$$\therefore p_i^{NE} = 1 - \frac{\lambda}{r_i} = 1 - \frac{1}{r_i} \times \frac{n-1}{\sum\limits_{j=1}^{n} 1/r_j}$$

$$(7.4)$$

On the other hand, we have

$$p_i^{NE} = \frac{w_i}{K + w_i}$$

$$\Rightarrow w_i = \frac{K p_i^{NE}}{1 - p_i^{NE}}$$

$$(7.5)$$

Without the loss of any generality, we can consider $w_1 = 1$. Therefore,

$$p_1^{NE} = \frac{1}{K+1} \Rightarrow K = \frac{1 - p_1^{NE}}{p_1^{NE}}.$$

$$\therefore K = \frac{\dfrac{1}{r_1} \times \dfrac{n-1}{\sum\limits_{j=1}^{n} 1/r_j}}{1 - \dfrac{1}{r_1} \times \dfrac{n-1}{\sum\limits_{j=1}^{n} 1/r_j}}$$

$$(7.6)$$

Using (7.4), (7.5), and (7.6) we have:

$$w_i = \frac{r_i - \dfrac{n-1}{\sum\limits_{j=1}^{n} 1/r_j}}{r_1 - \dfrac{n-1}{\sum\limits_{j=1}^{n} 1/r_j}} \qquad \forall i \neq 1$$

$$(7.7)$$

Discussion

The weightages given by Proposition 3 ensure that the NE given by (7.1) will result in fairness and maximize the throughput. This precludes the necessity for CNE. Moreover, as the NE is unique and self-enforcing, no user benefits by deviating from equilibrium point. Therefore, the equilibrium point is stable. However, the drawback with this approach is the existence problem of the weightages, as evidenced from (7.7). In cases where the existence condition is satisfied this approach is recommended.

We now consider the punishment model for achieving the same goal.

Punishment Model

In the previous mechanisms, if the weightages exist, the NE of the general scenario satisfies the desirable properties of the CNE in the fifth section. However, the existence of the suitable weightages is not guaranteed. Therefore, we propose another mechanism in this sub-section so that the NE of the "access game" coincides with the desirable point.

In order to do so, we adopt a punishment model whereby if the transmission probability of users is more than their optimal transmission probability, some punishment is meted out to the users. Let the optimal transmission probabilities be $(p^*_1 \ldots p^*_n)$. The utility functions are now modified as follows:

$$u_i = p_i \times \prod_{j \neq i}^{n} (1 - p_j) \qquad p_i < p^*_i \qquad (7.8a)$$

$$u_i = p_i \times \prod_{j \neq i}^{n} (1 - p_j) - k_i \times (p_i - p^*_i) \qquad p_i < p^*_i \qquad (7.8b)$$

k_i denotes the cost of transmitting at a higher probability. Following this model, we have the following result.

Theorem 4: *Using (7.8), a sufficient condition for $(p^*_1 \ldots p^*_n)$ to be the NE of the modified "access game" is that $k_i > 1 \; \forall i$*

Proof: In the modified game, user i can be thought to have three possible actions:

1.   transmitting with a lower probability than p^*_i, designated as action "1"
2.   transmitting at p^*_i, designated as action "2"
3.   transmitting with a higher probability than p^*_i, designated as action "3"

$$u_i(2, a_{-i}) - u_i(1, a_{-i}) = (p^*_i - p_i) \times \prod_{j \neq i}^{n} (1 - p_j) > 0$$

$$u_i(2, a_{-i}) - u_i(3, a_{-i}) = (p^*_i - p_i) \times \prod_{j \neq i}^{n} (1 - p_j) - k_i(p^*_i - p_i) = (p_i - p^*_i) \times (k_i - \prod_{j \neq i}^{n} (1 - p_j))$$

Clearly, a sufficient condition for $u_i(2, a_{-i}) - u_i(3, a_{-i}) > 0$ is that $k_i > 0$
Therefore, if $k_i > 0 \ \forall i$

$$u_i(2, a_{-i}) - u_i(3, a_{-i}), u_i(3, a_{-i}) \ \forall i$$

Hence, action "2" for all users is the unique pure strategy Nash equilibrium for the game considered. Therefore, $(p^*_1 ... p^*_n)$ is the unique Nash equilibrium of the game with the modified utility functions as in (7.8).

Discussion

In this approach, there is a cost associated with transmitting at a higher transmission probability. Therefore, it is in the best interest of the users to transmit at the desirable transmission probability. The question is how the punishment should be administered. It is plausible that the registration authority (RA) will monitor the activities of the users and will charge the deviating users if they transmit at a higher transmission probability. However, the intervention by the RA makes the system dependent on centralized intervention; thus violating the distributed property of system to some extent.

Conclusion

Summary

The objective of this chapter is to achieve fairness in bandwidth sharing in a distributed WLAN. The distributed medium access has been modelled as a non-cooperative "access game." The proposed model incorporates both quality of service (QoS) and battery power (BP) constraints in its description. Relative importance of QoS and BP were represented in payoff ratios of the access game. Three distinct cases representing important practical scenarios were considered. Cases 1 and 2 represent important special cases whereas Case 3 represents the general case. For all these cases, it was shown that the NE is not an efficient solution concept. Therefore, the concept of constrained Nash equilibrium was applied and corresponding results were obtained.

Future Research

1. In the above discussions and analysis, it was implicitly assumed that the system is stable. However, stability of the system would depend on the interaction between the packet arrival process and the performance of the MAC protocol (Fayolle et al., 1977). Simply put, for stability the number of unsuccessful packets should not become very large. The notion of stability has a direct bearing on the analysis and application of the protocol. As users choose a probabilistic transmission strategy in a given state, they would expect that state to repeat itself (assuming that users are long-term players). In other words, for the protocol to run correctly, the system should be ergodic.

2. Most of the CSMA protocols in application today use window-based transmission strategies. The CSMA/CD version used by the Ethernet has a one persistent strategy for transmission and adopts a random exponential back-off strategy when collision occurs. It would be useful to investigate if the results of this chapter can be extended to window-based schemes.

3. Another important issue is that of location-dependent error in a wireless environment. This is a major hindrance for achieving fairness in WLAN.

4. Finally, we propose distributed control as a stabilization mechanism to remove the issues associated with centralization aspect of the punishment model discussed in section 7.2

Acknowledgment

This work was partially supported by NSF under Grant EIA 0086251 and ARO under grant DAAD19-01-1-0502. The views and conclusions herein are those of the authors and do not represent the official policies of the funding agencies or the University of Central Florida.

References

Abramson, N. (1970). The ALOHA system -- another alternative for computer communications. *AFIPS Conference Proceedings, 37*, 281- 285.

Akella, A., Seshan, S., Karp, R., Shenker, S., & Papadimitriou, C. (2002). Selfish behavior and stability of the Internet: A game-theoretic analysis of TCP. In *SIGCOMM '02, Proceedings of the 2002 Conference on Applications, Technologies, Architectures, and Protocols for Computer Communications*, Pittsburgh, PA (pp. 117-130).

Bharghavan V., Demers, A., Shenker, S., & Zhang, L. (1997). MACAW: A media access protocol for wireless LANs. In *Proceedings of the Conference on Communications Architectures, Protocols and Applications* (pp. 212-225).

Binachi, G. (2000). Performance analysis of the IEEE802.11 distributed coordination function. *IEEE Journal on Selected Areas in Communications, 18*((3), 535-547.

Cali, F., Conti, M., & Gregori, E. (2000). Dynamic tuning of the IEEE802.11 protocol to achieve a theoretical throughput limit. *IEEE/ACM Transactions on Networking, 8*(6), 785-799.

Choudhury, G.L., & Rappaport, S.S. (1985). Priority access schemes using CSMA-CD. *IEEE Transactions on Communications, 33*, 620-626.

Demers, A., Keshav, S., & Shenker, S. (1989). Analysis and simulation of a fair queueing algorithm. *ACM SIGCOMM Computer Communication Review, 10*(4), 1-12.

El Azouzi, R., & Altman, E. (2003). Constrained traffic equilibrium in routing. *IEEE Transaction on Automatic Control, 48*(9), 1656-1660.

ETSI TS-RES 300 652. (1996, October). *Radio equipment and systems (RES); High performance radio local area networks (HIPERLAN); Type 1; Functional Specifications.*

Exley, G., & Merakos, L. (1987). Throughput-delay performance of interconnected CSMA local area networks. *IEEE Journal on Selected Areas in Communications, 5*(9), 1380-1390.

Fayolle, G., Gelenbe, E., & Labetoulle, J. (1977). Stability and optimal control of the packet switching broadcast channel. *Journal of the ACM, 24*, 375-386.

Fudenberg, D., & Tirole, J. (1991). *Game theory.* MIT Press.

Garcia, A.L., & Widjaja, I. (2000). *Communication networks.* MacGraw Hill.

Harsanyi, J. (1967-1968). Games with incomplete information played by Bayesian players. *Management Science, 14*, 159--182; 320--334; 486--502.

IEEE. (2002, November). *IEEE 802.11e, draft/D7.0, Part 11: Wireless medium access control (MAC) and physical layer (PHY) specifications: Medium access control (MAC) enhancements for quality of service (QoS).*

Jones, C.E., Sivalingam, K.M., Agrawal, P., & Chen, J-C. (2001). A survey of energy efficient network protocols for wireless networks. *Wireless Networks, 7*(4), 343-358.

Kleinrock, L., & Tobagi, F. (1975). Packet switching in radio channels: Part I - carrier sense multiple-access modes and their throughput-delay characteristics. *IEEE Transactions on Communications, 23*(12), 1400-1416.

Korilis, Y.A., Lazar, A.A., & Orda, A. (1995). The designer's perspective to noncooperative networks. In *INFOCOM '95. Proceedings of the Fourteenth Annual Joint Conference of the IEEE Computer and Communications Societies. Bringing Information to People*, Boston, MA (Vol. 2, 562-570).

Koutsoupias, E., & Papadimitriou, C. (1999). *Worst-case equilibria.* In *Proceedings of the 16th Annual Symposium on Theoretical Aspects of Computer Science* (pp. 404-413).

Kruys, J. (1992). HIPERLAN, applications and requirements. In *Proceedings of PIMRC '92, Third IEEE International Symposium on Personal, Indoor and Mobile Radio Communications*, Boston, MA (pp. 133-138).

Liu, Y-C., & Wise, G. (1987). Performance of a CSMA/CD protocol for local area networks. *IEEE Journal on Selected Areas in Communications*, *5*(6), 948-955.

MacKenzie, A.B., & Wicker, S.B. (2003). Stability of multipacket slotted Aloha with selfish users and perfect information. In *Proceedings of INFOCOM 2003, Twenty-Second Annual Joint Conference of the IEEE Computer and Communications Societies* (Vol. 3, pp. 1583–1590).

Nash, J. (1951). Non-cooperative games. *Annals of Mathematics, 54,* 286-295.

Nutt, G., & Bayer, D. (1982). Performance of CSMA/CD networks under combined voice and data loads. *IEEE Transactions on Communications, 30*((1), 6-11.

Orda, A., Rom, R., & Shimkin, N. (1996). Competitive routing in multiuser communication networks. *ACM/IEEE Transactions on Networking, 1*(5), 510-521.

O'Reilly, P., & Hammond, J., Jr. (1984). *An efficient simulation technique for performance studies of CSMA/CD local network. IEEE Journal on Selected Areas in Communications, 2*(1), 238-249.

P802.11, IEEE draft standard for wireless LAN medium access control (MAC) and physical layer (PHY) specification, D6.1. (1997, May).

Papadimitriou, C. (2001).*Algorithms, games, and the Internet.* STOC.

Qiao, D., & Shin, K.G. (2002). Achieving efficient channel utilization and weighted fairness for data communications in IEEE 802.11 WLAN under the DCF. In *Proceedings of the Tenth International Workshop on Quality of Service* (IWQoS'2002), Miami Beach, Florida.

Rakshit, S., & Guha, R. (2004, June). Optimal Mac Protocols. In *Proceedings of IEEE International Conference on Communications* (ICC) (CD ROM).

Rakshit, S., & Guha, R.K. (n.d.). Fair bandwidth sharing in distributed systems: A game-theoretic approach (Tech. Rep. CS-TR-04-07). University of Central Florida.

Rosen, J. (1965). Existence and uniqueness of equilibrium points for concave n-person games. *Econometrica, 33*, 520-534.

Roughgarden, T., & Tardos, E. (2002). *How bad is selfish routing?* Journal of ACM, *49*(2), 236-259.

Sharrock S.M., & Du, D.H. (1989). Efficient CSMA/CD-based protocols for multiple priority classes. *IEEE Transactions on Computers, 38*, 943-954.

Shenker, S. (1994). Making greed work in networks: A game-theoretic analysis of switch service disciplines. *IEEE/ACM Transactions on Networking, 3*(6), 819-831.

Vo-Dai, T. (1982). Throughput-delay analysis of the nonslotted and nonpersistent CSMA-CD protocol. In P.C. Ravasio, G. Hopkins, & N. Naffah (Eds.), *Local Computer Networks* (pp. 459–476). North-Holland, Amsterdam.

Vaidya, N.H., Bahl, P., & Gupta, S. (2000). Distributed fair scheduling in a wireless LAN. In *MOBICOM 2000, Proceedings of the 6th Annual International Conference on Mobile Computing and Networking,* Boston, MA (pp. 167-178). New York: ACM Press.

Visser, M., & El Zarki, M. (1995, September). Voice and data transmission over an 802.11 wireless network. In *Proceedings of PIMRC '95, Sixth IEEE International Symposium on Personal, Indoor and Mobile Radio Communications,* Toronto, Canada (pp. 648–652).

About the Contributors

Angappa Gunasekaran is a professor of operations management and the chairperson of the Department of Decision and Information Sciences in the Charlton College of Business at the University of Massachusetts (North Dartmouth, USA). Previously, he has held academic positions in Canada, India, Finland, Australia and Great Britain. He has BE and ME from the University of Madras and a PhD from the Indian Institute of Technology. He teaches and conducts research in operations management and information systems. He serves on the editorial board of 20 journals and edits a journal. He has published about 200 articles in journals, 60 articles in conference proceedings and 3 edited books. In addition, he has organized several conferences in the emerging areas of operations management and information systems. He has extensive editorial experience that includes the guest editor and editor of many journals. He has received outstanding paper and excellence in teaching awards. His current areas of research include supply chain management, enterprise resource planning, e-commerce, and benchmarking. He is also the director of Business Innovation research Center (BIRC) at the University of Massachusett—Dartmouth.

***

Tamara Babaian (http://cis.bentley.edu/tbabaian) received her MS in applied mathematics from Yerevan State University of Armenia, and a PhD in computer science from Tufts University, Medford, MA. She is currently an assistant professor in the Department of Computer Information Systems at Bentley College, Waltham, MA. Her research interests include artificial intelligence, human-computer collaboration and usability. She studies collaborative interfaces, knowledge representation, reasoning and planning. Her publications have appeared in the *Proceedings of the Intelligent User Interfaces*, *Artificial Intelligent Planning Systems*, *International Conference on Enterprise Information Systems*, and *Logical Methods in Computer Science*.

Leszek Borzemski of the Institute of Information Science and Engineering, Wroclaw University of Technology, Wroclaw, Poland, received his MSc, PhD and DSc (post-PhD habilitation) degrees in computer science from Wroclaw University of Technology, in 1976, 1980 and 1992, respectively. He is a professor in computer science at the Institute of Information Science and Engineering (IISE), Wroclaw University of Technology, Wroclaw, Poland. He holds the Chair of Distributed Computer Systems and IISE Laboratory. He is the vice-chairman of the Council of the Wroclaw Academic Computer Network. In 1993-2007 he was elected to the Committee on Informatics of the Polish Academy of Sciences. He is the author of 170 publications. His research interests include Web performance measurements and evaluation, data mining and Web quality. He is the member of the editorial board of the *Theoretical and Applied Informatics*. He has served as a PC member of several international conferences. He is the program chair of IEA/AIE2008 and ISAT2007. He is the member of KES International.

Ahern G. Brown is currently the assistant controller for Centex Homes in Charlotte, NC. He received his MBA and MS-ITM from Creighton University and holds an undergraduate degree from the University of Nebraska. His interests include information technology, marketing, strategy and accounting. Ahern has over 13 years of experience in applying technology and executing strategies that provide businesses with positive bottom-line driven results.

Catharine Curran, PhD (New Mexico State University), recently joined the Charlton College of Business as an associate professor of marketing. Her areas of specialization include marketing to children, privacy, public policy and the application of market orientation to traditionally non-market based professions. Her current research focuses on how becoming market driven has affected the traditional professions of law, medicine and education. Dr. Curran has published in journals such as *The Journal of Advertising*, *The Journal of Consumer Marketing*, *The Journal of Business Ethics*, and *Marketing Education Review*.

S.R. Devadasan is a professor in Production Engineering Department of PSG College of Technology, Coimbatore, India. He holds a bachelor's degree in mechanical engineering and a master's degree in industrial engineering. He received his PhD degree for his work on strategic quality management in the year 1996. He obtained all his degrees from Bharathiar University, Coimbatore, India. He has 17 years of teaching and research experience. He has published over 200 papers in the proceedings of the leading national and international conferences. He has published over 35 papers in international journals such as *Production Planning & Control, International Journal of Quality and Reliability Management,* and *International Journal of Operations & Production Management.* He is an editorial board member in the *European Journal of Innovation Management*, UK. His areas of research interest include strategic quality management, agile manufacturing and total quality management.

Tony Elliman is a senior lecturer in the School of Information Systems, Computing and Mathematics at Brunel University. He is active in research concerned primarily with the development of information systems for knowledge workers. He is a member of the IS Evaluation and Integration Group and has experience of using simulation techniques in modelling and evaluation projects. As a practicing software engineer he is a consultant on LRF funded medical research and has consulted for the Office of the Deputy Prime Minister (ODPM) on e-government projects. Originally trained as an electrical engineer with International Computers Limited, Dr Elliman has a broad background, having taught many aspects of computing including: information systems development, software engineering, distributed systems and hybrid simulation. As a chartered engineer, he has provided software consultancy services to government, academic and private sector organisations, including DERA and the EU.

Michael Griffin, MBA (Bryan College), CMA, CFM, ChFC, assistant dean of the Charlton College of Business, is a graduate of Providence College (BS 1980) and Bryant University (formerly Bryant College) (MBA 1982). Mr. Griffin has worked for a number of employers including Fleet National Bank, E.F. Hutton and Company, and the Federal Home Loan Bank of Boston. Mr. Griffin is the author of many business books and has developed several software packages both for commercial and academic use. He has been a consultant to a number of textbook publishers, including McGraw-Hill, Irwin, Addison Wesley, and Prentice Hall.

Ratan K. Guha is a professor in the School of Electrical Engineering and Computer Science at the University of Central Florida, Orlando. He received his BSc degree with honors in mathematics and MSc degree in applied mathematics from University of Calcutta and received the PhD degree in computer science from the University of Texas at Austin in 1970. His research interests include distributed systems, computer networks, security protocols, modelling and simulation, and computer graphics. He has authored over 150 papers published in various computer journals, book chapters and conference proceedings. His research has been supported by grants from ARO, NSF, STRICOM, PM-TRADE, NASA, and the State of Florida. He has served as a member of the program committee of several conferences, as the general chair of CSMA'98 and CSMA'2000 and as the guest co-editor of a special issue of the *Journal of Simulation Practice and Theory*. He is a member of ACM, IEEE, and SCS and served as a member of the Board of Directors of SCS from 2004 to 2006. He is currently serving in the editorial board of two journals: *International Journal of Internet Technology and Secured Transactions* (IJITST) published by Inderscience Enterprises (www.inderscience.com), and *Modelling and Simulation in Engineering* published by Hindawi Publishing Corporation (www.hindawi.com).

Tally Hatzakis is a lecturer for Brunel Business School. Her teaching areas include organisational theory and analysis, managing the digital enterprise and change management in digital enterprises. Her research interests include IT-driven organisational change, trust, and trust building, and has been chairing workshops and conference tracks in these areas under the auspices of the British Computer Society, European Congress of Organisational Studies, and the European Institute for Advanced Studies in Management. She holds a PhD in information systems, an MBA and a BSc in marketing management. Prior to returning to education, Tally spent a number of years in industry, where she has worked in project management, advertising, and marketing research.

Danie Jutras, MSc, is an information systems consultant, specializing in accounting and ERP systems for small business. Her research has been published in the *International Journal of Enterprise Information Systems*.

Ivan K.W. Lai, PhD, is an assistant professor in the Faculty of Management and Administration at the Macau University of Science and Technology. He has over 20 years industrial experience in the logistics and supply chain management. He has published many papers on the topics of ERP, IOS, and SCM. His current research focuses on Internet-based IOS, extended enterprise, ERP implementation, supply chain risk management, and action research in enterprise information systems.

Gilbert Y.P. Lin is a PhD student in the Department of Industrial Engineering and Engineering Management at National Tsing Hua University, Hsinchu, Taiwan. He also works in the R&D Division at Avectec, Inc. His research interests are global logistics management, e-business methodology and intelligent expert system. He has participated in several industrial projects with high-tech companies and non-profit R&D centers in Taiwan.

Wendy Lucas (http://cis.bentley.edu/wlucas) is an associate professor in the Department of Computer Information Systems at Bentley College in Waltham, MA. She received her MS from the MIT Sloan School of Management and her PhD from the Electrical Engineering and Computer Science Department at Tufts University. Her research interests include interface usability, information visualization, and Web search. She has published in *JASIST, European Journal of Information Systems, Information Processing & Management*, and *Theory and Practice of Object Systems*. Her primary teaching interests are programming languages, algorithms, and object-oriented technologies.

Purnendu Mandal is professor and chair at the Information Systems and Analysis Department, Lamar University, Beaumont, Texas. His teaching and research interests are in the areas of supply chain management with SAP, database management systems, e-commerce, strategic management information systems, and management information systems, system dynamics. He published over 150 journal and conference refereed articles. His research papers have appeared in *European Journal of Operational Research, International Journal of Production Economics, Management Decision, International Journal of Operations & Production Management, International Journal of Quality & Reliability Management, Logistics Information Management, Intelligent Automation and Soft Computing: An International Journal, International Journal of Technology Management, ASCE Journal of Management in Engineering, Decision, Applied Mathematical Modeling*, and so on.

S. Ragu Raman is working as a consultant in Genpact, Hyderabad, India. He pursued his bachelor of engineering (mechanical engineering) course at R.V.S. College of Engineering & Technology, Dindugul, TamilNadu, India.

He has published one paper in an international journal. His areas of research interest are quality information systems and total quality management.

Sudipta Rakshit received his bachelor's of technology (B.Tech) in aerospace engineering from Indian Institute of Technology, Kharagpur in 1998 and his PhD in computer science from University of Central Florida in 2005. He is presently employed with J.P. Morgan Chase Bank in New York. His research interests include computer networks, game theory, Brownian motion, and stochastic calculus.

Louis Raymond, PhD, is professor of information systems and holder of the Canada Research Chair on Enterprise Performance at the Université du Québec à Trois-Rivières. His research interests include IT use and management in the context of SMEs and network enterprises, ERP evaluation, strategic alignment, and performance measurement systems. His work has been published in various journals such as the *MIS Quarterly*, *Journal of Management Information Systems*, *Entrepreneurship Theory and Practice*, *Journal of Information Technology* and *International Journal of Operations & Production Management*.

Carl Reidsema is a senior lecturer in mechanical engineering design at the University of New South Wales, Australia. Following on from 12 years as a professional design engineer in industry, he obtained his PhD in mechanical engineering from the University of Newcastle, Australia. His research interests include knowledge-based engineering, AI approaches to CAD/CAE automation and decision support, and feature recognition technologies.

Suzanne Rivard, PhD, is professor of information technology and holder of the Chair in Strategic Management of Information Technology at HEC Montréal. Her research interests are in the areas of ERP implementation, outsourcing of information systems services, software project risk management, and strategic alignment. Her work has been published in various journals such as the *Communications of the ACM*, *MIS Quarterly*, *Journal of Management Information Systems*, *Journal of Strategic Information Systems* and *Organization Science*.

M. Sakthivel is a teaching research associate in Mechanical Engineering Department of Government College of Technology, Coimbatore, India. He obtained his bachelor's degree in mechanical engineering branch from Madras University, India in the year 1999. He obtained his master's degree in industrial engineering from the Bharathiar University in the year 2001. He has submitted his doctoral thesis on quality information systems to Anna University, India. He has five years of teaching experience. He has published seven papers in the proceedings of the leading national and international conferences. He has published three papers in international journals. His areas of research interest include strategic quality management, quality information systems and financial accounting systems.

Cesar Sanin has been working in the field of multi-disciplinary decision-making and intelligent technologies for the past 5 years. He obtained his administrative engineering degree (2000) from the National University of Colombia and a diploma in IT (2003) at the University of Newcastle, Australia. Afterwards, he pursued a PhD degree at the School of Mechanical Engineering of the University of Newcastle, and received his degree in the field of knowledge management and intelligent technologies (2007). Currently, he continues his work at the University of Newcastle as a researcher and lecturer. His research focuses on the areas of information/knowledge management, decision support systems and intelligent systems for engineering and business.

Alan Serrano is a lecturer in the School of Information Systems, Computing and Mathematics at Brunel University. His research concentrates on the area of information systems and business process design and simulation including topics such as business process integration and information systems modelling and techniques. Previous to his appointment as a lecturer, he has gained research experience in the areas of IS design and simulation through participation as a research assistant on a number of EU and UK funded projects. Dr Serrano is an active member of the Centre for Applied Simulation Modelling (CASM) and the Centre for Living Information Systems Thinking (LIST), both in Brunel. Dr Serrano has a wealth of expertise gained from his industrial experiences in Mexico, ranging from distributed systems analysis and design to computer network design and implementation.

Timothy Shea, DBA (Boston University), is an associate professor of management information systems. Dr. Shea first worked in industry and management consulting developing large systems applications and early CASE tools. He received his DBA in management information systems from Boston University. Dr. Shea's research has focused on the delivery and management of Web-based learning and teaching technologies, corporate universities, end-user training, implementation issues around ERPs, e-commerce, and communities of practice. He has over a dozen journal articles published, four book chapters, four training manuals, and dozens of conference presentations. He teaches advanced projects, database, networking, and quality information systems.

Alan D. Smith is presently university professor of operations management at Robert Morris University, located in Pittsburgh, PA. Previously he was chair of the Department of Quantitative and Natural Sciences and Coordinator of Engineering Programs at the same institution, as well as associate professor of business administration at Eastern Kentucky University. He holds concurrent PhDs in engineering systems/education from The University of Akron and in business administration from Kent State University. He is the author of numerous articles and book chapters.

S. Sriram is working as a software engineer in Infosys Technologies Limited, Chengelpet, India. He pursued his bachelor of engineering (mechanical engineering) course at Arulmigu Kalasilingam College of Engineering, Krishnankovil, TamilNadu, India. He has published one paper in an international journal. His areas of research interest are quality information systems, total quality management, thermal engineering and engineering mechanics.

Helena Szczerbicka received the MSc in applied mathematics and the PhD in computer science from the Technical University of Warsaw, Poland, in 1974 and 1982, respectively. In July 1985 she joined the Faculty of Computer Science at the University of Karlsruhe, Germany. In May 1994 she became a professor in computer science at the University of Bremen, Germany. Since May 2000 she has been a professor at the University of Hanover, Germany.

Edward Szczerbicki has had very extensive experience in the theory of information, autonomous systems analysis, knowledge management and decision support systems development over an uninterrupted 28 year period, 13 years of which he spent in the top systems research centers in the USA, UK, Germany and Australia. He has published over 240 refereed papers, 120 of which appeared in international journals covering the areas of systems science, decision support, autonomous systems modeling and simulation, and decisional DNA. His title of professor (2006) and DSc degree (1993) were gained in the area of information and knowledge management. His PhD (1983) was gained in uncertainty modeling for design and MSc (1976) in engineering management. He is now with The University of Newcastle, Newcastle, Australia.

Elisabeth Syrjakow was born in 1970 in the Federal Republic of Germany. She received the Dipl-Inform degree from the University of Karlsruhe, Germany in 1999. After that she was with the professional group Modeling and Simulation at the Institute for Computer Design and Fault Tolerance at the University of Karlsruhe. In June 2005 she received the PhD in computer science from the University of Karlsruhe. Since December 2006 she has been with the SWR Baden-Baden, Germany.

Michael Syrjakow was born in 1964 in the Federal Republic of Germany. He received the Dipl-Inform degree from the University of Karlsruhe, Germany in 1991. After that he was with the professional group Modeling and Simulation at the Institute for Computer Design and Fault Tolerance at the University of Karlsruhe. In February 1997 he received the PhD in computer science from the University of Karlsruhe. In July 2003 he finished his habilitation at the University of Karlsruhe about the topic "Web- and component technologies in modeling and simulation." In September 2005 he became a professor in computer science at the Wildau University of Applied Sciences, Germany. Since September 2007 he has been a professor at the Brandenburg University of Applied Sciences, Germany.

Heikki Topi (http://cis.bentley.edu/htopi) is associate dean of business for graduate & executive programs at Bentley College in Waltham, MA. His teaching interests cover a range of topics including advanced systems analysis and design, systems modeling, and data management. His current research focuses on human factors and usability issues in enterprise systems, information search and data management and the effects of time availability on human-computer interaction. His research has been published in journals such as *European Journal of Information* Systems, *JASIST*, *Information Processing & Management*, *International Journal of Human-Computer Studies*, *Journal of Database Management*, *Small Group Research*, and others. He has been actively involved in national computing curriculum development and evaluation efforts (including *IS2002*, *CC2005 Overview Report,* and as the chair of the current IS curriculum revision project). He is a member of the ACM Education Board.

Amy Trappey received her PhD degree in industrial engineering from Purdue University, Indiana, USA. She is a professor of industrial engineering and engineering management and the director of the Electronic Business Center (EBC) at the National Tsing Hua University, Hsinchu, Taiwan. Her research interests are in the areas of e-business methodology, knowledge engineering, product lifecycle management and e-automation. She is the editor-in-chief of *International Journal of Electronic Business Management*. Dr. Trappey is an ASME fellow.

S. Vinodh is currently a PhD scholar of Anna University working in the Department of Mechanical Engineering, PSG College of Technology, Coimbatore, India. He pursued his master's degree in production engineering at PSG College of Technology and obtained this degree recently from Anna University, Chennai, India. He studied at Government College of Technology, Coimbatore and obtained his bachelor's degree in mechanical engineering from Bharathiar University, India in 2004. He was a gold medalist in his undergraduate study. He has been awarded Best Outgoing Student by PSG College of Technology. He has now been awarded National Doctoral Fellowship by All Indian Council for Technical Education to support his doctoral work. He has published six papers in International Journals. He has published 18 papers in the proceedings of the leading national and international conferences. His research interests include total quality management, agile manufacturing, quality information systems and computer aided design.

D. Steven White, DBA (Cleveland State University), is a full professor of marketing. His research interests include seafood marketing, international services marketing, service exporting, global entrepreneurship, international marketing, global e-commerce and international business education. He has co-authored 29 articles published in refereed journals and over 20 refereed proceedings. Professor White teaches marketing principles and international marketing at the undergraduate level and international marketing and international business at the MBA level. Prior to entering academia, Professor White managed outdoor sporting goods stores/ski shops, served as an alpine ski instructor, and was the vice president of an advertising agency.

Quangang Yang is currently a research engineer at ResMed Ltd. and a PhD candidate at The University of New South Wales, Australia. He received his MEng from National University of Singapore in 2001 and BEng at Shanghai Jiaotong University in 1991. His research interests include FEM modelling, experimental modal analysis, multi-body dynamics, development of micro-systems, vibration and acoustic analysis and knowledge-based system for engineering design.

Yin-Ho Yao is an associate professor of industrial engineering and management department at the Ta Hwa Institute of Technology. He received his PhD degree in industrial engineering and engineering management from National Tsing Hua University, Hsinchu, *Taiwan*. His research interests are in the areas of electronic commerce applications, workflow management, service management and CRM.

Index